Conceptual readings in the marketing economy

Holt, Rinehart and Winston Marketing Series

PAUL E. GREEN, Adviser
WHARTON SCHOOL, UNIVERSITY OF PENNSYLVANIA

PHILIP KOTLER, Adviser
NORTHWESTERN UNIVERSITY

JAMES F. ENGEL, DAVID T. KOLLAT, ROGER D. BLACKWELL,
All of The Ohio State University
Consumer Behavior
Cases in Consumer Behavior
Research in Consumer Behavior

RONALD R. GIST,
University of Denver
Marketing and Society: A Conceptual Introduction
Readings: Marketing and Society

CHARLES S. GOODMAN,
University of Pennsylvania
Management of the Personal Selling Function

PHILIP KOTLER,
Northwestern University
Marketing Decision Making: A Model-Building Approach

JOHN C. NARVER,
University of Washington
RONALD SAVITT,
Boston University, National Economic Research Associates
The Marketing Economy: An Analytical Approach
Conceptual Readings in the Marketing Economy

THOMAS R. WOTRUBA,
San Diego State College
Sales Management: Planning, Accomplishment, and Evaluation

THOMAS R. WOTRUBA,
San Diego State College
ROBERT M. OLSEN,
California State College, Fullerton
Sales Management: Concepts and Viewpoints

Conceptual readings in the marketing economy

John C. Narver
University of Washington

Ronald Savitt
Boston University
National Economic Research Associates

HOLT, RINEHART AND WINSTON, INC.
New York · Chicago · San Francisco · Atlanta · Dallas
Montreal · Toronto · London · Sydney

Library of Congress Catalog Card Number: 71–126138

SBN: 03-079305-X

Printed in the United States of America

1 2 3 4   090   9 8 7 6 5 4 3 2 1

Dedicated to

E. T. Grether
David A. Revzan

Preface

This anthology is designed to accompany *The Marketing Economy: An Analytical Approach* although we believe that the selections as presented can stand on their own as vehicles for understanding the marketing economy. The articles were chosen with great care and placed in a sequence that provides the reader with a logical understanding of the relationships of structure and behavior. Each of the four parts is introduced by an essay which links the selections. These introductions also offer the reader specific background, which is necessary if the various selections are to have the most meaning. At the end of each part (and after every section in Part IV), we have included a list of Selected Readings, in recognition of the limitations of any anthology.

We feel—as authors should—that this collection is unique and valuable in that it furthers understanding of the conceptual aspects of marketing. We believe it is a useful collection for those who approach marketing from an analytical-conceptual point of view.

We gratefully acknowledge the contributions to our thinking from two friends and able scholars at the University of California at Berkeley, E. T. Grether and D. A. Revzan. The development of our interest in marketing structure and behavior, manifest in this book of readings and the companion text, *The Marketing Economy: An Analytical Approach*, was substantially inspired by our many contacts, over a ten-year period, with these two intellectually vigorous and stimulating people. To them we respectfully dedicate this book.

Seattle, Washington   —J. C. N.
Boston, Massachusetts   —R. S.
January 1971

Contents

Conceptual
readings in
the marketing economy

Conceptual foundation
of structure
and behavior

Marketing—all the prepurchase and postpurchase activities related to transactions—is composed of a complex set of parts. The participants in marketing range from individuals as buyers and sellers, to groups of buyers, to
groups of sellers, and even to groups of buyers *and* sellers. Thus, marketing
can be perceived and analyzed at several levels of aggregation—individuals
(units), groups of units, markets, and groups of markets.

In the decision-making process, the decision-maker, if rational, first
selects a goal and then decides upon the means to obtain it. Herbert A.
Simon, in the opening selection, "New Developments in the Theory of the
Firm," raises these issues in terms of economic and organization theory
aspects. The decision-maker, in focusing on his goal, estimates the effectiveness of the various means, taking into account some or all elements that are
going to affect his decision. These elements or considerations are known as
structure. We can specify structure elements in a market as well as within
any participant. Market elements of structure include: (1) concentration,
that is, the number and size of buyers and sellers, (2) product differentiation, (3) barriers to entry of new firms, (4) growth rate of market demand,
(5) price elasticity of market demand, and (6) ratio of fixed to variable costs
in the short run. For an individual buyer, for example, structural elements

1

include income, occupation, stage in life cycle, and social class. These are spelled out in greater detail in the introduction to Part III.

Structure is related to behavior. Behavior consists of two parts: (1) conduct, which is the policies and the decisions themselves; and (2) performance, that is, the net result of the decision in terms of utility and well-being for consumers, or profits or efficiency for other participants. The performance aspect of behavior is examined in some detail in Part IV, Sections B and C. The relationship between structure and behavior is of special interest here. In the static model, we say simply that structure influences behavior. In the selection by Edith T. Penrose, the firm is described in terms of its most basic structural elements, namely, its resources. The pool of productive resources available to a firm at any point in time gives direction to the decision-maker, in large part affecting his conduct and ultimately his performance.

Andreas G. Papandreou, in "Some Basic Problems in the Theory of the Firm," develops in greater depth the fact that the elements of structure for any one decision-maker typically do not arise only from his own level of aggregation, but also from other levels. Hence in many decision circumstances, a firm may have to take into account not only aspects of its own resource pool, but also aspects of the market (as described previously), and of outside creditors, governmental regulations, and stockholders. Papandreou is also concerned with overall performance of the decision-maker—and the dynamics of the structure-behavior interaction whereby behavior, in its performance aspect as well as its conduct aspect, affects structure in subsequent periods.

The number of elements in structure is a function of many factors. The complexity of structure is determined in part by whether a repetitive decision is being made. A decision once made may tend to be simplified in subsequent trials (see Howard and Sheth, "A Theory of Buyer Behavior," Part III), given reasonably satisfactory performance in each successive trial. It will also vary according to the time available for the decision and the nature of the market.

Structure frequently consists of compound elements such as organizations. The essence of an organization is a specificity of influence directed to the "members" of the organization. Individuals are members of many organizations, both voluntarily and involuntarily, where "organization" means simply a group that influences their activities. The group may be a family, a carpool, a bowling team, a coffee group; or it may be a formal organization such as a sales force, a trade association, a church, and so on. One is a member of a formal or informal organization when he identifies with it; in other words, when he applies the same general scale of values to his choices as do the other members of the group. The organization to which one relates at any one time has been called the "focal" organization by Almarin Phillips. The most subtle task and hence the most difficult in marketing analysis is trying to identify the focal organizations of the decision-maker, for only thereby can one approach accurate prediction of behavior.

Groups of sellers and buyers in a market can at times be seen as organizations themselves. That is to say, when the interdependence among sellers or the interdependence among buyers becomes sufficiently pronounced, informal if not ultimately formal organizations can arise. In general, interdependence grows when there is either increasing concentration among the sellers or increasing concentration among the buyers, or even because of increased contacts between firms which happens when diversified firms encounter each other more and more frequently across many markets. As a result, implicit and even explicit organization among the firms can occur.

David A. Revzan's "The Institutional Approach Revisited" develops the dynamics of structure-behavior relationships in terms of the marketing system. His point of view is dynamic in that he views marketing as a whole functioning through a variety of structures. The relationship is: Structure at one given period of time affects behavior, which in turn over time affects structure. In the long run, the functions or the activities in marketing become institutionalized in structure; that is to say, the activities become expressed in particular patterns or structural forms. This will be further developed in the readings in Part II.

In summary, the interrelationship of structure and behavior underlies all decision-making in or out of marketing. The first three readings in Part I establish the concepts of structure and behavior by focusing primarily on individual and firm decision-making. However, Simon, Penrose and Papandreou, in the discussions of the firm, provide many implications for marketing decisions—*whoever* or *whatever* the decision-maker. Phillips explicitly broadens the focus to include interfirm organization as decision-makers, and thereby he usefully extends the structure-behavior model. Finally, Revzan further enlarges the discussion to speak to the entire marketing system and the processes of change in marketing structures and behavior.

1

New developments
in the theory
of the firm*

Herbert A. Simon

Economics has often been defined as the study of the allocation of scarce resources. Shubik has observed that the definition is so broad as to fit psychiatry about as well as economics. In spite of his structure, which is probably right, I shall use this very broad definition to delimit the area of my remarks. I shall have something to say about both the normative aspects —the optimal allocation of resources—and the positive—the processes whereby resources actually are allocated. There are many well-known reasons why neither of these two aspects can easily be discussed without some attention to the other.

* I have borrowed freely from a forthcoming study, *The Behavioral Theory of the Firm*, by my colleagues Richard W. Cyert and James G. March, and have benefited also from their comments on earlier drafts of this paper.

From the *American Economic Review, Supplement*, Vol. 52, May 1962, pp. 1–15. Reprinted by permission.

ECONOMICS AND ADMINISTRATION

Economics (or psychiatry, if we accept Shubik's observation) is not the only science that claims an interest in resource allocation. A standard, often quoted definition of public administration reads:[1]

> Public administration is the management of men and materials in the accomplishment of the purposes of the state. . . . The objective of public administration is the most efficient utilization of the resources at the disposal of officials and employees.

If we delete the word "public" and substitute "firm" for "state," we arrive at a statement that could serve very well as a definition of normative micro-economics.

In international law, sweeping territorial claims are only made good by effective occupation. Similarly, definitions set the boundaries of a science only if they spell out the concepts it actually uses, the tools of analysis it has developed, and the knowledge it has attained. When we come to describe economics and administration, respectively, in these more specific terms, we soon see that they occupy very different territories within the general domain of resource allocation.

MECHANISMS FOR RESOURCE ALLOCATION

As a general rule, economics and administration have limited their investigations to particular, and distinct, classes of mechanisms and processes for resource allocation. Economics discovered the institution of the market, the price mechanism as a market-regulating process, and marginal analysis as a means of calculation. Administration discovered the institution of the formal organization, the mechanisms of authority and interpersonal influence to secure co-ordination, and planning as a means of decision making. The business firm became the boundary—I am tempted to say, the no man's land —between economics and administration. In our society—and perhaps even more generally in Western society of the last century—market mechanisms have been largely responsible for allocating resources among firms and among sectors of the economy, while authority and influence mechanisms have been largely responsible for allocating resources within firms.

To these two classes of allocative mechanisms we can add two more: democratic political processes and bargaining, which have received some

[1] Leonard D. White, *Introduction to the Study of Public Administration* (Macmillan, 1926), p. 2.

attention in both economics and administration.[2] Viewing these four mechanisms as functional equivalents, all concerned with resource allocation, raises all sorts of possibilities for investigation, and suggests numerous hypotheses, both normative and descriptive, about allocation. It also suggests a possible framework for classifying and interpreting the developments that have been taking place in the theory of the firm.

For example, we may consider explaining allocation in oligopolistic industries by bargaining rather than classical market mechanisms, as Galbraith, Shubik, and others have done. Conversely, we may pursue Anthony Downs's path of interpreting political behavior in terms of a generalized marginal analysis. We may seek parallels between the problems of control over political and administrative leaders by voters in a political democracy, and control over boards of directors and management by stockholders in a corporation. We may examine alternative arrangements for the joint use of prices and administrative controls to allocate resources in a wartime economy; or the consequences of using internal prices and divisional balance sheets to manage large multiproduct corporations.

Much of what is new in the theory of the firm has come from viewing allocation broadly, and from experimenting with the descriptive and normative application of the several allocative mechanisms outside the realms where they were initially discovered and employed.

PROSPECTUS

In my remarks I am going to describe developments in the theory of the firm under two main headings: first, developments arising out of the vigorous activity since the second World War in management science and operations research; second, developments arising out of descriptive, positive research on human behavior in organizations.

In each of these areas of work—management science and organization theory—I shall comment on what the new developments imply (1) for our theoretical models of the business firm, (2) for our understanding of allocative mechanisms, and (3) for techniques of investigating behavior in the business firm.

Finally, I shall take the liberty of adding a brief epilogue to the draft of this paper I sent to my discussants before the meeting—I shall be my own first discussant, as it were. In the epilogue I should like to indicate

[2] Robert A. Dahl and Charles E. Lindblom, in *Politics, Economics, and Welfare* (Harper, 1953), organize their analysis of resource allocation in terms of these four major types of processes: the price system, hierarchy (organization), polyarchy (democracy), and bargaining.

what consequences the new developments in the theory of the firm are likely to have for economic policy and welfare economics.

MANAGEMENT SCIENCE AND OPERATIONS RESEARCH

In sheer quantity, the man-hours that have been devoted to normative microeconomics—under such titles as "management science," "operations research," and "managerial economics"—outnumber those that have been applied to any other aspects of the theory of the firm in recent decades. Whether this has been an optimal allocation of effort is hard to say. It has certainly been productive. If optimizers are uncertain of its worth, satisficers can be content.

Since a whole session of last year's meetings of this Association was devoted to evaluating managerial economics' contributions to economic theory and vice versa, we need not go over the ground again in detail, but can base our conclusions on that previous discussion. The central fact is very simple: management science has brought economists in contact with the facts of business life, and businessmen in contact with the tools of economic analysis on a large scale, to the mutual advantage and surprise of both.

One of Mr. Wallis' colleagues has written that he already knows what an economist will find when he looks into a business firm, and that even if he finds something quite different it does not matter for economics.[3] He may be right on both counts, but since the looking will continue to go on, for quite practical reasons, we have no need to prejudge the result.

Management scientists are not concerned with systematic surveys of business practice. Their activity has not produced sample data from which one can extrapolate or aggregate a model of the behavior of firms in the economy. We should not underestimate, however, the impact upon economic theory of the anecdotal accounts of business decision making made available to economics by contact with business problems and practice.

THE ROLE OF INFORMATION IN THE MODEL OF THE FIRM

An example of this impact is the growing attention to search for information and transmission of information as vital steps in the decision-making process. Uncertainty is, of course, a venerable economic variable,

[3] Milton Friedman, *Essays in Positive Economics*, Chap. 1.

but the treatment of reduction of uncertainty as an economic activity is a relatively recent development. As Stigler observes:

> One should hardly have to tell academicians that information is a valuable resource: knowledge is power. And yet it occupies a slum dwelling in the town of economics. Mostly it is ignored: the best technology is assumed to be known; the relationship of commodities to consumer preferences is a datum. And one of the information-producing industries, advertising, is treated with a hostility that economists normally reserve for tariffs or monopolists.[4]

There is no difficulty in tracing this rediscovery of the economic significance of information back to activity in management science and operations research over the past two decades. Without attempting to reconstruct the history, I list some studies that gave information a central role and that are available to the economic theorist who wishes to re-examine the significance of this variable for the theory of the firm. An early example of the use of operations research techniques to solve a military problem was the application, discussed at length in the book of Morse and Kimball, of the theory of search to submarine warfare. Out of this application grew a more general theory of optimal search, developed by B. O. Koopman, Charnes and Cooper, and others.

Contemporaneously, consideration of games of imperfect information within the general framework of the theory of games led Marschak and Radner to develop an economic theory of teams, in which the cost of information and the value of information are the key variables.

Because management scientists became keenly aware of the imperfections of the data with which they worked, they early developed an interest in "sensitivity analysis." Sensitivity analysis is aimed at estimating the costs of making decisions with bad data and, correlatively, at estimating the value of procedures to improve the data. Cooper and Charnes and Dantzig developed techniques of sensitivity analysis as part of the apparatus for applying linear programming to management decisions. Sensitivity analysis and techniques for estimating the costs of inaccurate forecasts were developed for certain classes of dynamic programming models by Holt, Modigliani, Muth, and Simon in the United States and by Theil in the

---

[4] George J. Stigler, "The Economics of Information," *J.P.E.*, June, 1961. Even a casual perusal of the current journals will provide evidence for the rapidly growing popularity of information as an economic variable. The most recent example to come to my attention is Malmgren's paper, "Information, Expectations, and the Theory of the Firm," *Q.J.E.*, Aug., 1961.

Netherlands. Out of this and similar work came a new understanding of forecast horizons: the degree of independence of current decisions from information about distant events.

The examples cited are a sample, neither random nor systematic, of those that could be mentioned—almost all arising initially in the context of genuine practical decision problems. I might equally appropriately have mentioned the invention and development of sequential sampling theory by Wald, or Terborgh's analyses of optimal equipment replacement policies. (Professor Lintner, in the discussion, mentions another important example: the Renaissance of Bayesian statistical decision theory.) Or I could describe advances in the economic theory of distribution and advertising, no longer quite the neglected orphans that Stigler implies them to be in the passage quoted above.[5]

Now any or all of these developments could have come about without contact with practical decision-making problems. The theories are normative, not requiring data for their formulation or (in one sense, at least) their testing. The historical fact is that they were not discovered from an armchair. A proposition from search theory itself suggests the explanation for this historical fact: search begins when we are confronted with a problem for which no satisfactory solution presents itself.

Economists, statisticians, mathematicians, and natural scientists thrown up against concrete management problems discovered that the classical economic models paid little attention to the variables that were, in fact, crucial to rational practical action. All of us—economic theorists, management scientists, organization theorists—are satisficers when it comes to building our theories. We introduce new variables when we become aware that these variables are essential for explaining what we want to explain or solving what we want to solve. If information seeking is becoming significant for economic theory, it is because attempts to apply theory to the actual decision-making problems of the business firm have shown what a crucial role is played in decision by imperfections in our information and limits on our ability to calculate.

Attention to acquiring and processing information is only one way in which the decision models of management science have introduced new emphases into the theory of the firm. I may mention a few others. The new models are, of course, very much more detailed and disaggregated than the classical models. They introduce many decisions variables in addition to the quantities and prices of standard commodities. The multitudinous consequences of decisions are incorporated partly in the criterion function—

[5] See, for example, Frank M. Bass *et al.* (eds.), *Mathematical Models and Methods in Marketing* (Irwin, 1961).

usually a cost or profit function. They are incorporated also in policy constraints that can be introduced flexibly to handle "factors not elsewhere classified"—long-range considerations that are difficult to quantify, certain aspects of uncertainty, complications arising from external economies or diseconomies, and others.

IMPLICATIONS FOR RESOURCE ALLOCATION PROCESSES

What do the management science models tell us about the general theory of resource allocation, and the relative advantages of prices as compared with other allocative mechanisms? On balance, the introduction of formalized decision procedures incorporating such tools as linear programming and dynamic programming has tended to centralize the decision-making process. To be sure, the optimal solution of a linear programming problem can be interpreted in terms of classical marginalist principles, and quantities appear in the solution that have all the properties of prices. Nevertheless, in practice solutions are invariably obtained by centralized computations using algorithms like the simplex method and not by the *tatonnement* of a market. What are the reasons for this? Two are fairly obvious. First, with modern computing equipment, the solution-finding process is handled centrally at least as readily as it could be through decentralized price mechanisms. The decentralized procedures simply do not yield the savings in information-transmitting cost usually claimed for them. Second, since most of the internal "markets" involve bilateral monopoly, or something close to it, the exchange prices are administered and not competitive prices. Hence, most of the self-policing features of a competitive price system are absent.

There is a third important force toward centralization. In classical Marshallian theory, the principal reason for the existence of the firm, and for the use of administrative rather than market mechanisms for its internal decision making, is the presence of external economies in the operation of its parts. Frequently, the modern quantitative decision models of management science permit more careful attention to these external economies than was possible with simpler decision procedures, with the result that decisions are further centralized. It is common to find, for example, that without formal decision rules, almost independent inventory and production decisions are made by manufacturing and sales departments of companies. The resulting system behavior is far from optimal and often close to being dynamically unstable. Several quantitative studies suggest that such "arms-length" relations of manufacturing and sales departments in inventory policy can cause significant amplification of inventory cycles. Under these conditions, the co-ordination of policy permitted by centralized decision rules constitutes their major contribution to lowered costs.

Experience with the analytic tools of management science shows that the area in which marginalist principles are applicable is not coterminous with the area within which market mechanisms can be used effectively. The latter area is generally much narrower than the former. Under many circumstances, central planning authority and the other resources of organization are needed to secure the application of marginalist analysis to business decisions. Thus, the application of sophisticated marginal analysis within the firm is providing us with a great deal of information about the potentialities and limitations of prices and markets as allocative mechanisms—information whose usefulness for evaluating broader questions of institutional structure has yet to be exploited.

ORGANIZATION THEORY

I turn now to research of a less normative kind that has been directed largely toward understanding goal-forming, predicting, choosing, and control behavior in business firms. The classical theory has been criticized severely under all these heads. It has been asserted that the behavior of firms cannot be explained in terms of a profit-maximization goal; that classical frameworks for analyzing uncertainty are faulty; that the classical models falsify the process of choice; and that they ignore control processes entirely.

What are the facts? The central fact is that the facts are very scanty, indeed. Let us inventory them briefly:

1. There are anecdotal facts derived from the contacts of economists with business firms. Everything we know about how preconceptions color observations should lead us to mistrust these.
2. There are facts derived from sample studies of American business behavior. We have such facts on a variety of topics—business expectations and pricing practices, to mention two examples. The chief defect of these facts, and a very serious one it is, is that they are derived from questionnaires and, to a limited extent, interviews, and are consequently extremely sketchy. In surveys of practices, the facts are generally reports by businessmen as to how they make decisions, lacking independent checks of actual behavior.
3. There are facts obtained by intensive interviews and, to a limited degree, actual observations of behavior in individual business firms. The costs of intensive studies and the degree of co-operation required of the firms usually limit such studies to small and unrepre-

sentative samples of firms. Hence, there are major difficulties in extrapolating the findings to American business as a whole.

4. There are facts obtained by studying in the laboratory behavior that is (intendedly and allegedly) comparable to the behavior that occurs in business firms. The problem with such data is to establish the validity of the extrapolations.

In addition, simulation techniques—with or without computers—can be used to infer from any of these kinds of facts their implications for organizational behavior. (In his discussion of my paper, Professor Lazarsfeld has made some extremely valuable comments on several areas of sociological theory and method that are relevant to research on the business firm. Professor Lazarsfeld's suggestions are illustrative of the wealth of ideas for methods of investigation and theoretical concepts that the economist who wishes to study the firm at first hand can obtain from his colleagues in sociology.)

In enumerating the kinds of data that are available, I have emphasized limitations and gaps. There is a brighter side to the picture, to which I shall turn in a moment. First, however, I should like to emphasize strongly that neither the classical theory of the firm nor any of the amendments to it or substitutes for it that have been proposed have had any substantial amount of empirical testing. If the classical theory appeals to us, it must be largely because it has a certain face validity (e.g., "only those firms that maximize profits will survive in the long run") rather than because profit maximizing behavior has actually been observed. If we reject the classical theory, it must be largely because it appears to us to have a very low a priori probability (e.g., "firms don't have the information that would permit them to make profit maximizing calculations") rather than because any large body of data clearly refute it. As empirical scientists, we can only hope that in time the case will be different, that we will have the facts to test competing theories; it would be extravagant to claim that the time is now.

Developments in the theory of the firm have largely been of two kinds: (1) proposals for the revision of the theory to take care of objections that have been raised to it; (2) a variety of new techniques for securing data that would permit such proposals to be tested. These explorations have not yet been carried to the point where they give more than scattered indications of what the substantive answers will be.[6] Thus, in any assessment of

---

[6] Perhaps I am bending over backward in disclaiming knowledge of which version of the theory is correct. Obviously, I have my opinions, and even a certain amount of data that I regard as supporting them. However, one of the characteristics of the scientific endeavor is that it is not necessary to settle issues until enough evidence comes in—and even then they can always be reopened. In the present instance nothing is gained by claiming that the evidence is sufficient when it is so patently inadequate.

the progress that has been made over the past two decades, we need to emphasize progress in methods for studying human behavior in the business firm empirically, quite as much as the new facts discovered or the new theories to which these facts give rise.

To give substance to these general comments, I should like to review briefly four specific empirical studies, chosen to illustrate the range of techniques available for empirical research. In the first example, interviews in the business firm are the primary source of data; the second employs a laboratory experiment; the third includes direct observation of the decision-making process; in the fourth, computer simulation is used as a means of analyzing and interpreting the data.[7]

PRICING DECISIONS

The setting of prices plays a central role in classical theories of allocation—especially in theories of imperfect competition. It is not surprising, therefore, that pricing decisions have been studied empirically more than almost any others. The approach has generally been simple and straightforward: if you want to know how a businessman sets prices, ask him.

Obvious objections can be—and have been—raised to finding out about a decision-making process by asking the decision-maker. Does he know; and will he tell. Perhaps much of what the decision-maker does is "intuitive" and judgmental [and] resides in his subconscious when he does it; and perhaps not all, or most, of it can be recaptured even by retrospection. Moreover, how is the businessman motivated to reveal to the researcher his *modus operandi*? In certain circumstances, does not he even lay himself open to risks of antitrust prosecution if he describes how prices are set?

An increasing number of studies based upon extensive interviews in business firms show that these problems can usually be solved satisfactorily. For studies of pricing decisions, interviewing has many advantages over less intensive techniques using questionnaires. To be sure, both methods elicit answers to questions posed by the researcher. But the information gathered through interviewing in a firm can be orders of magnitude more detailed than the information obtained from questionnaires. Respondents probably provide less deliberate misinformation in a face-to-face interview than in a

---

[7] I have drawn most of my examples from work I know at first hand. Hence my discussion may well sound parochial. It is in no way intended as a survey of the field and I hope my discussants will help correct my myopia by citing some of the important work that has been done on other campuses.

mail questionnaire, and when they consciously warp the facts, they are more easily found out. The interview need not rely on general statements of practice but can probe these by applying them in detail to concrete examples or instances. The interviewer can explore, for example, the exact sequence of decisions and events in the most recent price changes the firm has made. He can see whether these events are consistent with the replies he has received about general pricing practices and procedures, and can ask for—and usually get—clarification when there are apparent discrepancies.

Finally, the interviewer need not rely on a single respondent in the firm but can usually get access to a number of executives and functionaries who participate in different aspects of the pricing decision. Almost everyone who does this for the first time is surprised to find how diffusely information about policies and practices is scattered among individual participants in a large business organization, and what a fragmentary picture each single individual has of the whole process. Thus, a major consequence of the use of interview techniques is to replace the classical reification of the firm as a single "entrepreneur" with a model of a complex organization comprised of many interacting parts. It is at this stage of inquiry that organizational considerations begin to play a major role in interpretations of the decision-making process.

For example, the authors of the Brookings study, *Pricing in Big Business*, make the observation that in large multiproduct firms it is one thing to adopt a policy of "maximizing return on investment" or even of "securing a satisfactory return and share of market"; it is quite a different matter to set up procedures that will reflect these and other relevant policies in setting the prices of the individual items the company sells.

The difficulties in relating procedures for pricing items to general price policies do not reside solely or mainly in conflicts of interest between the owners of the firm and subordinate managers. Even apart from such conflicts, price setting involves an enormous burden of information gathering and computation that precludes the use of any but simple rules of thumb as guiding principles. Through detailed study of pricing by multiple interviews throughout the firm we begin to get a picture of the informational and computational constraints that hedge in the pricing process and give it form. We learn, for example, that whatever the shape of the real world, the world that his accounting figures reveal to the businessman is usually one of constant marginal costs, virtually up to the point where output equals full capacity. With this knowledge, the businessman's wariness of price competition takes on a new interpretation, quite different from that given it by classical theories of monopoly and imperfect competition.

LABORATORY EXPERIMENTS ON ORGANIZATIONAL DECISIONS

Discovery of major discrepancies between the classical theory of the firm and the decision-making process as revealed by interviews whets the appetite for explanation. We can conjecture why these things are so—as we have just done in the last paragraph. But how test our hypotheses? The laboratory offers one possibility. From interviews, we reach the conclusion that executives who occupy particular positions in firms acquire estimating biases induced by, and characteristic of, those positions. We should be able to abstract the essential characteristics of the positions, say, of sales executives and production executives, respectively, and to create abstract analogues of these positions under laboratory conditions. If the explanation of the estimating biases is correct, then the corresponding biases should appear under the laboratory conditions. As in the natural sciences, we can sometimes test our understanding of a phenomenon by trying to produce that phenomenon in the laboratory.

Some experiments by Cyert, Dill, and March illustrate this approach. In one experiment, subjects were asked to estimate a quantity on the basis of two previous estimates purportedly made by other persons. Under one experimental condition the subjects were told they were "cost analysts" and that the numbers were predicted costs of a new product. Under the other condition, they were told they were "market analysts" and that the numbers were predicted sales of a new product. Both groups were given the same data from which to make their estimates. The "cost analysts" consistently made higher estimates than the "market analysts." In a somewhat more complex experimental design, the same investigators were able to induce estimating bias by motivating subjects to estimate high or low, but also to induce corrective processes as subjects anticipated and adjusted for the biases of the others who were collaborating with them.

Notice that in this way of using the laboratory as a data-generating device complementary to the field study, we met halfway the usual objections against extrapolating casually from laboratory to real-life situations. Generalizations are not extrapolated from laboratory to field. Rather the laboratory is used as a further check on our understanding of phenomena that we have already observed, and tried to explain, in the field.

THE OBSERVATION OF DECISION MAKING

Students who have progressed from the arm chair, to the questionnaire, to the interview, to the laboratory in their desire to discover how decisions are actually made in the business firm find it relatively easy to take the next step—actually to watch decisions in the course of their manufacture.

Decision-makers are, in fact, unconscious of many of their own judgmental processes. Moreover, even when their motives are of the best they are unreliable witnesses about what has happened in the past. The very positional biases that the study of executive thinking has revealed make their testimony suspect when it rests on memory of events that have passed through the selective filters of perception and interpretation. These deficiencies in the data can be reduced greatly if decisions are studied contemporaneously rather than retrospectively.

But what does it mean to "observe" decision making? The decision-making process is at best a stream of words and at worst a stream of thoughts. The former, if not the latter, can be captured and recorded. And now the fact that many persons participate in a business decision comes to the aid of the researcher. In individual human problem solving and decision making, the whole process can often take place inside a human skull, completely screened from observation. In organization problem solving, the stream of thoughts cannot go on very long without being accompanied by a stream of words. If the words can be recorded, a great deal can be learned about the process.[8]

As we proceed from the questionnaire through the interview to the observational study, we gain a great deal in the richness of the detail of process that we can observe. The price we pay is to give up any notion of sampling a universe of decisions in favor of making a careful record of one or a few. Both the cost of such studies and the problems of finding business firms that can and will permit them to be carried out make formal sampling notions inapplicable. Hence this approach rests on the assumption that we can reach an understanding of mechanisms through detailed study of processes without sampling in the ordinary way.

An example of this kind of intensive study of decision making is an investigation by Cyert, Dill, and March. They studied decisions by a steel company to invest in new capital equipment, in order to determine how expected return on the investment was estimated and how this factor was weighed against others in determining priorities among projects. The summary of this particular study will illustrate the picture of the decision-making process that is emerging from such work.

Three major features of this decision process are particularly interesting from the point of view of the place of expectations in a theory of

[8] In point of historical fact, some of the social psychologists who pioneered in the study of problem solving and decision making in groups did so not because they were interested in organizational phenomena, but as a means of externalizing the phenomena and making them accessible to observation.

business making. First, it is clear that search behavior by the firm was apparently initiated by an exogenous event, was severely constrained, and was distinguished by "local" rather than "general" scanning procedures. Second, the noncomparability of cost expectations and expected returns led to estimates that were vague and easily changed and made the decision exceptionally susceptible to the factors of attention focus and available organizational slack. Third, the firm considered resources as fixed and imposed feasibility tests rather than optimality tests on the proposed expenditure.

Clearly, we are viewing a resource allocating process here that is decidedly different from the price mechanism. One of its significant characteristics is that it is capable of operating in situations, like this one, where the relevant marginal quantities are not thought to be computable.

COMPUTER SIMULATION OF DECISION MAKING

As research moves toward more and more intensive and detailed observation of the decision process, it is soon faced with the historian's dilemma. How can this vast mass of fact be reduced to order as a first step toward interpreting it and generalizing from it? Although it is some centuries since astronomers have thought of the matter in this way, they too were once faced with the same dilemma. They had voluminous data on the locations of the heavenly bodies at many points of time. The first step was to describe these in terms of geometrical paths—the cycles and epicycles of the Ptolemaic system. A little later these paths were simplified to the circles of Copernicus and the elipses of Kepler. But the great simplification came, of course, with Newton, who showed that the scheme of the heavens could be represented far more parsimoniously by replacing the time paths of planets with the different equations that generated those paths.

For centuries after Newton, systems of differential or difference equations provided the model of "ideal" scientific explanation of dynamic systems. The modern digital computer, with its very general capacities for representing symbol-manipulating systems, opens to us the same possibility for explaining the time stream of a decision-making process by means of a computer program for simulating—i.e., generating—that stream.

The feasibility of reducing detailed historical data on decisions to programs capable of generating them has now been demonstrated by actually carrying it out in a number of instances. (On a much more macroscopic scale, the same approach has been adopted for theorizing about the economy. Orcutt's model of household behavior stands midway between classical macroeconomic dynamic models and the detailed microeconomic models we are discussing here.)

A program to explain the processes of a company deciding to install a digital computer was sketched out by Cyert, Simon, and Trow. A much more detailed program has been flow-diagrammed to represent the decision-making processes of a department store buyer. And recently, Clarkson has produced a computer program that predicts in great detail the decisions of the investment officer of the trust department of a bank. Although there are not yet many examples in the literature investigations of a comparable kind have now been carried out by other workers.

Thus, with the advent of the high-speed digital computer, economics has acquired a new theory-building and theory-testing tool that will enable it to handle far more detail of the firm's behavior than could be treated in the past. With optimism we may even hope that the demands of the institutionalists for faithfulness to the facts will no longer seem irreconcilable with the demands of theorists for facts that are manageable. We will feel less constrained to believe in a particular kind of world just because it happens to be a world that is easily theorized about.

CONCLUSION

In painting this picture of what has been transpiring in the theory of the firm, I have faced a difficult problem of selection and sampling, which I have solved largely by emphasizing the work with which I am most closely familiar. I have discussed a few general trends and developments that seem especially significant: the contact with problems of the firm that was induced by the growth of management science, and the increasing attention to problems of information flows that was engendered by that contact; the growth of techniques for studying the decision-making process in great detail and from vantage points within the firm; the study of the firm as a multiperson complex organization; the first steps toward exploring the use of computer programs as a new way of theorizing about complex systems.

On the substantive side, our new knowledge of the decision-making process betokens a major advance over the next few years in the general theory of allocation. Two centuries ago, economic theory discovered, in the price mechanism, an allocative procedure possessing quite remarkable properties. These properties and their application to the regulation of an economy have been pretty thoroughly explored by successive generations of economists. We are now becoming increasingly aware that the price mechanism is just one—although an exceedingly important one—of the means that humans can and do use to make rational decisions in the face of uncertainty and complexity. We are beginning to understand what some of the other mechanisms are and how they are used.

EPILOGUE

Those economists who are not specialists in the theory of the firm may well ask what implications these developments have for general economics —and particularly for the traditional core of the profession's interest in public policy and welfare economics. I think there are at least three kinds of implications that deserve attention.

First, conclusions about welfare in such areas as tax and antitrust policy depend in an important way upon the underlying postulates about the behavior of the individual firm. The picture of the firm that is emerging from the new research is that of a searching, information processing, satisficing, allocating mechanism. It is doubtful that the propositions that hold with the assumption of static, profit-maximizing firms under conditions of certainty also hold for such firms. Professor Baumol has already provided examples of how conclusions about tax incidence have to be modified if we assume the firm to be a sales maximizer rather than a profit maximizer.

Second, the great plan versus no plan debate hinges in considerable measure upon empirical propositions about how price mechanisms and planning mechanisms in fact operate: what costs they impose of information gathering and computing: how stably and rapidly they adjust the system to environmental change. Studies inside the business firm are providing us with a great deal of factual information about the costs and administrative problems associated with various allocative mechanisms. These facts are already calling into question beliefs that allocation through markets simplifies information processing as compared with centralized allocative processes.

Third, when we try to apply classical models to actual decision-making problems within the firm, we find that important modifications and improvements have to be made in these models if they are to operate successfully with the kinds of imperfect information that are available in the real world. From these necessities have emerged inventions like linear programming and modified concept of rationality like the satisficing concept. As we move from the decision-making tasks of the individual firm to the greater complexities of public decision making for the economy, we discover an even more pressing need for the improvement of the classical tools of analysis. The tool-building innovations in management science are already providing answers to some of these needs—witness, for example, the applications of linear programming to economic development by Tinbergen and his colleagues. The "new realism" in the approach to the firm's decision problems may also prove a major force toward moving welfare economics back from the position of rather excessive formalism it has reached in recent years to a more direct concern with, and ability to handle, concrete policy problems.

For these reasons, we may expect rather confidently that the rapid progress that has been taking place in our understanding of the business firm will induce secondary changes of considerable magnitude in the other branches of economic theory.

2

The theory of the growth of the firm

Edith T. Penrose

THE FIRM AS A COLLECTION OF PRODUCTIVE RESOURCES

The cohesive character that an administrative organization imparts to the activities of the people operating within it provides the justification for separating for analytical purposes such a group from all other groups. The activities of the group which we call an industrial firm are further distinguished by their relation to the use of productive resources for the purpose of producing and selling goods and services. Thus, a firm is more than an administrative unit; it is also a collection of productive resources the disposal of which between different uses and over time is determined by administrative decision. When we regard the function of the private business firm from this point of view, the size of the firm is best gauged by some measure of the productive resources it employs.

The physical resources of a firm consist of tangible things—plant,

From Edith T. Penrose, *The Theory of the Growth of the Firm* (John Wiley & Sons, Inc., 1959), pp. 24–42 and pp. 149–150. Reprinted by permission.

equipment, land and natural resources, raw materials, semifinished goods, waste products and by-products, and even unsold stocks of finished goods. Some of these are quickly and completely used up in the process of production, some are durable in use and continue to yield substantially the same services for a considerable period of time, some are transformed in production into one or more intermediate products which themselves can be considered as resources of the firm once they are produced, some are acquired directly in the market, and some that are produced within the firm can neither be purchased nor sold outside the firm. All of them are things that the firm buys, leases, or produces, part and parcel of a firm's operations and with the uses and properties of which the firm is more or less familiar.

There are also human resources available in a firm—unskilled and skilled labour, clerical, administrative, financial, legal, technical, and managerial staff. Some employees are hired on long-term contracts and may represent a substantial investment on the part of the firm. For some purposes these can be treated as more or less fixed or durable resources, like plant or equipment; even though they are not "owned" by the firm, the firm suffers a loss akin to a capital loss when such employees leave the firm at the height of their abilities. Such human resources may well be on the payroll for considerable periods of time even though their services cannot be adequately used at the time. This may sometimes be true also of daily or weekly workers. They, too, may often be considered as a permanent "part" of the firm, as resources the loss of whose services would involve a cost— or lost opportunity—to the firm.

Strictly speaking, it is never *resources* themselves that are the "inputs" in the production process, but only the *services* that the resources can render.[1] The services yielded by resources are a function of the way in which they are used—exactly the same resource when used for different purposes or in different ways and in combination with different types or amounts of other resources provides a different service or set of services. The important distinction between resources and services is not their relative durability; rather it lies in the fact that resources consist of a bundle of potential services and can, for the most part, be defined independently of their use, while services cannot be so defined, the very word "service" implying a function, an activity. As we shall see, it is largely in this distinction that we find the source of the uniqueness of each individual firm.

Ideally, the size of a firm for our purposes should be measured with respect to the present value of the total of its resources (including its personnel) used for its own productive purposes. This is almost impossible

---

[1] I am avoiding the use of the term "factor of production" precisely because it makes no distinction between resources and services, sometimes meaning the one and sometimes the other in economic literature.

to discover in practice, and in the absence of any really satisfactory measure of size we have a wide choice depending on our purpose. For the most part, though not always, the analysis of the growth of firms that is developed in the following chapters is most directly applicable to their growth measured in terms of fixed assets. This measure has its own disadvantages and there is no overwhelming reason for choosing it rather than another; adaptations of the analysis can be made to meet the requirements of nearly any measure, and at appropriate points in the following pages various problems of measurement will be discussed. As I have indicated, however, the use of total assets may distort the size of the firm as a productive unit because it includes the "placements"[2] of a firm which may be large simply because the firm is unable to expand its productive operations fast enough to make full use of its cash resources. This point will become clearer as we analyze the process of growth.

THE MOTIVATION OF THE FIRM

We cannot leave this discussion of the functions and nature of the firm without making a few remarks about the "motivation" of the firm—why it acts as it does. It is reasonable to assume that the people making decisions on behalf of a firm are acting in the light of some purpose, yet it is notoriously difficult to discover the true purposes of anyone. On the other hand, purposive behaviour cannot be understood if one does not know what the purpose is. Therefore if the economist is to understand the behaviour of firms he must make some assumption about why they do what they do. The more he believes that his assumption corresponds to the true motives, the greater will be his confidence in a theory designed to explain the behaviour of firms. It is possible that his theory may be very useful for analysis and for prediction, even if he is not very happy about the "realism" of his assumption, but the theory will not satisfy his desire to "understand," and his confidence in it will be correspondingly reduced.

Accordingly, a theory purporting to explain the process of growth of firms can be useful on two levels. It can be useful even if it only presents a logical model yielding conclusions which seem to correspond to actual events that can be "observed" in the growth of actual firms. But it will be even better if it helps us to understand the actions behind these events. For this, if we assume that firms act for a purpose, we must find an acceptable

---

[2] This ingenious term was proposed by Joan Robinson to denote "the purchase of titles to debts or shares," and is used here to mean investments outside the firm which, though perhaps conferring some power to influence the behaviour of other firms, do not bring the other firms into the administrative orbit of the investing firm. See Joan Robinson, *The Accumulation of Capital* (London: Macmillan, 1956), p. 8.

assumption as to *why* they act. In either case, the usefulness of the theory can only be tested against facts relating to particular firms.[3]

The Profit Motive

The assumption on which this study is based is simply that the growth of firms can best be explained if we can assume that investment decisions are guided by opportunities to make money; in other words that firms are in search of profits. But then the further question arises, why should a *firm*, or more accurately the managers of a firm, always want to make more profits? The "profit motive" when applied to individuals is usually based on the psychological assumption that increases in income and wealth have personal advantages for the individual which will spur him to obtain what he reasonably can.[4] The profits of a firm do not confer such advantages on individuals unless they are paid out as income to individuals. From this it is often concluded that a firm is interested in making profits in order to pay out dividends to owners. To be sure, some dividends must be paid to maintain the reputation of the firm and, in particular, its attractiveness to investors as the source of future funds, but why should a firm ever want to pay out more than this if owners are not in a position to force it to do so?[5]

Almost every large firm to-day is appropriately classed as "management controlled", that is to say, most firms that have grown large (according to any of the commonly accepted criteria of what is large) have reached a

[3] In this it differs fundamentally from the "theory of the firm," the primary usefulness of which lies in the extent to which it explains the response in the economy as a whole to those types of change which the theory leads us to believe will affect the price and output decisions of firms. The usefulness of this type of theory is not dependent upon whether or not it helps to explain the behaviour of any particular firm (although it may do so); consequently the appropriate test of its usefulness does not lie in its applicability to particular firms.

[4] For this reason, it has sometimes been held that the "profit motive" is weaker in the large corporations than in the small firm because the various managers of the former have less personal "stake" in the firm's profits. There may be some truth in this, but the extensive use of impersonal accounting records with which to judge the performance of the individual business executives in charge of the various operations of the large firms may have exactly the opposite effect; the "profit motive" may be sharpened simply because the personal preferences of businessmen are more rigidly controlled in the interests of the firm.

[5] ". . . the distribution of dividends . . . is a problem in the theory of the firm analogous to the problem of the distribution of a consumer's income between consumption and saving, and it presents similar analytical difficulties. From the point of view of the balance sheet a cash dividend represents a simple destruction of liquid assets. It is not an exchange, for no asset is created to correspond to the assets destroyed; it is, from the firm's point of view, an act of more or less voluntary consumption. It may be asked, therefore, why should the firm ever perform such an act?" Kenneth E. Boulding, *A Reconstruction of Economics* (New York: Wiley, 1950), p. 113.

size where either the ownership equity is widely shared, or the owners' control of operations is in practice effectively limited by the managerial bureaucracy.[6] Salaried managers have little or nothing to gain by paying out more than is necessary to keep existing shareholders from complaining in force, to attract any additional capital that may be needed, and in general to build up or to maintain the reputation of the firm as a good investment. On the contrary, the managers of a firm have much more to gain if funds can be retained and reinvested in the firm.[7] Individuals thereby gain prestige, personal satisfaction in the successful growth of the firm with which they are connected, more responsible and better paid positions, and wider scope for their ambitions and abilities. On this view, dividends would be looked on as a cost to be kept to a level no higher than necessary to keep investors happy; providers of capital, like providers of labour services, must be remunerated, sometimes handsomely, but a desire to remunerate them as handsomely as possible is not a plausible explanation of the behaviour of modern corporations.[8] Even owner-managers often seem to be more in-

[6] This is not only true in a country like the United States where firms have reached a very large absolute size, but also in some smaller countries as well. In the sample of large industrial firms that I studied in Australia, for example, not one was effectively owner-controlled in spite of the fact that no firm in Australia would be considered large in comparison with United States firms. The only exceptions were some of the wholly-owned subsidiaries of foreign corporations, and even here the influence of management was often very strong in all policy decisions.

[7] This does not mean that executives will keep their own salaries small in order to leave more for profits. On the contrary, the salaries of top executives will tend to get as high as the community will condone or as the conscience of the executives themselves will permit (and sometimes higher if the size of the remuneration can be concealed or "justified" by devices such a stock purchase options or other bonuses). The total remuneration of "top" executives in a large corporation will be such a small proportion of total profits that its effect on net profits has little practical significance, and the executives know this.

[8] It has been argued, for example, that an enterprise attempts to maximize net income to its owners, but that this is equivalent to maximizing the present worth of its assets, "for the significance of the assets to the firm is their ability to contribute to the realization of the desired stream of dividends," that is, "the stream of cash payments (dividends) to owners (shareholders) having the greatest present worth." N. S. Buchanan, *The Economics of Corporate Enterprise*. (New York: Holt, 1940), p. 209.

I am saying, on the other hand, that the enterprise must be considered separately from its owners from this point of view. In the calculation of the present value to owners of a dividend stream, dividend payments in the near future should be given more weight than dividend payments in the distant future. For the firm, however, dividend payments in the present may reduce funds available for investment and therefore reduce net earnings in the future, and there is no evidence at all that firms consider that the greater value of present cash payments to owners offsets in any degree the value to be attached to the prospect of higher earnings for the enterprise in the future. Furthermore, the "significance of assets to the firm" may just as well be considered to lie in their "ability to contribute" to meeting a "desired" payroll, a "desired" managerial bonus payment, or any other "desired" cost. Only if higher dividends in the present are expected to maintain

terested in the growth of their firm than they do in the income they with-draw from it. Small businessmen frequently tend to identify themselves with their firm and to view it as their life's work, as a constructive creation to which they can point with pride and which they can pass on in full strength to their children. To this end they often prefer to reinvest their profits in the firm rather than outside and to draw only moderately on profits for their personal consumption.

It seems reasonable, therefore, to assume that in general the financial and investment decisions of firms are controlled by a desire to increase total long-run profits.[9] Total profits will increase with every increment of invest-ment that yields a positive return, regardless of what happens to the marginal *rate* of return on investment, and firms will want to expand as fast as they can take advantage of opportunities for expansion that they consider profitable.[10] On this assumption, we would expect a marked tendency for firms indefinitely to retain as much profit as possible for reinvestment in the firm; we would also expect that funds that could not be profitably used would be invested instead of being used substantially to raise dividends, unless higher dividends were required to attract further equity capital. In other words, profits would be desired for the sake of the firm itself and in order to make more profit through expansion. The proposition, thus baldly stated, may to some seem to imply extreme and almost irrational behaviour. Yet it is, to my mind, the most plausible of the various possible assumptions.[11]

---

or increase the availability of capital funds in the future will the firm have an incentive to make them.

[9] Of course, no assumption about motivation will fit all firms. Indeed, there are many examples of firms that have been "milked" by those in a position to do so, and the firm destroyed because individuals in control were more interested in protecting their own interests than those of the firm or even of its owners. See, for example, the story of the destruction of the Amoskeag Manufacturing Company by a group of somewhat un-scrupulous trustees. Alan Sweezy, "The Amoskeag Manufacturing Company," *Quarterly Journal of Economics*, Vol. LII (May 1938), pp. 473–512.

[10] It should be noted that this in no way gets around the ambiguities inherent in the notion of a "most profitable" course of action in an uncertain world where businessmen possess different degrees of optimism and different attitudes toward risk and uncertainty. These questions are discussed in the next chapter.

[11] Compare, for example, the views of one of the more "popular" writers on business matters. Speaking of large corporations Herrymon Maurer remarks, "Such an enterprise is too big for any one owner or group of owners to control. It is run, therefore, not primarily for the stockholders, who have generally become used to a socially approved return on their investment, but for the enterprise itself. The aim of the enterprise is not immediate or even future maximum profits, once thought to be the goal of all enterprise, but healthy future existence, to which the size of profits is an important but secondary consideration." Herrymon Maurer, *Great Enterprise: Growth and Behavior of the Big Corporation* (New York: Macmillan, 1955), p. 186.

Long-Run Profits and Growth

The assumption that the managers of firms wish to maximize long-run profits derived from investment in the enterprise itself has an interesting implication for the relation between the desire to grow and the desire to make profits. If profits are a condition of successful growth, but profits are sought primarily for the sake of the firm, that is, to reinvest in the firm rather than to reimburse owners for the use of their capital or their "risk bearing,"[12] then, from the point of view of investment policy, *growth and profits become equivalent as the criteria for the selection of investment programmes.* Firms will never invest in expansion for the sake of growth if the return on the investment is negative, for that would be self-defeating. Firms will never invest outside the firm except eventually to increase the funds available for investment in the firm. To increase total long-run profits of the enterprise in the sense discussed here is therefore equivalent to increasing the long-run rate of growth. Hence, it does not matter whether we speak of "growth" or "profits" as the goal of a firm's investment activities.

There is no need to deny that other "objectives" are often important— power, prestige, public approval, or the mere love of the game—it need only be recognized that the attainment of these ends more often than not is associated directly with the ability to make profits. There surely can be little doubt that the rate and direction of the growth of a firm depend on the extent to which it is alert to act upon opportunities for profitable investment. It follows that lack of enterprise in a firm will preclude or substantially retard its growth, although "enterprise" is by no means a homogeneous quality, a problem to which we return in the next chapter.

THE PRODUCTIVE OPPORTUNITY OF THE FIRM AND THE ''ENTREPRENEUR''

The business firm, as we have defined it, is both an administrative organization and a collection of productive resources; its general purpose is to organize the use of its "own" resources together with other resources acquired from outside the firm for the production and sale of goods and services at a profit; its physical resources yield services essential for the

---

[12] Payout, under an ideal dividend policy in a growth situation, should not exceed the minimum amount necessary to maintain the market position and integrity of existing debt and equity issues and of issues contemplated in the near future." Harold Quinton, "Financing Growth Industries in an Inflated Economy: Standards, Theory and, Practice," in *Long-Range Planning in an Expanding Economy* (American Management Association, General Management Series, No. 179), p. 29.

execution of the plans of its personnel, whose activities are bound together by the administrative framework within which they are carried on. The administrative structure of the firm is the creation of the men who run it; the structure may have developed rather haphazardly in response to immediate needs as they arose in the past, or it may have been shaped largely by conscious attempts to achieve a "rational" organization; it may consist of no more than one or two men who divide the task of management; or it may be so elaborate that its complete ramifications cannot even be depicted in the most extensive chart. In any event, there need be nothing "fixed" about it; it can, in principle, always be adapted to the requirements of the firm—expanded, modified, and elaborated as the firm grows and changes.

The productive activities of such a firm are governed by what we shall call its "productive opportunity," which comprises all of the productive possibilities that its "entrepreneurs" see and can take advantage of.[13] A theory of the growth of firms is essentially an examination of the changing productive opportunity of firms; in order to find a limit to growth, or a restriction on the rate of growth, the productive opportunity of a firm must be shown to be limited in any period.

It is clear that this opportunity will be restricted to the extent to which a firm does not see opportunities for expansion, is unwilling to act upon them, or is unable to respond to them. We shall examine later the considerations

[13] The term "entrepreneur" throughout this study is used in a functional sense to refer to individuals or groups within the firm providing entrepreneurial services, whatever their position or occupational classification may be. Entrepreneurial services are those contributions to the operations of a firm which relate to the introduction and acceptance on behalf of the firm of new ideas, particularly with respect to products, location, and significant changes in technology, to the acquisition of new managerial personnel, to fundamental changes in the administrative organization of the firm, to the raising of capital, and to the making of plans for expansion, including the choice of method of expansion. Entrepreneurial services are contrasted with managerial services, which relate to the execution of entrepreneurial ideas and proposals and to the supervision of existing operations. The same individuals may, and more often than not probably do, provide both types of service to the firm. The "management" of a firm includes individuals supplying entrepreneurial services as well as those supplying managerial services, but the "competence of management" refers to the way in which the managerial function is carried out while the "enterprise of management" refers to the entrepreneurial function. The nature of the organization of a firm and the relationships between the individuals within it have often as important an influence on the competence and enterprise of management and on the kinds of decisions taken as do the inherent characteristics of the individuals themselves. The influence of "organizational structure" has been particularly stressed by the "organization theorists". See, for example R. M. Cyert and J. G. March, "Organization Structure and Pricing Behavior in an Oligopolistic Market," *American Economic Review*, Vol. XLV, No. 1 (Mar. 1955), pp. 129–139.

determining the kind of opportunity a given firm will perceive, and determining its ability to take advantage of what it does see; but at the very least we have to assume that the firm is eager and willing to find opportunities and is not hindered in acting on them by "abnormally" incompetent management. In other words the firms with which we shall be concerned are enterprising and possess competent management; our analysis of the processes, possibilities, and direction of growth proceeds on the assumption that these qualities are present in the firm.

It may be that most firms do not grow, that failure is more common than success, that over the long, long period, firms, like Schumpeter's lemmings, follow each other in succeeding waves into the sea and drown, or even that "death and decay" are "inherent in the structure of organization".[14] These things we do not know. We have neither the facts to disprove them nor convincing theoretical presumptions to support them.

We do know, however, that large numbers of firms *have* survived for long periods, and that there is at present no conclusive evidence that they have reached or are even near the end of the road—that they will not continue growing indefinitely. We know that other firms have been successfully established since the late 19th century, which, for our purposes, can be considered the beginning of the "corporate age" marking the end of a necessarily close connection between the fortunes of firms and the fortunes of families. Many of the relatively young firms show the same characteristics which mark the successful older firms. These are the types of firms we are concerned with; and the fact that we deal only with enterprising firms possessing or able to attract competent management does not prejudge any part of our argument. It merely provides us with a class of firms which are capable of growing. In the absence of such firms there would be no need for a theory of growth.

Enterprise, or "entrepreneurship" as it is sometimes called, is a slippery concept, not easy to work into formal economic analysis, because it is so closely associated with the temperament or personal qualities of individuals. This extremely personal aspect of the growth of individual firms has undoubtedly been one of the obstacles in the way of the development of a general theory of the growth of firms. It is important, therefore, to examine briefly the nature of "enterprise" and to indicate its significance and the role it will play in our analysis.

---

[14] As Kenneth Boulding has suggested in "Implications for General Economics of More Realistic Theories of the Firm," *American Economic Review* (Papers and Proceedings), Vol. XLII, No. 2 (May 1952), p. 40.

THE ROLE OF ENTERPRISE
AND THE COMPETENCE OF
MANAGEMENT

There are probably many ways of defining enterprise, but for our purposes it can usefully be treated as a psychological predisposition on the part of individuals to take a chance in the hope of gain, and, in particular, to commit effort and resources to speculative activity. The decision on the part of a firm to investigate the prospective profitability of expansion is an enterprising decision, in the sense that whenever expansion is neither pressing nor particularly obvious, a firm has the choice of continuing in its existing course or of expending effort and committing resources to the investigation of whether there are further opportunities of which it is not yet aware. This is a decision which depends on the "enterprise" of the firm and not on sober calculations as to whether the investigation is likely to turn up enticing opportunities, for it is, in effect, the decision to make some calculations. This is truly the "first" decision, and it is here that the "spirit of enterprise", or a general entrepreneurial bias in favour of "growth" has perhaps its greatest significance.

The assumption that firms are "in search" of profits already implies some degree of enterprise, for it is only in the special case where the profitability of expansion in a given direction is obvious and the decision to expand almost automatic that no particular quality of enterprise is required. One sometimes does hear businessmen insist that their firms "just grew", that there was no alternative—orders were coming in, demand was high and, pressed by circumstances, the firm simply "had to expand". Such conditions do not last indefinitely and the unenterprising firm ceases to expand as this type of opportunity declines. The enterprising firm, if it is a large one, will permanently commit part of its resources to the task of investigating the possible avenues for profitable expansion, acting on the general presumption, supported perhaps by past experience, that there are always likely to be opportunities for profitable growth, or that expansion is necessary in a competitive world. Smaller firms may only periodically be able to consider in what directions expansion might be profitable. In any case, the decision to search for opportunities is an enterprising decision requiring entrepreneurial intuition and imagination and must precede the "economic" decision to go ahead with the examination of opportunities for expansion.

Entrepreneurial versus Managerial Competence

"Enterprise" is obviously closely related to "ambition," but even if a firm is not very ambitious it may nevertheless be competently managed. This is particularly true of those smaller firms where there is a close relation between the "goals" of owners and the "goals" of firms. There are many businessmen, and very efficient ones too, who are not trying always to make more profits if to do so would involve them in increased effort, risk, or investment. In many industries and areas there are a considerable number of firms which have been operating successfully for several decades under competent and even imaginative management, but have refrained from taking full advantage of opportunities for expansion. Many of these are "family firms" whose owners have been content with a comfortable profit and have been unwilling to exert themselves to make more money or to raise capital through procedures that would have reduced their control over their firms.

It is not reasonable to expect all businessmen to devote their last ounce of energy to making money. In wage theory, it is well recognized that after a point higher wages may reduce, or at least fail to increase, the supply of labour. There is no reason to assume that businessmen and workers are fundamentally different in this respect. Hence we should not assume that the prospect of higher profits will always call forth the necessary effort from *all* firms in a position to earn them. Very good businessmen may well possess a personal scale of values in which an income greater than that necessary to provide a comfortable position in the community has a relatively low claim on time and effort.

Such men may have a high degree of managerial skill and imagination; they may be hard and efficient workers, but the ambition that would drive other men in the same circumstances to expand their operations in an unending search for more profit, and perhaps greater prestige, may be lacking. There is no inconsistency here: a good businessman need not be a particularly ambitious one, and so long as a firm is dominated by men who are not ambitious always to make profits it is unlikely that the firm will grow very large. Entrepreneurial preferences of this sort provide exactly the same kind of restriction of a firm's growth as does entrepreneurial inability to perceive or to act upon opportunities for profitable growth, for the most effective restriction on the quality of entrepreneurial services is that which stems from a lack of interest in experimenting with new and alien lines of activity, or in moving into new geographic areas. I say that this is the most effective restriction because mere specialization of managerial knowledge and ability is not of itself a serious bar to a firm's branching out into new lines of activity if existing executives are sufficiently interested and imaginative to bring into the firm people possessing the relevant knowledge and ability. Thus, the managerial competence of a firm is to a large extent a function of the quality of the entrepreneurial services available to it.

THE QUALITY OF ENTREPRENEURIAL SERVICES

"Enterprise" is by no means a homogeneous characteristic, and the "quality" of enterprise, that is to say, the particular types of entrepreneurial service available to a firm, is of strategic importance in determining its growth. Many of the most important services that a firm's entrepreneurs can produce are not the result of "tempermental" characteristics of the individual men but are shaped and conditioned by the firm itself; this point will be taken up in the following chapters, for the "production" within the firm of an important class of entrepreneurial services is a significant aspect of its changing productive opportunity. Here I want merely to discuss some of the "temperamental" aspects of the quality of entrepreneurial services which are not amenable to economic analysis, but which nevertheless cannot be ignored; all we can do is to note them here and at appropriate points consider their effect; we cannot explain them in economic terms.

Entrepreneurial Versatility

Entrepreneurial versatility is a somewhat different quality from managerial or technical versatility. The latter two qualities are primarily questions of administrative and technical competence; the former quality is a question of imagination and vision, which may or may not be "practical". To the extent that entrepreneurial ideas are inherently impractical, they are of little use to a firm; but if they are commonplace and short-sighted they are equally useless, and firms whose entrepreneurs are "dull" are by this fact alone restricted in their growth.[15] It often happens that the horizon of a firm, particularly of a smaller firm, is extremely limited. Content with doing a good job in his own field, the less enterprising entrepreneur may never even consider the wider possibilities that would lie within his reach if only he raised his head to see them. If occasionally he gets a glimpse of them, he may lack the daring or the ambition to reach for them, although he may be an ambitious, efficient, and successful producer in his chosen field or chosen geographical location. "Specificity" of entrepreneurial resources means that some of the productive services most essential for expan-

---

[15] Entrepreneurial services are probably required in some degree in most firms, for only if all the activities of a firm are carried out in a well-defined traditional way can one say strictly that no entrepreneurial function is being performed. It is, I think, important to recognize that there are varying degrees of qualities of "enterprise." The Schumpeterian "entrepreneur," though more colourful and identifiable, is too dramatic a person for our purposes. Schumpeter was interested in economic development and his entrepreneur was an innovator from the point of view of the economy as a whole; we are interested in the growth of firms, and here the entrepreneur is an innovator from the point of view of the firm, not necessarily from the point of view of the economy as a whole.

sion will not be available to the firm even though all managerial services which are required for efficient operation in a particular field are fully available.

There are many examples of firms with vigorous and creative management which have substantially altered their range of products, sometimes completely abandoning their original products and expanding their total output in spite of unfavourable demand conditions for the old products. But there are also many examples of other firms which have not been able to make the required adjustments. In such cases, failure to grow is often incorrectly attributed to demand conditions rather than to the limited nature of entrepreneurial resources.

The relation between "demand" and the growth of firms is discussed later (Chapter V). Plainly, however, to the extent that a firm is capable of producing only a given range of products, any limitations on the market for those products will restrict the firm's opportunities for expansion. A versatile type of executive service is needed if expansion requires major efforts on the part of the firm to develop new markets or entails branching out into new lines of production. Here the imaginative effort, the sense of timing, the instinctive recognition of what will catch on or how to make it catch on become of overwhelming importance. These services are not likely to be equally available to all firms.[16] For those that have them, however, a wider range of investment opportunities lies open than to firms with a less versatile type of enterprise, although the mere existence of "enterprise" is not sufficient, as we shall see, to enable a firm to move indiscriminately into any kind of activity.

It is not helpful to dismiss this lack of vision or of experimenting ambition as an example of a failure to attempt to "maximize profits", for it is intimately connected with the nature of entreprenurial ability itself and must be reckoned as a limitation on the supply of specific types of productive services.

Fund-Raising Ingenuity

Difficulties in obtaining capital are often given pride of place among the factors preventing the expansion of small firms, but this is legitimate in only a very limited sense. New, small, and unknown firms do not have the

[16] The history of the Farr Alpaca Company provides an instructive example not only of the effect of enterprising leadership on a small firm's ability to raise capital, create markets, alter its product lines as conditions change, and grow large and powerful, but also of the effect on a successfully established firm of the advent of unenterprising and short-sighted leadership when its original "productive opportunity" declines. Frances G. Hutner, *The Farr Alpaca Company: A Case Study in Business History* (Northampton, Mass.: Dept. of History, Smith College, 1951).

same facilities for raising capital as do established, large, and known firms. Of this there is little question. On the other hand, many small firms without adequate initial financial resources do succeed, do raise capital, do grow into large firms. And they do this, for the most part, by virtue of a special entrepreneurial ability. There are many examples testifying to the ingenuity of the superior businessman in obtaining the funds he needs, and only if the requisite entrepreneurial ability is lacking can one safely say that a firm cannot attract the required capital.[17]

To be sure, the type of entrepreneurial service needed to raise capital may not be closely related to the type of services needed to run a firm efficiently, for successful raising of capital depends on an entrepreneur's ability to create confidence. Thus small firms have often relied on a division of labour between an inventor or a skilled production manager, and a "businessman" able to raise capital and buy on credit. The statement that "shortage of capital" is the cause of failure of small firms often means merely that a very particular and possibly very rare sort of entrepreneurial ability is required to launch successfully a new firm on a shoestring or to keep up the rate of net new investment required to enable it to reach a size and position where its general credit standing is well established. On the other hand, even firms with substantial financial resources but indifferent managerial resources can escape trouble only if their entrepreneurs are sufficiently flexible and imaginative to know the kind of management needed by the firm and to attract it. Capital is a problem for the small and new firm in much the same sense that "demand" is a problem—the same kind of quality of "enterprise" that might be successful in a known and established firm, may not be successful in "selling" a firm or its product to cautious and sceptical investors or consumers.[18]

---

[17] Such, for example, was the ability of W. R. Morris (later Lord Nuffield), the well-known British automobile industrialist, to inspire confidence, that once when he asked for credit from a bank and was turned down, one of the directors of the bank threatened to sell his shares in the bank and finance Morris personally. Morris got the money, for, as Andrews reports, ". . . in the last resort, what really interests a bank is just this sort of judgment of personalities [and] it was prepared to give way. . . ." P. W. S. Andrews and Elizabeth Brunner, *The Life of Lord Nuffield* (Oxford: Basil Blackwell, 1955), pp. 105–6.

[18] A prominent management consulting firm has stressed the same point: "Among the resources which are scarce in the economic sense are certain psychological aptitudes including the spirit of enterprise and the ability to organize and run a new firm. There is reason to believe that only a small fraction of the working population possess these talents to an extent which is adequate for success. . . . The allocation of entrepreneurial skills is a controlling factor in the allocation of other scarce resources. A primary function of the entrepreneur is to persuade investors to put up their money. . . . If he does not possess adequate personal funds to launch the business he must then convince others that

It is, of course, true that "capital-raising ingenuity" is most easily recognized by its results, for it is difficult to say whether a given entrepreneur possesses the ability to raise capital if he has not yet demonstrated it by raising capital. Therefore, it would not be very helpful, even if true, to say that small firms fail to raise capital because they do not have the ability to do so, and I do not mean to argue in this way. There is little doubt that the most ingenious and persuasive of entrepreneurs are at times unable to raise critically needed finance.[19] I want merely to draw attention to the fact that there is a relation between entrepreneurial ability and the finance a firm can attract, and that difficulties attributed to lack of capital may often be just as well attributed to a lack of appropriate entrepreneurial services, in the sense that a different entrepreneur in the same circumstances might well achieve different results.

Entrepreneurial Ambition

The fact that businessmen, though interested in profits, have a variety of other ambitions as well, some of which seem to influence (or distort) their judgment about the "best" way of making money, has often been discussed, particularly in connection with the controversial subject of "profit maximization". From our point of view it will be useful to distinguish two broad types of entrepreneurial ambition, which are difficult to define with any precision, but which will be easily recognizable from a brief description of some of their characteristics.

There are some entrepreneurs who seem to be primarily interested in the profitability and growth of their firm as an organization for the production and distribution of goods and services. These we might call "product minded" or "workmanship-minded" entrepreneurs or "good-will builders." Their interests are directed towards the improvement of the quality or their products, the reduction of costs, the development of better technology, the extension of markets through better service to consumers, and the introduction of new products in which they believe their firms have a productive or distributive advantage. They take pride in their organization, and from their point of view the "best way" to make profits is through the improvement and extension of the activities of this organization.

Another type of entrepreneur, whom we might call the "empire-builder"

---

a differential advantage exists and can be exploited effectively at the proposed level of capitalization. *Thus the size of the capital requirement is not in itself a barrier if a genuine opportunity exists.* The larger the amount required, however, the smaller may be the number of prospective entrants who will be able to gain the confidence of investors either because of their persuasive powers or because of a personal record of success." Alderson and Sessions, *Cost and Profit Outlook*, Vol. VII, No. 11 (Nov. 1954), p. 2. (Italics added).

[19] For a discussion of the special problems of small firms see Chapter X below.

is of a different order. He is pushed by visions of creating a powerful industrial "empire" extending over a wide area. Though he may be concerned with product-improvement and development as a means of maintaining the competitive position of his firm, these activities are delegated to others in the firm, for he is much more interested in the extension of the scope of his enterprise through acquisition or the elimination of competitors by means other than competition in the market. He may hold fairly closely to a particular industrial field with the notion of obtaining a dominant position in that field, or he may range widely in his ventures, taking up anything that appears profitable. The successful empire-building entrepreneur must have initiative and be aggressive and clever in the strategy required to bargain with and successfully outmanoeuvre other businessmen; he requires a keen instinct for purely financial manipulations and a shrewd judgment in assessing not only the value of other firms but also the minimum costs at which they can be acquired, for often whole firms may be bought and sold merely for the "quick profits" to be obtained from them.[20] Above all, the empire builder, as the name implies, is a business politician and strategist—upon ability of this type his success depends.

The empire-builder will be of concern in this study only to the extent that he contributes to the process of growth of an industrial firm. Many empire-builders are, as individuals, nothing more than financial speculators, and the collection of firms they acquire never take on the characteristics of a single industrial firm as we have described it. We shall have occasion to examine the effects of "empire-building" on the process of growth of a firm, but for the most part the entrepreneurial services that will be of interest to us are of the "product-" or "workmanship-minded" variety.

Entrepreneurial Judgment

Unlike "versatility," "ingenuity," and "ambition." the quality of entrepreneurial judgment is only partly a question of the personal characteristics or temperament of the individual. So far as it does turn on the personal ability of the entrepreneur, we can only treat it as we have treated other types of individual ability, and content ourselves with the observation that firms whose entrepreneurs are not capable of reasonably "sound" judgments do not come within the class of firms with which we are concerned. That there are firms who consistently make mistakes, over-estimate what they can do, guess wrongly the future course of events, no one can doubt, but

[20] From one point of view, perhaps, these two types of entrepreneur are analogous to the "Stickers" and "Snatchers" that Hicks has described with respect to pricing policy. The former are concerned with building up a steady business, the latter with quick profits. See J. R. Hicks, "The Process of Imperfect Competition", *Oxford Economic Papers*, New Series, Vol. VI, No. 1, (Feb. 1954), pp. 41–54.

they do not interest us here; no theory of growth will explain their actions—only a theory designed to explain "mistakes" or failure.

To a large extent, however, the problem of entrepreneurial judgment involves more than a combination of imagination, "good sense", self-confidence, and other personal qualities. It is closely related to the organization of information-gathering and consulting facilities within a firm, and it leads into the whole question of the effects of risk and uncertainty on, and of the role of expectations in, the growth of firms. These aspects of the matter can be made an integral part of the analysis of the growth process, because the "expectations" of a firm—the way in which it interprets its "environment" —are as much a function of the internal resources and operations of a firm as of the personal qualities of the entrepreneur. This relationship we take up in the following chapters, but first a word about the significance of expectations.

THE ROLE OF EXPECTATIONS IN THE PRODUCTIVE OPPORTUNITY OF THE FIRM

Although the "objective" productive opportunity of a firm is limited by what the firm is able to accomplish, the "subjective" productive opportunity is a question of what it thinks it can accomplish. "Expectations" and not "objective facts" are the immediate determinants of a firm's behaviour, although there may be a relationship between expectations and "facts"— indeed there must be if action is to be successful, for the success of a firm's plans depends only partly on the execution of them and partly on whether they are based on sound judgment about the possibilities for successful action. In the last analysis the "environment" rejects or confirms the soundness of the judgments about it, but the relevant environment is not an objective fact discoverable before the event; economists cannot predict it unless they can predict the ways in which a firm's actions will themselves "change" the relevant environment in the future. In any event, what the economist sees may be very different from what an individual firm sees, and it is the latter, not the former, that is pertinent to an explanation of a firm's behaviour. Firms not only alter the environmental conditions necessary for the success of their actions, but, even more important, they know that they can alter them and that the environment is not independent of their own activities.[21] Therefore, except within very broad limits, one cannot

21 See my article "Biological Analogies in the Theory of the Firm," *American Economic Review*, Vol. XLII, No. 5 (Dec. 1952), pp. 814–15, and the subsequent *Rejoinder* to the *Reply* of A. A. Alchian, ibid. (Vol. XLII, No. 4 (Sept. 1953), pp. 600–609.

adequately explain the behaviour of firms or predict the likelihood of success merely by examining the nature of environmental conditions.

Within the unknowable limits placed by the environment on successful action there is a wide scope for judgment. We shall be interested in the environment as an "image" in the entrepreneur's mind, for we want, among other things, to discover what economic considerations, as contrasted with "temperamental" considerations, determine entrepreneurial judgments about the environment. The factors affecting the relation between the "image" and "reality" are not being ignored, but for an analysis of the growth of firms it is appropriate to start from an analysis of the firm rather than of the environment and then proceed to a discussion of the effect of certain types of environmental conditions. If we can discover what determines entrepreneurial ideas about what the firm can and cannot do, that is, what determines the nature and extent of the "subjective" productive opportunity of the firm, we can at least know where to look if we want to explain or to predict the actions of particular firms. If we can further establish that there are significant factors expanding the productive opportunity of a firm and causing it to change in a systematic way over time with the operation of the firm, we are on the trail of a theory of the growth of firms.

.   .   .   .

THE FIRM AS A POOL OF RESOURCES

The discussion of the role of diversification in the process of growth perhaps brings out more clearly than would anything else the significance of the statement made in an earlier chapter that a firm is essentially a pool of resources the utilization of which is organized in an administrative framework. In a sense, the final products being produced by a firm at any given time merely represent one of several ways in which the firm could be using its resources, an incident in the development of its basic potentialities. Over the years the products change, and there are numerous firms to-day which produce few or none of the products on which their early reputation and success were based. Their basic strength has been developed above or below the end-product level as it were—in technology of specialized kinds and in market positions. Within the limits set by the rate at which the administrative structure of the firm can be adapted and adjusted to larger and larger scales of operation, there is nothing inherent in the nature of the firm or of its economic function to prevent the indefinite expansion of its activities.

The continual change in the productive services and knowledge within a firm along with the continual change in external circumstances present the firm with a continually changing productive opportunity. Not all firms, to be sure, possess the qualifications which will permit them to take advantage of such opportunities, but it is sufficient for our purposes to have outlined the qualifications, to have analyzed the factors determining the direction of expansion of those firms possessing the requisite qualifications, and to have shown that there is no necessary limit to growth as time passes.

3

Some basic problems
in the theory
of the firm

Andreas G. Papandreou

The concept of the firm which is employed by economists in their teaching and research clearly reflects the frame of reference they have selected in dealing with the problems of their discipline. This frame of reference has been aptly called the *action* frame of reference.[1] It consists of five basic concepts: The *act*, the *agent*, the *end*, the *situation*, which includes both means (elements of the situation over which the agent exerts control) and conditions (elements of the situation over which the agent cannot exert control), and finally, the *norm*, that is, the principle which relates means to ends. The norm postulated by the economist is that of rationality. The agent is conceived as engaging in action which maximizes a utility index (an ordinally structured preference system), given the constraints inherent in the situation.

[1] Cf. Talcott Parsons, *The Structure of Social Action* (New York, 1937; 2nd ed., Glencoe, 1949), Ch. 2 for a discussion of the action frame of reference.

Reprinted with permission from Papandreou's "Some Basic Problems in the Theory of the Firm" in *A Survey of Contemporary Economics*, E. F. Haley (ed.), (Homewood, Ill.: Richard D. Irwin, Inc., 1952), pp. 183–222.

The concept of the firm has been built to fit the specifications of this frame of reference. This has been accomplished through the postulation of the concept of the entrepreneur, which to all intents and purposes displaces that of the firm in analysis. This result is attained in a fairly simple manner. The firm emerges as soon as the owners of productive services sell them to an entrepreneur for a definite price. When this set of transactions is consummated the owners of the productive services cease to be of analytic concern to us. We then turn to the entrepreneur, who thus becomes our sole object of analysis as far as the behavior of the firm is concerned. This tour de force enables the economist to retain his schema of an acting individual agent, even in the case of the firm, which may legitimately be regarded as a "collective" of some sort. This probably is the key to the interesting fact that the economist has not evolved a theory of conscious cooperation. On the contrary his main and lasting contribution lies in the formulation of the properties of unconscious cooperation via the system of markets.

The adequacy of the economist's frame of reference in dealing with the wide variety of behavior problems which do not involve conscious interdependence among the acting agents cannot be seriously subjected to question. As soon as we leave the realm of unconscious interdependence, however, and attempt to deal with problems of deliberate cooperation we find ourselves increasingly falling back on concepts and generalizations whose relationship with the main body of thought is more or less tenuous. The duopoly or oligopoly problem is a case in point. Although interesting work dating back to Cournot had been done on the "small numbers" case within the basic conceptual frame of reference employed by the economist, effective incorporation of these issues into the main body of thought did not seem feasible until the advent of the theory of games.[2] The same comment is in order in connection with the conscious cooperation which takes place within the firm. Whenever the economist becomes concerned with such problems as "union participation in management," or the "separation between ownership and control" he has to fall back on concepts and generalizations which are not part and parcel of his main frame of reference. Concern with such matters has been the province of the institutional economist, an economist, that is, who in one way or another employs much of the sociologist's or the social psychologist's method and vocabulary.

It will be argued in this essay that the literature of the last two decades has provided the means whereby the conceptual frame of reference of the economist can be widened to incorporate without strain the concepts which

[2] John von Neumann and Oskar Morgenstern, *Theory of Games and Economic Behavior* (Princeton, 1944; 2nd ed., 1947).

are necessary for the consistent treatment of problems of conscious cooperation. The contributions which are considered crucial in this respect are
three. There is, first, the contribution of Chester Barnard, who in his *The
Functions of the Executive*[3] has laid the foundations for a theory of conscious
cooperation which is consistent with the frame of reference employed by
the economist. There is next the monumental work of Neumann and
Morgenstern on the theory of games. Finally, Herbert Simon's work has
brought together under one conceptual roof Barnard's concept of organization and Neumann and Morgenstern's concept of a game of strategy.[4]

In the part immediately following, an attempt will be made to present
a frame of reference which will enable the economist to deal with problems
of intrafirm structure without doing violence to his main conceptual schema.[5]
This model will in turn lay the foundation for a systematic consideration of
two related problems: first, the relationship between social structure and
the structure of "power" and "control" over the firm, and secondly, the
relationship between the character of the preference system of the firm and
the cultural milieu in which it has grown.[6]

1. THE CONCEPT OF THE FIRM IN THE LIGHT OF THE THEORY OF ORGANIZATION

A. The Concept of Organization

The fundamental building block of a conceptual frame of reference
which assigns a central position to conscious cooperation is provided by
Chester Barnard's concept of *organization*. Organization is defined as a
"system of consciously coordinated activities or forces of two or more
persons."[7] It should be stressed that it is only the system of personal interactions that makes up the fabric of organization. Organization is not conceived, then, as a *group* of persons; rather it is conceived as an *action field*,
as a system of consciously interdependent actions of two or more persons.
When we consider persons in their roles as members of an organization, we
regard them in their purely functional aspects, as mere phases of coopera-

---

[3] Cambridge, Mass., 1938.

[4] H. A. Simon, *Administrative Behavior* (New York, 1945).

[5] The decision has been made not to consider in this essay the contributions of the social
psychologists or the industrial sociologists. Although their work is rich in empirical findings, the task of relating their conceptual frame of reference to that of the economist
cannot be carried out within the confines of this essay.

[6] It must be stressed at this juncture that these basic problems are the only aspects of
the theory of the firm which will be considered in this essay.

[7] *Op. cit.*, p. 73.

tion. The persons as such, whether they be conceived as physical, biological, or psychological and social entities, do not belong to organization.

Closely related to the concept of organization is the concept of a co-operative system. Organization is an element of the cooperative system; so are the persons whose activities constitute organization, and the physical plant which goes hand in hand with persons and organization. Persons and physical plant constitute a cooperative *system* (rather than an aggregate) by reason of the fact that the activities of the members are consciously coordinated toward the achievement of at least one definite end.[8]

The following conditions must be met for organization to emerge: first, persons must be willing to contribute activity to the system; secondly, they must share a common goal; thirdly, deliberate communication must be possible and present. The first two conditions must be met if the pattern is to be considered consciously cooperative. The third condition, deliberate communication, must also be met if conscious coordination and, therefore, organization is to merge. Herbert Simon, who on the whole accepts the Barnard schema, prefers to state the problem in the language of the theory of games.[9] The cooperative pattern emerges when the participants prefer the same set of consequences. If anticipations concerning one another's behavior are correct, all will act to secure these consequences. In the absence of deliberate communication, however, the pattern may be expected to be highly unstable. Conscious coordination is the device or process whereby each participant is informed as to the strategies selected by the others.

Organization in Barnard's sense obtains whenever the activities of two or more persons are consciously coordinated with a view of achieving a common goal.[10] Organization is, therefore, ubiquitous. It extends from the simplest and most unstructured cooperative activities to the most complex and imposing structures. The act of exchange may be chosen as an example of the simplest sort of organization. Willingness to participate, joint goal (in some sense), and deliberate communication are all present. To the act of exchange which constitutes simple organization can be contrasted the complex organization which typically obtains in the case of the firm. The firm is in fact a cooperative system possessed of an organization which is

---

[8] *Ibid.*, p. 65.

[9] *Op. cit.*, pp. 72–73.

[10] The reader must be warned that the discussion of the concept of organization in this essay is confined to what Barnard calls *formal* organization. To formal organization Bernard contrasts *informal* organization. The latter refers to the set of interactions among persons which are not governed by a common goal and which, therefore, are not consciously coordinated. The concept of informal organization is akin to the social psychologist's concept of the group.

both stable and complex. Stability in this connection refers to the non-ephemeral character of at least a part of the interactions which are included in the enterprise. Complexity refers to the fact that (typically) the firm's organization is made up of a system of simple or unit organizations. The process of communication in a complex organization cannot be left to chance. It becomes specialized in centers of communication. These fairly stable centers of communication make up the executive (sub-) organization of the firm. The executive-administrator is regarded within this frame of reference as a communication center, as the functionary who informs the participants of one another's strategies so that the cooperative goal may be achieved. Communication of the strategies involved in the process of co-operation is a necessary condition for the performance of the executive role. It is not a sufficient condition, however. The executive is not a mere center of communication. He also wields *authority* over the participants. The executive function, therefore, implies the issuing of coordinating *and* authoritative communications to those who contribute activities to the firm's organization. Authoritative coordination lies at the heart of the concept of the firm. Since authority plays such an important role in the concept of the firm selected in this essay, it is necessary to provide a definition of the term. Following Barnard and Simon we may define a communication as authoritative if the recipient accepts it as determining the premises of his choice of action "without deliberation on his own part on the expediency of those premises."[11]

B. The Process of Coordination

The conception of the firm as a cooperative system permits the organization theorist to set up a "rational" model of the firm closely resembling that of the economist; but, at the same time, it enables him to employ much of the available sociological and psychological material.

The rational model of the firm as constructed by the organization theorist resembles that of the economist in that rationality is attributed only to the executive organization or some segment thereof (corresponding closely to the economist's concept of the entrepreneur), while the economist completely removes from his model all agents other than the entrepreneur. The organization theorist, while including in his model the activities of the operative (nonexecutive) staff, views them as being partly rational and partly nonrational. In so doing, however, he does not destroy the purely

---

[11] Simon, *op. cit.*, p. 125. Simon has introduced, in this connection, the concept of the "area of acceptance." The area of acceptance may be defined as that subject of all actions which may be performed by an employee with respect to which he is willing to accept the executive communication as guiding his behavior.

rational character of the total construction. This is accomplished by regarding the activities of the operatives as manipulable components of the system. The sociological and psychological considerations enter the rational administrative action model as *data* in a means-ends problem, in the same fashion that end systems, technologies, and institutions enter the rational action model of the economist. Organization theory and the economist's theory of the firm are seen to converge, in fact, as soon as we introduce organizational techniques as data into the latter, side by side with the technological data.

Adoption of the rational model implies that we regard the executive organization of the firm or some segment thereof (which might be identified as the apex of the executive pyramid) as seeking to achieve ends with scarce means in a rational manner. This implies that administrative action is regarded (within the confines of the model) as efficient. Efficiency in turn implies that the means employed in the attainment of an end system are minimized or conversely that the ends attained from a given set of means are maximized.

The organization goals constitute the fundamental value premises of the system.[12] We are not concerned at this juncture with the manner in which these goals are formulated and the reasons for their acceptance by the executive as guiding his actions. This will concern us in detail at a later stage of the argument. All that needs to be emphasized here is that these goals are best regarded as being related to one another through a utility index of some sort. Nor is it necessary that we consider them to be ultimate ends; it would be preferable to consider them as intermediate stages in a means-ends chain in which they function as value indices of some sort. The goals of the firm—in the sense just described—must be contrasted sharply to what may be called the *function* of the firm. Function, in this sense, refers to the intended output of the firm, whether it is a service or a commodity. The function of a shoe manufacturing firm, for instance, is the production of shoes. It should be clear that when we talk about the utility index, the value premises accepted by the executive as guiding his actions, we make no commitment on the number or type of ends that enter the system nor do we make a commitment relating to the manner in which they are ranked. The statement is perfectly general, permitting any interpretation which is suitable in any concrete cases we care to study. It is conceivable, for instance, that the function of the firm may enter explicitly the value premises accepted by the executives as guiding their actions. Concern with "service" in this sense may, in fact, be prevalent in the case of government corporations, public utilities, etc. It is also possible that the conservation of the firm

---

[12] Cf. *ibid.*, Ch. 3.

may become one of the ends sought by the executives. Students of administration seem to be convinced that this is typical rather than unusual, at least in the case of the large concern.

Given the goals of the system, the (rational) executive engages in action which will enable the firm to attain them in an efficient way. This process involves (1) substantive planning, (2) procedural planning, and (3) execution of both plans.[13] Substantive planning essentially refers to the construction of the firm's budget,[14] whereas procedural planning refers to the construction of the psychological environment of decision necessary for the emergence of the organization. Substantive planning, procedural planning, and execution of the plans should not be conceived as a series of separate steps but rather as an integrated whole.

The structure of the system of communications and authority is the key to the procedural plan. This involves much more than the preparation of an organization chart specifying the channels of communication and authority. If the persons contributing activities to the firm's organization were regarded as rational agents, not much more than the organization chart would be needed. Under such conditions the operative could be considered as sub stituting organizational value premises for his private value premises and proceeding to act efficiently in a more or less automatic fashion. This construction implies that the operative (or, in fact, any contributor of action to the organization of the firm) substitutes a preference system communicated to him by the executive for his own personal preference system.[15]

The model of organization just presented is pegged upon the assumption of rational action on the part of all the participants in the organization of the firm. If it is recognized, however, that action is partly rational and partly subject to habit and the stimulus-response pattern, the procedural plans must elaborate the structure of internal influences as well as of authority which will provide the appropriate stimuli and lead to the establishment of the repetitive patterns which are necessary for the efficient attainment of the organizational ends. Learning theory and social psychology will provide the information necessary for the formulation of the appropriate procedural plan. The inculcation of loyalty to the organization and to the organizational goals, the development of efficient patterns of action and high morale become most important under these circumstances.

The distinction between influence and authority must be elaborated somewhat if we are to avoid making some of the conventional errors of

---

[13] *Ibid.*, p. 96.

[14] Cf. G. F. Thirlby, "Notes on the Maximization Process in Company Administration," *Economica*, Aug. 1950, XVII, 266–82.

[15] For a discussion of these issues, see Simon, *op. cit.*, Ch. 6, 10.

students of administration. In a complex organization, centers of communication are established which issue information to the participants concerning one another's strategies. When these communications are accepted by the recipient as determining the premises of his choices "without deliberation on his own part on the expediency of those premises,"[16] a relationship of authority exists between the issuer and the recipient of the communication. Authority, we have already seen, is of the essence in the structure of the firm. Authority in this sense, however, need not be exercised exclusively in a downward direction, though it is undoubtedly predominantly exercised in this manner. It may be exercised sideways and even in the upward direction. The structure of authority as it is depicted in organization charts refers not to the actual pattern of authority, but rather to that expected to prevail in the "normal" course of events. Influence implies suggestion and persuasion rather than command. The recipient of influence may accept a communication as governing his action; he does so, however, following "deliberation on his own part on the expediency" of the premises contained in the communication. The structure of influence is obviously of crucial significance in the functioning of an organization, especially in view of the fact that it is difficult to identify and control its sources.

Executive organizations in large or complex firms are themselves complex. This complexity expresses itself in a twofold manner. First, the lines of authority become elongated. Secondly, at any one level of this vertical scale of authority, executive work is divided into specialized function segments, giving rise to what may conveniently be called horizontal decentralization of authority. A large and complex firm, then, is almost invariably associated with an executive process which is decentralized both vertically and horizontally. With respect to the vertical decentralization of authority it is important to contrast *peak coordination* to inferior or subordinate coordinating activities. Peak coordination includes all the executive tasks performed at the apex of the executive pyramid. Authoritative and conscious coordination at its peak levels is carried on with a sense of the whole and in view of the total complex relationships of the firm to its social and physical environment. The internal and external equilibria of the system are sought simultaneously against the constellation of data confronting the firm. At levels inferior to that of peak coordination, this complex totality is lost. The outstanding characteristic of the peak coordination level of the executive organization is that it is not subject to horizontal decentralization. It should be clear, of course, that the fact that peak coordination is not subject to horizontal decentralization does not imply that the function must be performed by a single person. It is possible to allocate this function to a group

---

[16] *Ibid.*, p. 125.

rather than to an individual (an "organization" in Barnard's language). Although, then, peak coordination must be carried out by a single agency, the "singleness" of this agency must allow for subtle qualitative and quantitative variation in its composition.

G. F. Thirlby prefers the term *maximization center* for describing what has been called peak coordinator in this essay.[17] The substantive plan of the firm, according to Thirlby, is incorporated into the operating budget which is formulated by the maximizing center. The executive function at lower levels than that of peak coordination does not consist merely in the execution of the rigid orders of the peak coordinator. The task of selecting strategies, the task of selecting among alternative courses of action, is distributed, in general, throughout the organization. "Initiative may be exercised: (a) within the tolerance limits allowed by standing orders; (b) in the planning process leading to the board's decision which lays down standing orders."[18] The extent to which strategy selection is delegated down the lines of authority varies from case to case. What is crucial to keep in mind, however, is this: *the extent and character of the delegation is an integral part of the procedural plan selected by the peak coordinator.*[19]

C. The Process of External Influence

In the preceding section we considered the flow of authority and influence *within* the firm as they relate to the attainment of the firm's goals. Both the goals toward which the firm strives, however, and the manner in which they are attained are subject to powerful and all-pervasive influences

---

[17] *Op. cit.*, p. 267.

[18] *Ibid.*, p. 271.

[19] A number of empirical studies have been published during the last decade dealing essentially with the problem of location of the "decision-making" function in the contemporary enterprise. Clearly the outstanding study is R. A. Gordon's *Business Leadership in the Large Corporation* (Washington, D.C., 1945). It is mandatory reading for all concerned with problems of enterprise structure. P. E. Holden, L. S. Fish, and H. L. Smith's *Top-Management Organization and Control* (Stanford, 1941) is one exception to the run-of-the-mill management studies in that it combines a conceptual framework and case-study material. It seems on the whole, however, to be more normative than observational-analytical in character. The Harvard Graduate School of Business Administration studies of the board of directors, despite their informative character, completely lack a conceptual framework. Such generalizations as are presented in these studies merge with normative considerations to produce a list of more or less loosely stated recipes for running a business. I am specifically referring to J. C. Baker, *Directors and Their Functions* (Boston, 1945), M. T. Copeland and A. R. Towl, *The Board of Directors and Business Management* (Boston, 1947), and M. L. Mace, *The Board of Directors in Small Corporations* (Boston, 1948).

from outside the firm.[20] This is just another way of saying that the firm is a component of a much broader cooperative system which, in its informal aspects, becomes coextensive with what we call society. In a typical firm-and-market economy we are confronted with a process of cooperation which is partly conscious and partly unconscious. Within the firm, cooperation is of a deliberate character, with the conscious coordination of activities supplied by the firm's executive organization. In contrast to this, cooperation as it concerns the relations among firms (for that matter, as it concerns the relations among "units" in general), is unconscious; the interfirm or interunit cordination is supplied by the system of markets.[21]

No less important is the unconscious influence provided by the mores, folklore, customs, institutions, social ideals, and myths of a society which lay the foundation for formal organization. More immediately relevant to any one firm's behavior are the standards and values of the groups and communities with which it comes into contact as an organization, as well as the groups, communities, and organizations to which its members belong. It should be clear that the preference system of the firm, as well as the attitudes of the participants in the firm's organization toward such things as cooperation, authority, efficiency, innovation, etc., must be profoundly affected by the broader community within which the firm operates.[22]

Side by side with these unconscious societal influences we find influences exercised consciously by a variety of organizations, groups, and persons which in one way or another are affected by the firm's behavior (i.e. constitute "interest-groups"). This set of influences is highly heterogeneous; in order to make some headway, therefore, in the analysis of their consequences upon firm behavior some attempt at classification must be made.[23] To begin with we are concerned here with conscious *external* influences rather than those of an *internal* nature. The latter have already been discussed in some detail in the preceding section. An influence is regarded as being internal if it is exercised by a participant in the organization (in the Barnard sense) during the process of conscious cooperation. It follows that the highest level of authority (in the sense of channels of

---

[20] The reader should be warned that the term "influence" is used in this connection in the loose lexical sense rather than in the technical sense imparted to it by Simon's definition. Hereafter, whenever we employ the term in its technical sense, we shall italicize it.

[21] In this connection see R. H. Coase, "The Nature of the Firm," *Economica*, Nov. 1937, IV, 386–405.

[22] For an excellent presentation of these issues the reader is urged to see H. A. Simon, D. W. Smithburg, and V. A. Thompson, *Public Administration* (New York, 1950), Ch. 3.

[23] See Gordon, *op. cit.*, Ch. 7, and G. C. Means in National Resources Committee, *The Structure of the American Economy* (Washington, D.C., 1939) Pt. 1, Ch. 9, for two attempts at presenting a consistent system of concepts.

authority expected to hold under "normal" conditions) from which internal influences can be exercised over the organization is that of the peak coordinator. The peak coordinator may himself be influenced by communications (or anticipations of communications) issued by stockholders, creditors, a union, and so on; such influence, however, will not be regarded as internal since it is not a component of the system of activities which are coordinated by the organization's executive.

Conscious external influences may be broken down into two categories: (1) the exercise of *influence* and (2) the exercise of authority. External *influence* and authority may be exercised over a firm by: (*a*) the government (in its sovereign aspects); (*b*) groups earning income by contributing factor services to the cooperative system (i.e., owner-stockholders, lenders of money, suppliers of goods on lease, operative labor, executive and professional labor); (*c*) buyers of the firm's product; (*d*) sellers of products and services to the firm; (*e*) competitors in the factor and product markets; (*f*) other persons, groups, or organizations which take interest in its operations. The degree of influence that such groups are in a position to exercise probably varies with their "power," whatever this ambiguous term may be taken to mean.

One final distinction seems necessary at this juncture. When the exercise of influence has as its immediate object the peak coordinator, it may either affect his conception of the broad value premises, the preference system of the organization, or it may affect the objective environment, the factual premises of his decision.[24] In the former case the results sought by the organization are modified or even radically changed as a result of the influence exercised. This implies that a new strategy will be selected. In the latter case the results sought are not affected, but, since the factual premises are changed, the strategy will have to be modified.[25]

D. Some Implicit Issues

Although no attempt has been made to define the firm, it must be clear from the context that the firm is considered as a cooperative system possessed of a unique executive organization—an organization, that is, which con-

[24] The distinction between factual and value premises is discussed at length in Simon, *op. cit.*, Ch. 3.

[25] It should be stressed that the value premises of enterprise strategy selection may be significantly affected as a result of the exercise of internal influence and authority in the upward direction. Executives at levels below that of peak coordination may at times be very influential in the formulation of the preference system of the firm. Such influence is regarded as internal since it is exercised by participants in the firm's organization in their capacity as participants rather than as a "bargaining" group. In this connection see E. S. Mason, "Price and Production Policies of Large-Scale Enterprise," *Am. Econ. Rev., Proc.*, Mar. 1939, XXIX, 61–74.

verges to a peak coordinator.[26] The awkward term "peak coordinator" has been chosen advisedly in order to avoid associating the functionary with any one agent or group of agents designated by some conventional title, such as president, or chairman of the board, or executive council or the finance committee, etc. Just as we avoid all commitments as to the title borne by the peak coordinator in any one concrete case, we make no commitment as to the legal status of the firm. The firm may be a corporation or a group of corporations or a part of a corporation, or it may be a partnership or a proprietorship or some combination of some or all of the above.

This discussion raises the question of the *frontier* of the firm. We must be able to recognize whenever we are confronted with a concrete institution or legal entity, whether we are dealing with a plant (a segment of a firm), a firm, or a multifirm. The economist's basic criterion in establishing the frontier of the firm is provided by the notion of profit maximization. In the words of Robert Triffin "the frontier of the firm will be the frontier of the maximizing unit."[27] It is preferable, however, not to employ the concept of profit maximization inasmuch as this begs a number of questions which will be considered subsequently. The concept of the profit-maximizing plan of the firm may be replaced by the concept of *a* plan, in general, with a corresponding operating budget. A plant's plan must of necessity be a subset of the firm's plan. The firm's plan or budget, however, is *not* a subset of some other plan. The objection might be raised, however, that in the case of a multifirm this is exactly what takes place. The issue is important enough for the frame of reference under discussion to merit consideration.

When a group of firms subjects some segment of its behavior to the coordinating influence or authority of the group (or some organization which in some sense or other represents the group) a multifirm may be said to exist. The legal form selected and the source of the "power" to coordinate may vary from case to case. Typically both cartels and combines constitute multifirms. It is argued here that the member firms' plans are *not* subsets of the multifirm's plan; rather the multifirm's plan should be regarded as a composite of mutually consistent subsets of the participating firms' plans. The interfirm coordinating communications are aimed at modifying some of the factual premises of firm strategy selection, and thus lead to the exclusion of some of the strategies which otherwise would have been available to the member firms. In any case it must be clear that the plan of the

---

[26] A question may be raised concerning the status of a one-man "firm." Since in this case organization is absent, and since organization is an element of our definition of the firm, it follows that a one-man "firm" is not a firm at all. For some purposes this implication of the definition is undesirable. For our purposes it is of no consequence.

[27] *Monopolistic Competition and General Equilibrium Theory* (Cambridge, Mass., 1940), p. 94.

multifirm cannot contain the plan of the firm. If it did, the multifirm would become a "firm" and its member units would become "plants."

2. THE STRUCTURE OF EXTERNAL INFLUENCE

The preceding part was devoted to the formulation of a conceptual frame of reference which assigns a central position to conscious cooperation. In this part we propose to consider some of the empirical evidence available on the matter of external influence over the firm. There can be no doubt that the structure of external influence is of central concern to the student of firm behavior. The preference system of the firm is intimately related to the origin and character of *influence* and authority exercised over the firm. Therefore, the selection of an appropriate model for the analysis of firm behavior will be greatly facilitated by knowledge concerning the structure of influence over the firm.

In attempting, however, to arrive at some empirical generalizations concerning the character of the influence exerted by various interest groups over the firm, we are forced to sacrifice the generality of the model of organization presented, and to make definite commitments concerning the empirical counterparts of some of the concepts developed in the model. These commitments will, in general, become evident as the argument progresses. It is probably sufficient at this juncture to state that the firm is identified with the large modern corporation. The tentative empirical generalizations put forth in this part are subject to this restriction.

A. Stockholders and Creditors

The thesis, so dramatically enunciated by Berle and Means, that ownership has been separated from "control" as a result of the diffusion of stock ownership—a consequence of the growth of the large corporation—has not gone completely unchallenged.[28] The Securities and Exchange Commission arrived at the conclusion that approximately three-fourths of the corporations studied were "more or less definitely under ownership control."[29] Robert Gordon has successfully argued, however, that the conclusions of the Securities and Exchange Commission are based on a more or less

[28] A. A. Berle, Jr. and G. C. Means, *The Modern Corporation and Private Property* (New York, 1932). See also James Burnham, *The Managerial Revolution* (New York, 1941), for a somewhat different interpretation of the same phenomena.

[29] Temp. Nat. Econ. Com., *The Distribution of Ownership in the 200 Largest Nonfinancial Corporations*, Monog. 29 (Washington, 1940). Paul Sweezy, "The Illusion of the 'Managerial Revolution,'" *Sci. and Soc.*, Winter 1942, VI, 1–23, also has challenged the thesis that ownership has been separated from control. Consideration will be given to the broader implications of the controversy in Pt. IV.

mechanical manipulation of statistical data on the distribution of stock-ownership.[30] Both Gordon's study and an independent investigation by the author of this essay tend to support the Berle and Means thesis that the "property atom" has been split as a consequence of the growth of the large corporation.[31] To be sure, the data on the distribution of stockownership support both the thesis that there is diffusion of ownership and the thesis that there is concentration of ownership. There is nothing contradictory in this. To establish, however, that stockholdings are distributed in a strikingly unequal fashion and that there is substantial concentration of stockowner-ship in the hands of minority groups of stockholders does not automatically imply that "control," "leadership," "authority," and "influence" are exercised by these minority groups. Gordon's careful study of the role of the stock-holder in the large corporation furnishes some of the answers to these vexing questions. We shall attempt to summarize his findings, though presenting them whenever possible within the frame of reference developed in this essay.

At the start, a distinction must be made between small stockholders and large stockholders or stockholder groups, the terms "large" and "small" referring to the proportion of stock outstanding owned rather than the absolute dollar figures. The prevalence of the small stockholder in the large or giant corporation is not open to dispute. Stockholdings of less than 1 per cent aggregated well over half the value of the common stock of 176 giant corporations.[32] With respect to the small stockholder we are forced to the conclusion that his capacity to exert influence over the large corporation is insignificant. This is the result of the lack of interest in and/or ability to organize for the exertion of influence in stockholders' meetings. The proxy machinery, though largely a management instrument, "becomes a partial—and by no means completely satisfactory—substitute for complete dis-franchisement."[33] The growth of nonvoting stock and the narrowing of the range of matters on which stockholder vote is legally necessary have both contributed to the passivity of the small stockholder.

One sort of influence of the small stockholder over the corporation must be recognized, however. There are undoubtedly limits beyond which no management would care to go in disregarding the interests of the small

[30] Gordon, *op. cit.*, Ch. 2, 8.

[31] A. G. Papandreou, *The Location and Scope of the Entrepreneurial Function* (Cambridge, Mass., 1943), unpublished thesis in Harvard University Library.

[32] Gordon, *op. cit.*, p. 159.

[33] *Ibid.*, p. 161. The SEC has attempted to improve practices relating to the use of the proxy machinery under power granted to it by section 14(a) of the Securities Exchange Act of 1934.

stockholder. If these limits were transgressed, management could well expect "activation" of the passive small-stockholder group (possibly under the leadership of some small but powerful minority) and censure of its actions. The peak coordinator, to state the matter more formally, must take account of this potentiality as a factual premise in the development of enterprise strategy.

It is not easy to arrive at generalizations concerning the degree to which large minority interest groups exert influence over the large corporation in the formulation of its strategy. It must be admitted, however, that practically all degrees of influence can be found—ranging from the most passive to active participation in the executive process. In some cases members of large minority interest groups participate actively in the performance of the executive, and possibly even the peak coordination, function. In such cases the minority group may be regarded as affecting substantially the value premises (the preference system) of executive decision making. Where this is not true, it is likely that minority groups exert *influence* (ranging from "substantial" to "little") affecting the factual premises of executive decision making. Seldom do minority groups exert authority, and when they do it is unlikely that they exercise it with respect to the value premises of decision making (except, of course, in the cases where they actively participate in the peak coordination function).

Intimately associated with the problem of ownership "control" is the question of the role of the board of directors in the large corporation. The degree of influence exercised by the stockholder group must needs be related to the manner in which boards of directors are instituted, to their composition and to the role which they play vis-à-vis the executive organization of the firm. Gordon's findings on the functions of directors support the view that seldom do boards of directors perform the peak-coordination function. The board of directors does not, in general, constitute a group independent from and superior to, the executive group. Its membership is partly drawn from the executive ranks—and, even when this is not true, its constitution is largely determined by the executives. In many cases, therefore, the board of directors may be conceived as a management instrument, i.e. as an organization subject to the coordination supplied by the executives for the attainment of the goals of the enterprise. This interpretation of the role of directors in the large corporation does not imply that they exert no influence over the peak coordinator. It does imply, however, that, in general, boards of directors exercise *influence* rather than authority, and that insofar as they do exercise *influence* they tend to affect the factual rather than value premises of enterprise strategy selection.

The general picture of the relationship between ownership and influence in the large corporation clearly supports the view that the importance of the owner group has declined substantially with the advent of the giant corporation. This conclusion, however, is open to misinterpretation and misuse. Although it is certain that ownership in the large corporation generally lacks the position necessary to influence significantly the structure of the preference system of the enterprise, it does not follow that the peak coordinator will fail to attach a significant weight to the interest of the stockholders in the formulation of the preference system of the firm. The peak coordinator and, more generally, the executives of the enterprise are subject to the subtle but all-pervasive influences exercised on them by the standards, values, and myths of the broader community in which they function. In a private enterprise society these standards, values, and myths can be relied upon to influence the executive to take "due account" of the interests of the owner. Unfortunately, it is impossible to assess the significance of this factor: this should not lead us, however, to a casual underestimation of its importance. Another element in the picture which should not be neglected is the extent of stockownership on the part of the executive group. Absolute, not relative, measures are relevant in this context. Any executive who has a substantial "dollar stake" in an enterprise is apt to be influenced to some extent by his role as an owner. The ownership stake of executives in the large industrials is substantial. It is somewhat less substantial in the utilities, and tends to be rather negligible in the case of the railroads.[34] The importance of this consideration should not be exaggerated, of course, since executive compensation is quantitatively much more important than earnings from stockownership. Still, it serves to modify rash generalizations concerning the insignificance of the stockholder interest in enterprise strategy selection.

The importance of the creditor or financial group also seems to have declined in recent years. Included in the financial group are the commercial, private, and investment bankers. The power of the financial group to influence the behavior of business firms derives primarily from two sources. To begin with, bankers can employ their bargaining power to establish some degree of continuing influence over firms which either borrow from them or make use of financial services supplied by them. Secondly, bankers in any city (especially large commercial banks) are apt "to be the rallying point and to provide the leadership for the city's financial interests."[35] In this leadership role bankers may be in a position to exert substantial influence

---

[34] *Ibid.*, pp. 297–304. See also R. A. Gordon, "Ownership and Compensation as Incentives to Corporation Executives," *Quart. Jour. Econ.*, May 1940, LIV, 455–73; J. C. Baker, *Executive Salaries and Bonus Plans* (Boston, 1938).

[35] Gordon, *Business Leadership*, p. 189, n. 1.

over management of both small and large corporations. This leadership role shades imperceptibly into the relatively high status which bankers must have in any community, at least from the point of view of the business executive.

Gordon recognizes the importance of these considerations; he feels, nevertheless, that the degree of influence exercised by the banker over the large enterprise has been exaggerated. Generally speaking, bankers are apt to exert much influence over firms during periods of financial stress, reorganization, merger, and rapid expansion, i.e., in situations that enhance the bargaining power of the banker. Under such conditions and, in most cases, for the duration of the period of great need of funds, they may exercise some authority as well as *influence*. Almost invariably, however, their authority and *influence* are restricted to the range of problems which are generally referred to as "financial." It is, therefore, probably correct to surmise that bankers, insofar as they exercise any influence over the firm by reason of their bargaining power, tend to affect the factual premises rather than the value premises of strategy selection. At times, however, they may be successful in affecting the value premises, the preference system of the firm, particularly in respect to the liquidity attitudes of the executive.[36] In their role as a high status group they may be able to exert moderate influence over the enterprise by affecting not only the factual premises but also the value premises of enterprise strategy selection.

It is generally agreed that the influence of the banking interests over the firm has declined significantly during our times.[37] Increased reliance of the large successful corporation of internal financing may partly account for this. The growing participation of insurance companies and other financial institutions in the investable funds market has undoubtedly contributed to this decline in the importance of the banker. Increasingly important is the role of government as a supplier of funds. The advent of World War II accelerated this tendency, and preparation for meeting the eventuality of a third world war may be expected to carry the process even further.

B. Labor

The appraisal of the role of labor as an interest group vis-à-vis the business firm, especially in relation to its influence on the executive of the corporation, is somewhat obstructed by the heated verbal debate between the spokesmen of management and labor which has accompanied the power struggle between organized labor on the one hand and management on the other. The broader social implications of this conflict will be considered at

---

[36] *Ibid.*, p. 201, n. 24.

[37] *Ibid.*, pp. 214–21; Paul Sweezy, *The Theory of Capitalist Development* (New York, 1942), Ch. 14.

a later stage of this essay. We are presently concerned with the evaluation of the degree to which labor is in a position to exercise influence over the executive organization of the firm.

The outstanding document on the subject has been written by Neil W. Chamberlain.[38] The ability of labor, as an interest group, to exert influence over the firm is dependent upon the degree to which it is organized for such action. The mechanism of collective bargaining, supported by the power to strike, renders the exercise of its power legitimate within the framework of our legal institutions. It is well known, of course, that labor has achieved dramatic success (not without significant setbacks, however) on both the political-legal level and on the level of utilization of its legal power in its dealings with employers. Although there are reasons for expecting that the growth of its power over the firm will continue, the feeling is quite general that it will proceed somewhat more slowly and less dramatically.

The main direct source of influence of labor over the executive organization of the firm is the employment contract. This has been defined by Simon as a contract in which the employee agrees to accept the authority (in the Barnard-Simon sense) of the employer and the employer agrees to pay the employee a stated wage.[39] The union, representing labor at the bargaining table, can affect not only the wage rate, but also the area of acceptance of authority, i.e. the range of behavior with respect to which the employee will accept executive communications as guiding his actions. The union can go even beyond this, however, by specifying the "physical" and "social" conditions under which executive communication will be accepted as guiding the action of its members. As soon as these possibilities are appreciated, it becomes evident that labor, if effectively organized, can establish substantial authority over the peak coordinator of the firm, extending over as wide a range of matters as it deems relevant to its interests and as its power permits it to invade. The experience of the last twenty years can leave no doubt about the determination and ability of labor to widen this range. The extent to which it has been successful is evidenced by the great concern of management over the "encroachment on its prerogatives" by the unions.

It is highly likely that the growing ability of labor to exercise authority

[38] *The Union Challenge to Management Control* (New York, 1948). This book constitutes mandatory reading for those who wish to gain valuable insights into the nature of the problem. Other relevant contributions are: Gordon, *Business Leadership*, pp. 255–58; C. E. Lindblom, *Unions and Capitalism* (New Haven, 1949); S. H. Slichter, *Union Policies and Industrial Management* (New Haven, 1949); C. S. Golden and H. J. Ruttenberg, *The Dynamics of Industrial Democracy* (New York, 1940).

[39] H. A. Simon, "A Formal Theory of the Employment Relationship," *Econometrica*, July 1951, XIX, 293–305.

over the firm's peak coordinator is restricted to the factual premises of enterprise strategy. Despite the high degree of union pentration of "management areas," the socio-cultural climate mitigates the likelihood that unions can exert significant influence in the process of formulation of the value premises of enterprise strategy. This seems to be the case today, though it must be admitted that future developments may bring significant changes in this respect.

The influence we have just examined is exercised directly by labor over the peak coordinator of the firm, and is analogous in many respects to the influence exercised over him by the other interest groups. Labor unions, however, are in a position to exercise influence at the lower levels of the executive hierarchy as well as directly on the operatives. This raises serious problems of coordination which have been debated vigorously by representatives of unions and management. Insofar as the influence exercised by the unions at these lower organizational levels contradicts the authority of the executive the efficiency and even the life of the concern may be seriously endangered. Chamberlain is convinced that this feature of the conflict between labor and management can be eliminated by the acceptance by both contestants of the need for "functional integration."[40] This essentially amounts to recognition by the union that its representatives can act at the lower levels only within the limits established by the peak coordinator in conformance with his agreement with the unions. The clear implication of this notion is that union representatives, insofar as they participate in the process of coordination of the activities which make up the firm's organization, must assume the responsibilities of the role of the executive along with its privileges.

C. Government

The influence of government has increased in a striking fashion during the last quarter century. Government means so many things, however, and its influences take such a variety of forms that the discussion here must of necessity be restricted to the broadest and most general considerations.

Government, in this context, includes federal, state, and local governments in their legislative, executive, and judicial aspects. The government in its sovereign aspect exercises authority over all its citizens and subordinate organizations. With respect to the private firm not "affected with a public interest" government's authority is aimed at affecting the factual premises of strategy selection whether its communications ("laws," "orders," "decisions") take a prohibitory or a prescriptive form. With respect to

---

[40] Chamberlain, *op. cit.*, Ch. 10–12.

government corporations, however, and firms "affected with a public interest" its authority clearly extends to the formulation of the value premises, the preference system of the organizations.

Government exercises indirect influence on all firms by participating actively in the economic process, i.e., by directly affecting the flow of funds and the counterflow of goods and services. Developments of the last quarter century have given special importance to this type of influence. Fiscal policy has come to be considered as the most essential instrument of national planning.[41] Government has also increasingly engaged in influencing its constituency by means of modern methods of mass communication. Public opinion climate formation and direct appeals to businessmen and other interest groups may elicit behavior patterns somewhat more consistent with the interests of government.

Government is itself subject to the pulls and pressures exerted on it by the various national interest groups. It may be hypothesized, in fact, that its behavior is a vector of this multitude of influences or forces exercised upon it.[42] One of the most important functions of government is the maintenance of the centripetal cooperative aspects of society despite the centrifugal or conflict forces in operation. The resolution of important conflicts or the development of a *modus vivendi*, if resolution is not likely, undoubtedly constitutes one of the central tasks of government. It is clear, therefore, that the problem of "control" over the business firm must be of immediate interest to government. Some of the authority it exerts over the firm is aimed at resolving the conflict of the interest groups which are vying for the "control" of the firm. A great deal of labor legislation, of the regulation of the securities market, and even some of the antitrust laws are aimed at this resolution of conflict over the "control" of the firm.[43] However, the more actively government participates in the resolution of conflict over the firm the more likely it is that the contestants will shift their battleground from the firm level to the political level. "Control" of the government may then become the means for establishing "control" of the firm. There are signs that we are steadily moving in this direction. Needless to say such a development will undermine most of the institutions associated with a "decentralized society."

[41] See Arthur Smithies, "Federal Budgeting and Fiscal Policy," *A Survey of Contemporary Economics*, Vol. 1, H. S. Ellis, ed. (Philadelphia and Toronto, 1948), Ch. 5; also, the present volume, Ch. 9.

[42] A stimulating analysis of the problem of influence exercised on government by business groups can be found in R. A. Brady, *Business as a System of Power* (New York, 1943).

[43] It should not be forgotten, of course, that the law of property still is the main instrument for resolving issues of this order.

D. Conclusions

The brief survey of the structure of external influence over the large, modern enterprise strongly supports the following conclusions: (a) the influence of stockholders has declined with the advent and growth of the modern corporation; (b) the influence of financial groups also has declined; (c) labor's influence has grown by leaps and bounds and may be expected to continue growing with the passing of time; (d) government's influence has also increased spectacularly; (e) management has become the focus of forces pulling the enterprise in different directions.

These empirical findings have been presented within a conceptual framework with the following general features: (a) The peak coordinator is conceived as the highest level of intrafirm authority. He formulates the operating budget of the firm. This amounts to the selection of a strategy. The selection of a strategy, in turn, requires the specification of some value premises (preference system) and factual premises. (b) The peak coordinator is subject to a variety of influences some of which affect the value premises while others affect the factual premises of his decisions. (c) The preference system accepted by the peak coordinator as guiding enterprise behavior is regarded as being a resultant of all the influences which affect the value premises of enterprise strategy selection. If the peak coordinator were free of immediate, direct, conscious influences, his own value system and, therefore, the ethos of his own culture and subculture would be dominant in the formulation of the value premises of enterprise strategy selection. If the peak coordinator must accept the authority of one or more groups (with respect to value premises), their value system and, therefore, the ethos of their culture and subculture will be dominant. The developments of the last half-century support the hypothesis that the peak coordinator has been subjected to a changing structure of conscious influence.

The changes in the structure of enterprise which attend the growth of the modern corporation in size and national importance have been discussed quite intensively in the literature of the last two or three decades. Much has been written on the "separation of ownership and control," on "management control," and the "encroachment upon management prerogatives" by unions. These developments raise serious problems both of analysis and public policy.

There is general awareness of the developing contradiction within the structure of public policy. Our law of property and laws of incorporation (supported by judicial decision and interpretation) still support the construction that the board of directors plays a role of agent, trustee, or fiduciary to the stockholders of the corporation. The fundamental legal limitation on the action of the board is merely one of intent. Insofar as they take the interest of the stockholders into account they are free practically to do anything they wish with company property. We are familiar with the fact, however, that, at least in the majority of the corporations, the board of directors is rather passive. We are also aware of the fact that the connection between the mass of stockholders and the board of directors is a very loose one, to say the least. Some of the legislation enacted (namely laws pertaining to securities markets, reorganizations, public utility structure, etc.) aims at preserving the power of the stockholder and the traditional relationship between director and stockholder. Other types of important legislation, especially labor legislation, have tended to give legal status "to an interest in the affairs of the corporation by a party other than the stockholders."[44]

It is interesting to note that even business executives and business students are increasingly giving lip service to the notion that the boards of directors (or management) are trustees for the owners, *and* labor, *and* customers, *and* the public. It must be recognized, of course, that statements by managers or directors to that effect need not imply adherence to such principles in decision making—at least as far as the value premises of decision making are concerned. They do imply, however, that the forces of change have been so successful that new verbalizations, slogans, and myths are necessary for the daily conduct of business.

Government policy is undoubtedly largely the resultant of the pressures and counterpressures of the various interest groups vying for "control" of the firm. Insofar as this is true we may expect government to sanction developments which are supported by the new "balance of power" in the economy. Although this approach may lead to interpretation of current government policy it cannot provide us with criteria as to what government policy *should* be from the point of view of the economy or the nation as a whole. Before we are in a position, however, to establish optimum policy measures we must be acquainted with the *behavior consequences* of the structural changes which we are presently considering.

3.   DO FIRMS MAXIMIZE PROFITS?

A.   Rationality and Profit Maximization

The assumption that firms maximize profits has dominated economic analysis for a long time. Nevertheless, the concept of profit maximization is seldom stated unambiguously; and, even when it is stated with precision, its relation to the broader body of theory is rarely made explicit. In recent

[44] Chamberlain, *op. cit.*, p. 19, n. 18.

years, however, the assumption has come under fire as being unrealistic, especially in the case of "management controlled" corporations. Increasingly, economists tend to qualify the assumption by listing conditions under which it might not be true. In what follows we propose to consider the issue in some detail.

It is worth pointing out at the outset of the discussion that we are not concerned primarily with the question of whether firms do *in fact* maximize profits. Excessive concern with the realism of the assumption—in the sense of direct correspondent with the "facts"—suggests an inadequate conception of the role of theory construction. The validity of the assumption must be judged primarily by reference to its capacity to lead to tentatively valid derived propositions about empirical data.

It is often supposed that the assumption of profit maximization rests on the same universal grounds as the assumption of utility-index maximization or rationality. This is not correct however. Profit maximization does imply rationality of course; but rationality is consistent with maximization of other things as well as profits. Profit maximization can be derived from utility-index maximization only through the imposition of a restriction on the character of the index. As soon as the distinction between profit maximization and utility-index maximization is carefully drawn it becomes possible to distinguish between *efficiency* and profit maximization in an unambiguous fashion. Efficiency relates to rationality, that is to maximizing a utility index. It implies maximization of ends with a given set of means or the minimization of means in the attainment of a given set of related ends. Efficiency is implicit in profit maximization, but efficient behavior need not be profit-maximizing behavior. A business firm may be efficient without seeking to maximize profits.

Ideally rationality implies that the actor has a well-ordered preference system, that he has perfect knowledge concerning the means-ends relationships, and that he acts to maximize his end system. Actually he is confronted with a means-ends chain. Each link in the chain must be considered as an intermediate end (with respect to the preceding link) and as an intermediate means (with respect to the succeeding link). In general, we prefer not to state the preference system in terms of the ultimate ends. The higher the level of the ends in the means-ends chain, the more difficult it becomes to establish the relationship between means and ends and hence the more difficult it becomes to ascertain whether action is rational or not.[45] Profit may be regarded as a value index in terms of which we rank the ends which enter our preference systems. As soon as we select profit as the *ranking criterion* of an end system, rational behavior must involve profit maximiza-

[45] See Simon, *Administrative Behavior*, Ch. 4.

tion.[46] Thus profit-maximizing behavior can be derived from rational behavior when we specify that the ranking criterion of our preference system is profit.[47]

Profits may be introduced into the theory of choice in a somewhat different way. Profit may be regarded by the theorists as one among many related goals sought by the entrepreneur. In such constructions profit maximization is replaced by the more general notion of preference-function maximization. Hicks' classic statement that "the best of all monopoly profits is a quiet life" was made in this vein.[48] This suggestion has led to a fuller treatment by Benjamin Higgins, Tibor Scitovsky, and Melvin Reder.[49] Higgins points out that profit maximization is a survival condition in perfect competition. Its force is much weaker, however, in the case of nonperfect competition since under such conditions the entrepreneur may be expected to have margins with which to work and with which to satisfy desires other than the desire for profit. Higgins proceeds to classify the desires or forces which lead to nonprofit-maximizing solutions into three categories: those which lead the entrepreneur to produce at a point below the profit-maximizing output; those which lead him to product at a point above that output; and, finally, those that make him stay where he is, whether he is producing an output above or below the profit-maximizing output. Leisure (Hicks' "quiet life") leads to the first case. Desire to own a large firm, power, prestige, etc., may account for the second case. The third case arises either as a result of "just price" ideas or as a result of reluctance to experiment. Higgins' formal presentation involves the introduction of indifference curves (relating profit to output) into the standard textbook dollars-output diagram. Tangency of the net-profits curve to an indifference curve maximizes the entrepreneur's utility index.

Scitovsky's paper deals more specifically with the leisure *versus* income problem as it relates to the entrepreneur. The leading conclusion of Scitovsky's argument is that profits will be maximized only if the entrepreneur's choice between more or less activity—or between more income and more

---

[46] Where profit is the ranking criterion not ranking but measurement takes place. It seems best, however, to use the expression "ranking criterion" even in this case is order to maintain the generality of the concept.

[47] In this connection, see Talcott Parsons, "The Motivation of Economic Activity," *Can. Jour. Econ. Pol. Sci.*, May 1940, VI, 187–202; reprinted in *idem, Essays in Sociological Theory Pure and Applied* (Glencoe, 1949), Ch. 9.

[48] J. R. Hicks, "The Theory of Monopoly," *Econometrica*, Jan. 1935, III, 1–20.

[49] Benjamin Higgins, "Elements of Indeterminacy in the Theory of Non-perfect Competition," *Am. Econ. Rev.*, Sept. 1939, XXXIX, 468–79; Tibor Scitovsky, "A Note on Profit Maximization," *Rev. Econ. Stud.*, Winter 1943, XI, 57–60; Melvin Reder, "A Reconsideration of the Marginal Productivity Theory," *Jour. Pol. Econ.*, Oct. 1947, LV, 450–58.

leisure—is independent of his income. In all other cases utility-index maximization leads to outputs which do not maximize profits. Reder's paper contains a wealth of suggestions. He, too, claims that profit maximization must be regarded as a very special case.[50]

B. Profit Maximization and Uncertainty

As soon as we introduce dynamic and uncertainty considerations, new issues arise in connection with the profit-maximization construction. It should be noted at the outset that the introducion of time (even in a trivial or perfunctory way) reduces the potency of the profit-maximization assumption in producing operationally meaningful theorems. Since the entrepreneur must now be assumed to be maximizing the present value of his assets (or some related magnitude) his horizon and expectations must be known before statements concerning his behavior in any one period can be derived from the profit-maximization assumption. In other words, any number of current outputs may be consistent with profit maximization even in the case of single-valued expectations—expectations, that is, which are held with certainty. In the absence of knowledge concerning entrepreneurial horizon and expectations the profit-maximization construction becomes an empirically irrelevant tautology.[51]

• Recognition of the fact that expectations are not single-valued will generally force us to substitute preference-function maximization for profit-maximization analysis. Gerhard Tintner's work has illuminated this aspect of the problem considerably.[52] IIis approach is structured on the generally accepted frequency-ratio analysis. Tintner distinguishes four cases: (1) subjective risk with respect to prices and interest, with the assumption of perfect knowledge concerning technical-technological conditions; (2) subjective uncertainty with respect to prices and interest, also on the assumption of perfect knowledge concerning technical-technological conditions; (3) subjective risk with respect to technical-technological conditions; (4)

---

[50] An interesting discussion of the problem can also be found in William Fellner, *Competition among the Few* (New York, 1949), pp. 169–74.

[51] The Lester-Machlup controversy is relevant at this juncture. See B. F. Haley, "Value and Distribution," *A Survey of Contemporary Economics*, Vol. I, pp. 11–13, for a discussion of the issues involved and for bibliographical references.

[52] Gerhard Tintner, "The Theory of Choice under Subjective Risk and Uncertainty," *Econometrica*, July–Oct. 1941, IX, 298–304; *idem*, "A Contribution to the Non-Static Theory of Choice," *Quart. Jour. Econ.*, Feb. 1942, LVI, 274–306; *idem*, "The Theory of Production under Non-Static Conditions," *Jour. Pol. Econ.*, Oct. 1942, L, 646–67; *idem*, "A Contribution to the Non-Static Theory of Production," in *Studies in Mathematical Economics and Econometrics*, Oscar Lange, Francis McIntyre, T. O. Yntema, ed. (Chicago, 1942), pp. 92–109.

subjective uncertainty with respect to technical-technological conditions.[53] Risk refers to a situation in which the entrepreneur is confronted with a joint probability distribution of the anticipated prices, interest rates, and (in the third case) technical-technological conditions, where the parameters of the distribution are known with certainty (probability of 1). Subjective uncertainty is present if the parameters of the joint probability distribution are not anticipated with certainty. In this case there exists an *a priori* probability distribution of the joint probability distribution. Tintner's solution of the choice problems consists in the postulation of a *risk preference functional*, in the case of subjective risk, and an *uncertainty preference functional* in the case of subjective uncertainty, which must be maximized by the entrepreneur. The implication of the solution clearly is that the mathematical expectation of anticipated discounted profits (the weighted arithmetic mean of discounted net profits with the probabilities as weights) will not be maximized except in a special case. This means, in somewhat different words, that the entrepreneur may be just as concerned with other features of the probability distribution of anticipated net profits (such as its dispersion, kurtosis, skewness, etc.) as he is with the mathematical expectation.

G. L. S. Shackle's recent contribution to the theory of expectations deserves comment.[54] Shackle takes strong exception to the traditional approach of dealing with the problem of expectations. His basic objection to the traditional approach is that numerical probability calls for both uniformity of some sort in the conditions of experiment and a "large" number of such experiments. Even if this difficulty were to be overcome somehow, the entrepreneur would still be faced in many cases with decisions which for *him* are virtually *unique*.[55] Shackle's novel way of attempting to deal with the problem takes the following general form: He formulates first a *potential surprise function*, $y=f(x)$, which gives, for each value of x (where x stands for the "values" of hypothetical outcomes), the surprise y, which the entrepreneur expects himself to feel if x turns out to have that value.[56] It must be emphasized that zero potential surprise need not mean certainty; it merely means that the entrepreneur would not be surprised at all if that particular value of x were realized. With an interesting tour de force, Shackle proceeds to epitomize the potential surprise function. For any given degree of surprise, the greater the absolute (either gain or loss) value of x, the more our attention will be aroused; while, for any given value of x, the

---

[53] Tintner, "The Theory of Production under Non-Static Conditions," *loc. cit.*

[54] *Expectation in Economics* (Cambridge, Eng. 1949).

[55] *Ibid.*, Ch. 7.

[56] See Ralph Turvey, J. de V. Graaf, and W. J. Baumol, "Three Notes on 'Expectation in Economics,'" and Shackle's reply in *Economica*, Nov. 1949, XVI, 336–46.

greater the degree of potential surprise, the less our attention will be aroused. Thus indifference curves can be drawn such that all points on any one of them have equal capacity to arouse interest or attention. In general, we should expect two points of tangency (one in the gain, the other in the loss region) between the potential surprise curve and the indifference curves. These two points are named *focus-gain* and *focus-loss*. According to Shackle the entrepreneur's attention will be *focused* exclusively upon these two hypothetical outcomes. Finally, we can construct an "indifference map of uncertainties," from which, given the focus-gains and the focus-losses of any two courses of action, we can identify the course of action which will be preferred by the actor. The indifference curves relating focus-gains to focus-losses are assumed to be positively inclined, since presumably increases in focus-losses must be compensated for by increases in focus-gains.

Shackle's treatment of the subject of expectations is both promising and stimulating. It is clear, however, that its value remains to be demonstrated in empirical work. In this respect, of course, it is neither superior nor inferior to the traditional approach. What is important from our point of view, however, is this: even if we adopt the Shackle approach the profit-maximization construction must yield to a broader statement.[57]

C. Conclusions

Concisely stated, the few preceding paragraphs mean that we should proceed to substitute general preference-function maximization for profit maximization. No doubt this procedure will reduce our chances of being wrong. This protection from error, however, is gained at a cost. It is much harder to derive operationally meaningful theorems concerning firm behavior from a construction which is directly based on preference function maximization than to do so from the profit-maximization construction. The relative development of the theory of the firm (based on profit maximiza-

[57] It is not possible to consider here other developments in the theory of expectations and uncertainty. It seems advisable, however, to call the attention of the reader to some outstanding performances in this field. Among the earlier statements of the problem the following might be mentioned: Helen Makower and Jacob Marschak, "Assets, Price and Monetary Theory," *Economica*, Aug. 1938, V, 261–88; Jacob Marschak, "Money and the Theory of Assets," *Econometrica*, Oct. 1938, V, 311–25; A. G. Hart, "Anticipations, Uncertainty, and Dynamic Planning," *Jour. Bus. Univ. Chicago* (Special Supplement), Oct. 1940, XIII, 1–98. Among the more recent performances the following deserve special mention: Milton Friedman and L. J. Savage, "The Utility Analysis of Choices Involving Risk," *Jour. Pol. Econ.*, Aug. 1948, LVI, 279–304; Jacob Marschak, "Role of Liquidity under Complete and Incomplete Information," *Am. Econ. Rev., Proc.*, May 1949, XXXIX, 182–95, and Milton Friedman's, R. M. Goodwin's, Franco Modigliani's and James Tobin's discussion of the paper, *ibid.*, pp. 196–210; Jacob Marschak, "Rational Behavior, Uncertain Prospects, and Measurable Utility," *Econometrica*, Apr. 1950, XVIII, 111–41.

tion) as contrasted to that of the consumer (based on utility-index maximization) testifies to the validity of this argument. If economists wish to replace profit maximization with preference-function maximization, they must take steps to make certain that their procedure will not be rendered meaningless from an empirical point of view. It is necessary to experiment with ideal types in which specific commitments are made about the shape of the preference function maximized by the entrepreneur. This calls, of course, for substantial work both in the general area of expectations (and the manner in which they are related to the flow of events) and in the area of "structure of control" over the firm.

It is a major thesis of this essay that the preference function maximized by the peak coordinator is itself a resultant of the influences which are exerted upon the firm. The peak coordinator is conceived as performing the integrating function; he is conceived as formulating the preference system of the enterprise. He does so, however, under the "weight" of the unconscious and conscious influences exerted upon him. This formulation contains one disturbing possibility. It must be evident that if influence takes the form of authority, and if authority is simultaneously exercised by two or more interest groups in a contradictory manner, the peak coordinator will not be able to formulate a consistent preference system.[58] It may be necessary, under such conditions, to drop the action frame of reference in favor of a behavioristic interpretation.

In this connection we should mention Kenneth Boulding's recent book which contains many interesting suggestions concerning the concepts of utility and profit maximization.[59] *Homeostasis*—or maintenance of the "state" of the organism—is, according to Boulding, a construction more general than that of maximization. The concept of equilibrium, in other words, is more general than the concept of maximum. A maximization approach, as a special case of the equilibrium approach, yields useful results only in cases where the agent (organism, in Boulding's terminology) *consciously* recognizes a divergence from the maximand as a stimulus to action. Boulding thinks that preference-function maximization as an analytical device can be employed successfully in the case of the firm. The labor unions, however, are an outstanding example (among others) of organizations whose behavior could be approached more effectively through the more general nonmaximum analysis. A nonmaximum approach is tantamount to a behavioristic approach. A relationship among variables can be postulated as soon as the nature of the "state" which is to be maintained is specified.

---

[58] In this connection see K. J. Arrow, "A Difficulty in the Concept of Social Welfare," *Jour. Pol. Econ.*, Aug. 1950, LVIII, 328–46.

[59] *A Reconstruction of Economics* (New York, 1950), Ch. 2.

Empirical generalizations concerning behavior may be conceived as variants of the homeostatic approach.

Armen A. Alchian's "Uncertainty, Evolution, and Economic Theory,"[60] is worthy of special mention in connection with the formulation of behavior models. The economic system is conceived as containing a process of selection of the fittest; it is conceived as adopting those firms which, in a world of uncertainty, have happened to have made the appropriate decisions regardless of the process. Positive profits are the mark of success and viability. The process of reasoning or motivation through which this success was achieved is not significant. Alchian offers two models in his paper. The first is an "adoptive model dominated by chance." It is skillfully asserted that random behavior, involving no conscious adaptation, may lead to predictable resource allocation, given the adopting mechanism of the economic system. The second model includes conscious adaptation which takes the form of imitation of the successful and/or trial and error. Alchian arrives at the interesting conclusion that the economist can employ the tools he has developed for dealing with conditions involving certainty to "predict the more adoptable or viable types of economic interrelationships that will be induced by environmental changes even if individuals themselves are unable to ascertain them."[61]

Whether we choose a behavioristic or an action frame of reference we must always take pains to impart empirical meaningfulness to our model. The way to achieve such meaningfulness, if we restrict ourselves to the action frame of reference, consists in formulating a variety of ideal types, making commitments in each case about the shape of the preference function to be maximized, and testing (whenever possible) the operationally meaningful hypotheses which can be derived from them. Whether we like it or not, it seems that we are on the road to developing and testing a variety of formulations rather than a single set of postulates.

4. ENTERPRISE IN A CHANGING WORLD

A. The Concept of Entrepreneurship

The term *entrepreneur* has heretofore been used as interchangeable with the term *peak coordinator*. Emphasis was placed throughout on the *function* which was identified as peak coordination rather than on the person or persons performing it. The peak coordinating function has been defined

[60] *Jour. Pol. Econ.*, June 1950, LVIII, 211–21.

[61] *Ibid.*, p. 220. In this connection we should also mention Boulding's ecological approach, *op. cit.*, Ch. 1.

as the supply of conscious and authoritative coordination at the apex of the organizational structure. Coordination, in turn, is conceived as the deliberate provision of communications which "integrate" the strategies of the co-operating participants in order to produce the system of actions which we have named *organization.*

This particular definition of entrepreneurship is, of course, arbitrary. It is consistent, however, with the general properties of the organization frame of reference presented in this essay. It is unfortunate that the term entrepreneur has come to mean so many different things and to be associated with so many different conceptual frames of reference.[62] This is especially disturbing in view of the fact that the role assigned to the entrepreneur is a crucial one in almost all the dominant conceptual schemata. The entrepreneur as the "organizer-manager," the entrepreneur as the "risk-bearer," the entrepreneur as the "innovator," are concepts which have played and are still playing an important role in economic analysis.[63] Beyond their variety of analytical uses the terms entrepreneur and enterprise have come to be most important in the structure of American "ideology." Enterprise almost invariably suggests "freedom," "progress," "change," and "dynamic leadership." Under these circumstances it becomes extremely difficult to use the concept of entrepreneurship in a value-neutral and analytical meaningful manner. There can be no doubt that the goals of scientific investigation would be served well if we were to drop the term entrepreneur from the professional vocabulary. In view of the fact, however, that the chances of this occurrence are almost nil, we should strive to become as precise and exacting in the use of the term as conditions permit.[64]

Though the subject cannot be discussed at length here, a few comments may point the direction in which conceptual clarification of the term entrepreneur might proceed. A distinction is needed between the concept of the entrepreneur as a *function* and as an *ideal type.* When we talk about risk-bearing or innovating or combining the factors of production, we are thinking of functions performed within a structural-functional system.[65] Again,

---

[62] For a concise review of the meanings attributed to the term see J. H. Strauss, "The Entrepreneur: The Firm," *Jour. Pol. Econ.,* June 1944, LII, 112–27.

[63] The two classics in this area are F. H. Knight, *Risk, Uncertainty and Profits* (Boston and New York, 1921), and J. A. Schumpeter, *The Theory of Economic Development,* trans. Redvers Opie (Cambridge, Mass., 1934).

[64] The Research Center in Entrepreneurial History, Harvard University, has been doing much stimulating work in this area. The reader is referred to their serial publication, *Explorations in Entrepreneurial History,* R. R. Wohl and H. G. J. Aitken, ed. (mimeographed). See also, A. H. Cole, F. H. Knight, J. M. Clark, and G. H. Evans, Jr., "Symposium on Profits and the Entrepreneur," *The Tasks of Econ. Hist.,* Dec. 1942 (Suppl. to the *Jour. Econ. Hist.,* Vol. II), pp. 118–46.

[65] See Parsons, *Essays in Sociological Theory Pure and Applied,* Ch. 1–2.

when we talk about the "owner-manager-risk-bearer" or the "owner-manager-innovator" or the "nonowner-manager," and so on, we are constructing ideal types which are handy for expository and heuristic purposes. It should be clear, for instance, that the separation of ownership and "control" need not be construed as eliminating the function of the entrepreneur in the Knightian sense. The peak coordinator in a "management-controlled" corporation may be likened to Knight's "independent" entrepreneur (who in this case also performs the management function). The entrepreneur, in this case, does not have to persuade the contributors of capital that he is capable of performing the entrepreneurial function. His power position vis-à-vis the contributors of capital is such that he does not need their approval or consent. Knight's formulation does contain, however, an ideal type corresponding to the function of bearing the risk in a world of uncertainty, namely, that of the *capitalist-entrepreneur*. It cannot be doubted that the separation of ownership and "control" is fatal to this ideal type. Similarly, Schumpeter's innovation is a function which may be performed in institutional settings completely different from the private-property and decentralized-economy setting which is crucial, however, for Schumpeter's entrepreneur as an ideal type.[66]

If the distinction between function concepts and ideal-type concepts is made with clarity and precision, any number of constructions of the term entrepreneur may be made, each one of them useful in its own context and in relation to its own domain of concepts. The definition of entrepreneur proposed in this paper is clearly a function definition. It can be used in a variety of ideal-type constructions. In fact, for each set of external influences a different ideal type can be constructed which can be employed meaningfully in the analysis of the behavior of the firm under the specified set of influences.

B. Social Change and Business Enterprise

It has been clear, particularly in Part II, that there is an historical dimension to the issues presented in this essay. The advent of the large or giant enterprise with the attending increase in the area of conscious coordination of economic activity, the rapid growth of the executive or managerial and white-collar classes, the separation of ownership and "control," the growth of labor and government into significant sources of influence over enterprise—all these and other developments are rightly claimed to have altered both the character of enterprise and the social structure within which enterprise operates. Journalists, sociologists, political scientists, and economists have produced a voluminous literature dealing

---

[66] J. A. Schumpeter, *Capitalism, Socialism, and Democracy* (New York and London, 1942), p. 134.

with various aspects of these developments. We can do no more here than concern ourselves with two issues which seem to be immediately relevant to the topic of this essay: first, in what way have these changes in the institutional setting affected enterprise behavior? Secondly, does the cumulation of all these changes amount to a new and significantly different societal structure? If it does, we must adjust our thinking with respect to both analysis and policy to the new social realities.

With respect to enterprise behavior a number of suggestions have been made. It is often claimed, for instance, that the time horizon of the large modern enterprise is much wider than that of the small-scale enterprise which (typically) preceded it. Easterbrook goes so far, in fact, as to suggest that for the "bureaucratic" organization maximization of the period of existence may be the appropriate "principle of selection."[67] The notion that time horizon is positively correlated with size of enterprise is plausible. It will not help us much, however, either from an analysis or a policy point of view, if we leave matters at this stage. The implications of a widening time horizon must be worked out with precision and must lead to commitments concerning the shape of the preference functions maximized (typically) by the "bureaucratic" enterprise, before we can appraise the significance of the change and put it to good analytical or policy use.

The large or giant modern enterprise is also claimed to be more rational than its small-scale predecessor. The methods of scientific management and accounting techniques employed by the former constitute evidence, it is argued, of its greater efficiency. Insofar as this is true it should make the economist's action frame of reference (with the implicit commitment that action is rational) more meaningful today than it has been in the past. At the same time, however, it is claimed that a giant enterprise is subject to inefficiencies which are associated with the "dead weight" and inflexibility of its "bureaucratic" structure.[68] In the same vein it is argued that the "professionalization of management" which attends the growth into dominance of the modern enterprise must affect the character of the end system formulated for the enterprise by the entrepreneur. Also, the growing independence of the "managers" from the contributors of capital, the increasing power of labor unions, and the spectacular growth of government participation in economic life must have affected the preference system of the firm significantly. It must be repeated, however, that it is insufficient to point the direction in which these developments are apt to affect the behavior of the firm. It is necessary to proceed to the formulation of models

[67] W. T. Easterbrook, "The Climate of Enterprise," *Am. Econ. Rev., Proc.*, May 1949, XXXIX, 323–35.

[68] In this connection see Gordon, *op. cit.*, Ch. 14, and TNEC Monog. 11, *Bureaucracy and Trusteeship in Large Corporations* (Washington, D.C., 1940).

which lead to operationally meaningful propositions. Until then our thinking will, of necessity, be restricted to the speculative and expository levels.

One last suggestion may be discussed in this connection because of the wide support it has been receiving of late. Many authors have proposed that organizational preservation or conservation or maintenance of market position are more relevant "principles of selection" than profit maximization.[69] In an economy of oligopolistic markets and giant firms, maintenance of organization and position must be of crucial importance to the peak co-ordinator. Though this cannot be doubted, effective analytical use of these insights must await the elaboration of their implications for firm behavior. Some suggestions are in order in this connection. The maintenance of organization or maintenance of market position insights may be developed systematically within either an action (maximization) or a homeostatic (nonmaximum) frame of reference. Boulding's asset-ratio preference theory seems to fit best the maximization formulation, provided we include among the assets of the firm such things as market position, etc. The behavioristic approach would be restricted to working out the implications of maintaining a given "state."

To the second question or issue we raised, namely, whether or not the changes that have taken place in the structure of our economy amount to a new society, the answer given by most seems to be, "Yes." Clearly the outstanding contribution in this field is Schumpeter's *Capitalism, Socialism, and Democracy*. Schumpeter's argument is so elaborately spun and touches on such a variety of issues, economic, cultural, and social, that it is impossible to do it justice in this essay. One aspect of his analysis, however, is so immediately relevant to our argument that we cannot afford to pass over it. The new society, for Schumpeter, is the product of successful capitalism. Employing an analysis which resembles in many respects the Marxian schema, he argues that the very success of capitalist enterprise has laid the foundations of its own withering away. The rise of the new bureaucratic and scientifically oriented large enterprise, itself the result of the creative genius of the capitalist-entrepreneur, has led to the routinization of innovation, to the "expropriation" of the owners, and to the emergence of a large and powerful bureaucracy which does not regard itself as the servant of the *rentier*-owner. In his words, "Dematerialized, defunctionalized, and absentee ownership does not impress and call forth moral allegiance as the vital form of property did. Eventually there will be *nobody* left who really cares to stand for it—nobody within and nobody without the precincts of the big

---

[69] See Oswald Knauth's *Managerial Enterprise* (New York, 1948). R. B. Heflebower has developed an intriguing analysis of firm behavior in terms of market position in a manuscript which has not been published as yet.

concerns."[70] Social revolution is taking or has taken place. The "battle-ground" is the enterprise itself. The "revolutionary" is the capitalist-entre-preneur, himself the victim of his own "revolution." The heir apparent is the "manager," the "planner," the "bureaucrat."

James Burnham's *The Managerial Revolution* does not compare well with Schumpeter's brilliant work. Burnham's main theme is provoking, but his argument on the whole is thin and insensitive to the complexities of the problem he has set himself to resolve. Burnham has missed completely what Schumpeter has so aptly called the "Cultural Indeterminateness of Social-ism."[71] Much too much is deduced from a rather simple set of assumptions. Burnham's argument is cast in the language of dialectic materialism. He travels the same road as the Marxists as far as the future of capitalism is concerned, but he parts company with them concerning the interpretation of the process of the "struggle for power" which is involved in the demise of capitalism and, therefore, concerning the character of the society which is to succeed (or has succeeded) capitalist society. Not the working class but the managers will displace the capitalist ruling class. The new society is, therefore, not a classless but a class society. Despite the shortcomings of the Burnham thesis it undoubtedly contains a kernel of truth. Despite the pronounced cultural differences between the Nazi society and the U.S.S.R., and between both of them and the British and American social structures, their development in the last two or three decades suggests the presence of a common leitmotiv. The emergence of a large bureaucracy in both the private and the public spheres, and the tendency toward centralization in the over-all direction of the economic process are common to all of them. But we don't need the argument of the "managerial revolution" to under-stand these developments. Schumpeter's analysis is both more exacting and more plausible than Burnham's thesis. It is important to note, however, that both Burnham and Schumpeter base a major part of their argument on the separation of ownership and "control." Almost all studies of current social change give a very prominent place to the Berle and Means thesis.[72] Few are those who are prepared to discount its importance.

If it is true that we are undergoing a social revolution of such magnitude the question of policy toward such problems as the separation of ownership and control, or labor participation in "management," or the ineffectiveness of the board of directors in the large corporation, must be regarded in a new light. To begin with we cannot seriously entertain the notion that we can

[70] *Op. cit.*, p. 142.

[71] Schumpeter, *op. cit.*, p. 170.

[72] Peter Drucker's *The New Society* (New York, 1949) is an outstanding example among them.

reverse the process. A good many of these developments must be accepted as more or less permanent features of the new *status quo*. Then again, even if we are willing to accept some of these developments as inevitable elements of our new social environment, and even if we are quite clear in our minds about the appropriate objectives of public policy, we cannot formulate policy until we have taken stock of the behavior implications of the new social structure. Herein lies the task of the economist.

4

An attempt
to synthesize some
theories of the firm

Almarin Phillips

INTRODUCTION

After attempting to mediate an academic argument between two of his friends by pointing out that each was correct in a limited sense, a man discovered that he had emerged distinctly third best in the encounter. Both of his friends had turned their arguments against his efforts to reconcile their differences. The erstwhile mediator summarized the lesson he had learned: "Blessed are the peacemakers; for they shall be called meddlers."

This paper considers three general approaches found in recent contributions to the theory of the firm and compares these to the traditional, profit-

From Almarin Phillips and Oliver E. Williamson (eds.), *Prices: Issues in Theory, Practice, and Public Policy* (Philadelphia: Univesrity of Pennsylvania Press, 1967), pp. 32–44. Reprinted by permission.

maximizing approach.[1] The attempted synthesis of the theories combines them—not with total success—into a more complex view of the determinants of market behavior and performance. In the synthesis it is argued that each of the theories is valid in particular circumstances, but that none by itself applies universally. The theories appear not as contending substitutes but rather as complements to one another, each dealing with a subset of factors which affect the behavior of firms. The argument could be regarded as one intended to illustrate the harmony of the theories. But, given the dangers inherent in meddling with others' arguments, it is intended as an expression of an independent view, not as a gesture toward peace.

The mode for synthesization is based on an enlarged view of organization structures within and among firms. With the new emphasis on organizational aspects of firm behavior contained in theories under consideration, it is not obvious that the criticism should be made that their organizational approach is inadequate. Yet that is an underlying argument of the paper. The older, profit-maximizing tradition typically ignored organizational considerations.[2] The newer theories have been based on research treating single, focal organizations and sometimes treat these in limited environmental conditions. In the present paper, the approach based on the single, focal organization is discarded. Emphasis is placed instead on complex, multi-organizational structures of firms. The firm, its subgroups, and interfirm groups are all recognized as being potentially important in the explanation of market behavior. Focus shifts within the organizational complex depending on the characteristics and locus of achievement problems.

The argument proceeds by a brief summary of the principal variants of contemporary theories. Following this, an attempt is made to adduce generalizations concerning the behavior of individuals and their organizations when there may be simultaneous identification by indivduals with multiple, interrelated organizations and shifts over time in organizational coalescence. These generalizations are then used to illustrate the possibilities for integrating and synthesizing the several organizational and, to a lesser degree, the profit-maximizing theories of firm behavior.

---

[1] The principal references are to R. M. Cyert and J. G. March, *A Behavioral Theory of the Firm* (Englewood Cliffs: 1963); O. E. Williamson, *The Economics of Discretionary Behavior: Managerial Objectives in the Theory of the Firm* (Englewood Cliffs: 1964); R. Marris, *The Economic Theory of 'Managerial' Capitalism* (New York: 1964) and W. J. Baumol, *Business Behavior, Value and Growth* (New York: 1959). The paper also considers my *Market Structure, Organization and Performance* (Cambridge, Mass.: 1962) and O. E. Williamson, "A Dynamic Theory of Interfirm Behavior," *Quarterly Journal of Economics* Vol. 79 (1965), pp. 579–607. For a broader review of related literature, see J. W. McGuire, *Theories of Business Behavior* (New York: 1964).

[2] An early exception is R. H. Coase, "The Nature of the Firm," *Economica*, N. S. Vol. 4, pp. 386–405.

FOCAL ORGANIZATIONS AND ENVIRONMENT IN THEORIES OF FIRM BEHAVIOR

To clarify the comparison of current theories, assume the following conditions. First, there is a group of multi-product firms. The number of firms in the group, their relative sizes, and the number and specification of products need not be detailed for present purposes.[3] The firms are a "group" in the sense of their having mutually dependent demand functions. At least one product of every firm is subjectively regarded by those making pricing decisions as having a significantly high cross-demand elasticity with a product of a least one other firm in the group.

Second, within each firm the productive functions for the products are such that each uses a scarce productive factor which is also necessary for the production of at least one other of the firm's products.

Third, associated with each firm there are distinguishable groups of individuals. One group is composed of persons whose incomes and, hence, levels of satisfaction vary directly with the profits of the firm. This is the "ownership group." A second group consists of those in positions to direct the activities of the entire firm and whose rewards come from salaried incomes and other perquisites and emoluments connected with their positions. This is the "top management group." Another set of groups is composed of persons with positions and utility functions such that individual satisfactions are directly related to the activity of particular product lines of the firm's output, with a different group for each line. These are called "product management groups." A final set of groups—though little attention will be given to them here—is made up of persons whose satisfactions vary directly with the wage bills for producing the product. These are called the "wage employee groups."

Fourth, it is assumed that legal arrangements provide the ownership group with the authority to hire and fire top management personnel. It is not assumed, however, that this authority is necessarily easily exercised. Similarly, it is assumed that legal authority exists for the top management group to hire and fire personnel in the product management groups and for the latter to hire and fire in the wage employee groups.

By these assumptions, several sorts of intergroup conflict may exist.[4] First, there may be conflict among the firms in the market group because

---

[3] These are, nonetheless, important considerations in any application of our results.

[4] Conflict is used here to mean "a breakdown in the standard mechanisms of decision-making so that an individual or group experiences difficulty in selecting an action alternative." See J. G. March and H. A. Simon, *Organizations* (New York: 1958), pp. 112ff. Conflict resolution need not eliminate inconsistency between goals; resolution does clarify decision rules.

of their demand interdependence. This conflict may be perceived first by the product-line management for those products involved in competitive rivalry, but the effects are on the ownership groups' rewards as well as on those of the top management and product management groups. Any or all of these groups—jointly or severally—may perceive themselves as being involved in interfirm conflict.

Second, there may be conflict among the product management groups within single firms. This conflict originates in their joint use of a scarce resource and in satisfaction deriving from product-line activity levels. Their interdependence is of a kind such that changes in output mix tend to make one group better off at the expense of others.

Third, there may be conflict between the hierarchically arranged groups within firms. Top management and owners may be in conflict; product management groups and top management may be in conflict; wage employees and product management or top management may be in conflict. Here, the basic source of conflict is the inconsistency in sources of satisfaction. Profits, management salaries and perquisites, product-line activity levels, and wages cannot be simultaneously optimized nor, indeed, are there likely to be many opportunities to make decisions within the firm of which the direct effects will be to increase all of these simultaneously.

The assumed structure of firms and the various forms of potential intergroup conflict can now be used to compare the conventional, managerial, behavioral, and interfirm theories. While the conventional approach does not ordinarily give explicit treatment to any group as an organizational entity, it is clear that in that theory it is the ownership group which is determinative of firm behavior. This is the focal group, with technology and the rewards systems of others operating only as constraints to profit-maximization. Conflict internal to the firm is totally resolved by the universality of the maximizing assumption. As employees (or "labor") with technically defined contributions to production, persons in other groups are provided with opportunity cost satisfaction and participate only so long as there are no preferable alternatives for themselves. Conflict among firms is totally unresolved by the "competitive" assumptions which run with the theory; it is totally resolved when the "collusion" versions are employed.[5] The owners *are* the firm so far as behavior is concerned.

Managerial theories, as Williamson points out clearly in his essay, focus principally on the behavior of the top management groups of particular firms in what is essentially a "no-conflict" environment. Whether the top management group seeks to maximize a multidimensional utility function,

[5] It is more accurate to restrict this conclusion specifically to those variants of traditional theory which utilize the calculus to analyze behavior.

as in the Williamson versions, or to maximize sales or rates of growth, as in the Baumol and Marris versions, their having the necessary latitude in directing the firm to achieve their goals depends on other groups' not attempting simultaneously to optimize with respect to their goals. Williamson observes that the theory is applicable only where competition "is attenuated so that survival is not a pressing concern for the firm."[6] Baumol sees firms attempting to maximize sales subject to a minimum profit constraint. Marris credits security considerations with being the constraining force in the firm's efforts to maximize growth rates.

In the terms used here, these limiting or constraining conditions, when operable, imply a conflict between the top management group and some other group in its environment. If unresolved, this conflict leaves the behavior of the firm uncertain. Unless the resolution completely favors the achievement of management goals, the managerial theories lose their relevance. A group other than the top management group affects the firm's behavior and moves it in a direction inconsistent with maximal satisfactions for the management group. Threats to survival (Williamson), to security (Marris), or to profits (Baumol) create potential conflict between owners and managers. Threats to satisfactory achievements for product-line managers would presumably create conflict among them or between them and top management. Thus, generally, the managerial theories are pertinent only where top management groups behave as maximizers and all other groups—whether because of limited opportunities, imperfect knowledge, or satisficing forms of behavior—do not intervene in directing the firm. Given these conditions, the top managers *are* the firm.

The Cyert and March behavioral theory is considerably less restricted with respect to organizational focus and environmental conditions. As presented by Cyert and March, the firm's subgroups are not identical to those assumed above, but, consistent with those used illustratively here, they do have different and not necessarily consistent subgoals. The levels of achievement for these subgoals are considered in slack (i.e., no-conflict) and no-slack (i.e., conflict) conditions. Further, rather than viewing some groups as inherently satisficers and others as inherently maximizers, the theory posits that all groups behave as satisficing organizations. The problems which arise from less than satisfactory performance and from intergroup conflict are resolved—but less than optimally resolved—by patterns of behavior characterized by uncertainty avoidance, problemistic search, and organizational learning.

---

[6] See above, p. 12. Note, however, that Williamson does trace out some behavioral implications for conditions in which managers recognize relations between current behavior and future environmental states.

Unlike any of the other theories, the focal organization in the Cyert and March approach varies with the nature and locus of achievement problems. The focal organization may be one (or more) of the suborganizations of a firm or the over-all organization of the firm itself. Search for problem solutions is stimulated "in the neighborhood of the problem symptom." "Initial reaction . . . will be in the department identified with the goal," and "the organization uses increasingly complex . . . search" only when simple and local search fails.[7] It is true, nonetheless, that the focal organization is, at least by emphasis, restricted to the firm and intrafirm groups. While firms in the Cyert and March approach attempt to "devise and negotiate an environment so as to eleminate uncertainty . . . through the establishment of industry-wide conventional practices,"[8] this kind of behavior is not incorporated into the otherwise sweeping organizational analysis.[9]

The interfirm organizational theory treats a group of market-related firms in a manner quite analogous to the treatment of firms in the Cyert–March approach. That is, it stresses relations among firms and their interfirm organizations as the intrafirm theory stresses relations among subgroups within firms and the organization of the firm. Hostile (conflict) and friendly (no-conflict) environment and structural situations which lead to low (unsatisfactory) and high (satisfactory) achievement levels are considered in an organizational context. But, just as the intrafirm theories focus on the firm and its subgroups with little attention to interfirm relations, so does the interfirm theory focus on the latter, with no attention to the individual firm and its subgroups.

In summary, the differences in the conventional, managerial, intrafirm behavioral and interfirm behavioral theories lie largely in differences in organizational focus and in differences in assumptions with respect to the environment of the focal organization. The managerial theories consider the behavior of top management in an environment in which internal and external conflict are resolved. The intrafirm behavioral theory deals with the firm as a coalition of subgroups with conflicting goals and internal conflict but in the context of a generally no-conflict relationship with other firms. The interfirm theories are concerned with organizations of firms in relation to varying market environments and varying organizational structures. All of these depart from conventional analysis in their recognition of at least some groups which fail to behave in an optimizing fashion and

---

[7] Cyert and March, op. cit., p. 116.

[8] Ibid., p. 120.

[9] Note, however, that in their simulation of the market behavior of oligopolistic firms, specific attention is given to the probable reactions of other firms to the behavior changes of the focal firm. Ibid., pp. 149–236.

in their treatment of nonownership groups in the determination of the behavior of firms. But, as is emphasized below, all of the more recent approaches contain elements in which individuals and groups coalesce in the resolution of conflicts when the achievements of an organization of which they are a member and, hence, their own achievements are threatened. In this limited and apparently unrecognized sense, there is a weak concurrence in the system of behavior portrayed in all of them. Further, in this concurrence is found the possibility for synthesization and, more particularly, for the definition of circumstances in which threats to achievement occur in terms of profits for individual firms and in which coalescence would appear as profit-maximizing behavior.

A MULTIORGANIZATIONAL VIEW

An organization is "a set of social relations deliberately created, with the explicit intention of continuously accomplishing some specific goals or purposes."[10] In terms of the structure of firms assumed above, each firm, ownership group, top management group, product management group, and wage employee group is an organization. But this hardly exhausts the list of possible organizations included in that structure. Because conflict among themselves or with top management might tend commonly to reduce the achievements of product managers within a firm, there may be an organization composed of the managers of the several lines explicitly intended to avoid conflict resolutions that are unsatisfactory in terms of the goals of the product managers. For similar reasons, there may be an organization of wage employees which crosses product lines. For some purposes, owners and top managers may be an organization; for others, top management and product management may combine in a purposive set of social relations. Thus, just within a single firm and without considering groups composed of subsets within the broad functional groups that have been assumed, many organizations are possible. Individuals simultaneously belong to, contribute to, and receive inducements from a complex of intrafirm groups.

Other organizations may exist among the firms. The wage employees may be "industrially" organized. The product managements of the separate firms may be organized. The top management and ownership groups may also have organizations for a variety of purposes. Again, a single person, as well as belonging to organizations within a given firm, may belong to one or more interfirm organizations.

[10] A. L. Stinchcombe, "Social Structure and Organizations," in J. G. March (ed.), *Handbook of Organizations* (New York: 1964), p. 142.

These multiple and overlapping "organizations of organizations" all relate quite directly to goals and purposes accomplished through essentially economic and market activities. Here the multiple organizations to which individuals belong are generally combinations of individuals and groups that are horizontally or vertically connected within and among firms. It should be noted, also, that individuals and, to a lesser degree, perhaps, organizations may be members of several organizations which are quite unrelated. The individual is a member of a firm, a social club, a church, an alumni society, and a bowling team. Firms may belong to local chambers of commerce, industrial development corporations, industry trade associations, national manufacturers' associations, etc. As stated before, the individuals and firms will tend to identify with and make contributions to the individually unrelated organizations, depending on the goal or purpose to be accomplished.

Two related hypotheses—already strongly implied—are advanced with respect to behavior in a multiorganizational context:

1. Changes in an environment common to, or conflicts among, two or more interacting individuals or organizations which are perceived by these individuals or organizations as a cause of less than satisfactory levels of achievement tend to cause stronger identification with and coalescence in an organization of higher order which includes the commonly affected individuals and organizations.

2. New organizations tend to be established when changes in the environment common to interacting individuals or organizations or when conflicts between individuals or organizations are perceived as a cause of less than satisfactory achievements, and when no existing organization is perceived as being effective in improving achievements.

These hypotheses are not meant to imply that coalescence in or formation of an organization of a higher order involves the abandonment of membership in and identification with the lower order or previous organizations. These and the goals and purposes they are designed to achieve remain. What is hypothesized is simply a shifting in the relative strength of identification with and contribution to the many organizations, depending on the nature and locus of achievement problems. Neither are the hypotheses meant to imply that a particular higher order of new organization will necessarily be effective in offsetting the adverse environmental change or in reducing the conflict so as to raise achievement. As becomes clear below, however, the tendency toward coalescence will be stronger the more it is perceived by all commonly affected members that the union is the most effective alternative.

The results of existing organizational research are used below to give support to these hypotheses. The difficulty in stating them succinctly and, indeed, of summarizing the relevant literature are cause for a more homely form of argument, however. The hypotheses are nothing more than clumsy statements of the maxims, "United we stand; divided we fall," or "In union there is strength." They represent not at all the exclusive behavior of economic units but rather behavior characteristics of humans and their tendencies to group. By way of illustration, one would anticipate little cooperation (i.e., organization) among individual Boy Scouts in a fire-building contest with a prize for one scout in each patrol and with rules against prize-sharing. If the game were changed to a contest among patrols, with one prize for whichever is the winning patrol of a troop, intrapatrol organizations will tend to rise. In a similar contest among several troops in a city, intratroop (and interpatrol) organizations will appear. That is, the primary and focal organizations will tend to shift depending on the nature (fire-building, dishwashing, tent-pitching) and the locus (intrapatrol, intra-troop, intracity) of the achievement problem.

More formally, the hypotheses are fully consistent with and, in a sense, simply an extension of the Cyert–March–Simon feedback process of prob-lemistic search—search which is motivated by a problem and which proceeds to more complex possibilities for solution only as simple ones fail. Here, however, the search extends to that for organizational arrangements which will be effective in solving a common problem.

The described tendencies are also supported by closely related organizational theories. One of these is the Barnard–Simon theory of organizational equilibrium, modified to the context of equilibria in strengths of identification with two or more organizations.[11] The change in environment or the conflict postulated in the propositions lowers the inducements received from the affected organizations, weakening the willingness of participants to contribute to those organizations relative to visible alternatives. An alternative—and one which may not involve the exit "costs" of leaving any organization completely—is to identify more strongly with and contribute more to another organization which, by combining the commonly affected individuals, promises higher inducements because of its more effective control over the environment or its ability to rationalize internal group conflict. Thus, the hypotheses describe tendencies for the strengths of identifications of participants in more than one organization to shift among organizations depending on the locus and nature of the problem which

[11] March and Simon, *op. cit.*, pp. 83–111.

causes less than satisfactory achievement. The shifts occur as the perceived inducement-contribution balances from the several organizations change.[12]

Support for the propositions can be found also in a combination of other two-way generalizations.[13] Initially, a decrease in the munificence of the environment may result in increased conflict among the affected groups. If anything, this conflict will reduce the control of the groups over the environment and further reduce achievement. With or without the further deterioration of achievement due to increased conflict, the effect of the environmental change on achievement is, when perceived, to increase the felt need for joint decision-making. This is because the groups recognize themselves as being mutually dependent on the same hostile environment, because the similarities in their positions leads to increased perceptions of goal-sharing, and because of the consequent increase in the frequency of their interactions. There tends to be a decrease in internal conflict, an increase in the uniformity of opinions concerning effective actions, and greater control over (or ability mutually to adapt to) the environment. In sum, what tends to happen is that the affected individuals or organizations coalesce in an organization of higher order in response to the environmental change or conflict which commonly reduces achievement.

There will, of course, be reverse tendencies in the event that the environment becomes more munificent. But once the shift in identifications to a particular larger organization has been experienced as an effective way to offset environmental hostility, it will tend to be used more quickly and will lessen internal conflict in future circumstances of the same sort. The larger organization, that is, tends to become used as a programmed response by its suborganizations in certain circumstances.[14]

The second proposition relating to new organizations comes into play only when the first has proven ineffective. The establishment of a new organization represents a form of innovation. It is an alternative used when search among and efforts by existing organizations have yielded no satisfactory solutions to the achievement problems. New organizations are apt to emerge, it is hypothesized, as an eventual response to adverse environ-

---

[12] Inducements are "payments" received from the organization by participants; contributions are "payments" made to the organization by participants.

[13] These generalizations are explained more fully and their empirical foundations are summarized in March and Simon, op. cit. See pp. 53–111, 121–131, 172–199.

[14] Compare Williamson, "A Dynamic Theory of Interfirm Behavior," op. cit. We add the observation that the response sometimes seems to be repetitive despite a change in the nature of the hostility in the environment. Old organizations do not die easily.·

mental conditions of a sort not previously encountered and against which no existing organization is effective.[15]

The propositions lead to the conclusion that no single organization is appropriately focal in all circumstances. In particular, "environment" becomes a concept entirely relative to the group being considered. Analysis of environmental influences depends critically on determining the nature and locus of sources of pressures on achievement and the subsequent use of theory at the organizational levels which are likely to be involved in the primary responsive behavior. Hence, analysis at the level of, say, the firm may be quite appropriate for certain classes of problems. But for other classes of problems the analysis should be at the level of subgroups within the firm, groups of firms, or groups of subgroups from several firms. Theories of firm, intrafirm, and interfirm organizations must each be only partial explanations of the full array of organizational influences on market behavior. The critical issue, then, is to relate the several influences to various classes of achievement problems in a systematic way.

A clarification is first necessary. The addition of the multiorganizational propositions has been couched in terms of satisficing rather than optimizing behavior. Shifting strengths of identification among organizations, organizational coalescing in response to common problems, and the creation of new organizations are seen in the light of responses to less than satisfactory levels of achievement. The shifting is not viewed as a process tending constantly toward a unique optimum. Indeed, in a multiorganizational framework, even the definition of an optimal situation is difficult because of the mixture of interdependent individuals, organizations, and goals.

It is true, nonetheless, that in this framework individuals and separate organizations often have alternatives in achieving their own goals which do not appear in the single, focal organizational approach. Because of the variety of possible organizational affiliations, contributions may be made to and inducements received from the organizational mix in a manner which satisfies the participants. That is, the differences in goals and value systems of individuals lead to different inducement-contribution responses among the many organizations. Strong identification would tend to run to those organizations which, from the point of view of the member, share similar goals and are prestigious and effective. To the extent that this

---

[15] Stinchcombe, op. cit., p. 146, lists conditions which motivate the formation of new organizations. These are consistent with the hypothesis here, but, as stated, they do not include the satisficing aspects of behavior and the formation of new organizations as a feedback from less than satisfactory achievement. Stinchcombe points out that a "liability" of newness is that "New organizations must rely heavily on social relations among strangers." In a multiorganizational context, a new organization is often just a new set of social relations among persons well known to one another.

occurs, the quasi-resolution of conflict which characterizes behavior in a single organization interferes less with the maximizing of satisfactions of individuals than is apparent in the single, focal organizational approach.[16]

Observations of individuals and organizations during periods in which the strengths of identifications are changing and new coalitions are arising will, of course, be difficult to distinguish from optimizing behavior. The changes are being made to improve achievement. If, for example, one observed a set of interdependent subgroups in a firm identifying more strongly with the firm and its profit goal during a period when the survival of the firm was threatened, one could hardly distinguish this behavior from that of the firm acting as a profit-maximizing unit. In other circumstances, however, the behavior of the firm's subgroups may be quite at variance with profit-maximization. An opportunity for additional profits is apparently forgone or "traded off" in order to achieve more of another goal. Unless it is argued that there is a recognition of the rates of trade-off among goals and of the relations of these trade-offs to a composite, multidimensional utility function (with implicit interpersonal and intergroup comparisons of utility), the satisficing behavioral assumption seems preferable to one which requires optimization.

AN ATTEMPT TO SYNTHESIZE

Static aspects of the complementarity of the conventional, managerial, behavioral, and interfirm theories should at this point have become quite obvious and can be dealt with briefly. Conventional, profit-maximizing analysis of firm behavior is quite appropriate if the group of firms individually face relatively continuous threats to survival in the form of less than satisfactory levels of profits, if the management and wage employee groups have no visible and preferred alternative employment, and if there is no effective interfirm organization. In these circumstances, the tendency to coalesce will be at the level of the firm since—because of these assumptions —there are no alternatives for higher achievement regardless of the level of the aspirations of the various individuals and groups.

---

[16] We reject, therefore, characterizations such as that of R. J. Monsen, Jr., and A. Downs, "A Theory of Large 'Managerial' Firms," *Journal of Political Economy*, Vol. 73 (1965), pp. 221–236, that owners tend to act as "satisficers" while managers tend to be "maximizers." In the first place, even in their owning and managing roles, their behavior will depend on achievement levels relative to aspirations. In the second place, any individual—owner, manager, or worker—may appear as a "satisficer" in an organization which, in terms of *his* utility function, offers few inducements relative to contributions and as a "maximizer" or "achiever" in other organizations with a more favorable inducement–contribution balance.

In similar fashion, the theories of managerial discretion are appropriate where there is no threat to survival originating external to the firm, where the profit levels are adequate to prevent intervention from owners, and where the satisfactions of all other subgroups within the firm are high enough to induce their continued participation without attempts to affect the firm's behavior. The intrafirm behavioral theory is applicable where there is failure to achieve satisfactorily by at least one subgroup within the firm or by the firm itself but where, either for reasons of market structure or market organization, the effective remedy for achievement failures does not extend beyond the level of the firm. Finally, the interfirm theory may be used where the sources of achievement difficulties are common to a group of firms and where unilateral action by single firms is ineffective.

This is hardly a fruitful synthesis. In terms of the purposes of this volume, it yields no knowledge about the specifics of price behavior which could not be gained from the theories individually. But the more intriguing aspects of synthesis are dynamic. While efforts to produce dynamic relationships among the theories have not yielded a rigorous model, even a loose, verbalized form indicates that some predictive and explanatory powers may be gained from a combination of the theories. The predictions or explanations of market performance which emerge from the use of any one of the theories in static form imply enough about conflicts and environmental states to predict—qualitatively, to be sure—some dynamic tendencies not otherwise apparent. A few illustrations can be offered here.

One example can be found in Williamson's essay above. In explaining managerial decisions where the environment of future periods is dependent, among other things, on the behavior of the firm in the current period, it is observed that "adopting a managerial posture yields high current satisfaction but only at the expense of 'shrinking' future choice sets." That is, the results of maximization by managers at one point in time may be to reduce managerial rewards at succeeding points of time. In the Williamson version, managers recognize the probably future consequences of current decision alternatives and continue to maximize over time with the time-environment relations included in their behavioral rules. He thus retains the essence of a purely managerial theory. If, however, one assumed alternately that managers do not fully recognize the future consequences of today's behavior, different results obtain. Most obviously, short-term behavior which increases the satisfactions of managerial groups may, as Williamson says, produce long-term tendencies for the profits of the firm to be less than satisfactory for the ownership group. The firm becomes a "loose ship." If this occurs, the behavior typified by the managerial theories at one point in time tends to cause more active intervention by ownership groups at future points in time. And in those times, the behavioral theory or, perhaps, an outright profit-maximizing theory might better explain and predict the firm's be-havior.[17] Less obviously, continuously high and rising achievement by the top management group may raise the aspirations of the lower echelons of management and of other employees. This, in addition to having an adverse effect on profit, would tend to create internal conflict in the firm for which the behavioral theory might again be more appropriate.

In a dynamic context, many similar feedbacks can be traced from the performance predictions of the theories. The profit results predicted for an atomistically structured, noncollusively acting group of firms indicate that tendencies to collude or combine will arise over time. Unresolved conflict is perceived by the firms as a cause of less than satisfactory achieve-ments. According to the hypotheses above, this perception would cause tendencies to coalesce in higher-order organizations, with results which are better predicted by consideration of the variables and assumptions of the interfirm theory than by those of competitive theory. If evidence that such a feedback operates is necessary, consider that all of the famous American antitrust cases involving overt price conspiracy have arisen from market situations in which independent behavior—often in conjunction with de-creases in demand—have produced first a low profit record and then attempts to organize on an interfirm basis.[18]

What, then, does the synthesis offer with respect to explanations or predictions of price and output behavior? Not a great deal, it must be admitted. But it can hardly offer less than do the separate theories used without reference to one another. It may offer a bit more in that the com-bined form of the theories at least raises questions concerning the dynamic —or "real time"—stability of any assumed mode of behavior. Since it appears that firms (and subgroups within firms and groups of firms) do behave over time as though different objectives were being pursued, one could hope that a more rigorous synthesization will be developed which makes the changes in goals and changes in behavior endogenous to the market system to which the theories relate. At the moment, such a synthesis seems unlikely.

---

[17] This corresponds approximately with Carl Kaysen's suggestion that the apparent goal of the firm may vary over time. "Another View of Corporate Capitalism," *Quarterly Journal of Economics*, Vol. 79 (Feb. 1965), p. 43. Note that Williamson's model is partly responsive to this suggestion.

[18] See Phillips, *op. cit.*, especially Chaps. 4 to 9, for discussion of several significant cases.

5

The institutional approach revisited

David A. Revzan

This paper is designed to present an extended view of the Duddy-Revzan institutional approach.[1] In this extended view, the institutional approach will be related to the following topics: a view of the dimensions of the marketing system; the role of the institutional approach—a restatement; and the implications of the discussion for selected research areas.[2] Of special importance to this workshop is the extent to which the contents of this paper can serve to stimulate research of the types to be suggested.

[1] See'Edward A. Duddy and David A. Revzan, *Marketing: An Institutional Approach*, 2nd Ed. (New York: McGraw Hill Book Co., Inc., 1953), Chap. II and Appendix C for the original, detailed statement as such.

[2] A selected bibliography related to the institutional approach and other aspects of this paper is attached at the end.

From David A. Revzan, *Perspectives for Research in Marketing: Seven Essays* (Berkeley: Graduate School of Business Administration, University of California, Berkeley, Institute of Business and Economic Research, 1965). Reprinted by permission.

THE DIMENSIONS OF THE MARKETING SYSTEM

The marketing system which exists today to trade in hundreds of billions of dollars of goods and services (in gross transactional terms) is an evidence of significant economic specialization; while, at the same time it may be viewed as a mass mechanism operating within the dimensions of a mass society. It is an evidence of an ever-changing complex system of varying degrees of economic competition working and made effective, if at all, through an array of wholesale and retail markets.

These forms of competition generate from these markets, and interact, in turn, on them. In addition, they interact with other forms of human activities in various degrees of satisfactory performance, depending upon the sector of the marketing system studied, and the criteria of "satisfactory performance" utilized. The marketing system has evolved, further, in a geographical environment; and, in one as well, of a political philosophy which, in this country, has left its individualistic markings. Through this marketing system, and especially the framework of the price structure, the coordination of specialists continually is achieved with varying degrees of effectiveness.

The major dimensions of the marketing system to be discussed more fully in this section, are as follows:

1. A system of marketing and facilitating agencies;
2. A continuous expansion of a series of product assortment alternatives;
3. An ever-changing geographical environment;
4. The evolution and maturation of a series of wholesale and retail markets, with an accompanying system of formal and informal market news communication;
5. Based in turn upon (4), the evolution of a continuing complex wholesale and retail price structure;
6. The evolution of increasingly complicated managerial attempts at non-price competition;
7. The *integration* of all of the foregoing dimensional components into a marketing system through the *coordination and control* aspects of the price structure, management, people acting as ultimate consumers, and government;
8. A continuous struggle between attempts, on the one hand to introduce changes and to maximize buyer and seller alternatives in the marketing system, as opposed to attempts to reduce or eliminate such changes and to minimize the range of alternatives; and

9. Finally, running parallel to the above, the resultant levels of economic and social performance of the marketing system.

A System of Marketing and Facilitating Agencies

At the heart of any well-developed marketing system is an ever-changing and evolving series of specialized wholesale and retail middlemen who have a prime responsibility for the movement and exchange of goods and services from points of various producers' origins (extractive and manufacturing) to various intermediate and final users. In addition, there are numerous types of facilitating agencies (also ever-changing and evolving) engaged in essential transportation, storage and auxiliary functions. All of these agencies (and their respective functional elements) are linked together in various channel groupings oriented towards the marketing of particular product and service assortments. This continuous emergence of an agency structure is interrelated with the ever-emerging mass marketing system handling ever-widening volumes and assortments of goods and services, and providing for increased buying and selling alternatives.

Expansion of Product Assortment Alternatives

Marketing exists in its modern context, and by its very nature, on the continuous buying and selling of goods and services (with related functional aspects). One of the most explosive elements in any marketing system, therefore, is the extent to which the available product assortments multiply. These waves of expansion rarely are orderly, or capable of being forecasted accurately. And, the development of one change in a given product assortment frequently reacts chainwise in creating additional product assortments. Over the long pull, it should be noted that those assortments comprising the non-ultimate consumers' goods group have tended to exceed the ultimate consumers' goods group both in complexity and importance.

In this environment of change, especially significant for the marketing system is the relationship between product assortments in the basic sense, and the impact of these expansions upon the frantic search for individual identification of each production and for middleman source of the products in the channels of distribution. Further, at the ultimate consumer level, complexity results from the increasing obliteration, in a mass society, of what represents the basic rock-bottom level of necessities, and what represents "conspicuous consumption" and "waste." Another complexity results from the increasing difficulties of buyers at any level of the marketing channel to be able to make meaningful differentiations between the competing products in the ever-widening assortments.

Changing Area Structures

The story of the development and dimensions of the modern marketing system is, partially, the story of changing geographical dimensions. These dimensions must begin with a recognition of the basic condition of the unequal spatial distribution of the basic extractive industry resources.[3] It includes, also, a consideration of the variable success between the regions of the earth in conquering surface space by means of ever-improved transportation. Further, geographical factors are ever-changing in their relationships to where people select to live and pursue economic (or other) activities. Accordingly, changing spatial patterns emerge for the location of enterprises carrying on various economic and related activities.

Thus, each marketing enterprise is faced with a continuous problem of deciding where to locate each establishment; and to a systematic determination of the boundaries of the surrounding trading areas which furnish the most fertile sales prospects, compared with alternative opportunities. In certain marketing situations, the collective locational pull of all clustering establishments is dominant; while, in other situations, each agency must compete with every other agency in the same kind of business in terms of primary geographical outreach.

A System of Wholesale and Retail Markets

In rudimentary societies, no highly formalized system of wholesale markets and retail markets is either needed, or emerges. But a modern system of marketing requires increasingly specialized trading markets in both sectors in which the types of competition are determined; in which the conditions of buying and selling are specified; and in which the determination of prices and terms of sale takes place. These combinations of wholesale and retail markets vary in importance and in systematic organization from commodity category to commodity category. They vary, also, in their geographical patternings, and in the sequence of marketing relationships.

Price Structures

Modern production and marketing are organized, and the specialists engaged in each, coordinated through the price system. The preceding dimensions are very essential in effecting a series of prices which become interrelated, in turn, into a price structure. Then this price structure, through its wholesale and retail segments, becomes important in the coordination and controlling role specified. This price structure grows in complexity with the evolution of each of the other dimensions of a mass marketing system, and is, as well, at the very center of the ever-evolving marketing system.

[3] This inequality varies in nature from resource to resource.

Evolution of Non-Price Competition

While the marketing system consists, in part, in the organization and coordination of specialists through the price structure, increasingly, managerial attempts have been directed towards escaping from the rigors of competition, especially price competition. Thus, a continuous tug of war results between managerial attempts at price competition, and offsetting managerial attempts at retreating from such competition. And, the role of governmental regulation in this connection has not been consistently in the direction of maintaining or improving price competition.

Apart from interfering with the use of the price structure as the basis for marketing efficiency, the increasing intrusion of non-price competition has resulted in a series of repercussions in the marketing system not recognized in early evolutionary periods. Perhaps the most criticized of these repercussions has been the role of advertising. Functions and new agencies have emerged which are related inextricably to the increased development of non-price competition.

Coordination and Control

With the increasing complexities of the marketing system, provisions have to be made for formal coordination and controls in addition to that furnished by the price structure. Thus, the widening scope of coordination and control becomes evident in the decision-making activities of business executives at all channel levels; in the authority of the various users of product assortments; and in the increasing insertion of control by laws administered by government agencies.

These widening circles of coordination and control activities create increasing evidences of the lack of unification between the various agencies so engaged. This lack of unification reacts, in turn, upon the coordination and control activities in terms of which aspect will attain dominance at any given period of evolution.

Change versus Stability

Marketing is eminently concerned with change. Indeed, marketing may be visualized as that part of business enterprise activities which seeks continually to instill change into the marketing system in an attempt to maximize buyer and seller alternatives. However, not all marketing institutions can or will accept this over-all tendency towards change. Accordingly, many devote their managerial efforts towards trying to achieve stability in one or more of the marketing dimensions in which they are involved. In one sense, then, marketing history is concerned with the continuing struggle between pressures making for change, versus the pressures attempting to initiate or to achieve relative stability.

A somewhat different aspect of this dimension is the effect that this struggle has upon the formal life cycle of a marketing institution. Some go through a relatively short life cycle, and then disappear from the marketing system. Others reach a peak, and then taper off in reduced relative importance without ever completely disappearing. Those with greater flexibility and adaptability, and superior managerial resources, may evaluate the pressures making for change correctly, and, thereby, achieve a new cycle (or cycles) of growth. Finally, some institutions may achieve a given peak of growth, and, thereafter, level off at that peak in a pattern somewhat resembling relative stability. The cumulative cycles of change versus stability have shown no tendency towards uniform periodicities, nor has the amplitude of each tended to be uniform compared with other cycles.

Other Aspects

While the preceding discussion has dealt with the major dimensions of the present-day marketing system, four other dimensions need to be kept in perspective. Without any attempt at assigning any system of priorities, these may be listed as:

1. The evolution of a body of common, equity, and statutory law designed to facilitate sales contracts, agency relationships, formations of businesses, *et al.*, with the outlining of corresponding responsibilities;
2. The evolution of a modern system of money and banking, and related banking and credit facilities and agencies to furnish, so to speak, the "life blood" of the marketing system;
3. The evolution of systems of grades and standards for commodities, designed to effect benefits in market news communication and price relationship among other things; and
4. The origins and evolution of a mail and parcel post system, with corresponding benefits for communication and delivery.

THE ROLE OF THE INSTITUTIONAL APPROACH: A RESTATEMENT

The General Meaning and Framework of the Institutional Approach

This approach represents a view, first of all, of the marketing system in the dimensions discussed above, as an *organic* whole, in which the anatomical and physiological structure of the "marketing body" are isolated and studied within the framework of the above discussions.

The structural components of this organic system consist, first of all, of an *agency structure*; i.e., the various business units which perform the entire range of marketing functions, together with their interrelationships through channels of distribution within an over-all marketing organization (as defined in a later section). These, individually, are the "cells" of the marketing body; and, in their interrelationships with other "cells," constitute the functional parts of the marketing body. The meaningful activities performed by each are part or all of the component elements of the marketing functions; and groupings of these functions comprise the marketing processes of concentration, equalization, and dispersion.[4]

This ever-changing agency structure operates within an environment of goods and services, and adapts itself, as well, to the environment of area structure. *Area structure*, as noted above, calls attention, first of all, to the basic geographical specialization of extractive industry resources, and to the expected marketing returns based on them—the basic conditions of locational inequality. Building on this inequality, it next emphasizes that for each agency in the over-all agency structure, there is the necessity of selecting a particular location. These locational alternatives have exclusive trading areas, respectively, in which each is dominant in terms of buying and/or selling importance—*the primary trading area.*

A zone surrounding the primary trading area offers less-than-proportionate marketing returns, and is designated as the *secondary trading area.* A final zone may exist in certain area structures in which the particular locational (trading) center has no outstanding advantages over competing locational centers—the *zone of indifference.* As the urban structure becomes more complex, a hierarchy of super trading areas may encompass several subordinate trading areas in a metropolitan area context. These trading area boundaries, in the organic tradition of the institutional approach, are dynamic and not static, as prices, freight rates, and other determinants change their geographical relationships.

The next structural element, *the price structure*, deals with the "brain" and "nervous" system of the marketing organism. As has been indicated, this price structure is the integrating force through which the exchange of goods takes place within a mass marketing system. Thousands upon thousands of individual prices are interrelated to form threads of prices; and these, in turn, are woven together into an intricate fabric of price structures in the wholesaling and retailing sectors, respectively.

The importance of each price varies within each strand of thread; and the strands of thread vary in thickness, in turn, within the fabric. And, while the over-all price structure tends to be dynamic, the individual prices may show wide variations in their respective responsiveness to change over time.

---

[4] The terminology and content vary from author to author.

Their determination takes place in organized and non-organized markets under conditions ranging from some form of workable competition to conditions of absolute monoply, with many intermediate gradations.

Just as the individual parts of the human body work together in an integrated whole when the body is healthy, or to restore such balance, so do the structural components of the marketing body become coordinated with an over-all body or system. This concept of *homeostasis* in human biology has aspects of the functioning of higher animal organisms which has some transferability to the concept of the marketing body in the Duddy-Revzan institutional approach.[5] Some aspects of this concept of homeostasis are especially valuable here:[6]

1. The existence of a *fluid matrix* (equivalent to the roles of transportation, and money and credit).
2. The existence of *a margin of safety*; i.e. "allowances for contingencies."
3. The ability of the organism to store more than is needed at a moment of time, and, when necessary, to eliminate surpluses.
4. The existence of a series of complementary interactions.
5. The existence in the organism of defenses against unfavorable attack.
6. As in the human organism, the consistency of certain basic characteristics of the marketing system, and the continuous attempts made to maintain these conditions.
7. The recognition of (6) as basic to necessary conditions of freedom and independence.
8. The necessity for the organism, internally, to respond positively or negatively to every external change.
9. The existence of a set of automatic sentinels or indicators.
10. The tendency to be resistant to change, in the presence of change.
11. The tendency for certain effects to spiral.
12. The tendency for homeostasis to oppose natural instability.
13. Finally, the tendency for homeostasis to permit the organism to maintain itself at maximum efficiency under conditions which are naturally unstable.

---

[5] See Walter B. Cannon, *The Wisdom of the Body*, rev. and enlarged ed. (New York: W. W. Norton and Co., 1939) for the definitive statement. This book has been reprinted as a Norton Library paperback N-205 (1963). Also of value is Jules Henry, "Homeostasis, Society, and Evolution: A Critique," *The Scientific Monthly*, 81 (December, 1955), 300–309.

[6] Henry, *op. cit.*

To the extent that the concept of homeostasis has validity for the present discussion, it can be said that from within the marketing body come various signals of balance and imbalance often reflected, as has been noted, through the "nervous and brain functions" of the price structure. In addition, the managerial decisions of each agency working within the framework of this price structure become of key significance. More will be said about this later in a discussion of the meaning of marketing organization. These decisions, it should be noted, involve individual business units and group action in an environment both of competition and cooperation.

But, as has been noted, these internal organizational activities of the managerial personnel are only part of the complete coordinating and controlling aspects. There are the external forces of the combined population acting as ultimate consuming units in many patterns; and the force of government acting through its agencies (regulatory and other) to carry on its regulatory activities. The collective force of the ultimate consumers may act in positive fashion by making purchases, or, by actual participation in the agency structure as in the case of consumers' cooperatives. Negatively, this group by collective unwillingness to purchase particular goods or services, or to patronize particular business establishments, or to even spend money at all, have powerful effects on the marketing system.

The government agencies building upon the varying participation of the electorate, also have important positive and negative coordinating and controlling roles by means of various laws, *et al.* Increasingly, these tend to follow highly variable and often conflicting patterns. But, additionally their position has been extended by virtue of their further role as important buyers of goods and services; and, because frequently they become active owners and operators of marketing agencies.[7] Certainly, in the present defense and space programs, the Federal Government not only ranks as the largest single buying power in the United States, but, also, as the single greatest threat to its own anti-trust legislation.

Some Elements of Institutional Theory[8]

Some of the component elements of institutional theory as used here in this biological-sociological-economic context stem, in part, from the structural elements already discussed. And, while the institutional approach to marketing serves to conform most closely to things as they are or as they change, institutional theory in its present state of development has important limitations recognized by its advocates and followers.[9]

---

[7] This would include facilitating agencies as well.

[8] See the attached bibliography for many valuable ideas on institutionalism and institutional theory, as well as for additional readings.

[9] See Duddy and Revzan, *op. cit.*, Appendix C.

Its basic philosophy seems to be largely pragmatic. Institutional theory is content to deal with particular problem situations and limited objectives, although it should be noted that these may be broader in perspective than other theories. The vagueness of its concepts, and its general lack of precision in certain elements, proceed largely from the inclusion of the data of other than the purely economic disciplines in an effort at a closer approximation to reality and an over-all integrating viewpoint.

Its passion for concreteness and realism is, so far, an obstacle to achieving scientific status as measured by the standards of such disciplines as Newtonian physics and mathematics. There is an obvious need for techniques of measurement which will take account of psychological and sociological forces to supplement the quantitative measurements now available.[10] In this, however, the institutionalists certainly are at no greater disadvantage at the present time than the empirical model builders of the more orthodox school or others. With its emphasis on the effect on individual decisions of environmental and cultural factors, institutionalism is in danger of a lapse into economic determinism, on the one hand; while, on the other, its emphasis on the concept of coordination and control exposes it to the danger of authoritarianism.

At its best, institutionalism leans away from the chaos of individualism towards the order of limited freedom in a society of competing groups operating under a voluntarily assumed discipline. Institutional theory rejects the notion of fixed laws which ignore the possibility of change in human behavior; and it moves toward the concept of improving society as human behavior responds more and more to changing cultural conditions and to improved techniques of control.

In viewing the marketing system as an organic whole, institutional theory sets up a social standard of value by means of which the functioning of any part of that system must be measured by its contributions to the aims and purposes *not only* of the marketing system but to the economic order and all of society as well. Thus, it helps to locate responsibility which, under an impersonal individualized scheme of organization, is diffused to the point where no one can be held responsible because no one has enough power supposedly to influence the total result.

The problems with which an institutional theory must deal are clearly those which grow out of the conflicts of interest of competing economic groups, and those which reflect the impact on the marketing structure of forces making for change. These problems must be approached from the point of view of management operating in a particular kind of cultural environment. The results of such study will have much practical value, and,

---

[10] In this connection, note the present day efforts of the behavioral scientists.

when fitted into an institutional framework, may ultimately very well provide a theory of marketing.

The following propositions, eight in number, may be of additional help in understanding the elements of institutional theory:

Proposition #1.

The marketing organization is thought of as the functioning of a system of interrelated structures or organisms; and, its function is conditioned by the cultural patterns of the geographic region in which it operates at any given period of time.

Proposition #2.

The marketing organization, in the above context, cannot be segmented and considered effectively apart from its broader relationships to the whole economy.

Proposition #3.

Each institution operating in the over-all marketing system must be analyzed in terms of an evolutionary pattern—a life cycle, so to speak—which has pertinency only with reference to a particular socio-economic-cultural environment.

Proposition #4.

The individual, instead of considered as acting independently in making judgments, is considered instead to operate as a member of a group; and his actions and decisions are conditioned, and sometimes determined, by the standards of the group to which he belongs.

Proposition #5.

Individuals, as members of these institutional groups, sacrifice some of their respective individual freedom, while continuing to maintain and exercise a large degree of self-interest, in a search for cooperation and security through group action.

Proposition #6.

The tendency towards group action leads to an effort at conscious control of various types: (a) imposition of group authority on the individual's freedom of action; (b) exercise of control by government at various administrative levels; (c) by the force of customs and traditions operating for various groupings within the pressure of a mass market; (d) ever-growing evidences of monopoly power; and (e) through cooperative organizations.

Proposition #7.

The substitution of group action for much of individual action leads inevitably to conflicts between group actions in various capacities. These conflicts may intensify the need and demand for increased government control; and, in turn, they create rivalry among economic groups seeking either to exercise or control such authority.

Proposition #8.

Finally, if institutions exercise various forms of coercion and control, then ethical problems of responsibility for such actions arise and need to be evaluated.

The Meaning of Marketing Organization

In the preceding section of the discussion of the institutional approach, reference has been made from time to time to the concept of marketing organization: The author's treatment of this concept of marketing organization is as follows:[11]

> . . . The concept as it is used . . . is not concerned with the internal aspects of a particular firm. What is being emphasized here is the way in which many different kinds of individual firms and establishments array themselves in *formal, systematic* manner within various producing, buying, selling, and facilitating agencies in making possible the systematic, continuous movement of goods and services from producing to using units, together with the necessary determination of prices and terms of sales for their exchange. Depending upon the ideology of the political environment, the maximization of alternatives for final users may or may not result, and the operation of the organization within some framework of "efficiency" may or may not take place.
>
> The marketing organization is formal and systematic in the sense that there has evolved over a long period of time: (a) specialized production units both at the extractive and manufacturing levels which account for the highest percentage of all goods produced; (b) a series of specialized middlemen who, together with the integrated types, operate in various types of wholesale primary and intermediate markets; (c) a series of specialized retail middlemen who, together with the integrated types, operate similarly in retail markets; and (d) many types of facilitating agencies affecting services to establishments at all levels, and who act in a buying capacity as well, including pro-

[11] David A. Revzan, *Wholesaling in Marketing Organization* (New York: John Wiley and Sons, Inc., 1961), pp. 17–18.

fessional transportation, storage, financial, communication, research, and related facilitating functions.

Thus, to summarize, the marketing organization is a cross-sectional or dissectional study of the agencies and mechanisms of marketing as they array themselves in systematic fashion each to the other in moving goods and services from producing units.

IMPLICATIONS FOR SELECTED MARKETING RESEARCH AREAS

This Workshop is concerned importantly with generating, stimulating, and extending marketing research among the participants, and through them, to a larger professional group. Let me, then, conclude this paper with a discussion of some significant marketing research problems areas related to the discussion of the institutional approach. Time will permit me only to outline these suggested areas as a basis, perhaps, for further discussion during this Workshop.

1. *A comparative analysis of the conceptual frameworks inherent in alternative approaches to the study of marketing with the institutional approach.*

    My colleagues will present two alternative approaches to the institutional approach during ensuing sessions. Other approaches are available in the literature. This area of research would investigate the comparative merits of each approach in integrating the study of marketing, and in furnishing a basis for evaluating the results of special problem research. Contributions to an evolving theory of marketing would also be examined.

2. *Restatements and redefinitions of various marketing terms and concepts.*

    There is a growing need for a detailed professional investigation under this heading designed to derive uniformity of statements wherever possible; and, in establishing meaningful ranges of differences wherever necessary.[12]

3. *Study of the biological analogies inherent in the institutional approach, especially in the concept of homeostasis.*

    This project is more or less self descriptive in view of the preceding discussion.

---

[12] The efforts of the American Marketing Association have not, in my opinion, been very successful along these lines.

4. *Study of the cultural environment inherent in the institutional approach.*

    This project is more or less self descriptive.

5. *An analytical view of the comparative position of wholesale middlemen in the wholesaling sector; and of retail middlemen in the retailing sector.*

    In order to know more about the complexities of agency structure, including channels of distribution, this project could emphasize not only the changing relative importance of each type, but answers to such questions as: the degree of competition between types of operation? the relationships between types of operation and kinds of business in detail not presently found in the *Census of Business?* the relative impact of managerial integration on each type? their relative role in channels of distribution? etc.

6. *The significance for marketing of the changing relative importance of the wholesaling and retailing sectors.*

    This research project could investigate such topics as the extent to which the marketing system is becoming less and less ultimate consumer oriented; the changing product assortment and other complexities of each sector; and the implications for the study of marketing.

7. *An analysis of the spatial aspects of marketing in trying to formulate a basic geography of marketing.*

    This research project could attempt, further, to systematize and improve in analytical and integrated content the study of area structure inherent in the institutional approach.

8. *An evaluation of channels of distribution in a spatial framework.*

    My own research and writings on channels of distribution indicate that we need to know more about the relations of channels to area structure. Apart from the works of Breyer and a few other writers, little has been done to show patterns of channels in a spatial framework; or, to correspondingly study channel competition in a spatial framework. This research project has many important relationships with project #5.

9. *A reevaluation of the role of organized wholesale markets in marketing; and of systematic versus non-systematic price structures.*

    This project, again, is highly self-descriptive, and is very fundamental to a better understanding of the institutional approach.

10. *The dynamics of the Federal government both as multi-purchaser of goods and services; and as a seller of goods and services.*

    This research project would investigate the direct effects of the emergence of the Federal government as purchaser and seller on the marketing system; and the implications for governmental control. Some aspects have been briefly noted above, but the full sweep of this evolution, within the framework of the institutional approach, has yet to be understood and evaluated fully.

11. *A theory of the significance of change in the institutional approach.*

The concept of change is fundamental to the institutional approach. This project could investigate, among other things, the following: the concept of change in an institutional framework; the manifestation of change in an evolutionary framework; variations in change between the various structural components and institutions of the marketing system; and institutional barriers acting as blockages to change.

12. *The ethical responsibility of the marketing system.*

This project would investigate the implications of proposition #8 indicated above.

This list of suggested marketing research projects has focused attention on some selected needed areas of research which are closely related to the Duddy-Revzan institutional approach. They are broad and sweeping in scope; but they hold forth the reward of possible significant breakthroughs in understanding the marketing system, and improving the professional results. There is no assumption, however, that these can or should only be studied in the perspective of the institutional approach. We merely have a bias in favor of that approach.[13]

SELECTED REFERENCES

Books

Ayres, Clarence E., *The Theory of Economic Progress.* Chapel Hill, N.C.: University of North Carolina Press, 1944.

Cannon, Walter B., *The Wisdom of the Body*, rev. and enlarged ed. New York: W. W. Norton and Co., 1939. (Also reprinted as paperback N-205, 1963.)

Clark, John M., *Economic Institutions and Human Welfare.* New York: Alfred A. Knopf, 1957.

Commons, John R., *Institutional Economics.* New York: The Macmillan Co., 1934.

[13] A later session in the final week of the Workshop will discuss a proposed Berkeley marketing faculty group research project, *The Structure of the Marketing System.*

Copeland, Morris A., *Fact and Theory in Economics: The Testament of an Institutionalist*. Ithaca, N.Y.: Cornell University Press, 1958.

Duddy, Edward A., and David A. Revzan, *Marketing: An Institutional Approach*, 2nd ed. New York: McGraw-Hill Book Co., Inc., 1953, Chap. II and Appendix C.

Gruchy, Allan G., *Modern Economic Thought: The American Contribution*. Englewood Cliffs, N.J.: Prentice-Hall, Inc., 1947 (see pp. 631–655 for an extensive bibliography).

Revzan, David A., *Wholesaling in Marketing Organization*. New York: John Wiley and Sons, Inc., 1961.

Articles, etc.

Ayres, Clarence E., "The Co-ordinates of Institutionalism," *The American Economic Review*, XLI (May, 1951), 47–55; discussion, 78–84.

Boulding, Kenneth E., "A New Look at Institutionalism," *The American Economic Review*, XLVII (May, 1957), 1–12; discussion, 13–27.

Burns, E. M., "Institutionalism and Orthodox Economics," *The American Economic Review*, XXI (March, 1931), 80–87.

Commons, John R., "Institutional Economics," *The American Economic Review*, XXI (December, 1931), 648–657.

Copeland, Morris A., "Economic Theory and the Natural Science Point of View," *The American Economic Review* (March, 1931), 67–79.

————, "Institutionalism and Welfare Economics," *The American Economic Review*, XLVIII (March, 1958), 1–17.

Hamilton, Walton H., "Institution," *Encyclopedia of the Social Sciences*, Vol. VIII, pp. 84–89.

————, "The Institutional Approach to Economic Theory," *The American Economic Review*, IX (March, 1919).

Harris, A., "Types of Institutionalism," *The Journal of Political Economy*, XL (December, 1932).

Henry, Jules, "Homeostasis, Society, and Evolution: A Critique," *The Scientific Monthly*, 81 (December, 1955), 300–309.

Homan, Paul T., "The Institutional School of Economics," *Encyclopedia of the Social Sciences*, Vol. V, pp. 387–392.

Hoover, Calvin B., "Institutional and Theoretical Implications of Economic Change," *The American Economic Review*, XLII (March, 1954), 1–14.

Knight, Frank H., "Institutionalism and Empiricism in Economics," *The American Economic Review*, XLII (May, 1952), 45–55; discussion, 67–73.

Mann, F. K., "Institutionalism and American Economic Theory: A Case of Interpenetration," *Kyklos*, 13(3) (1960), 307–326.

Penrose, Edith T., "Biological Analogies in the Theory of the Firm,"
   The American Economic Review, XLII (December, 1952), 804–819.
Revzan, David A., "What is 'Theory in Marketing'?" (article-review of
   Reavis Cox and Wroe Alderson, editors, *Theory in Marketing*),
   The Journal of Marketing, XV (July, 1950), 101–109.
Stocking, George W., "Institutional Factors in Economic Thinking,"
   The American Economic Review, XLIX (March, 1959), 1–21.
Witte, Edwin E., "Institutional Economics as Seen by an Institutional
   Economist," *The Southern Economic Journal*, XXI (October, 1954),
   131–140.
Wolf, Charles, Jr., "Institutions and Economic Development," *The
   American Economic Review*, XLV (December, 1955), 867–883.
Wright, David McC., "What is the Economic System?" *Quarterly Journal
   of Economics*, LXV (May, 1958), 198–211.

SELECTED READINGS

Wroe Alderson, *Dynamic Marketing Behavior* (Homewood, Ill.: Irwin,
   1965).
Wroe Alderson, *Marketing Behavior and Executive Action* (Homewood,
   Ill.: Irwin, 1957).
Joe Bain, *Industrial Organization* (New York: Wiley, 2d ed., 1968).
Richard Caves, *American Industry: Structure, Conduct, Performance*
   (Englewood Cliffs, N.J.: Prentice-Hall, 1964).
Norman Collins and Lee Preston, *Concentration and Price-Cost Margins*
   (University of California Press, 1968).
John C. Narver and Ronald Savitt, *The Marketing Economy: An Analytical
   Approach* (New York: Holt, Rinehart and Winston, 1971), especially
   Chapters 1-4.
Almarin Phillips, *Market Structure, Organization and Performance*
   (Cambridge: Harvard University Press, 1962).
David A. Revzan, *Perspectives for Research in Marketing* (IBER,
   University of California, 1965).
Herbert A. Simon, *Administrative Behavior* (New York: Macmillan,
   2d ed., 1958).
Herbert A. Simon and James March, *Organizations* (New York:
   Wiley, 1958).

II Agency and channel: structure and behavior

Firms or other marketing agencies make offerings in markets in order to satisfy the wants of demanders and thereby fulfill their own goals. In common parlance, we call the offerings goods or services. These offerings are in essence bundles of utilities with potential for want satisfaction. A seller, in order to make a sale, must present a good or service so that a buyer perceives his own want (that is, his total set of physical and nonphysical elements believed necessary to satisfy the need to be satisfied by the particular offering. If two sellers are competing, the one who more completely matches the buyer's perception of what he wants is the seller who gets the order. A product—a specific offering—is the buyer's total percepts of what a supplier is offering for sale or for lease. This relationship between what sellers offer for sale and what buyers purchase is the basis of seller or buyer rivalry, as well as the resulting buyer and seller alternatives, and the framework for assessing consumer sovereignty. This latter is a function of the structure of buyers and sellers throughout all markets. The readings in Part II deal with the market behavior of firms, especially as sellers.

The selection from Edward H. Chamberlin's *The Theory of Monopolistic Competition* builds upon the concept of products as "bundles of utilities," in which the physical product is but one of several elements in the total product. The fact that sellers recognize that demanders frequently desire

107

more than the physical product provides much of the basis for the complex marketing structure and behavior of many firms. What we have, then, is a direction for the utilization of the resources discussed in the Penrose selection in Part I, where it was stressed that firms as pools of productive resources can and do supply a wide range of type of offerings, at any time choosing to offer that combination of products with the highest expected value.

Based on Chamberlin's analysis, firms are disposed to seek differential advantage, the belief of a demander that one supplier's offerings possess more want-satisfying ability than other suppliers' offerings. One way in which a seller can gain differential advantage is to manipulate his physical product, thereby physically differentiating himself from his rivals. This can be done by changing its shape, its components, or by generally altering its functional abilities. If the seller does not want to change the physical product, he may try to change buyers' perceptions of the firm, that is to effect "enterprise differentiation," such as by changing the character and quality of the sales force, the tone of promotion, and/or the outlets through which the firm distributes its product.

It was argued in the previous selections that firms exist as long as they are able to find sufficient economic profits in the provision of want-satisfying activities. M. A. Adelman discusses the revenues and profits received by firms. His argument is based on the premise that firms are rewarded for the value which they add to the product for the buyer. This article builds upon the differentiation concept raised in the previous selection.

The third selection, "Some Functions of Marketing Reconsidered," focuses on the activities of marketing agencies. It does not dwell upon the "physical product" but focuses instead on those activities which are necessary for transactions to occur. Edmund D. McGarry reviews the approaches to functional analysis and then provides his own list of functions.

Stanley C. Hollander's "Who Does the Work of Retailing?" should be read with an eye toward seeing the general arguments as clearly as possible, rather than merely noticing the specific cases which are illustrated. He is concerned with developing an understanding of the activities that a firm will choose to perform. These choices—which are continuously reevaluated in the rational profit-seeking firm—are a function of the economies or, in general, profit possibilities associated with new activities. A major factor in the determination of whether or not to perform a function is the availability of external economies in the form of other more efficient agencies in relation to the internal price. It should be noted as well that firms may choose to perform one or more of these functions simply as a means of enterprise differentiation, aside from simply factors of cost.

Because many firms do not perform all functions (that is, they are not fully integrated), there are vertical relationships among firms. The marketing channel is the collection of agencies and the flows associated with transactions for any given good or service. These develop when trading relations are established between or among agencies, making possible the passage of legal rights or possession (usually both) of goods and services. Ralph F. Breyer examines the origin of such arrangements in terms of various channel systems.

The last two selections in Part II, "The Concept of Marketing Organization Through the Channel" by David A. Revzan, and "Non-Price Competition at the Department-Store Level" by Perry Bliss, are provided as a means of adding detail to the overall framework. Revzan develops the concept of the marketing channel in great depth and provides specific examples for the more general analysis raised earlier in Chamberlin and Breyer. Bliss accomplishes much the same thing by relating the functional activities to the concept of differentiation, thereby specifically illustrating Chamberlin's argument.

In summary, Chamberlin provides the rationale and bases for firm differentiation. In a logical extension of Chamberlin's argument, Adelman discusses the meaning of price and shows the intimate relationship between "product" and "price" as sources of customer value. Next, McGarry considers the basic activities or functions which must be performed for transactions to occur. From these three discussions, one notes the strong and important connection between differentiation, value added, and the functions to be performed. Hollander extends the preceding arguments in a discussion with many general implications for indirect as well as vertically integrated channels. He considers internal versus external economies in the choice of who will perform the necessary activities. Channel formation and various empirical patterns of middlemen and channels are then specifically set forth by Breyer and Revzan respectively. Bliss ties together many aspects of the discussions of differentiation, functions, and the close relationship between price and product.

6

The
differentiation
of the product

Edward Hastings Chamberlin

1. THE MEANING OF DIFFERENTIATION

The interplay of monopolistic and competitive forces now to be considered
is of a different sort from that described in the previous chapter. It arises
from what we shall call the differentiation of the product. This chapter
introduces the subject by explaining what differentiation means, and how
and in what relationship it involves both monopoly and competition.

A general class of product is differentiated if any significant basis exists
for distinguishing the goods (or services) of one seller from those of another.
Such a basis may be real or fancied, so long as it is of any importance whatever to buyers, and leads to a preference for one variety of the product over
another. Where such differentiation exists, even though it be slight, buyers
will be paired with sellers, not by chance and at random (as under pure
competition), but according to their preferences.

Differentiation may be based upon certain characteristics of the product itself, such as exclusive patented features; trade-marks; trade names; peculiarities of the package or container, if any; or singularity in quality, design, color, or style. It may also exist with respect to the conditions surrounding its sale. In retail trade, to take only one instance, these conditions include such factors as the convenience of the seller's location, the general tone or character of his establishment, his way of doing business, his reputation for fair dealing, courtesy, efficiency, and all the personal links which attach his customers either to himself or to those employed by him. In so far as these and other intangible factors vary from seller to seller, the "product" in each case is different, for buyers take them into account, more or less, and may be regarded as purchasing them along with the commodity itself. When these two aspects of differentiation are held in mind, it is evident that virtually all products are differentiated, at least slightly, and that over a wide range of economic activity differentiation is of considerable importance.

In explanation of the adjustment of economic forces over this field, economic theory has offered (a) a theory of competition, and (b) a theory of monopoly. If the product is fairly individual, as the services of an electric street railway, or if it has the legal stamp of a patent or a copyright, it is usually regarded as a monopoly. On the other hand, if it stands out less clearly from other "products" in a general class, it is grouped with them and regarded as part of an industry or field of economic activity which is essentially competitive. Thus, although patents are usually classed as monopolies, trade-marks are more often looked upon as conferring a lesser degree of individuality to a product, and hence as quite compatible with competition (sometimes even as requisite to it). By this dispensation, the value of patented goods is explained in terms of the monopolist's maximizing his total profit within the market which he controls, whereas that of trademarked goods is described in terms of an equilibrium between demand and supply over a much wider field. All value problems are relegated to one category or the other according to their predominant element; the partial check exerted by the other is ignored.

This procedure has led to a manner of thinking which goes even further and denies the very existence of the supposedly minor element. Monopoly and competition are very generally regarded, not simply as antithetical, but as mutually exclusive. To demonstrate competition is to prove the absence of monopoly, and vice versa. Indeed, to many the very phrase "monopolistic competition" will seem self-contradictory—a juggling of words. This conception is most unfortunate. Neither force excludes the other, and more often than not both are requisite to an intelligible account of prices.

2. PATENTS AND TRADE-MARKS

The general case for a theory which recognizes both elements con-
currently may be presented by inquiring into a particular problem: does
any basis really exist for distinguishing between patents and trade-marks?
Patents (and copyrights) are ordinarily considered as monopolies. They
are granted under the authority vested in Congress by the United States
Constitution to secure "for limited times, to authors and inventors, exclusive
rights to their respective writings and discoveries." The privilege granted
is *exclusive*—the inventor has the sole right to manufacture and sell his
invention for seventeen years. The monopoly nature of this privilege is
generally recognized both in the literature of patents and in that of general
economics.[1] To be sure, the issue is usually not sharply drawn, but one
gains the impression that here are instances where the principles of
monopoly value are true without qualification.

On the other hand, the competitive element has been pointed out, and
it has even been claimed that patents are, in their essence, competitive
rather than monopolistic. Vaughn argues that "Patented products may be in
competition both with patented and unpatented goods. In fact, the patent
law is conducive to competition in that it stimulates individual initiative
and private enterprise."[2] Seager points out that "a large number of them
[patents] are for the protection of rival processes and serve to stimulate
rather than to diminish competition among those employing the different
methods."[3] The Committee on Patents in the House of Representatives
reported in 1912 that before the era of trusts and combinations in restraint
of trade "the monopoly granted by the patent law, limited as it was, in time
tended to stimulate competition. It incited inventors to new effort, and
capitalists and business men were encouraged to develop inventions. Under
these conditions a patent, while granting a monopoly in a specific article,
had rarely a tendency to monopolize any branch of the trade, because few
inventions were so fundamental in character as to give the owner of the
patent a monopoly in any branch of the trade, and every great financial
success arising from an individual patent was sure to result in rival inventions."[4] The report goes on to demonstrate the competition normally present

---

[1] A few references are chosen at random: Elfreth, *Patents, Copyrights and Trade-Marks*,
p. 33; Prindle, *Patents as a Factor in Manufacturing*, p. 16; Mill, *Principles of Political
Economy*, Book V, Chap. X, Sec. 4; Ely, *Outlines of Economics*, 5th ed., p. 561; Garver
and Hansen, *Principles of Economics*, p. 258.

[2] *The Economics of Our Patent System*, p. 26.

[3] *Principles of Economics* (1917), p. 414.

[4] House Report No. 1161, 62nd Congress, 2nd Session, pp. 2, 3. (Cited in Vaughn, *op.
cit.*, p. 27.)

if patents are separately held, in the following words: "Capital seeking to control industry through the medium of patents proceeds to buy up all important patents pertaining to the particular field. The effect of this is to shut out competition that would be inevitable if the various patents were separately and adversely held."[5] Evidently, when they are so held, the fact that they are monopolies does not preclude their being in competition with each other. Every patented article is subject to the competition of more or less imperfect substitutes.

It is the same with copyrights. Copyrighted books, periodicals, pictures, dramatic compositions, are monopolies; yet they must meet the competition of similar productions, both copyrighted and not. The individual's control over the price of his own production is held within fairly narrow limits by the abundance and variety of substitutes. Each copyrighted production is monopolized by the holder of the copyright; yet it is also subject to the competition which is present over a wider field.

Let us turn to trade-marks. Their monopolistic nature has not been entirely ignored. Says Johnson, "Somewhat analogous to the profits arising from a patent are the profits arising from the use of a trade-mark or from the 'good-will' of a concern." These returns "fall under the general head of monopoly profits."[6] The tone of hesitancy should, however, be noted, for it is characteristic. These profits are not *the same* as those arising from a patent; they are only "somewhat analogous." Ely classifies trade-marks as "general welfare monopolies,"[7] and, although "it may be questioned whether they ought to be placed here,"[8] he argues that they should be. "They give the use or monopoly of a certain sign or mark to distinguish one's own productions. . . . Of course, another person may build up another class of goods, and may establish value for another trade-mark." He therefore concludes that "it is a monopoly only in a certain line, marking off the goods of one manufacturer." Veblen speaks of monopolies "resting on custom and prestige" as "frequently sold under the name of good-will, trade-marks, brands, etc."[9] Knight puts "in the same category of monopoly . . . the use of trade-marks, trade names, advertising slogans, etc., and we may include the services of professional men with established reputations (whatever their real foundation).[10] The list might be extended further.

On the other hand, trade-marks and brands are commonly regarded

---

[5] *Ibid.*, p. 5.

[6] *Introduction to Economics*, pp. 246–247.

[7] *Monopolies and Trusts*, p. 43.

[8] P. 48.

[9] *The Theory of Business Enterprise*, p. 55.

[10] *Risk, Uncertainty and Profit*, p. 185.

in the business world as a means of enabling one seller to compete more effectively with another—as congruous with and even necessary to competition. The view is implicitly sanctioned in economic literature by a common failure to take any cognizance of trade-marks whatever. They are simply taken for granted as a part of the essentially competitive régime. Frequently patents and copyrights alone are mentioned as monopolies; the implication is that trade-marks are not. A positive stand is taken by the late Professor Young in Ely, *Outlines of Economics*, where the elaborate classification found in Ely, *Monopolies and Trusts*, is reproduced with the significant change that trade-marks are omitted. "Trade-marks, like patents, are monopolies in the strictly legal sense that no one else may use them. But, unlike patents, they do not lead to a monopoly in the economic sense of giving exclusive control of one sort of business." By means of a trade-mark a successful business man "may be able to lift himself a little above the 'dead level' of competition . . . he is able to obtain what might be called a quasi-monopoly. But because his power to control the price of his product is in general much more limited than that of the true monopolist, and because competition limits and conditions his activities in other ways, his business is more properly called competitive than monopolistic."[11] Against this position it may be argued, first, that single patents, as has been shown, do not ordinarily give exclusive control of one sort of business and do not confer a monopoly in this sense of the term; and secondly, that, even granting that patents do give *more* control, this is simply a matter of degree, reducible to relative elasticity of demand. Both patents and trade-marks may be conceived of as monopoly elements of the goods to which they are attached; the competitive elements in both cases are the similarities between these goods and others. To neglect either the monopoly element in trade-marks or the competitive element in patents by calling the first competitive and the second monopolistic is to push to opposite extremes and to represent as *wholly* different two things which are, in fact, essentially alike.

An uncompromising position as to the competitive nature of trade-marks is found in Rogers, *Goodwill, Trade-Marks and Unfair Trading*. "These things [patents and copyrights] are monopolies created by law. . . . A trade-mark is quite a different thing. There is no element of monopoly involved at all. . . . A trade-mark precludes the idea of monopoly. It is a means of distinguishing one product from another; it follows therefore that there must be others to distinguish from. If there are others there is no monopoly, and if there is a monopoly there is no need for any distinguishing."[12] Here explicitly is the dialectic behind the attitude widely prevalent in economic

---

[11] 5th ed., pp. 562, 563.
[12] Pp. 50–52.

and legal thinking, to which preference has already been made, that monopoly and competition must be regarded as alternatives. Evidently, it applies equally well to patents, for, to paraphrase the argument, no matter how completely the patented article may be different from others, there are always others, and therefore no monopoly. Monopoly becomes, by this reasoning, a possibility only if there is but one good in existence. What is the difficulty? Assuredly, two things may be alike in some respects and different in others. To center attention upon either their likeness or their unlikeness is, in either case, to give only half of the picture. Thus, if a trade-mark distinguishes, that is, marks off one product as different from another, it gives the seller of that product a monopoly, from which we might argue, following Rogers, that there is no competition. Indeed, Rogers himself falls into the trap and refutes his own argument a few pages further on, where, speaking of a buyer's assumed preference for "Quaker Oats," he says, "It is a habit pure and simple, and it is a *brand* habit, a *trade-mark* habit that we and others like us have, and that habit is worth something to the producer of the goods to whose use we have become habituated. It *eliminates competition*, for to us there is nothing 'just as good.' "[13] If trade-marks "preclude monopoly" and "eliminate competition," one may well ask the nature of the remainder.

Are there any bases, after all, for distinguishing between patents and trade-marks? Each makes a product unique in certain respects; this is its monopolistic aspect. Each leaves room for other commodities almost but not quite like it; this is its competitive aspect. The differences between them are only in degree, and it is doubtful if a significant distinction may be made even on this score. It would ordinarily be supposed that the degree of monopoly was greater in the case of patents. Yet the huge prestige value of such names as "Ivory," "Kodak," "Uneeda," "Coca-Cola," and "Old Dutch Cleanser," to cite only a few, is sufficient at least to make one sceptical. It would be impossible to compute satisfactorily for comparison the value of the monopoly rights granted by the United States Government in the form of patents and copyrights, and the value of those existing in the form of trade-marks, trade names, and good-will. The insuperable difficulty would be the definition (for purposes of deduction from total profits) of "competitive" returns, and of profits attributable to other monopoly elements. Allowance would also have to be made for the difference in duration of patents and trade-marks, for the enhanced value of patents in many cases by combination, and for other factors. But merely to suggest such a comparison is to raise serious doubts as to whether the monopoly element in patents is even quantitatively as important as that in trade-marks.

[13] *Ibid.*, p. 56. (Italics mine.)

Let us apply the reasoning to the second phase of differentiation mentioned above,—that with respect to the conditions surrounding a product's sale. An example is the element of location in retail trade. The availability of a commodity at one location rather than at another being of consequence to purchasers, we may regard these goods as differentiated spatially and may apply the term "spatial monopoly" to that control over supply which is a seller's by virtue of his location. A retail trader has complete and absolute control over the supply of his "product" when this is taken to include the advantages, to buyers, of his particular location. Other things being equal, those who find his place of business most convenient to their homes, their habitual shopping tours, their goings and comings from business or from any other pursuit, will trade with him in preference to accepting more or less imperfect substitutes in the form of identical goods at more distant places; just as, in the case of trade-marked articles and of goods qualitatively differentiated, buyers are led to prefer one variety over another by differences in their personal tastes, needs, or incomes.

In this field of "products" differentiated by the circumstances surrounding their sale, we may say, as in the case of patents and trade-marks, that both monopolistic and competitive elements are present. The field is commonly regarded as competitive, yet it differs only in degree from others which would at once be classed as monopolistic. In retail trade, each "product" is rendered unique by the individuality of the establishment in which it is sold, including its location (as well as by trade-marks, qualitative differences, etc.); this is its monopolistic aspect. Each is subject to the competition of other "products" sold under different circumstances and at other locations; this is its competitive aspect. Here, as elsewhere in the field of differentiated products, both monopoly and competition are always present.

Speaking more generally, if we regard monopoly as the antithesis of competition, its extreme limit is reached only in the case of control of the supply of all economic goods, which might be called a case of pure monopoly in the sense that all competition of substitutes is excluded by definition. At the other extreme is pure competition, where, large classes of goods being perfectly standardized, every seller faces a competition of substitutes for his own product which is perfect. Between the two extremes there are all gradations, but both elements are always present, and must always be recognized. To discard either competition or monopoly is to falsify the result, and in a measure which may be far out of proportion to the apparent importance of the neglected factor.

Hence the theory of pure competition falls short as an explanation of prices when the product is (even slightly) differentiated. By eliminating monopoly elements (i.e., by regarding the product as homogeneous) it ignores the upward force which they exert, and indicates an equilibrium price which is below the true norm.[14] The analogy of component forces, although not exact, is helpful. Actual prices no more approximate purely competitive prices than the actual course of a twin-screw steamship approximates the course which would be followed if only one propeller were in operation. Pure competition and pure monopoly are extremes, just as the two courses of the ship, when propelled by either screw separately, are extremes. Actual prices tend towards neither, but towards a middle position determined with reference to the relative strength of the two forces in the individual case. A purely competitive price is not a normal price; and except for those few cases in the price system where competition is actually pure, there is no tendency for it to be established.

It might seem that the theory of monopoly would offend equally in the opposite sense by excluding the competitive elements. This would be true, however, only in the case of *pure* monopoly, as defined above—control of the supply of all economic goods by the same person or agency. The theory of monopoly has never been interpreted in this way. It applies to particular goods, and as such always admits competition between the product concerned and others. Indeed, we may go so far as to say that the theory *seems* fully to meet the essential requirement of giving due recognition to both elements, and the interesting possibility is at once suggested of turning the tables and describing economic society as perfectly monopolistic instead of as (almost) perfectly competitive. Subsequent chapters will carry the refutation of this view. Meanwhile the issues are clarified by displaying the large element of truth it contains. Let us see upon what grounds it may *not* be refuted.

Product differentiation
and the theory of value

Under pure competition, the individual seller's market being completely merged with the general one, he can sell as much as he pleases at the going price. Under monopolistic competition, however, his market being separate to a degree from those of his rivals, his sales are limited and defined by three new factors: (1) his price, (2) the nature of his product, and (3) his advertising outlays.

[14] The full explanation of this will appear in subsequent chapters.

The divergence of the demand curve for his product from the horizontal imposes upon the seller a price problem, absent under pure competition, which is the same as that ordinarily associated with the monopolist. Depending upon the elasticity of the curve and upon its position relative to the cost curve for his product, profits may be increased, perhaps by raising the price and selling less, perhaps by lowering it and selling more. That figure will be sought which will render the total profit a maximum.

The adjustment of his product is likewise a new problem imposed upon the seller by the fact of differentiation. The volume of his sales depends in part upon the manner in which his product differs from that of his competitors. Here the broad sense in which the word "product" is used must constantly be held in mind.[15] Its "variation" may refer to an alteration in the quality of the product itself—technical changes, a new design, or better materials; it may mean a new package or container; it may mean more prompt or courteous service, a different way of doing business, or perhaps a different location. In some cases an alteration is specific and definite—the adoption of a new design, for instance. In others, as a change in the quality of service, it may be gradual, perhaps unconscious. Under pure competition a producer may, of course, shift from one field of activity to another, but his volume of sales never depends, as under monopolistic competition, upon the product or the variety of product he chooses, for he is always a part of a market in which many others are producing the identical good.[16] Just as his sales may, under pure competition, be varied over a wide range without alteration in his price, so they may be as large or as small as he pleases without the necessity of altering his product. Where the possibility of differentiation exists, however, sales depend upon the skill with which the good is distinguished from others and made to appeal to a particular group of buyers. The "product" may be improved, deteriorated, or merely changed, and with or without a readjustment of price. To it, as well as to the price, the conventional assumption of profit maximization will ordinarily be applied.[17]

Thirdly, the seller may influence the volume of his sales by making expenditures, of which advertising may be taken as typical, which are directed specifically to that purpose. Such expenditures increase both the demand for his product, and his costs; and their amount will be adjusted, as are prices and "products," so as to render the profits of the enterprise a

[15] To this end, it will frequently be inclosed in quotation marks.

[16] To put the matter in another way, slight differences are not inconsistent with pure competition, provided that *for each variety* there be a large number of producers competing in a single market.

[17] For an extended discussion of product variation, see my article, "The Product as an Economic Variable," *Quarterly Journal of Economics*, Vol. LXVII (1953), p. 1. (Essay 6 in *Towards a More General Theory of Value*.)

maximum. This third factor is likewise peculiar to monopolistic competition, since advertising would be without purpose under conditions of pure competition, where any producer can sell as much as he pleases without it. But it does not necessarily make its appearance with the monopoly elements already introduced. It will be argued later that gains from this source are possible because of (a) imperfect knowledge on the part of buyers as to the means whereby wants may be most effectively satisfied, and (b) the possibility of altering wants by advertising or selling appeal. It will be helpful to proceed slowly, postponing this range of considerations until after the consequences of differentiation *per se* have been traced. For the present, then, advertising as a competitive activity is put to one side, and attention confined to the two variables of price and "product." This may be done by proceeding explicitly on the assumption of given wants and perfect knowledge concerning the means available for satisfying them.

Where both prices and "products" may be varied, complete equilibrium must involve stability with respect to both. The notion of a "product equilibrium" needs explanation, and its importance may not at once be apparent. The theory of value, concerning itself with the price adjustment for a given product, has passed it by completely, and it seems to have occurred to no one[18] that the inverse problem might be put of the product adjustment for a given price. Price adjustments are, in fact, but one phase, and often a relatively unimportant phase, of the whole competitive process. More and more is price competition evaded by returning the buyer's attention towards a trade-mark, or by competing on the basis of quality or service (or by advertising, excluded for the present). The fact of such competition should at least be brought into the open by including the "product" as a variable in the problem.

For a complete picture, indeed, each element of the "product" should be regarded as a separate variable. What, for instance, is the adjustment with regard to location when price and the *other* aspects of the "product" are given? Quality, service, etc., might be isolated in the same way.[19] Some indication of the peculiarities to which such analysis might lead is given in Appendix C, where an attempt is made to isolate the factor of location. Aside from this, however, variation of the "product" is considered only in its most general aspects.

[18] With the single exception of Hotelling, "Stability in Competition," *Economic Journal*, Vol. XXXIX (1929).

[19] It may be remarked at this point that there seems to be no reason why competition which is compounded with monopoly elements should necessarily tend to improve the "product" in these or other respects. The result will depend upon circumstances. Just as a seller may, under monopolistic competition, gain by raising his price and selling less as well as by lowering his price and selling more, so he may gain by deteriorating his product as well as by improving it.

The markets for goods which are substitutes for each other being closely interrelated, the position and elasticity of the demand curve for the product of any one seller depend in large part upon the availability of competing "products" and the prices which are asked for them. The equilibrium adjustment for him, therefore, cannot be defined without reference to the more general situation of which he is a part. However, it is not inconsistent with recognition of this interdependence that the conditions with respect to his competitors which define his own market be held constant while his own adjustment is considered in isolation. A complex system may be better understood by breaking it into its parts, and the problem of individual equilibrium will serve as a helpful introduction to the more complicated one of the adjustments over a wider field.

Aside from this purpose, which may be regarded as entirely expositional, a solution of the equilibrium adjustment for the individual enterprise has other justification in that it is often directly applicable to the facts. Theory may well disregard the interdependence between markets wherever business men do, in fact, ignore it. This is true (1) in a multitude of cases where the effects of a change inaugurated by any one seller are spread over such a large number of competitors that they are negligible for each. It is also true (2) when there are no very direct substitutes for the product, so that the increase in its sales brought about, say, by a lowering of its price, is not predominantly at the expense of any closely competing product or group of products, but rather at the expense of goods of all kinds. Here we have the implicit assumption of "isolation" underlying the traditional theory of monopoly; indeed the phase of the problem here considered may be regarded merely as an extension of the theory of monopoly to include the adjustment of "product" as well as of price. In sum, the theory of individual equilibrium is significant (1) in itself, and (2) as an introduction to the problem of equilibrium over the wider field embracing what is usually regarded vaguely as an "imperfectly competitive" market.

7

The "product"
and "price"
in distribution*

M. A. Adelman

The "price" and output of any "product" are brought into some kind of relationship with cost through the competitive process, and a discussion of any of them is inevitably linked with the others. Adam Smith was of the opinion that nothing special needed to be said about distribution; he answered the perennial complaint about too many stores in a famous passage which asserted in effect that the number of firms and the prices charged were subject to the normal competitive laws and could not, under competition, exceed the optimum.[1]

Later economists, without being too clear about it, seemed to feel that somehow competition and price making in distribution were subject to certain disturbances. More than a century of grumbles and insights scattered

* I am indebted to Edwin Kuh for helpful comments on an earlier draft, but he is not responsible for any errors.

[1] *Wealth of Nations* (Modern Library Ed.), Book II, Chap. V, p. 342.

From the *American Economic Review, Supplement* XLVII (May, 1957), pp. 266–273. Reprinted by permission.

through the literature were summed up by Knut Wicksell, who noted that retail prices "are frequently regarded as exceptions . . . generally to every rational process of price formation." Wicksell thought they could be explained by joint costs and location monopoly. Unusual profits were absorbed by additional entrants crowding into the trade, so that the normal effort to maximize profits led to excess capacity and higher costs.[2] Years later came the well-known article by Hotelling,[3] and shortly afterward the modern theory of monopolistic or imperfect competition. Chamberlin was to formulate Wicksell's sequence rigorously, as the "tangency solution,"[4] one of the most useful pieces of apparatus which the economic theorist has given to workers in applied fields.

It is worth remembering that the modern theory originated in large measure out of the conflict between the normal competitive assumptions and the facts of daily life of which everyone is willy-nilly aware. The unease we feel about the distributive trades is reflected in our speech patterns. We speak of "value added by manufacture"; but we ask, "Does distribution cost too much?"[5] Clearly this double standard makes no sense unless we suspect that the value added in trade includes something unnecessary or undesirable. Now some of this may be the physiocratic prejudice that doubtless affects us all in some degree. At a much higher level, there is the feeling that much of our distribution activity is really part of the overhead cost of a commercial and urbanized civilization rather than a net increment to welfare. Undoubtedly, there is much truth in this view, but it is easily exaggerated and I fear has been. For it is in the underdeveloped—or, to use the newly fashionable euphemism, developing—economies that sellers come to market with a few second-hand oil cans, expending a man-day or more in marketing them;[6] it is in developed but certainly poorer economies than the American that the housewife buys one egg at a time; it is in the prosperous suburbs of the United States that she buys a week's supply or more and provides delivery, inventory (including refrigeration) facilities, and breaking bulk, so that the retail market services of poorer countries become part of the household economy of wealthier ones and pass out of the money national income. For the United States, Hall and Knapp have shown

[2] Knut Wicksell, *Lectures on Political Economy* (London: Routledge, 1938), Vol. I, pp. 86–88.

[3] Harold Hotelling, "Stability in Competition," *Economic Journal*, 1929, p. 41.

[4] Edwin H. Chamberlin, *The Theory of Monopolistic Competition* (Harvard University Press, 6th ed., 1948), Chap. 5, Figs. 12, 17.

[5] P. W. Stewart and J. Frederic Dewhurst, *Does Distribution Cost Too Much?* (Twentieth Century Fund, 1939).

[6] P. T. Bauer and Basil S. Yamey, "Economic Progress and Occupational Distribution," *Economic Journal*, 1951, p. 745.

that state per capita income is positively correlated with the number of stores per 10,000 population but is negatively correlated with the number of food stores—the largest single group.[7] I think the same tendency exists, although less strongly marked, as among the metropolitan areas of the United States and Canada. The relationship ought to be explored for census tracts, although my attempt with the special retail census of Dallas for 1953 was not successful. The complete results of the census of 1954 should permit much more intensive work to be done here. But even the fragmentary data at hand show that there is no simple connection between per capita income and the importance of distributive services, and they suggest that distribution is more a matter of additional utility than an overhead cost. They do not bear directly on the impression that the competitive process is somehow not working properly in distribution and is not tending to any optimal price-quantity solution. In trying to solve such problems, we need to ask what we mean by price and product in distribution.

Measurement of a single distributive price or product culminates in a highly aggravated form of the index-number problem, because of the great variety of goods handled in nearly every kind of establishment, compounded by the change in the assortment through time. A price index is usually, therefore, of doubtful meaning. On the side of cost of the product, true joint costs are rare in distribution, but common costs are everywhere, and their separation is not usually very effective. A recent investigation of gross and net margins in the Dutch grocery trade is particularly interesting.[8] It covered a sample of fifty stores and about 100 items within each store and analyzed costs under ten categories, making considerable use of time studies. The sampling problems and the accounting methods invite comment, but we must neglect them. Two results claim our attention. The average purchase per customer per store varied from 1.06 to 2.56 guilders, which on its face would indicate that a very different bundle of services was being sold. Furthermore, average (for all stores) gross margin varied among products from 5 per cent to over 45 per cent and average net margin from minus 54 per cent to plus 34 per cent. How do we explain such variations? There are probably some elements of genuine price discrimination—either the active exploitation of several demand curves or passive adjustment to whatever

[7] Margaret Hall and John Knapp, "Number of Shops and Productivity in Retail Distribution in Great Britain, the United States and Canada," *Economic Journal*, 1955, pp. 83–85.

[8] S. C. Bakkenist and D. E. Deutick, *Onderzoek naar de Distributiekosten in de Detailhandel in Kruidenierawaren in Nederland* ("Investigation Into Retail Distribution Costs of Groceries in the Netherlands"), issued by Preijer & DeHaan (Amsterdam and The Hague, 1950). I am indebted to my colleague and former student, John L. Enos, for more than the translation.

lines appear to be most in demand at the moment. The first is a symptom of monopoly, the second of active if nonperfect competition, but in the latter case these differentials relate to an ever changing group. Some of this variation is simply haphazard and based on rules of thumb which—as will be seen in a moment—it may yet be irrational to modify. It also seems to be the rule, in this country and Europe, that staples like sugar and flour are often sold at prices which will not return the cost of sales; and other items may be similarly "footballed" from time to time. This tradition in part reflects a chronic relapse into competition, to be explored later; but for the most part it is a sort of low-grade advertising—the selection and flaunting of a biased sample which is supposed to mislead the consumer, and doubtless often does. Yet we have the record of a large food chain which carried through a very profitable changeover to supermarkets by controlling the gross and net margins and paying no attention to individual prices. The theory was clearly stated by one official: "It would be futile to expect us to undersell everybody on everything. . . . Find some way of impress[ing] upon the public that in the long run they will be money ahead if they spend all their food dollars in our super-markets." (*U.S. v. A. & P.*, 173 F. 2d 79, 7th Cir. 1949, Govt. Exhibit 226.) The example is not unique. Price of the individual item simply drops out, and the store is regarded as selling a single service.

On the whole, the best concept of wholesale and retail price is value-added or gross margin, the payment for furnishing the product, wholesale or retail service, or both. It offers great advantages in simplicity and in accuracy, for it mirrors all the forces of demand and cost that impinge upon the distributive operation, and it permits us to measure costs, prices, and output over time. But it brings certain problems in its train.

1. For one thing, it would be both a pecuniary and a social diseconomy if the individual distributive firm disregarded variations of cost and revenue as among goods or lines of goods and was contented if total receipts more than covered total costs. This would tend to perpetuate the pattern existing at any moment; it would afford no clue or incentive to lower cost and more profitable behavior. The optimum is somewhere between a single undifferentiated service and a large number of products each with an arbitrarily allocated cost. For the firm, the problem really becomes how to acquire, at reasonable cost, information on its several activities which is as good as, or better than, its competitors—even if by an absolute standard it is quite inaccurate. The problem of economies and diseconomies of scale and of horizontal and vertical integration is largely a matter of devising the smallest possible number of meaningful product-groups or distributive activities within the firm and obtaining some data on them.

2. The second kind of problem arises in the study of costs, prices, and output over time. Barger[9] applies an estimated average markup to the deflated value, at the producer's level, of output passing through distributive channels to obtain an estimate of output of wholesale and retail service. His is a notable contribution but subject to at least two kinds of qualifications. One is the changing bundle of services rendered under the catchall name of retail and wholesale distribution. Producers at one end of the channel or consumers at the other may absorb or relinquish some of the services of packaging, warehousing, breaking bulk, delivery, advertising, financing, etc. Even aside from these vertical shifts, distributive firms may do more or less. Therefore, there is no reason to suppose that a dollar's worth of producer's output takes a larger, smaller, or constant distributive service over time. Secondly—and perhaps more important—our use of value measures is distorted by the very process under investigation. Suppose there was a considerable increase in productivity generally but not in distribution. The payment for any given factor tends to equality of net advantage in all uses. Over time, the value of a unit of labor or of any other factor used in distribution would increase because its value in other uses had increased. The gross margin and the apparent output of the distributive product would also increase (at a rate depending on various elasticities), although there was in fact no real increase in the quantum of services rendered. Perhaps a deflation by an index of real wages and the prices of inputs might help; none has been devised. I suspect that any such attempt would lead in a circle; and that this is an area where the basic logical defects of index number construction serve not merely to qualify the result but prevent it, because the aggregate product has been defined in terms of the aggregate price, and there is no independent measure of each. But further thinking is certainly needed.

3. The abandonment of direct price comparisons also makes it more difficult to reach a judgment about the operations of competition and monopoly. Thus, uniform prices throughout a large market or large number of submarkets, such as a standard metropolitan area, are prima facie evidence not of competition but of its absence, for conditions of demand and cost vary from place to place. But particular prices may be almost the least important thing to compare; they may be set by rule of thumb because the raising or lowering of the price of retail service or wholesale service can take place anywhere along the price front and is best accomplished, indeed, by price changes on lines or types of product rather than by individual items.

4. The final qualification for value-added data is the extent to which

---

[9] Harold Barger, *Distribution's Place in the American Economy since 1869* (Princeton University Press, 1955), Chap. 2.

they may be distorted by inclusion of monopoly gains. Unfortunately, we know little enough about competition in distribution. There is plenty of scope for collusive oligopoly in wholesaling. As an example we may take grocery wholesaling.[10] In 1948 the largest one-sixth of general-line wholesalers accounted for nearly 60 per cent (58.5) of sales. This overstates the degree of concentration somewhat, by excluding specialty-line wholesalers, and also understates it, since the total number of firms is about 30 per cent below the number of establishments.[11] In the largest metropolitan area, New York-Northern New Jersey, there are 189 such wholesalers, and one-sixth would be around 31, doubtless more than sufficient for active competition in the absence of collusion. But the number drops off rapidly as we go down the list, and past the largest nine Standard Metropolitan Areas, at most 3 or 4 wholesalers would account for 60 per cent of sales; in about fifteen S.M.A.'s the nearest whole number is 1. Other commodity lines are less concentrated; others more so. Wholesalers are generally small grass-roots folk not politically vulnerable, and hence not so afraid of antitrust enforcement; and there are generally few innovations to induce vigorous competitive behavior.

As for retailing, the inherent differentiation because of location, the inelasticity of demand with respect to the price of retail service (which is only a fraction of total price), and the inertia and ignorance of the individual customer are the elements of a monopoly power which is usually

[10] The following comments are based on the *Census of Business, 1948: Bulletin No. 3-1, The Grocery Trade*, Table 5, pp. 11, 12–A.

[11] *The Grocery Trade, op. cit.,* Table 11, p. 63, shows 4,205 general-line grocery wholesalers. It shows also the number of establishments owned by firms owning 2, 3–5, 6–9, 10–14, 15–24, and 25 or more establishments. We have divided the number of establishments in each group by the middle number or by the nearest lower whole number. The last group has been divided by 25. An interpolation formula would have yielded a smaller number of firms; our procedure yields 3,013. One can say in round numbers that there were not more than 3,000 such firms in the United States.

Table 12-A divides general-line into sponsoring and nonsponsoring voluntary groups. Among sponsoring wholesalers, the sales of the largest 72 were 687.7 million dollars, of the next largest 172, 529.2. Among nonsponsoring the sales of the largest 63 were 542.1 million dollars, of the next largest 293 were 837.5 million. Approximately, therefore, the largest 600 establishments, or 16.6 per cent of the total of 3,633, sold 2,956.5 million dollars, or 58.5 per cent of total sales of 5,049.8 sold by sponsoring and nonsponsoring combined. The degree of concentration would have been slightly higher if it had been possible to consolidate the lists of sponsoring and nonsponsoring. (We cannot tell whether it would have been affected by including unavailable data for the 632 retailer-owned and other wholesalers.)

According to the *Preliminary Trade Report: 1954 Census of Business, Wholesale Trade, Series PW-3-47* (October, 1956), the number of general-line wholesale grocery establishments (with paid employees) declined from 4,253 in 1948 to 3,320 in 1954. Information by size was not available when this paper was written.

substantial, at least in the short run. Of course, the locational "monopoly" is only the obverse of a wide dispersion of establishments close to consumers which is the very essence of the retail service. But with marginal cost inevitably below average, there is an abiding desire for more volume by any and all means except price reduction. Hence the process of "trading-up," as Professor McNair has called it—more advertising and service constantly added. One retailer's extra services may do no more than offset the expenditures of the other, with everybody worse off—profits down to bare normal for retailers so long as there can be entry and too many resources being drawn into distribution.

Such a judgment does not require any distinction of the truly necessary costs of distribution from the frills, or selling costs from production costs. It would be difficult to consider the annual model change in automobiles as a production cost, for example. Except in one sense, to be explored presently, the distinction is illusory. An additional service, whether or not embodied in any physical object, means an increment to cost and to revenue, and if the latter exceeds the former, the service is rendered. The basic question, which lies at the heart of our interrelated problem of price, product, and competition, is whether the market is providing an objective measure of the value of the particular incremental service. Unless the consumer has the alternative of choosing the increment of service at a higher price or the lesser service at a lower price, we cannot tell whether that increment is worth its cost in a free market. But this appraisal process does not work smoothly or well. In the first place, the desired and the undesired services are commingled in the general lump of retail and wholesale service which the consumer buys and which, it was previously urged, really constitutes the product. Secondly, even if every single increment to service were desired by the consumer, it does not necessarily follow that he would prefer all of them or any particular combination of them, for the marginal utility neither of money nor of the distributive services is constant. And since experimentation with lower prices is difficult and risky to begin with, there must be a considerable bias toward more services than the consumer wants, and the wrong kind.

It is not a cheerful picture of the retailer constantly pushing up his costs in the hope—often mistaken—of raising the demand function even more; and then seeing above-normal profits slowly disappear because of imitation or entry, whereupon the whole process is repeated. The end result, as the textbooks indicate in the chapter on monopolistic competition, is a smaller scale of output, a higher price, and a larger volume of services than would exist if the consumer could pick and choose in a more competitive market. But this does not prove that the waste is great, nor that the element of monopoly gain and monopoly restriction is a large part of value-added in distribution. For the greater the size of the gap between what the consumer wants and what he is getting, the greater the inducement to the bolder spirits to offer the leaner and better product. The barriers to entry are low, though the market is probably small. The most important obstacle to the innovator is that his entry would add so much to the local supply that price would be driven far down. The solution lies in either spreading over so many markets that the effect on price is greatly damped; or in having so great a cost advantage that existing firms will be driven out.

The thesis suggested here is that competition in distribution often works slowly and with a lag. Since pent-up forces act with some violence, it often takes a somewhat cataclysmic form. The high rate of turnover in distribution is well known and also the innovations that from time to time overtake one branch or another. The distinctive mark of these innovations is that they were carried out by the large establishment (not necessarily the large firm). At one time department stores did unto specialty shops as discount houses were to do unto them; the old-fashioned grocery store was largely displaced by the economy store and it by the supermarket; while the impact of the mail-order house has been recorded for all time in the invective of its rivals. In fact, a useful if not a very precise index of the strength of competition in distribution is the resentment of the unsuccessful competitors; and thanks to their ready access to publicity and legislation, the documentation is usually good. The characteristic theme is that the consumer is simply misguided when he prefers—to take the examples best known today because of Congressional hearings—lower priced gasoline or lower priced automobiles; what he ought to prefer is rivalry in service alone rather than in service and price considered together. The consumer, in their view, should not be given what he wants because he wants the wrong things; this is a useful index of the kind of competitive pressure now being exerted in gasoline retailing and automobile retailing and a good clue to the monopoly element in retail value-added.

The general conclusion is that there are elements of monopoly in wholesale distribution and retail distribution which tend to raise the distributive margin above what it needs over the competitive optimum, but that low entry requirements generate countermovements whenever the excess builds up to some critical point. This conclusion is not necessarily optimistic or pessimistic. For the crucial questions are those of fact and therefore of degree: how far the distributive margin is raised before it is undermined by competition and how fast the process works. I hope we can look forward to research in particular trades and markets, in size distributions, and in the determinants of distributive margins. The price and product in distribution have perhaps more than their share of peculiarities; but this should be a motive, not a barrier, to exploration.

8

Some functions
of marketing
reconsidered

Edmund D. McGarry

1. WEAKNESS OF THE FUNCTIONAL ANALYSIS

From the beginning of the systematic study of marketing, a great deal
of attention has been given to the analysis of marketing functions. A large
number of articles have been published on the subject in various professional
journals, and practically every textbook on marketing attempts to make some
use of such an analysis in its presentation.[1] Yet, despite all these writings,
there is little general agreement as to what the functions are or as to the

[1] For an excellent summary of different points of view concerning marketing functions,
see E. S. Fullbrook, "The Functional Concept in Marketing," *Journal of Marketing*, IV
(January, 1940), 229–37.

From Reavis Cox and Wroe Alderson (eds.), *Theory in Marketing* (Homewood,
Ill.: Richard D. Irwin, Inc., for the American Marketing Association, 1950), pp.
263–279. Reprinted by permission.

purpose of defining them. Nevertheless, the importance of discovering the functions and of using them to analyze marketing problems is generally recognized. Agnew, Jenkins, and Drury state that "one of the most urgent needs of the present time is the accurate analysis and evaluation of different functions."[2] Alexander says: "Writers on the subject are by no means agreed as to the precise activities which belong to this category [marketing functions]. The lists that have been suggested contain from as few as eight to as many as twenty or thirty such functions. There is no standard group of them."[3]

Dissatisfaction with the present status of functional analysis is evidenced by the following statement recently distributed by the Committee on Definitions of the American Marketing Association:

> It is probably unfortunate that this term [marketing function] was ever developed. Under it students of marketing have sought to squeeze a heterogeneous and non-consistent group of activities. For example, the functions of assembling, and dividing, if such functions exist, are performed through buying, selling, and transporting. Grading, standardization, and packaging are adjuncts of selling. Merchandising, when performed by the manufacturer, is partly a production and partly a manufacturing activity. Such functions as assembling, storage, transporting, are broad general economic functions, while selling, and buying are essentially individual in character. All these discrete groups we attempt to crowd into one class and label marketing functions.[4]

It is the purpose of this essay (a) to point out some of the discrepancies and inconsistencies in the use of the term "function," (b) to clarify some of the concepts regarding marketing, and (c) to set forth tentatively a list of functions that—for the purpose of making more understandable the part that marketing plays in modern society—appears to be more comprehensive and more useful than those now used. In order to accomplish this purpose, it is necessary to redefine marketing and to reorient the approach to the subject on a broad scale. Fortunately, marketing is one of the youngest of

---

[2] H. E. Agnew, R. B. Jenkins, and J. C. Drury, *Outlines of Marketing* (New York: McGraw-Hill Book Co., Inc., 1942), p. 47.

[3] R. S. Alexander, F. M. Surface, R. F. Elder, and W. Alderson, *Marketing* (Boston: Ginn & Co., 1940), p. 89. Actually, Ryan, in attempting to give a complete and detailed picture of the distribution process, lists 120 functional elements grouped into 16 functional categories, as "one of the many possible ways of presenting the elements of marketing" (F. W. Ryan, "Functional Concepts in Market Distribution," *Harvard Business Review*, XIII [January, 1935], 205–24).

[4] From a tentative mimeographed statement distributed by the Committee in 1947.

the disciplines that have grown out of economics, and there should be no encrusted reasoning or vested interests to inhibit the student from making such changes as the analysis requires. The very fact that there is wide disagreement lays the basis for experimental thinking.

It should not be necessary to point out that, in suggesting a new and different basis for functional analysis, the writer of this essay anticipates neither general acceptance of his ideas nor general agreement as to their value. Disagreement is healthful in so far as it stimulates thought. The purpose of this article is exploratory, and it is hoped that its conclusions will be sufficiently controversial to stimulate discussion of the fundamentals of the science of marketing. With this end in view, the writer himself reserves the privilege of changing his mind should his position prove untenable.

2. DEVELOPMENT OF THE FUNCTIONAL CONCEPT

The first application of the term "function" in connection with marketing is commonly attributed to Shaw, who, in 1912, enumerated the functions of middlemen as follows: sharing the risk; transporting the goods; financing the operations; selling (communication of ideas about the goods); and assembling, assorting, and reshipping.[5] L. D. H. Weld applied the functions of middlemen—as developed by Shaw, with some changes of his own—to the process of marketing as a whole, because, as he explained, "they are not always performed by middlemen, but often to a greater extent by producers themselves," and "it should be noted that the final consumer performs part of the marketing functions."[6]

With the coming of textbooks, functional analysis became popular. Most writers, following Weld, took over bodily the functions of middlemen and applied them with certain changes in terminology to the process of marketing in general. It was not until Breyer called attention to the need for a different approach in the treatment of marketing as an institution from that used in studying marketing agencies that students came to realize that some reorientation was necessary.[7]

Actually, there is no more reason to consider the functions of middlemen to be necessarily the same as the functions of the marketing process

[5] A. W. Shaw, "Some Problems in Market Distribution," *Quarterly Journal of Economics*, XXVI (August, 1912), 703–65.

[6] L. D. H. Weld, "Marketing Functions and Mercantile Organization," *American Economic Review*, VII (June, 1917), 306–18.

[7] R. F. Breyer, *The Marketing Institution* (New York: McGraw-Hill Book Co., Inc., 1934), p. 8.

than there is to consider the functions of a carburetor to be the functions of a car. The use of the functional terminology interchangeably for different parts of the system and for the system as a whole points to two errors in definition. One involves the definition of the term "marketing," and the other the definition of the term "function."

"Marketing," according to the Committee on Definitions of the American Marketing Association, "is a series of activities which are involved in the flow of goods from production to consumption";[8] or, to use the definition presently proposed by the same Committee, marketing is "the performance of business activities that direct the flow of goods and services from producer to consumer or user."[9] In both these definitions, there is a vague implication that marketing begins at the factory door (or the farm gate or the mine head) and ends at the turnstile of the supermarket. In other words, marketing is the work that middlemen usually do. Neither of the definitions embraces the idea that marketing is often a major directive factor in production and that it extends its influence into consumption; nor does either comprehend that conceivably the consumer might also be the producer, as would theoretically be possible in a fully integrated co-operative institution.[10] In short, there is no recognition of the part that marketing plays in the economic system or in social behavior generally.

"A marketing function," according to the Committee on Definitions, "is a major specialized activity performed in marketing."[11] Thus, it appears that marketing is simply a bundle of activities in the flow of goods, and a marketing function is any one of the bigger activities in the bundle.[12] One might readily draw the analogy of a wheel in a machine. The activity of the wheel consists, of course, in turning around and around. This, then, is its function; and the machine itself may be defined as a lot of wheels going around and around. Clearly, this describes the machine in a primitive sort of way, and it may conceivably be of aid in some types of analysis; but it is questionable that it leads to any profound understanding of the machine. Is it any wonder

---

[8] "Definitions of Marketing Terms," consolidated report of the Committee on Definitions, *National Marketing Review*, I (Fall, 1935), 156.

[9] "Report of the Definitions Committee," *Journal of Marketing*, XIII (October, 1948), 202–17.

[10] For a further discussion of this point see the essay by D. F. Blankertz on "Consumer Actions and Consumer Nonprofit Co-operation" elsewhere in this volume.

[11] *Report of the Definitions Committee, 1948*, p. 210.

[12] Ryan, in his "pragmatic" approach to the problem, explains that he uses the word "function" in its ordinary meaning as the name of each of the recognizable items or elements of marketing activity because it is the most widely used and the most acceptable English word available. It means the normal activity of the thing, its actual performance (Ryan, *op. cit.*, p. 213).

that the most persistent criticism of marketing is that it is purely descripive?

One must not, however, minimize the difficulty of developing a sound definition of "marketing," particularly when it has to run the gauntlet of the numerous and individualistic members of a large committee. It is generally conceded that, in our present economy, the essential element in marketing has to do with the passing of title, since ownership is required for use. But how can a definition be formulated that will be equally applicable (a) to an economy of free enterprise; (b) to an economy based on purely communistic principles, where ownership is theoretically held by the state; and (c) to a purely co-operative economy, where ownership and operation of production facilities are in the hands of consumers? To meet these problems, as well as the problem of broadening the concept to include the overall purpose of marketing, the following definition is proposed:

> *Marketing is that phase or aspect of an economy that has to do with and results in the changes in custody of, responsibility for, and authority over goods, to the end that goods produced by many agencies are made available for the convenience and satisfaction of different users.*

It will be noted that "marketing," as defined above, is not limited to two points, production and consumption; instead, it is a phase or aspect of the entire economy, the implication being that it is a pervasive element that penetrates every part of the economy.[13] The term "responsibility for" is meant to include not only changes in private ownership in a capitalistic economy, but also changes of custody from person to person, even where ownership is maintained in a single organization. The definition also includes the main purposes of marketing, the essential reasons for the process.

3. THE MEANING OF ''FUNCTION''

With the above definition of "marketing" in mind, it is possible to turn to the problem of defining the functions of marketing. To secure a sound definition for the term, it is well to ask, first: What should be the purpose of functional analysis? The answer is that, by breaking the process down into its functions, it is possible to separate the essential from the nonessential elements. Functional analysis should enable the analyst to evaluate the

---

[13] "Exchange of goods occurs in the most primitive of societies and trade between nations has flourished throughout history, but under modern capitalism marketing has become not only all pervasive but central to the whole economic system" (Leverett S. Lyon, "Marketing," *Encyclopaedia of the Social Sciences*, X, 133).

activities that are performed in terms of ultimate objectives and thus to emphasize those that are necessary and subordinate or eliminate those that are not. Such an analysis should give perspective to the study of marketing and make clear the place of the process in the conceptual scheme of the economy. Through the study of functions, changes in the structure of marketing caused by shifting, combining, or eliminating activities from one agency to another should be made understandable.

Obviously, such purposes as these cannot be attained as long as functions are defined merely as certain activities, even when an attempt is made to separate the good from the bad or the major from the minor activities. When this is done, all that is accomplished is a description of the process involved; and activities such as looking into the future, guessing as to what is in the consumer's mind, and so on ad infinitum, might just as well be called "functions" as the activities usually selected. No one will deny that these are important activities of marketers and that description is a necessary first step in analysis, but it is difficult to see how any particular purpose is served by enumerating them as separate functions.

The term "function" should be so defined as to meet the purpose for which it is used. The function of the heart is not simply to beat, which is its activity, but rather to supply the body with a continuous flow of blood. The term "functional architecture" implies that a building is designed for a purpose. In like manner, "functions of marketing" should denote a purpose-fulness in the marketing process; and the term should be used only in connection with activities that must be performed in order to accomplish the general purpose. Thus, accounting is not a function of marketing, although no one would think of carrying on business without it. The term "function" should be restricted to the *sine qua non* of marketing, those things without which marketing would not exist.[14]

The ideal to which marketing aspires is to distribute to consumers all the goods that full employment of all resources makes possible in such a way that each can secure what he wants within his income, with a minimum of delay and inconvenience. Under these circumstances, in a capitalistic economy, each would be able to buy what he could afford, and the money received from his buying would result in the financing of further production without waste. The continuous flow of goods to consumers and the continuous flow of money back into production are implied.

A careful study of the so-called "functions of marketing," as stated by the various writers on the subject, reveals that the most difficult problem is to be found in those activities having to do with changing of title, which

---

[14] It is recognized, of course, that different sets of functions may be formulated for different levels of analysis and for different purposes.

practically all authorities agree is the central core of the marketing process. Most writers have denominated these activities "the buying function" and "the selling function." Some have brought the two together under the head of "exchange functions" or "bargaining functions." Others have tried to get away from the buying and selling concepts by calling them, respectively, "assembly" and "dispersion."

In 1934, Breyer broke sharply with the recognized authorities and proposed a fundamentally new approach to the whole problem. He insisted "that the searching work and the negotiation work rather than who performs them (seller or buyer) are the fundamental, distinctive charactertics of the marketing task involved, and that selling and buying are merely two different aspects of these two primal types of activity. . . . When viewing the marketing institution as an integral unit . . . our functional conceptions, contactual and negotiatory, are more useful for purposes of analysis and synthesis than are the customary selling function and buying function concept."[15]

It is apparent that Breyer's analysis, excellent as it is, is essentially a subdivision of "the bargaining transaction," as developed by Commons.[16] Its conclusions are based heavily on legal considerations, and it does not comprehend what would happen to the marketing process under a purely authoritarian or collectivist regime. Further, it fails to come to grips with one of the most subtle and pervasive elements in modern marketing, viz., the use of persuasion in influencing the bargaining transaction. Using Breyer's concepts as a starting point, however, it is possible to set up a list of functions that will satisfy these objections, as well as those mentioned previously.

4 . A NEW LIST OF MARKETING FUNCTIONS

Before taking up the functions here developed individually, it is desirable to outline the list in the order of the progression in which they are usually undertaken, as follows:

1. Contactual (Breyer)—the searching out of buyers and sellers
2. Merchandising (Alexander)—the fitting of the goods to market requirements
3. Pricing—the selection of a price high enough to make production possible and low enough to induce users to accept the goods

[15] Breyer, *op. cit.*
[16] J. R. Commons, *Institutional Economics* (New York: Macmillan Co., 1934).

4. Propaganda—the conditioning of the buyers or of the sellers to a favorable attitude toward the product or its sponsor
5. Physical distribution—the transporting and storing of the goods
6. Termination—the consummation of the marketing process

The Contactual Function

The contactual function, according to Breyer, is the process of searching out the market. In the American economy, it consists of finding out either who the potential buyers are or who the potential sellers are, where they are located, and how they can be reached. It also includes media analysis that aims to discover which type of medium is likely to be most effective in reaching that segment of the market that affords potential customers for a particular item. Likewise, it includes the analysis of distribution channels to discover which outlets are most likely to be patronized for a particular good. Thus, the contactual function comprehends not only the staking-out of the segment of the market that it is desirable to exploit but also the making and maintaining of such contact with potential customers as is necessary to discover their desires. In cases where the buyer takes the initiative, the function consists in finding the most acceptable sources for the goods. In the case of consumer co-operative integration, the contactual function may represent both a searching-out of sources and a searching-out of potential members of the co-operative.

The Merchandising Function

The Committee on Definitions, in its earlier statement, gave as a definition of "merchandising" the following: "The adjustment of merchandise produced or offered for sale to customer demand. It involves the coordination of selling with production or buying for resale . . . It involves the selecting of the product to be produced or stocked and deciding such details as the size, appearance, form, dressing of the product (packaging, etc.), quantities to be bought or made, time of purchase or production, price lines to be carried or made, etc."[17]

Copeland and Learned have defined "merchandising" as follows: "Merchandising is product planning. The job of merchandising is to ascertain the characteristics of the merchandise for which there is a potentially profitable demand, to prepare instructions for the manufacturing plant in

---

[17] "Report of the Committee on Definitions" (1935), 156. As its latest definition of "merchandising," the Committee on Definitions recommends the following: "The planning involved in marketing the right merchandise, at the right place, at the right time, in the right quantities and at the right price" (*Report of the Definitions Committee, 1948*, p. 211).

order that it may be able to produce goods for which a demand exists, to aid in developing plans for promoting the sales, and to supervise the various routine operations in connection with these activities. It includes the determination of what to make, how much, at what time, and at what price."[18]

The writer of this essay prefers to omit pricing from the merchandising function and to consider it as a function in itself. Thus, the merchandising function includes all the adjustments made in the goods and in their presentation to meet the needs and desires of potential consumers or users. It includes quality determination as well as measurement, packaging, branding, and display at strategic points to stimulate consumer interest.

There is an implication in the definitions quoted that merchandising is wholly carried on by the seller. However, the activities enumerated can, with equal validity, be carried on by the buyer, as is done when he sets up specifications to guide his source in processing the items. And they may be performed in an integrated totalitarian system in which the state or some other organization determines just what will be produced and how it will be presented.

The Pricing Function

Even though both of the definitions quoted above include pricing as a part of merchandising, it seems that pricing is far too important to be relegated to such a minor role. A considerable part of the time and thought of the marketer is given to the problem of what price to pay or what price to accept. The suggestion of Breyer that "the forces which shape the amount of [that] price are the supply and demand forces of the market" and that pricing is therefore not a function of the marketing institution, can be given little weight, since these factors do not operate in a vacuum, but actually consist of evaluations made and expressed by buyers and sellers.[19] It is the making of these evaluations that constitutes the function of pricing in marketing.

It should be made clear that the pricing function has to do with the determination of reservation prices, offering prices, or acceptance prices, and that these are not necessarily the same as the prices at which the goods actually move. The decisions on prices here contemplated depend on the purposes the various parties have in mind. In the case of free trading on organized exchanges, the decisions depend largely upon the individual estimates of future price changes. On the other hand, where the prices are

---

[18] M. T. Copeland and E. P. Learned, *Merchandising of Cotton Textiles* (Cambridge: Harvard Bureau of Business Research, 1933).

[19] Breyer, *op. cit.*, p. 11.

administered by management, a large number of factors is involved—for example, the expected demand, the cost of production and selling, the price of competing articles, and the pricing policies of other concerns in the trade. "A change in price," says Knauth, "is a nervous affair. The perfect price cannot be reasoned out. The only guide is public reaction which is discovered by trial and error."[20]

The Propaganda Function

The term "propaganda," originally had to do with the propagation of "the faith." It has come to mean, however, any scheme or plan for the propagation of a belief or an opinion in which the progagandist has an interest. Objections may be offered to the term because it now carries a connotation that is somewhat invidious. However, since the invidiousness itself appears to be derived from the fact that the propagandist has "an ax to grind," and since this is in no place more evident than in the business world, the word seems to be all the more appropriate for describing the marketing function.[21]

Under the propaganda function would fall all the methods used by the seller to influence people to buy from him and all the methods used by the buyer to induce sellers to sell to him. Thus, it would include all advertising, whether product or institutional; publicity of various kinds; and personal selling. In short, propaganda includes all the efforts put forth in business for the purpose of persuading and inducing a person in the market to act in a way that is favorable to the interest of the propagandist. It is a conditioning process organized to focus on the recipient all those environmental factors favorable to the interest of the propagandist. It aims not only to secure the attention and the favorable attitude of the recipient but also to persuade and induce him to act in a favorable way.

The Physical Distribution Function

Under the merchandising function, one may include time and space elements implied in the words "right time" and "right place." This use of the term would imply that the physical distribution function, which includes transportation and storage, is a part of the merchandising function. How-

---

[20] O. W. Knauth, *Managerial Enterprise* (New York: W. W. Norton & Co., Inc., 1948), p. 118. See also his articles "Marketing and Managerial Enterprises," elsewhere in this volume, and "Considerations in the Setting of Retail Prices," *Journal of Marketing*, XIV (July, 1949), 1–12.

[21] Borden uses the term "merchandising function," i.e., "the function of determining product form," and the term "promotional function," i.e., "the function of stimulating and fashioning consumers' desires for his product" (N. H. Borden, *The Economic Effects of Advertising* [Chicago: Richard D. Irwin, Inc., 1942], p. 36).

ever, since this function is almost universally recognized, either as a single function or as "transportation" and "storage," and is adequately defined in practically all textbooks, there is little need to discuss it at length here.

The Termination Function

Breyer says that "after the contact between the producer and consumer has been made it becomes necessary to arrive at an agreement . . . on at least three essentials: the quality, the quantity and the price of the services to be exchanged." Since these three elements are subject to negotiation, he terms the process "the negotiation function."[22] As stated above, Breyer's concept is fitted into the framework of the purchase-sale transaction in a free economy and thus lacks the breadth necessary to encompass marketing under a fully controlled economy. If the functions are to be made all-inclusive, it is necessary to find a term much broader than "negotiation." Such a term should embrace not only those factors that culminate in a contract, but also the carrying-out of the terms of the contract to the point at which marketing ends. To fulfill these requirements, the term "termination function" has been chosen. This term has an advantage in that it has come into rather extensive usage, particularly with reference to government contracts.

If one assumes, as is done here, that the adjustment of the goods to the consumers and the adjustment of the consumers to the goods takes place largely through the functions of merchandising and propaganda, then the area of negotiation is considerably reduced. However, the negotiation of the actual sale—the meeting of the minds of the parties—still remains. And, in our economy, after the terms of sale are agreed upon, there is usually the overt legal act of transferring title. The termination function, then, is the consummative act for which all of the other functions have been preparatory. Under it falls the determination of the terms of sale for each specific transaction, including delivery dates, credit arrangements, guarantees, and service policies that have been agreed upon. However, it must be remembered that marketing does not end with the payment for and the acceptance of the goods, because, in practice, there often remains a contingent moral and (sometimes) a legal obligation on the part of the seller that the goods be satisfactory. In cases of a fully controlled economy, the termination function would include all the processes necessary to place the goods under the responsibility of those who are to use them, to bring to an end the responsibility of those who have brought the goods this far, and such other contingent actions as the economy may require.

[22] Breyer, *op. cit.*, p. 6.

5. THE CO-ORDINATION OF MERCHANDISING AND PROPAGANDA FUNCTIONS

The merchandising and propaganda functions are in this analysis conceived as co-ordinate in adjusting products to their prospective users, on the one hand, and in adjusting potential users to the products made for them, on the other. The necessity for these adjustments grows out of the general thesis (*a*) that products—whether made by man or produced by nature—seldom, and perhaps never, completely meet the preconceived notions of what those who are to use them want,[23] and (*b*) that wants for specific goods with definite characteristics are determined largely by environmental factors that are to some extent controllable. Since this conception departs most widely from the accepted doctrine, it is necessary that its basis be carefully examined.

In classical economic theory, there was an assumption (implied or expressed) that for every economic good a demand existed; for, by definition, an economic good was something that was wanted and that was scarce.[24] Wants were usually explained as stemming from biological or physiological needs—for example, the needs for food, clothing, and shelter. Essentially, then, wants for goods existed; they could not be created; and they ripened into demand as the wanter secured purchasing power. This concept of demand as something existing had a much more realistic basis in the market at the time of the early economists, when it was formulated, than it has today.[25] Under conditions of low-level consumption and a sellers'

---

[23] "The fact that consumers buy certain things does not necessarily mean that they are satisfied with them, or that there was a plan in buying them. Psychologists who realize that wants are irrational feel that it is their task to explain, and perhaps to predict, consumer behavior; but their explanations cannot very well run in terms of specific goods and services. In their analysis, what is wanted may be something that will satisfy a half-dozen different cravings, and the number of alternatives is almost infinite—if the consumer has enough money" (W. E. Atkins *et al.*, *Economic Behavior* [rev. ed.; Boston: Houghton Mifflin Co., 1939], p. 761).

[24] For a clear statement of the inadequacy of the older point of view and the development of a comprehensive theory applied to modern conditions, see E. H. Chamberlin, *The Theory of Monopolistic Competition* (Cambridge: Harvard University Press, 1933). Chamberlin's analysis includes changes in product and in selling costs, as well as in prices and quantities. His product and selling costs correspond, respectively, to merchandising and propaganda as used in the present analysis.

[25] "As a people we have become steadily less concerned about the primary needs—food, clothing and shelter. . . . Our wants have ranged more widely and we now demand a broad list of goods and services which come under the category of 'optional purchases'" (Committee on Recent Economic Changes of the President's Conference on Unemployment, *Recent Economic Changes* [New York: McGraw-Hill Book Co., Inc., 1929], I, xv).

market, there was little need for and little possibility of discrimination on the part of consumers among products with small differences; consequently, product differentiation had but little appeal.[26] However, it is another story when we consider an economy in which most of the basic wants of practically all the people are continuously satisfied. As the level of consumption rises, more attention is paid to small differences—differences often imperceptible in so far as the inherent physical properties of the goods are concerned.[27]

From the standpoint of marketing under modern conditions, the demand for products is largely created. Man chooses one item rather than another because of a more favorable attitude toward the chosen item than toward the item that is not selected. This attitude is not something that is native and in existence; rather, it is created by a multitude of environmental factors. Among the most potent of these factors are those derived from what the individual himself has experienced or observed about the item and what has been communicated to him by others. Whether he knows it or not, a person's mind is largely made up from a complex of rational and irrational, tangible and intangible factors, many of which are imponderable and impossible to define. Furthermore, these factors, taken together, often have an importance greater than price in the making of choice.[28] For this reason, the two-dimensional logic of those economists who use price and quantity as the sole analytical measures for their problems is wholly inadequate for the understanding of the multidimensional demand factors that face the marketer under conditions of high-level consumption.

Marketing writers, however, have tended to follow the lead of the older economists without much qualification and with practically no criticism. They have failed to emphasize the difference between what is wanted or desired in a generalized way and what is wanted as to a specific

---

[26] The term "low-level consumption" characterizes an economy in which consumption rises but little above "the level of bare subsistence for the many plus some gewgaws for the wealthy few." It represented the "simple process of grasping for whatever food, clothing and shelter could be produced and making them last as long as possible." The term "high-level consumption" denotes "an economy in which the output of goods is considerably more than enough to provide for the prime needs of the population." For a full discussion of high-level consumption see W. H. Lough, *High Level Consumption* (New York: McGraw-Hill Book Co., Inc., 1935).

[27] "The satisfactions, in an economic sense, which the consumer seeks in merchandise are only partly concerned with intrinsic properties" (P. H. Cherington, *People's Wants and How to Satisfy Them* [New York: Harper & Bros., 1935], p. 166).

[28] "It is arguable that under modern conditions a firm enlarges its market more frequently and more effectively by increasing expenditure on marketing devices to capture consumers than by that price cutting to woo customers which was assumed by the classical theory of competition to be the normal procedure" (Maurice Dobb, "Middleman," *Encyclopaedia of the Social Sciences*, X, 417).

product. It is, of course, the particular product that is sold in the market—a fact that should constitute one of the main differences of approach between marketing and economic theory. The marketer deals with individualized items, usually standardized within low tolerances, and each transaction is undertaken under a more or less different set of circumstances. He attempts to fit his particular product to the desires of a large number of different individual personalities, each of which is beset with different necessities, whims, and attitudes.

Under mass production, a high degree of product standardization is necessary, and little attention can be paid to the narrow differences in the desires of individual consumers except as they form a pattern for a group. If a producer cannot find or influence a sufficiently large segment of the population to accept his product, he cannot afford to underwrite the facilities that will enable him to sell at prices consumers will be willing to pay.[29] He is therefore under compulsion to build into the product characteristics that a sufficient number of customers will want, or to use the influences at his disposal to persuade them to want what he has made, or to do both. What the consumer wants or may be induced to want is often impossible to define in terms of physical characteristics, not only because there are no adequate measures of the characteristics that different consumers consider important, but also because the many alternatives the consumer may consider in his particular case are unknown and practically unknowable in advance of production. For this reason, the producer must constantly rely upon a process of trial and error in the market to discover what is wanted, and upon a process of indoctrination and propaganda to persuade consumers to accept what it is practicable to produce.[30]

6.   MARKETING AND ECONOMIC REFORM

Under communism, socialism, and most other reform movements, marketing is in the hands of the state. Usually, this means that a central bureaucracy of so-called "experts" is set up for the purpose of determining

[29] "Advertising and selling effort in so far as they influence demand may create uniformities of desires so that mass production of specialized articles may be disposed of. . . . Unless sufficient uniformities exist or are created, his (the businessman's) product cannot be sold at a profitable price" (H. R. Tosdal, "The Advertising and Selling Process," *Annals of the American Academy of Political and Social Science*, CCIX [May, 1940], 66–67).

[30] "Significant differentiations to the consumer are those things which give him satisfaction, and he expresses his judgment of them by buying or refusing to buy. Hence in a free economy whether or not differentiations are meaningless or inconsequential must be determined in the end by consumers' behavior" (Borden, *op. cit.*, p. 660).

what the public is to have in the form of goods and services that are distributed according to some preconceived plan. Theoretically, free choice of goods by the public is possible and could be implemented by directives from the board.[31] Innovations in goods are initiated by the board on the basis of objective tests, and "the wastes of competition" are thus eliminated. Advertising, except for simple statements concerning new products available, is generally prohibited; and propaganda, usually under the guise of education, takes the form of indoctrinating the public with the idea that only by these means can the maximum satisfactions be secured.

Inherent in the reasoning of these reforms is the theory that definite and objective wants exist that must be satisfied, and that it is possible for properly trained experts to determine what these wants are and to manage the economy in such a way that they can be supplied. The problem of adjusting goods to the consumer so that nice differences, which only the consumer himself can evaluate, can be secured, is largely ignored except in so far as the people can reject or accept what is offered them. Goods presumably are to be so standardized as to fit the needs of the people. People, rational beings as they are presumed to be, will attain the highest standard of living by accepting the goods that are designed for them by the experts. And, since much of the differentiation among products in capitalistic countries represents conspicuous consumption, it is considered unnecessary and undesirable.

Assuming the validity of all the arguments that the proponents of these reforms put forth as to the workability of their plans, it is conceivable that systems of this type might provide the basic needs of consumers; and, if free choice is permitted, it is possible that a certain amount of flexibility could be attained. However, the absence of any strong incentive on the part of the committee of experts to discover new types of wants, even though they act under directives to do so, seems to preclude the development of

---

[31] Lange, a leading authority on the economics of socialism, claims that a system "with neither free choice in consumption nor in occupation" would be undemocratic in character and incompatible with the ideals of the socialist movement. "Such a system would scarcely be tolerated by any civilized people. A distribution of consumers' goods by rationing was possible in the Soviet Union at a time when the standard of living was at a physiological minimum and an increase in the ration of any food, clothing, or housing accommodation was welcome, no matter what it was. But as soon as the national income increased sufficiently, rationing was given up, to be replaced to a large extent by a market for consumers' goods. And, outside of certain exceptions, there has always been freedom of choice of occupation in the Soviet Union. A distribution of consumers' goods by rationing is quite unimaginable in the countries of Western Europe or in the United States" (O. Lange, *On the Economics of Socialism*, ed. by Benjamin Lippencott [Minneapolis: University of Minnesota Press, 1938], p. 95).

want-making as distinguished from want-satisfying machinery. Unless some such machinery is set up to perform the functions of merchandising and commercial propaganda, it is difficult to conceive how the system could lead to high-level consumption, the very essence of which is the close adjustment of particular goods to the individual's personality—the indulgence of whims and idiosyncrasies that, from our point of view, make life worth living. This is not to say that the population might not be propagandized into a sense of satisfiedness and even smugness; but, under these conditions, the individual could never develop the self-expression in terms of goods that is so necessary to one's personal adjustment to his environment.

7. SUMMARY AND CONCLUSION

The so-called "functions" of marketing, as enumerated and explained in most marketing textbooks, are really certain activities performed by different agencies in marketing. They describe somewhat mechanistically the processes through which goods pass from the producer to the consumer, with emphasis upon the relationships among the different marketing agencies. Such an analysis is inadequate for the purpose of explaining marketing in its broader aspects and defining its place in the social structure. To accomplish this latter objective, it is necessary to define functions in terms of purposefulness for society and to focus attention on the relationship of the marketing system to the environmental field in which it operates.

If it is assumed that people's wants, in so far as they apply to specific items of goods, are created by environmental factors and that goods cannot be made under conditions of mass production to meet all the varying specifications of individual consumers or users, then it becomes a major task of marketing to reconcile the notions of potential users as to what they desire with the products that businessmen find it practical to provide. This means, on the one hand, that goods must be found or devised that will, as nearly as possible, meet the preconceived notions of users as to nature, quality, and price, and that these goods must be presented at the proper time and under the most congenial conditions to appeal to users; and it means, on the other hand, that potential users must be conditioned to accept the goods as the best possible compromise between what they think they want and what they can get.

When considered from this point of view, the marketing task can be broken down into six different necessary functions, each of which contributes to the over-all purpose expressed above, as follows:

1. The contactual function, which has to do with the searching-out of potential customers or suppliers and the making of contact with them.
2. The merchandising function, which comprises the various activities undertaken to adapt the product to the users' ideas of what is wanted.
3. The pricing function, which has to do with the prices at which goods are offered or at which they will be accepted.
4. The propaganda function, which includes all the methods used to persuade the potential users to select the particular product and to make them like the product once they have it.
5. The physical distribution function, which comprises the transportation and storage of the goods.
6. The termination function, which has to do with the actual change in custody of and responsibility for the goods and is the culmination of the process.

These six functions cut vertically through the channels of distribution. They are performed in part by the various agencies of distribution and in part by producers and consumers. The development and refinement of these functions have been major factors in the attainment of high-level consumption in free-enterprise countries, and it is difficult to conceive that any system of economy can reach such high levels without developing machinery to perform these functions.

In the light of this approach, marketing is something more than mere buying and selling at a profit; it is something more than a machine for matching supply with demand for the purpose of determining price; it is something more than a system of institutions for the distribution of goods. In a comprehensive sense, marketing is all of these; but in addition, and more fundamentally, it is the phase of the economy through which, in large part, man in the modern world makes his adjustment to his environment in terms of psychic desires and physical goods.

9

Who does the work of retailing?

Stanley C. Hollander

We often think of a marketing channel as a sort of "bucket brigade" that passes goods from manufacturers to consumers. Moreover, we can easily come to think of that brigade as if it were composed of a limited number of institutional types who perform relatively standardized duties and who are represented by little boxes bearing the conventional letters "M," "W," "R," and "C" for manufacturer, wholesaler, retailer, and consumer.

From *Journal of Marketing*, national quarterly publication of the American Marketing Association, 28 (July 1964), pp. 18–22. Reprinted by permission.

About the author. Stanley C. Hollander, who holds a Ph.D. from the University of Pennsylvania, is Professor of Marketing at Michigan State University.

He is editor of EXPLORATIONS IN RETAILING, and has recently completed a study of one form of contracting out which Michigan State University has published under the title, BUSINESS CONSULTANTS AND CLIENTS.

The author is indebted to Professors Perry Bliss of the State University of New York at Buffalo and Eli P. Cox of Michigan State University for some very helpful suggestions.

Thus, we often tend to assume that most retailers perform relatively similar tasks. We usually assume that their work includes such activities as operating and maintaining stores, selecting and purchasing merchandise from wholesalers and manufacturers, determining prices, setting up displays, persuading customers to buy, collecting and receiving money from customers, furnishing incidental services, and in general making many decisions concerning the operations of their businesses.

This type of thinking is demonstrated in the census and other governmental statistical reports on retailing, in which merchants are very rarely classified on the basis of duties performed, but usually are divided only on such bases as size, location, and merchandise handled.[1]

Similarly, many comparative studies of retail efficiency in different environments have assumed homogeneity in the retailers' activities.[2]

FOUR ALTERNATIVES

It would be unfortunate if this type of conventional thinking blinded us to the heterogeneity of American business.

If, for example, we examined the actual work done by the employees and owners in each retail business, we would find some very striking inter-firm differences. Some retail firms are involved in a host of activities that we normally consider as wholesaling, manufacturing, or processing functions. The staffs of other firms are involved in only a fraction of the activities that are part of the total retail function.

Retailers have four major alternatives with regard to any conceivable activity:

1. They may *perform* the work; that is, they or their employees may actually do it.
2. They may *contract out* the work to specialized functionaries, such as contract-delivery companies, building-maintenance organizations, management consultants, and sales-finance companies.

---

[1] See Robert D. Entenberg, "Suggested Changes in Census Classifications of Retail Trade," JOURNAL OF MARKETING, Vol. 24 (January, 1960), pp. 39–43, for some thoughtful recommendations for changes in even these standard classifications.

[2] See William H. Starbuck, *Sales Volume and Employment in British and American Retail Trade*, Institute Paper No. 24 (Lafayette, Indiana: Institute for Quantitative Research in Economics and Management, Purdue University, 1962), especially pp. 42–53, for a criticism of the use of this assumption in Margaret Hall, John Knapp, and Christopher Winsten's otherwise monumental study, *Distribution in Great Britain and North America* (Oxford, 1961).

3. They may, and in a limited number of instances do, *share* the work with other competitive or noncompetitive retailers.
4. They may *shift* the work, either back to wholesaling and manufacturing suppliers or forward to consumers.

The choices among these alternatives are important to retail management in two ways.

The firm's total costs may be reduced by contracting out, sharing, or shifting activities. These three alternatives often provide attractive economies of scale.

But simultaneously they may reduce the firm's opportunities for differentiation. Hence, in deciding whether to perform a given activity, management should balance costs against the value of the activity's contribution to the store's individuality.

Influence on Productivity

The availability and use of these alternatives may also influence the productivity of the distributive system as a whole. Thus, a major study of European retail productivity strongly recommended the increased use of functional specialists and groups in procurement and other operations:

> "As standardisation of the [buying] operations within the medium sized [retail] enterprise is possible to only a minor degree and specialisation hardly at all, a solution lies in the collective organisation of many of these tasks by groups of retailers, and the complete or partial transfer of function from the individual retailer to group organisation.
>
> ". . . There is the need for all organisations and firms concerned with distribution to develop specialisation of function in their activities . . . Functions that are directly competitive with one's neighbour must be retained by the individual unit itself, but the more that other functions ranging from buying to expert advice on shop layout can be undertaken collectively by groups of distributors thereby increasing specialisation, the greater the increase in productivity."[3]

As one student of marketing development has pointed out, the American economic environment has particularly encouraged the growth of specialized service institutions, "without which the broader forms of economic activity . . . would have great difficulty in existing."[4] The growth of these

[3] James B. Jeffreys, Simon Hausberger, and Goren Lindblad, *Productivity in the Distributive Trade in Europe: Wholesale and Retail Aspects.* (Paris: Organisation for European Economic Co-operation, 1954), pp. 61, pp. 104–105.

[4] Kenneth H. Meyers, "ABC and SRDS: The Evolution of Two Specialized Advertising Services," *Business History Review,* Vol. 34 (Autumn, 1960), pp. 302–326, at p. 303.

ancillary or specialized functional institutions has been a major contributor to American business performance.[5]

More directly concerned with retailing, a department store historian has noted:

> "There is hardly any phase of store operation which is not covered by a specialist [organization] in that field. These experts are available to any store which is struggling for better operations, and they constitute one of the main reasons for the steady advance in American merchandising."[6]

Pervasiveness of the Alternatives

American retailers have many opportunities to select from among the four basic alternatives, which seem to apply to almost every retailing activity except perhaps the basic decisions to enter and leave business.

For example, many different combinations of the four are used in merchandising. Some retailers share or shift much of their merchandising work under such common institutional arrangements as voluntarily or wholesaler sponsored cooperative chain plans, franchise retailing, and/or rack jobbing. Some department-store and specialty-shop merchandising is contracted out to independent resident buying offices, while in other cases the work is shared through cooperative buying offices.

The amount and range of the work that is delegated to the resident office varies greatly. Some merchants accept only information and advisory services from the resident buyers; some delegate authority to execute routine reorders; and some contract out authority and responsibility for organizing basic central buying programs. Even when store owners and employees perform the buying work, their tasks may range from simple acceptance or rejection of salesmen's offers to almost complete control of the manufacturing process, as in specification buying.

Occupancy and building maintenance is another aspect of retailing with a wide range of alternatives. Some retailers, particularly in department-store and supermarket fields, have carried performance to the point of becoming shopping-center developers. Other retailers have limited their real estate activities to stores that they own and maintain themselves.

In some fields, such as gasoline retailing, many of the shelter activities have been shifted to merchandise suppliers. Still other retailers have con-

---

[5] Arthur H. Cole, "An Approach to the Study of Entrepreneurship," *Journal of Economic History*, Supplement 6 (1946), pp. 1–16, at p. 11.

[6] F. M. Mayfield, *The Department Store Story* (New York: Fairchild Publications, 1949), p. 220.

tracted out building and housekeeping activities to landlords and maintenance companies. Perhaps the extreme version of contracting out is found among leased department operators, who merely acquire floor space in stores.

The retailers who feature private brands tend to perform most of the promotional tasks, although they may contract out specific activities to such specialists as advertising agencies, window-trimming companies, and package designers.

Other retailers tend to shift varying amounts of promotional work back to suppliers. The promotional assistance offered by the suppliers may include point-of-sale materials, cooperative advertising programs and supplies, and the furnishing of demonstrators, in addition to developing basic demands for the product.

Specialized contractors are sometimes used for house-to-house selling campaigns and for the solicitation of charge accounts. The use of trading-stamp companies is a form of contracting out.

Voluntary and cooperative chain members frequently share promotional tasks. Other retailers do not share this type of work very frequently. However, there are some examples of their sharing joint advertising and promotional campaigns sponsored from time to time by shopping center groups and by community merchants' associations.

The informational aspects of credit are generally shared or contracted out through cooperative and independent credit bureaus. The financial aspects may be contracted to a host of specialized institutions; collection work may be delegated to collection agencies; or the whole task may be shifted, through cash sales, to the consumer.

After-sale service may be handled by the retailer, shifted backward to the manufacturer or forward to the consumer, or turned over to specialized contractors. Many small retailers contract out bookkeeping and financial work; large retailers often turn to specialized contractors for temporary tabulating work, particularly at inventory time. Similar choices are available in connection with practically all other retail activities.

BASES FOR SELECTING ALTERNATIVES

We really do not have an adequate theory of what the business firm does, that is, of what governs its range of functions and activities.[7] The available literature, particularly in analyses of channel relations and vertical

[7] George J. Stigler, "The Division of Labor Is Limited by the Extent of the Market," *The Journal of Political Economy*, Vol. 59 (June, 1951), pp. 185–193, at p. 185.

integration, does contain some extensive discussions of the fourth alternative, that of shifting tasks backward or forward.[8]

But unfortunately the alternatives of contracting out and sharing have received much less attention. Thus, we know surprisingly little about the growth and roles of the many specialized service institutions that help to support modern retailing.

Similarly, most studies of activity sharing among retailers have been limited to analyses of cooperative chains and of joint political ventures.[9] We do not know, for example, why some shopping centers have highly successful merchants' associations, while other centers have developed only the barest minimum group activity. Many other aspects of retail sharing also remain unstudied.

However, some identifiable factors do seem to influence the choice of alternatives.

1. American retailing is a fertile field for *the development of centralized activities, either through contracting or sharing*, because of the existence of so many noncompetitive firms with common interests.

Sometimes even contiguous retailers find that their cooperative interests outweigh competitive considerations. This is particularly likely to be true in the case of modern shopping centers where the amount of inter-store competition is controlled through restrictive leases.

However, one of the major opportunities for centralizing organizations in retailing comes from the purely local nature of many retail markets and the physical separation of stores. A resident buying office in New York, for example, may serve 20, 50, or more independent department stores that have little competitive impact upon each other.

A British productivity team concluded some years ago that the use of such offices was more suited to American department stores than to English ones, largely because of spatial considerations.[10] The available time and expense saving from reduced store-buyer travel to the central market (London) was less significant in a compact country such as England; and

[8] See, for example, Richard M. Clewett, editor, *Marketing Channels* (Homewood, Illinois: Richard D. Irwin, Inc., 1954); Robert H. Cole and others, *Vertical Integration in Marketing* (Bulletin 74) (Urbana, Illinois: Bureau of Economic and Business Research, University of Illinois, 1952); Wroe Alderson, *Marketing Behavior and Executive Action* (Homewood, Illinois: Richard D. Irwin, Inc., 1957), Chap. 11.

[9] See James C. Palamountain, *The Politics of Distribution.* (Cambridge: Harvard University Press, 1955); Ewald T. Grether, "Solidarity in the Distributive Trades in Relation to Price Competition," *Law and Contemporary Problems*, Vol. 4 (June, 1937), pp. 375–391; Hector Lazo, *Retailer Cooperatives* (New York: Harper & Brothers, 1937); Williard F. Mueller and Leon Garoian, *Changes in the Market Structure of Grocery Retailing* (Madison: University of Wisconsin Press, 1961), Chap. 6.

[10] British Productivity Team on Retailing, *Retailing* (Report), London: Anglo-American Council on Productivity, 1952), p. 48.

similarly, inter-city department store competition seemed more pronounced.

However, the growth of chain organizations, the development of department store branches, and the spread of interurbias may change the American picture to include more competition between retailers who are now quite separate.

2. The *size of the firm* undoubtedly plays an important role in the selection of alternatives.

Large retailers often can integrate backward and thus perform more activities than can medium-sized ones. But the relationships between size and number of activities performed are complex. Small retailers may not need sufficient quantities of many services to attract potential contractors, and thus may be forced to perform (or omit) many activities that large retailers can contract out.

Many very small retailers do not have sufficient breadth of interest, or perhaps enough to gain, to participate in the type of sharing exemplified by trade association work.

Finally, there seems to have been an historical tendency for large retailers to concentrate upon impersonal price appeals. Thus, large retailers probably have shifted more tasks forward to the customer than have the smaller merchants.

3. *Vertical disintegration may be the typical, but not inevitable, development in growing industries,* while integration is characteristic of declining industries, as Stigler has pointed out.[11]

According to this view, growth provides increasing opportunities for specialization, whereas decline offers a temptation to consolidate functions in an attempt to maintain position. Although more information would be needed to test the applicability of this generalization to retailing, department store experience seems an exception to this observation. Vertical disintegration in the department store field occurred after, rather than during, the years of great growth.

In 1954, considerably after the major period of department store expansion in both England and the United States, it was noted:

"But these vertical integrations on three levels are relatively rare in the department store field, and one may say that the trend during these last decades has been in the opposite direction, *i.e.*, several department stores have liquidated their interests in the manufacturing field, as they have found that such an extension of their activity to manufacturing was a source of weakness rather than of strength."[12]

---

[11] Stigler, same reference as footnote 7, at pp. 189–191.

[12] H. Pasdermadjian, *The Department Store: Its Origins, Evolution and Economics* (London: Newman Books, 1954), p. 111.

4. Some sharing and contracting rests upon *physical production functions*, that is, upon the economies of scale inherent in some retailing operations. Thus, centralized delivery services, whether operated cooperatively or by independent contractors, tend to reduce redundant truck mileage.

5. *Contracting technical tasks to outside specialists*, such as consultants, attorneys, and architects, often provides other economies of scale. Many retail firms have only intermittent need for these specialists. Hence, attempts to perform the work within the firms through employment of the appropriate staffs would involve prohibitive underutilization of expensive personnel.

6. Other economies and diseconomies that lead to performance, sharing, shifting, and contracting decisions arise from man-made *price schedules*, rather than from engineering or production functions.

Retailers in a number of cities now participate in shippers' pools, because of a current and perhaps temporary large differential between freight consolidators' charges and available carload rates. Retailers tend to perform a larger percentage of their advertising tasks than manufacturers do, in part because agency commissions are not paid on local-rate time and space. In an economic sense, no national advertiser really has to consider whether to prepare his own advertisements instead of employing an agency. Retail advertisers have the choice, and frequently elect to perform the work. At the same time, the local-national rate differential helps to create a situation in which many retailers perform space-buying tasks for their suppliers.

7. Some activities are feasible only on a *group basis*.

Inter-firm exchanges of operating ratio statistics (a very common research technique in retailing) and exchanges of information on credit applicants' past payment behavior are two examples of these activities. Such exchanges are often shared or contracted through trade associations, credit bureaus, and similar institutions.

8. *Legal and semilegal requirements* determine the choice of alternatives in a limited number of instances.

Publicly owned retail corporations must delegate their annual audits to outside accountants. Opinions of independent appraisers may be desirable or necessary in connection with insurance and damage claims. State or local licensing requirements may keep some retail corporations from direct performance of such service-trade activities as optometry and theater-ticket brokerage. Social security expenses, wage-and-hour controls, and chain store licensing fees seem to be among the factors that have kept some suppliers (for example, gasoline refiners) from absorbing all retail functions. These suppliers have found both legal and operating advantages in franchise distribution systems where a portion of the work is performed by quasi-independent dealers.

9. Some *unavoidable retail activities*, including bad-debt collection and

attempts to curb shoplifting, tend to engender ill will. Sometimes some of this ill will is transferred to a collection agency, a private detective service, or some other outside scapegoat.

10. The alternatives that are available to individual retailers will be determined in part by *the presence or absence of reliable contractors* charging reasonable fees within particular communities.

Probably, over time, the supply of contractors adjusts reasonably well to retailer demand, but certainly the adjustment is not instantaneous. Similarly, the willingness or nonwillingness of fellow retailers to participate in joint activities will help to determine how much sharing any one retailer can do. Among the conditions that are conducive to this formation of groups are personality factors, historical accidents, and the influence of individual leaders.

11. Only some of the selections from among the four alternatives seem to result from *explicit decisions*.

Often there seems to be almost an innate acceptance of a way of doing business. Hence, some retailers may continue to perform activities that could profitably be transferred to consumers, or to suppliers. Other activities seem to get shifted or transferred by default, rather than through conscious action. Many manufacturers claim that much of their own pre-retailing work has been created by dealer apathy.

12. *Noneconomic factors*, particularly the attitudes of retailers, suppliers, and customers, may be important in decisions to perform, to share, to shift, or to contract out.

Some analysts who have looked at "make or buy" questions in manufacturing feel that executives often elect to make rather than to buy, because of misguided desires for security and independence. Somewhat similar desires may induce retailers to perform things that could best be left to others. However, retailers also know that excessive delegation, sharing, and shifting can destroy the individuality of the store. The problem is to find the appropriate balance.

10

Some observations on "structural" formation and the growth of marketing channels

Ralph F. Breyer

Embedded everywhere in the enormous complex of activities and agreements that characterize the marketing institution is an elemental piece of structure, the so-called marketing channel. In the broadest sense of the term, not only *trading* concerns engaged primarily in selling and buying—producers, wholesalers, retailers, brokers, selling agents, commission houses, etc.—but also *nontrading* concerns engaged principally in other types of marketing activity—commercial banks, transportation and storage companies, insurance companies, and so on—are found in a marketing channel. In this essay, we are concerned only with the trading channel, which consists of various sequences of the former group of "concerns." This channel is, of course, a system, and we shall often refer to it as such. For purposes of this essay, it is sufficient merely to define the term "system" in a broad sense:

From Reavis Cox, Wroe Alderson, and Stanley Shapiro (eds.), *Theory in Marketing* (Homewood, Ill.: Richard D. Irwin, Inc., for the American Marketing Association, 1964), pp. 163–175. Reprinted by permission.

This essay is part of a study of marketing channels being conducted under a grant of Ford Foundation research funds made available to the author by the Wharton School.

"A system is a set of objects together with relationships between the objects and between their attributes."
Being composed of both human beings and machines, the channel is what is often termed a "man-machine" system. This essay is an attempt to answer the following two questions: When does a channel come into existence? What are the more useful indices of overall channel growth? Standing alone, the observations on channel structure presented in this article should help somewhat in the development of more precise concepts than can be used in the study of marketing channel phenomenon.[1]

To qualify as a channel in this essay, the vertical sequence of trading concerns must bridge the *entire* gap between production and the consumer.[2] The vertical positions of the trading concerns are referred to as "levels"—the producer level, the broker level, the wholesaler level, etc. Any vertical section short of the entire length of the channel is termed a "segment"—producer-to-wholesaler, or wholesaler-to-retailer, or producer-to-wholesaler-to-retailer, and so on. Upon occasion, we shall refer to "type" channels, "enterprise" channels, and "business-unit" (often shortened to "unit") channels. The first is a channel identified solely by *types* of concerns, such as manufacturers, brokers, wholesalers, and retailers; the second, by specific independent *ownerships*, termed enterprises. The business-unit channel is defined in terms of each separately named and/or spatially separated *operating unit* of a trading concern (or enterprise). Thus, two trading businesses under *one* ownership, even though located at the same place, would each constitute a "business unit" in a channel if they operated under different trade names. A branch warehouse located at some point other than the headquarters of the parent trading concern would also constitute a separate business unit.[3]

The need for the "business-unit" concept is most obvious in a completely integrated trading channel. Although such a channel is composed of but one enterprise and would be represented as a *P–C* channel, the goods may

[1] This monograph summarizes one part of a broader study of marketing channels which has not yet been completed. In the context of the entire study, the material presented here should take on more meaning and value.

[2] This phrase sounds somewhat "clumsy." If we changed it to "production and consumption," it would literally mean that marketing is carried on right up to the actual time and place of consuming the goods, which is, of course, rarely true. On the other hand, "producer and consumer" fails to indicate specifically that marketing starts *after* production is completed. However, when speaking of channel structure, we are generally dealing with trading *concerns* and shall hereafter use the phrase "producer and consumer" in a sense synonymous with "production and consumer."

[3] Even though this branch house did no selling but merely received, stored, and shipped the goods, it would still be considered part of the *trading* channel, because it is an integral part of a *trading* concern.

actually be "moved"[4] from the producer's plant to one of its wholesale ware-houses and then to one of its retail stores and finally to the consumer. Obviously, in structural terms, the $P–C$ designation is entirely inadequate, as it does not show those business units owned by the producer that are operated at the wholesale and retail levels. In terms of business units, the channel is a $P–W_p–R_p–C$ channel, the subscripts indicating ownership by the producer in this case. Where only partial structural integration exists, as, for example, a warehouse owned by a retailer that received all shipments from producers, the enterprise channel concept should be expressed by $P–R–C$, but structurally, the channel should be represented by $P–W_R–R–C$. Although, strictly speaking, a channel so structured is a hybrid containing enterprise and business-unit elements, it will be termed a "business-unit channel" as long as it contains at least one business unit. The term "trading concern" or "concern" can refer to a nonintegrated ownership such as P in the channel immediately above, or to the concern R which also owns the warehouse W_R, or to the business unit W_R itself, or to all collectively, de-pending upon the context.

For the time being, we shall ignore the "type" channel and assume that the enterprise and business-unit channel happen to be identical. Therefore, we will deal with them as one channel. Usually, we shall use the $P–W–R–C$ channel (producer to wholesaler to retailer to consumer) for illustrative purposes.

A trading channel is formed when trading relations making possible the passage of title and/or possession (usually both) of goods from the producer to the ultimate consumer is consummated by the component trading concerns of the system. Let us assume that producer P_1 franchises or agrees to permit a wholesaler, W_1, to handle his product, and W_1, in turn, franchises or agrees to permit a retailer, R_1, to retail this same product. A trading channel exists once the terms of the franchises or agreements spanning the whole gap from producer to consumer are concluded between concerns assumed to possess the necessary marketing capabilities. Theoretic-ally, not a single unit of the product(s) may be actually marketed by this specific sequence of trading concerns. Nevertheless, in a practical and important sense a channel was formed, since the capacity to "move" the product(s) was brought into being by establishing the requisite trading relations between competent concerns. Except for certain industrial goods, such explicit agreements between the retailer and the *consumer* at the terminal segment of a channel are rare.

Let us now assume that a dealer, R_1, receives an order from an indus-

---

[4] The term "moved" is employed here as a synonym of "marketed" and is *not* restricted to physical movement of the merchandise.

trial consumer for an industrial product manufactured by P_1; a product R_1 has never handled before. Knowing that he cannot deal directly with P_1, R_1 contracts to buy the product from a wholesale distributor, W_1, who also has not handled this product before. W_1 then contracts to purchase it from P_1. As soon as these contracts (orders) are consummated, including the contract (order) between R_1 and the consumer, a trading channel has been formed even though the parties had never traded with one another before and a set of trading relations was not explicitly agreed upon. In this case, the channel system was initiated by the closing of contracts containing firm orders to buy certain amounts of specific goods. This is true even though the product may not actually move through the channel and no passage of title may occur for six months, because the product must be manufactured to order. Although there is no explicit agreement upon trading relations, the establishment of such relations is implicit in the fact of entering into sales-purchase contracts.[5]

The two illustrations provided involve channel formation, because the *intent* is that goods shall move. In the example given in the prior paragraph, suppose that the parties had already established trading relations and were trading in *other* goods under these "agreements." Could we say then that the trading channel for the *new* product already exists? If the *new* product does not require any changes in those trading-relation agreements, we would say "yes." If it does require such alterations, the answers is "no." In any case, one must recognize that although explicitly established trading relations may cover a group of products, a separate and distinct channel exists for each product that actually flows down this particular sequence of trading concerns. In this sense, a new channel is formed *productwise* when a new product moves through an established sequence.[6] A channel is formed, of course, wherever a single product or group of products moves through a new combination of trading concerns. This is true even where the goods are merely consigned or leased at various stages of the channel.

INDIVIDUAL CHANNEL FORMATION

Individual channels usually exist as components of a channel group. Such a group is characterized by a network of trading interconnections which link the trading concerns or units of the group. A single new trading-

---

[5] At times, the goods may be consigned to a trading unit or leased to a consumer. In such cases, sale-purchase contracts of the product per se may never materialize (i.e., lease without purchase option) or are delayed (i.e., consignment sale or lease with purchase option). Here, explicit agreement on trading relations is almost always required.

[6] A further discussion of this situation is found in the following section.

relation agreement is sufficient to establish at least one new channel in such a channel group. To avoid getting bogged down at this stage with the intricacies of channel groups, we shall first take up the *single* channel. A single channel is one that has but one trading concern or trading unit at each level. At times, we shall talk of this channel as if it were "isolated" or "free-standing" rather than one of the constituent channels of a channel group. The "isolated" single channel is defined as one with trading concerns or units that trade *only* with one another. Having finished with the single channel, we will then move on to the channel *group* (network), treated as a given, integrated, "structured" system of which the single channel is a mere subsystem. To qualify as a channel *group*, at least one trading concern or trading unit must have established trading relations with a minimum of two other trading concerns or units operating on the same level. (Whether we should include the consumer, who is, of course, a part of the channel, in these formulations is optional. For some industrial products it may be worthwhile or even imperative. In this essay, unless otherwise stated, the consumer is excluded from the channel in all subsequent discussions.)

One can maintain that a channel exists when and only so long as goods actually flow. It appears more useful, however, to view a channel system as being formed as soon as new trading relations are established and as continuing to exist so long as these trading relations hold.[7] The actual flow of a product through a channel is almost always intermittent. This is even true for large groups of products that are highly seasonal. If we insisted upon an actual flow of goods, we should, strictly speaking, have to accept the view that the channel is dissolved during even brief periods of a few days when no product(s) move through all or part of the channel and, conversely, a new channel is born on each resumption of the flow. Or, less strictly interpreted, such a requirement would compel us to stipulate the maximum time interval of the intermittency permitted before the channel would be classified as having dissolved. This would perforce be a rather arbitrary decision. On the other hand, we must consider the situation where agreements on trading relations continue in force but no goods have "moved" through the channel for an abnormally long period of time. In such case, we might term this a "passive channel system" in contrast to an "active channel system" where intermittency in goods flow is "reasonable" or "normal." When one of the trading concerns of a channel stops handling the product(s), such action, of course, dissolves the channel.

The formation and dissolution of marketing channel systems is a ubiquitous phenomenon which we shall examine first under the assumption

[7] Here, the term "channel system" refers to a single channel, either "isolated" or a constituent of a channel group.

that we have a reasonably large, fixed pattern of trading concern, that is, a large fixed number of producers, of wholesalers, and of retailers available for a P–W–R–C channel structure. We can discern at once at least three different situations. In a highly flexible situation, the trading concerns can and readily do switch their sources of supply or their outlets with minimum inconvenience and cost. If one resource or outlet is readily substituted, such action destroys one channel and creates a second. If a resource or outlet is added or dropped without substitution, there is a net gain (or loss) of one channel. A very considerable part of all consumer-goods marketing, especially that of low unit value, constant demand items, is characterized by flexible trading relations with changes in suppliers and outlets comparatively frequent and widespread.

In contrast to the situation just discussed above is one where more or less continuing trading relations prevail over a considerable period of time. Such stability may be due to true, in contrast to pseudo, franchise arrangements and exclusive distribution agreements. If such arrangements do not embrace the entire channel, they still leave much flexibility for channel formation or dissolution in the remaining segments. But where such agreements exist, the qualifications of both outlet and supplier are carefully examined in advance; fairly detailed stipulations are usually set forth in a written agreement; and substantial commitments respecting selling methods, advertising, service, merchandising help, etc., are made. These tend to cement the relationship more firmly so that dissolution of the channel by abrogation of the agreement is less easily accomplished, and channel formation is generally a slower process. In any case, many such contracts require thirty to ninety days' notice of an intention to cancel.

Finally, only a qualified flexibility respecting channel formation and dissolution exists in the fully integrated channel where production, wholesaling, and retailing units are all owned by one concern.[8] Such complete integration involves a very considerable investment. A large organization must be developed, and great control exercised throughout the length of the channel. Consequently, the substitution of an outside, independently owned, trading concern for one of the owner's own units is much less likely. In this case, as well as where only part of the channel is integrated, the enterprise channel, contrary to our prior stipulation, does differ from the business-unit channel. There is some degree of flexibility in adding or dropping certain of the *business units* owned by any one concern, and such action *could* result in the formation and dissolution of *business-unit* channels.

---

[8] If the producer's plant can, or does, not supply all the goods handled by its wholesale and retail units, then so far as these goods are concerned, the channel is not fully integrated and hence considerable flexibility may exist.

However, since changes in the business-unit channel require considerable investment (or, conversely, the liquidation of a sizeable investment with some possibility of loss), the degree of flexibility in an integrated channel will be rather low, unless the owning agency is supported by considerable financial resources. Where only certain segments of the channel are integrated, the other segments are free of the constraints previously mentioned.

It should be emphasized here that "flexibility" has been used to refer primarily to the ease with which channels are formed and dissolved. Although it is usually the case, such of the channels that exist where conditions are highly flexible may not be of shorter life than those established under less flexible conditions.

For a marketing channel to exist, there generally must be at some time a flow of goods from producer to consumer. "Goods" may mean just one product or several products taken together. In its ultimate sense, the channel concept should be centered on the *single* product. Where several different products flow through the same set of trading concerns, there are an equal number of separate channels productwise. Also, each new product that is introduced creates a new channel productwise, even though no new trading relations are explicitly established. Similarly, the dropping of one product dissolves at least one channel productwise. This view of a channel is justified by the following factors: consumers and traders buy *individual* products; different products may possess markedly different marketing characteristics (selling, merchandising, servicing, pricing, costs, etc.); and individual product identification by such factors as brand or trademark constitutes the nucleus for a unique pattern of competitive effort, even though there will be many other aspects of competition between products.

We have previously assumed that the trading-concern population is fixed in size and pattern. In reality, however, some trading concerns are always going out of business and others entering. With the advent of one new trading concern—manufacturer, wholesaler, or retailer in our $P–W–R–C$ structure—at least one and almost always a considerable number of new channels are formed. Conversely, one or more channels are destroyed as each concern exits. Thus, new concerns and new products are great channel multipliers, with the number of channels increasing much faster than the number of firms or products.

Let us now turn to the "type" channel and contrast it with the enterprise and business-unit channels previously considered. As soon as a new *type* of trading concern enters a given marketing sector, at least one and perhaps several new "type" channels are created. The proliferation of new "type" channels resulting from the development of a new type of marketing agency is, however, much more limited than the increase in enterprise and unit channels that occurs when new trading concern or trading unit makes its appearance. "Type" channels may range from broad to narrow depending upon the "type" classification under which the trading concerns are grouped. The *P–W–R–C* channel is obviously very broad as *all* of the varying kinds of pertinent producers are included in *P*, all wholesalers in *W*, all retailers in *R*, and all consumers in *C*. On the other hand, a *multiple-line* manufacturer to a *full-line, full-service* wholesaler to a *limited-line, limited service* dealer to the consumer would be a much narrower "type" channel. "Types" could be based on the distinctive product or product group handled—an *automobile* manufacturer, a *grocery* wholesaler, a *lumber* dealer—but since we generally have a certain product or product group in mind when analyzing channels, such classification comes into the picture automatically. Even so, where product mix problems at various levels in the channel are important, the "product" classification is inadequate because such mixes may vary widely within any one such classification.[9]

"Type" channel systems are hardy and often compete sharply with one another. In this struggle, some wax, others wane, and the "type" channels which fall in either category may vary from one sector of marketing to another. But it is rather seldom that the "type" channel, especially those based on the broader "type" classifications, go out of existence altogether. Also, the formation of a new "type" channel is a rather infrequent occurrence. Such changes of "type" channels are of much greater consequence than the formation and dissolution of enterprise and business-unit channels, because of the direct effect on a large train of individual trading concerns.

MEASURES OF OVERALL GROWTH FOR THE INDIVIDUAL CHANNEL

Perhaps the best measure of overall growth or decline of a marketing channel (or channel group) could be developed from some kind of sophisticated input-output analysis. Such an analysis is a complex and time-consuming undertaking. What we need at the moment is a more readily computed measure of overall growth. The two best measures appear to be (*a*) the physical units of product "moved" through the channel and (*b*) the dollar spread of the channel for a given time period. Both are at best approximate and are none too satisfactory measures. The physical unit measures the "put-through" of the channel system, as that term is generally used in engineering. Such a measure has the advantage of eliminating price fluctuations. But where the channel handles several products with varying

---

[9] "Sorting" concepts, originally developed by Wroe Alderson, are very important in this connection. See Wroe Alderson, *Marketing Behavior and Executive Action* (Homewood, Ill.: Richard D. Irwin, Inc., 1957), chap. vii, "Matching and Sorting—The Logic of Exchange."

characteristics, it may be impossible to devise a single unit of measure. Moreover, such a measure would not take into account material changes from year to year in the total "service delivered"[10] by the channel for its customer, the consumer. These services, for example, include such factors as product warranties, consumer credit extension, lessening of "outs" at the retail level (which may well require producer and/or wholesaler co-operation), etc.[11]

The dollar spread of the channel should reflect such "service" changes. It would be computed by subtracting from the *retail* dollar volume of the channel—a figure which is the same as the total sales of the retailer R_1—the production costs of the producer P_1 plus the net profits of the producer allocable to production in contrast to marketing. This subtrahend is here termed "production takeout." The allocation of net profit to production would admittedly be quite arbitrary. Perhaps the best method would be to allocate it in the ratio which direct production costs bore to direct marketing costs. This would avoid the difficult task of apportioning overhead between production and marketing. To cancel out the effects of price changes, appropriate deflators would have to be used.

Let us assume retail dollar volume could not be obtained directly, a condition which is much more likely to prevail when channel groups rather than single, isolated channels are studied. One might then derive the retail dollar volume figure by using producer dollar sales volume with wholesaler and retailer margins expressed as percentages of the producer sales dollar; or, if more convenient, by using the wholesaler dollar sales volume and the retailer margin expressed as a percentage of it. Having established the dollar spread figure for the channel, one can compute both absolute and relative growth of the channel. Should relative growth alone be desired, the retail dollar volume alone could be used with the assumption that the percentage which the "production takeout" bore to the retail dollar volume remained the same from year to year.[12]

In all of these computations of channel growth, adjustments would have

[10] The phrase "service delivered" constitutes *all* of the marketing services performed in getting the goods from producer to consumer. It includes that done by the *non*trading agencies, even though they are not part of the *trading* channel. The justification for this interpretation is that it is the *trading* channel (or more accurately, the individual *trading* concerns that compose it) that authorizes and pays for such "nontrading" marketing work.

[11] Variations of service extended by the trading concerns to one another are not relevant, as these merely involve alterations in allocation of such services among the traders. It is true that such reallocations may bring about lower cost, but this is not at the moment a pertinent issue.

[12] In fact, if "production takeout" percentage and all margin percentages downstream remain the same, one could use the producer dollar volume or wholesaler dollar volume figure alone for the computation of *relative growth* (or decline).

to be made for any differences in inventories at each level of the channel at the beginning and at the end of the period.

CHANNEL GROUP FORMATION

Only one factor justifies the attention given to the single, *isolated* channel, a phenomenon almost nonexistent in practice. Knowledge of such a channel is helpful in understanding certain "structural" features of those multiple-channel networks of marketing which were previously termed channel-group systems. Single channels do, of course, exist in practice but as components of a channel group. In fact, we can view a channel group as being made up of a collection of individual channels. These single channels, however, are not isolated because each one of their trading concerns has trade dealings with two or more concerns within the given channel group, and often with outside concerns as well. If channel members deal solely with other trading concerns *within* the given channel group, that channel group is then an "isolated" one. Such "isolated" channel groups exist, and some are very important. The channel group that handles the domestic distribution (and this study is confined to domestic marketing) of the automobiles of one domestic manufacturer is, for example, an isolated one, although with the advent of foreign-made cars this situation is rapidly disappearing.

The channel group is obviously more than a mere collection of individual channels. It is in the nature of a network, the structural configurations of which are well known. The formation of the single, isolated channel is structurally defined in the sense that as soon as the requisite trading relations between the full complement of trading concerns spanning the gap from producer to consumer has been consummated, the channel is formed. By definition, no trading concerns or units may be added or subtracted. But for the channel *group* there is no such definite and fixed point marking the completion of its formation. The channel group configurations that merit analysis are generally the resultant of the interplay of the interests of the various trading concerns embraced by the group. Hence, we would generally "set up" a channel group for study by establishing the interests of one or another trading concern or the common interest of a group of trading concerns as the central focus of the study, such as the interest of a particular producer, or wholesaler, or retailer, or of a certain group of producers making a certain product, or of a group of producers, wholesalers, and retailers all of whom are members of a joint product certification program. The identification of this central focus of interest serves to map the pertinent channel group. The primary interest of a sizeable producer is to establish that network of channels[13] for the marketing of his product(s) which will most effectively exploit the ultimate potential markets and at the same time promise him maximum long-run profits.[14] But for almost any product, qualitative, quantitative, and geographic changes in market-demand patterns, product innovations, entrepreneurial innovations (new types of trading concerns), etc., continually occur. This causes a constant flux in the channel composition of the group as it responds to such alterations.

A producer who seeks 100% distribution makes practically no effort to shape his channel-group structure. Instead, he tries to "pump" his product(s) through whatever channels he can with the hope that nearly all potential ones will finally take on the product(s). The configuration of such a channel group will be highly sensitive to changes in such factors as market conditions and competitive tactics. With the possible exception of some staple manufactured products, such channel groups will exhibit a relatively high degree of instability. Agricultural staples are marketed through highly unstable channel groups. The same holds true for manufactured products sold through agents at some stage in their flow down the channels of the group. If the channel group is a $P–B–W–R–C$ one, and B represents brokers, then the channel configuration will probably be very unstable, as the producers make successive offerings and brokers sell now to certain wholesalers, now to others. A channel is formed every time a wholesaler buys for the first time. When wholesalers who previously purchased refuse to buy, a channel is dissolved if the period of intermittency of purchase is "unreasonably" long.

Very often, however, producers of branded and vigorously promoted items will select the channel group that handles their product(s) with great care and exercise some degree of control over the different trading concerns. Broad gauge marketing policies, objectives, and plans are developed, and an attempt is made to fashion the channel group accordingly. Such "engineered" channel groups are found especially where selective or exclusive distribution policies are followed. In such instances, the formation of the channel group is a comparatively well thought-out and carefully applied process. In this process, however, emphasis is not usually centered as much on *channel* formation as on the individual trading concerns or units to be included. This is true because the trading concern or trading unit is the primary "activating" unit and possesses a closely knit specialized organization with central direction and control. Also, each such concern or unit generally constitutes a common center used by a large number of individual constituent channels of the given channel group. Moreover, as will

[13] See, however, the second following paragraph.

[14] Assuming, for simplicity's sake, that this is his only objective, which is rarely true.

be made clear in a subsequent paragraph, a trading concern or unit is at times only *directly* interested in its *immediate* sources of supply and its *immediate* customers. If the producer decides to add or drop such an individual concern, then *ipso facto* at least one and usually several channels are respectively formed or dissolved. Of course, there are times when unauthorized trading concerns get hold of the producer's product(s), in which case the channel so formed might be termed a "bastard channel." In varying degrees and at varying times, wholesalers and retailers also attempt *full-span* "engineering" of their channel group.

MEASURES OF OVERALL GROWTH FOR THE CHANNEL GROUP

As was true for the single, isolated channel, the most useful measures of overall growth of the channel group are the number of physical units of product(s) put through the channel group and the dollar spread for the channel group. Adaptations and cautions similar to those expressed for the single, isolated channel are also relevant. The application of either of these measures to the channel group is generally more complicated than their application to the single, isolated channel. Usually, a number of the trading concerns in such a group will also be dealing with outside trading concerns. Such dealings must be excluded from the computations, because only those goods which "moved" through channels, all of whose trading concerns are a part of the group, can be considered in measuring that channel group's put-through. Consequently, the nonisolated channel-group measurement of growth would require considerable product coding and many separate records. Even in an isolated channel group, where none of the trading concerns deal with concerns outside the group, if the retail dollar volume figures required for computing dollar channel spread by the use of relative margins is to be derived, such margins would need to be properly weighted. In any case, the considerable differences in growth or decline generally present in the various parts of the channel group would be lost in the *overall* measure for the group. Hence, a great deal of "subgroup" or "subsystem" analysis would be required.[15]

The number of consumers served by the channel group, the types of consumers served, the geographical area of the consumer market, the number of products handled, the number of trading concerns in the group, and the number of constituent channels in the group have but limited useful-

---

[15] See, for example, Reavis Cox and Charles S. Goodman, "Marketing of House-building Materials," *Journal of Marketing*, July, 1956, pp. 36–61. In this original study, the authors develop seven measures of work done in each marketing "flow."

ness as measures of overall channel-group growth.[16] Contrary to appearances, it is not easy to use the number of products handled as a measure of growth. All parts of the channel group may not handle each and every product, and the number of items not universally carried may fluctuate from time to time.

The number of individual constituent channels and the number of trading concerns and/or trading units are two possible measures of growth that would not apply to the single channel. However, both have very little usefulness, as they give ambiguous measures of channel-group growth. For instance, an increase in the number of constituent channels might be caused by the following factors: an increase in the interconnections between the same number of trading concerns handling the same products; an increase in the number of products handled by all or part of the channel group; or an increase in trading concerns or units. Also, growth in the number of trading concerns or units in a channel group may or may not mean an increase in the volume handled or an increased number of constituent channels.

To measure the growth of the individual constituent channels of a channel group would seldom be worthwhile. It would always be more difficult than measuring the growth of single, isolated channels. Products are not easily traced through the many channel routes that tie into *each* trading concern or trading unit. Moreover, a specific trading concern, especially in the nonintegrated channel group, usually has little direct interest in the growth or decline of each specific channel of which it is a part. Its attention is rarely focused beyond its immediate supplier upstream and its immediate outlet downstream. As stated before, however, the measurement of growth by subgroups of channels of a channel group, based on "type" of channel, product(s) handled, geographic areas, etc., might well be worthwhile.[17]

A complicating factor in all cases are the changes that occur over time in the composition of the channel group. Some trading concerns drop out and others come into the group. Consequently, the year-to-year measures of growth or decline are not made with reference to an identical channel-group structure. Even where the set of trading concerns remains the same, the pattern of the interconnections between them, i.e., the individual constituent channel pattern, may be altered. This is especially true for those

---

[16] The author developed a method for establishing such costs for channels and channel groups in his study "Quantitative Systemic Analysis and Control: Study No. 1—Channel and Channel Group Costing," 1949, although his purpose at the time was not the use of such costs for measuring growth.

[17] Here, the channel group is a "mixed" one in that it contains more than one type of channel, such as a channel group with both *P–W–R–C* and *P–R–C* types.

groups where freedom and ease in changing connections are not restricted by selective or exclusive distribution arrangements.

INTEGRATED AND MIXED CHANNEL GROUPS

The formation of fully integrated channel groups is, of course, completely controlled by the single ownership. Although the constituent business units may have limited freedom in determining with whom they will deal, all changes in the structure are dictated by the owner. The channel structure pattern of such a group is comparatively stable. The same measures of growth would apply to it as apply to nonintegrated groups and could probably be computed with less difficulty, because the records kept by the owner would cover the entire channel group. Much the same can be said for the integrated portions of partially integrated channel groups.

Finally, a channel group, unlike the one used for illustrative purposes, may be composed of two or more types of channels. Such a group has already been termed "mixed." A channel group with a mixed structure will be more adaptable to the requirements of varying marketing situations. In addition, it is generally known that some of the most severe competition in marketing occurs between the various types of channel groups. Much the same situation with respect to formation and growth exists for the "mixed" and the "simple" (one-type) channel group.

11

The structure of wholesaling
in the United States:
channels

David A. Revzan

THE CONCEPT OF MARKETING ORGANIZATION
THROUGH THE CHANNEL

Ordinarily, marketing organization would be visualized mainly in its internal aspects: that is, primarily how individual business enterprises engaged in the work of marketing allocate responsibilities among the various personnel in relation to authority; what type of organizational framework is applicable; what span of executive control is visualized; and whether or not decentralization of authority is utilized. These aspects and their relationship to policy formation and functional arrangements are analyzed completely in later chapters.

Within the content of this chapter, marketing organization is studied only in its external aspects. In this perspective, it is concerned with how agencies related directly, semidirectly, or indirectly to the functions of marketing are so intertwined with each other that some semblance of orderly

From David A. Revzan, *Wholesaling in Marketing Organization* (New York: John Wiley & Sons, Inc., 1961), Chapter 5. Reprinted by permission.

relationship can be detected. The main vehicle for this orderly relationship, as will be seen, is the channel of distribution. But the concept of marketing organization in these external aspects also connotes the existence of systematic relationship in terms of the geographic units involved. In this sense, it has a very close tie-in with the motion of area structure discussed in the preceding chapter. Thus, the external view of marketing organization is a result of the concept of level of business activity, of specialization of labor, and of function and process (marketing) as they relate to structure.

Within this context of marketing organization, the most important factors acting as influencing agents are: The physical and dollar volume of goods and services to be marketed; the varietal composition of the goods and services included in the preceding; the evaluation of specialized management abilities within the marketing framework; the increasing diversification of types of users of products; the increasing diversification of locations of buyers and sellers; the increasing diversification of the auxiliary marketing functions; the changing sizes and policies of business firms; and the effects of government activities.

The Meaning of Channel of Distribution

The word "channel" has its origins in the French word for canal. It thus connotes, in its marketing application, a pathway taken by goods as they flow from point of production to points of intermediate and final use. But in these flows there is a further connotation of a sequence of marketing agencies; namely, the wholesale and retail middlemen who perform, type by type, various combinations of marketing functions at various points in the channel in order to facilitate such flows. In addition, there is a connotation of a sequence of facilitating agencies which perform auxiliary functions at one or more points within the channel. Some writers view each functional or subfunctional grouping as giving rise to flows. The channel is, therefore, the vehicle for viewing marketing organization in its external aspects and for bridging the physical and nonphysical gaps which exist in moving goods from producers to consumers through the exchange process, including the determination of price.

The channel thus bridges the gap, geographically speaking, between producers and users. In this sense, distance is involved not only in the usual terms of miles (or an equivalent measure) but also in terms of the times involved and the costs of communication and transportation. In addition to time in this aspect, the channel has a function to perform in bridging time gaps in the pure storage sense. Thus, within the channel, certain types of middlemen and certain special agencies arise to carry physical inventories (and to change their physical characteristics) over periods of time. In addition, the channel is useful in bridging gaps in product assortment patterns by matching sellers' inventories—in physical and qualitative aspects—with buyers' inventory intentions. More will be said of this function of channels in later sections. Finally, the channel is a means of bridging gaps in knowledge and in the communication of that knowledge. It becomes, accordingly, a structural arrangement whereby sellers (or their middlemen representatives) search for customer prospects with whom to communicate and to whom sales can ultimately be made, and whereby buyers, in turn, search for sellers carrying the assortments desired from whom purchases ultimately can be made.

The concept of the channel of distribution involves, in addition to these characteristics, sets of vertical and horizontal relationships between various types of wholesale and retail middlemen. As such, it can be used as the keystone for the analysis of various "circuit" and "flow" arrangements centering around these management aspects. Based upon all of these considerations, there can evolve systematic analysis of such problems as: (a) the characteristics of various types of channel structures; (b) the power focus of the management element in each kind of channel structure; (c) comparisons between these as to relative short-run and long-run efficiency; (d) comparative costs of keeping and defending existing channels of distribution as against selecting new types.

From this lengthy definition of the channel and its characteristics, it follows that the channel is composed of the following:

1. A series of more or less complicated connections between business units or groups of business units by means of which the center of marketing activity is effected; namely, the transfer of legal possession or right or use by means of buying and selling activities. At the wholesaling sector there may be more than one cycle of buying-selling relationships in the channel.
2. A pattern of physical flow of the commodity or commodities involved which may parallel the business connections in (1) or move through different business unit arrangements.
3. Further patterns designed to show flows of other auxiliary activities.[1]

The business units involved in channels of distribution, other than the wholesale and retail middlemen as such, may be classified as follows:[2]

---

[1] R. Vaile, E. T. Grether, and R. Cox, *Marketing in the American Economy* (New York: The Ronald Press Co., 1952). These authors speak of *forward flows* of physical possession, ownership and negotiation; *backward flows* of ordering and payment; and *combination flows* of information, financing, and risking.

[2] In this classification scheme, any one of the groups may appear in the channel as an originating seller; as an intermediate or final buyer; as a provider of some primary or auxiliary function within the channel; or a combination of these.

I. *Extractive Industry Establishments*
   A. Agriculture.
   B. Forestry.
   C. Fisheries.
   D. Mining (metal, anthracite coal, bituminous coal, crude petroleum and natural gas, and nonmetallic mining and quarrying).
II. *Contract Construction*
III. *Manufacturing Establishments*[3]
IV. *Finance, Insurance, and Real Estate Agencies*
   A. Banking.
   B. Securities brokers, dealers, exchanges.
   C. Finance agencies, n. e. c.
   D. Insurance carriers.
   E. Insurance agents and combination offices.
   F. Real Estate.
V. *Transportation Agencies*
   A. Railroads freight and passenger.
   B. Local and highway passenger.
   C. Highway freight transportation and warehousing.
   D. Water.
   E. Air.
   F. Pipelines.
   G. Services allied to transportation.
VI. *Communications and Public Utilities Agencies*
   A. Telegraph telephone, and related.
   B. Radio broadcasting and television.
   C. Utilities—electric and gas.
   D. Local utilities and public service, n. e. c.
VII. *Services*
   A. Hotels and other lodgings.
   B. Personal.
   C. Private households.
   D. Commercial and trade schools and employment agencies.
   E. Business services, n. e. c.
   F. Miscellaneous repair services and hand trades.
   G. Motion pictures.
   H. Amusement and recreation (except motion pictures).
   I. Medical and other health services.
   J. Engineering and other professional services, n. e. c.

[3] See the classification used in Chapter 4.

The Channel and Linkages and Blockages

In terms of physical analogies, the channel has been referred to as a canal in which is contained the variegated physical flow of goods. But in view of the complex array of business units as classified which may be involved in one or all aspects of channel functions, the channel may be visualized also as a chain-link arrangement in which each business is in effect one link. Thus, the channel may be here visualized as a series of linkages which vary as to the number of links, as to the functions to be performed by each link and the entire set of linkages, and according to the "thickness" and strength of each link. Some links are dominant, as will be discussed in the next chapter, whereas others play a subordinate role. Closely related to this is the situation wherein some links are engaged in the primary functions of marketing, whereas others function merely as facilitating or auxiliary links.

It is in the functioning of the channel as a series of linkages that there arises also the phenomenon of blockages. In a sense, blockages may be visualized as the activities of one or more links (business units) in a particular channel to protect the economic status of that channel by placing barriers (blockages) in the way of competing channels. These blockages may consist of such legal devices as an exclusive agency franchise arrangement preventing any links in the channel from handling competitive products; they may consist of various forms of legislation designed to restrict the units permitted to market particular products; they may represent manufacturers control over resale prices; or they may represent collusive activity within or outside the letter and the spirit of the law. Such blockages may have only very temporary success, or they may have elements of permanency, or they may generate their own destruction by giving alternative channels and their own linkages considerably more motivation than might be otherwise expected.

The Relationship of the Channel of Distribution to the "Funnel" Concept

The channel is the concrete marketing organizational framework in which the abstract concept of the funnel is executed. The funnel depends on one or more of the types of channels to be discussed later to become a reality. Depending upon the channel and the sum total of the functioning of its component links, the funnel concept may or may not be completely realized. The sum total of the functioning of all channels becomes the basis, in turn, for the approximation of the funnel concept in its total abstract meaning.

Types of Notation Systems for Channel Diagrams

As a final preliminary to the discussion of types of channels, a word needs to be said about how channel diagrams are constructed. In general, the components of the channel diagram consist of: (a) a box enclosing the title of and the type of agency making up a link; (b) a solid or broken line indicating, accordingly, either physical or nonphysical flows; (c) an arrow indicating the direction of the flow; and (d) a box enclosing the title and type of each using agency at the end of the channel. In addition, notation schemes may be used to indicate and differentiate primary agencies from auxiliary or facilitating agencies. By means of varying widths of lines, the proportionate importionate importance of each segment flow through each agency combination can be shown.

Some simple diagrams may indicate each of these aspects of the notation systems. Figure 11.1 illustrates some kinds of notation systems which may be used to designate the agencies (links) involved in channel diagrams. Any geometric design is permissible, although in actual practice there is no hard and fast line of distinction. Figure 11.2 shows the notation systems typically used for designating the type and direction of flows. Solid lines are the orthodox notational scheme for indicating the physical flow of the commodity or commodities involved. Broken lines generally denote the nonphysical flows and may be further coded to reflect each type of such flows.

Figure 11.3 shows a concrete illustration of an actual channel for fresh California tomatoes in which the width of the lines shows the relative importance of the flows based upon the total volume sold. It will be noticed that no detailed breakdowns are given of the agency links; but it should be noticed, also, that the area of each circle is proportionate to the volume handled.

In the absence of any standardized notational system, it is obvious that the numerous channel diagrams available show a wide variety of notational framework found in the discussion of types of channels which follows. Any one using channel diagrams ought to be in a position of obtaining from such diagrams the kind of information which may be useful in understanding channel structure.

FIGURE 11.1

NOTATION SYSTEM FOR AGENCIES IN CHANNEL.

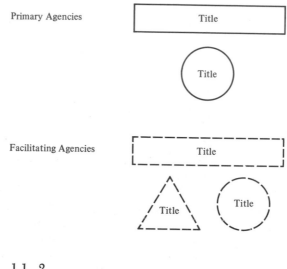

Primary Agencies

Facilitating Agencies

FIGURE 11.2

NOTATION SYSTEM FOR TYPES AND DIRECTION OF FLOWS.

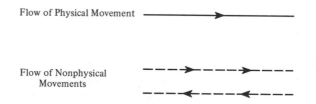

Flow of Physical Movement

Flow of Nonphysical Movements

One other aspect of channel diagram notation may be useful, namely, the indication of the direction and extent of management control. The form used is by Duddy and Revzan[4] (see Figure 11.4) and is used to explain the evolution of more complex forms of channel organization.

TYPES OF CHANNELS OF DISTRIBUTION

There are perhaps five important variables which affect the classification of types of channels: (1) Channels may be distinguished according to the

[4] E. A. Duddy and D. A. Revzan, *Marketing: An Institutional Approach,* 2nd ed. (New York: McGraw-Hill Book Co., Inc., 1953), p. 266.

FIGURE 11.3

DEALER TYPES HANDLING FRESH TOMATOES SOLD AT RETAIL IN NORTHERN AND CENTRAL CALIFORNIA SUMMER AND FALL, 1948.

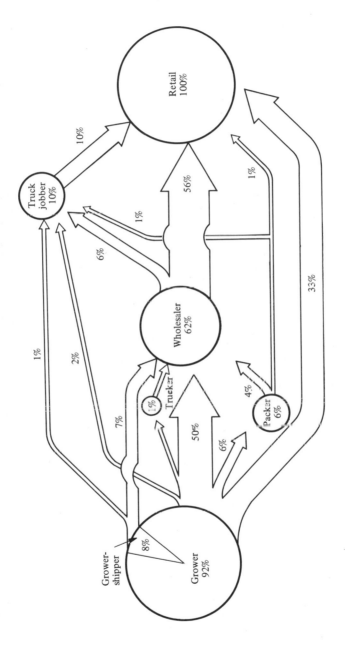

(*Source:* Walter D. Fisher, *California Fresh Tomatoes—Marketing Channels and Gross Margins from Farm to Consumer—Summer and Fall, 1948*, University of California, College of Agriculture (Berkeley), mimeographed Report No. 113, June 1951.)

number of links (intervening business agencies) involved; (2) channels may be differentiated according to their relative level of importance or their position within the entire framework of marketing; (3) channels may be differentiated according to the type of managerial control manifested; (4) channels may be separated according to the breadth of business penetration which may be presented; and (5) channels may be designated according to the types of flows indicated above.

FIGURE 11.4

PROGRESSION FROM SIMPLE TO COMPLEX CHANNELS.

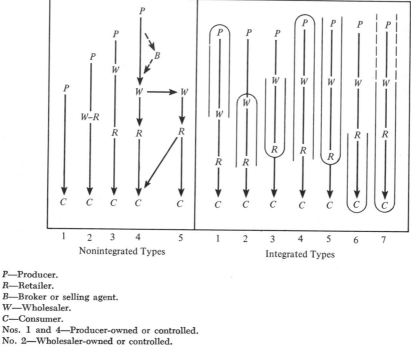

Nonintegrated Types   Integrated Types

P—Producer.
R—Retailer.
B—Broker or selling agent.
W—Wholesaler.
C—Consumer.
Nos. 1 and 4—Producer-owned or controlled.
No. 2—Wholesaler-owned or controlled.
Nos. 3 and 5—Retailer-owned or controlled.
Nos. 6 and 7—Consumer-owned and operated.

Obviously, this classification format is so cross-related that any collection of channel diagrams may have to undergo multiple assortment. Presumably, a sixth classification basis could emphasize, by evaluating the five types indicated above, the relative degree of simplicity or complexity found in any given channel situation. But this is a far less satisfactory basis for classification than any of the preceding five indicated.

Channels, By Number of Links

This is the oldest and most orthodox classification scheme used in the marketing literature. Based on the number of links, it distinguishes between direct, semidirect, and indirect channels, and, in addition, has both a commodity and functional aspect. A *direct channel* is characterized by the existence of a single-link pattern; namely, direct contact between manufacturer (or other producer) and user. The producer may assume full responsibility for the marketing functions and for the establishment of communication between himself and the users; or the user may assume full responsibility for the functions and communication. There may be, and usually are, facilitating agencies involved; but the main characteristic is the directness of both the physical and nonphysical flows. The producer may send his salesmen directly to the customers' place of business or residence; the customer may send his buyer to the producer's place of business; or a specialized facility may be used, such as a roadside stand or a mail-order catalog.

Indirect channels represent the opposite spectrum from that of the direct channel. By indirect is meant the insertion between producer and user of more than one type of wholesale middleman if the commodity is of the industrial goods type, and of more than one type of each of wholesale and retail middleman if the commodity is of the consumers' goods category. Indirect channels represent, accordingly, the most complex arrangements from the point of view of both the number of linkages and blockages and the variety of types of middlemen involved.

Semidirect channels represent an intermediate situation between these extremes. Only one type of wholesale middleman may be involved in the case of industrial goods, or only one type of wholesale and of retail middleman may be involved. There is no hard and fast dividing line between the semidirect and indirect channels.

In each of these cases, the characteristics as to number of links are modified by the kinds involved and by the middlemen's adaptations of the functions which need to be performed. For example, both roadside stands and municipal farmers' markets become physical parts of the direct channels for certain kinds of agricultural products. They are not found, on the other hand, in the direct channels either for industrial or manufactured consumers' goods. Again, certain types of organized wholesale market facilities become part of the indirect channels for certain types of agricultural goods but not for the other categories. It may be stated somewhat categorically that the direct channels usually involve the performance of a much wider range of primary and auxiliary functions by the middlemen included than is likely to be the case either for indirect or semidirect channels.

Channels According to Level of Importance

Where a channel exists which makes use of more than one combination of agencies, a differentiation may be made between that part of the channel which is a primary level of importance and that part which is of auxiliary importance. Thus, in Figure 6, it is apparent that the primary channel for fresh California tomatoes consists of (a) the movement from grower → to wholesaler → to → retailer; and (b) the direct movement from grower → to → retailer. The same diagram shows at least six auxiliary channels which account for substantially minor proportions of the total movement of the product.

Channels, By Type of Control

This classification scheme introduces the element of managerial integration, and subdivides channels into producer controlled, wholesale-middlemen-controlled and retailer-middlemen-controlled. Subclassifications can be introduced by the type of operation found within each group. However, a much more useful subclassification scheme can be based upon the type of horizontal and vertical integration found in the channel.[5]

The horizontally integrated channel includes two types. Type A involves a single management which controls a number of units all handling the same general assortments of commodities on the same business plane, viz., production, wholesale market, or retail market. Type B involves a similar arrangement of units, but these units together or separately handle either complementary product lines, or completely unrelated lines, or combinations of both. In both types, the controlling management pursues a unified profit policy.

The *vertically integrated* channel is subdivided into two types, and each of these is, in turn, further subdivided into three groups. Type A represents a channel arrangement in which the vertically integrated firm controls a number of different operations in production and/or marketing of *similar* commodities on successive business levels. This type is subdivided into: (a) the *backward vertical integration* form, in which the controlling business firm is further away from the ultimate consumer in the channel than any other agency link; (b) the *forward vertical integration* form, in which the controlling business firm is further away from the ultimate consumer in the channel than any other agency link; and (c) the form which is a combination of (a) and (b). Subgroup (a) may be termed retailer-controlled for edible agricultural products and manufactured consumers'

---

[5] The discussion which follows is based to a considerable extent upon Werner Z. Hirsch, "Toward a Definition of Integration," *The Southern Economic Journal*, XVII (October 1950), 159–165, and his longer version of the article in typed manuscript form.

goods products, while subgroup (b) may be subdivided into producer-controlled or wholesale-middleman-controlled.

Type B of the vertically integrated channel consists of the complementary vertically integrated firm which controls a number of different operations in the marketing and/or production of complementary products on successive business levels. This type also is subdivided into three groups as follows: (a) the *divergent forward variety*, in which a firm begins with one or a few commodities and then divides these into numerous complementary products as they flow closer and closer to the consumer; (b) the *convergent backward variety*, in which a firm "pulls" in numerous raw materials and services in order to manufacture and place in the channel one or just a few commodities; and (c) the *forward parallel variety*, in which firms merely begin with a given number of complementary products and push these along in the channel without any significant change in number.

There are in addition to these groupings two types of a combination of the horizontally integrated and vertically integrated channel. Type A consists of a joint horizontally and vertically integrated firm which controls a number of vertically integrated units all handling *similar* products at successive levels of the channel. Type B consists of the same kind of arrangement in which the controlled vertically integrated units all handle *complementary* products. Each of these types may be subdivided into the same subgroupings as type B of the vertically integrated channel.

Some discussion may be pertinent at this point of the main devices used by business firms to achieve complete or partial integration of the forms noted. The most obvious and completely successful device is for the controlling business unit to acquire the direct ownership and management of all units involved in the channel of distribution. Control may also be acquired through ownership of the patents of the basic machinery used in the production process or through legal control over an entire product or family of products. Policies may be dictated through the many-sided forms of interlocking directorates or other financial-organizational controls.

A much more informal but, nevertheless, very effective control may be achieved by aggressive sales promotion by any agency in the channel which is designed to enhance that agency's control over part or all of the channel. These tactics may establish strong brand preferences which may "force" the product through the channel over the opposition of intermediate channel agencies; or they may open other areas of informal integration. Any agency may attempt to secure informal integration by prepackaging policies and by such inventory tactics as full-line forcing. The extension of credit arrangements and the use of such legal devices as exclusive dealer franchise contracts may act as the basis for informal integration. The use of resale price maintenance agreements extends the manufacturer's control through the length and breadth of the channel. Finally, such tactics as sharing-the-market agreements or cartels act as very potent integrating forces in the channel until dissolved by the extension of government regulation.[6]

Channels, By Breadth of Business Penetration

It is obvious that channel structure begins with the individual channel arrangement which exists for the product (or products) produced by a given producing unit. From this beginning arrangement, there may emerge as many such channels as there are producing units. Every change in the number of producing units or in the number and types of products produced can lead to changes, in turn, in the number and format of each of these individual producers' channels.

These individual producers' channels may be combined, in turn, into two different group arrangements. Products of homogeneous marketing characteristics can be grouped together into a *product family* channel. Thus, all the individual producers' channels for soaps and detergents may be grouped into a soap-and-detergent group channel. Or, using the classification scheme discussed in Chapter 4, individual producer channels may be grouped, in turn, into industry channels, using either the two-digit basis of classification only or adding the three-digit and four-digit subgroupings. Finally, product group and/or industry channels may be further combined into channels for extractive industry products, channels for industrial goods products, and channels for manufactured consumers' goods products.

Channels, By Types of Flows

It has been indicated that, so far as flows are concerned, most marketing studies separate the physical from the nonphysical flows. But, as has also been indicated, some writers subdivide the nonphysical flows into several component types. Although not much attention will be given to these subdivisions in this book, the reader should be aware that some writers devote a considerable amount of detailed description and diagrammatic representation to these flows.[7]

THE GEOGRAPHIC STRUCTURE OF CHANNELS OF DISTRIBUTION

Although the usual notation systems used for channels of any of the types discussed in the preceding section do not indicate their geographic characteristics, it should be obvious that channels reflect all of the geo-

---

[6] At this point, the reader should keep in mind the relationship between this discussion and the previous discussion of linkages and blockages.

[7] Vaile, Grether, Cox, *op. cit.*, Chapters 5, 7.

graphic characteristics discussed in Chapter 4. The agencies involved in any channel of distribution represent, among other things, a series of individual decisions by individual business firms as to where to locate a particular establishment. Each establishment in the channel has a geographic zone of influence which represents decisions of some individual firm or group of firms as to what the wholesale and, in the case of consumers' goods, retail trading areas are, measured potentially and in actuality. It has been indicated that these areas change in boundaries with varying degrees of frequency based upon many variables.

Since so much information has to be included in the notation systems for channel diagrams, it should be obvious as to why the geographic aspects are frequently excluded. This exclusion is done for purposes of making the channel diagrams manageable both in physical size and in comprehensibility.

This short section has been included for those readers interested in the full complexity of channel diagrams, and to point out that there is a wealth of complicated geographic data which have not been omitted simply because no notation has been made.[8]

CHANNEL STRUCTURE, THE NATURE OF THE COMMODITY, AND COMMODITY FLOWS

The purpose of this section is to sketch the approach to be taken in succeeding sections in adapting the general outline of channel structure, as discussed in previous sections, to the particular position occupied by wholesale middlemen in channels found in particular commodity situations. It should be apparent that little or no attention can be given here to those types of channels used in marketing the products of individual producing firms.

In the following sections the discussions will center around the channels of distribution for the following industry and product groupings:

I. *Channels of Distribution for Agricultural Products*
   A. Products to be processed.
      1. Moving to industrial users.
      2. Moving to ultimate consumers.
   B. Products moving to ultimate consumers without processing.
II. *Channels of Distribution for Other Extractive Industry Products*

---

[8] R. F. Breyer has a very interesting way in which to diagram a geographic pattern. See his *The Marketing Institution* (New York: McGraw-Hill Book Co., Inc., 1934), Chapter X, and especially Figs. 14–20 therein. But even these diagrams are only suggestive of the complete range of agencies which can be included in a limited representation of the geographic detail. However, the treatment is in the usual highly imaginative and valuable style of Breyer's writings on marketing organization.

III. *Channels of Distribution for Manufactured Industrial Goods*
 A. Products entering directly into the production of other products.
 B. Products facilitating further production.
 C. Products for nonmanufacturing types of customers.
IV. *Channels of Distribution for Manufactured Consumers' Goods*
 A. Durables.
 B. Semidurables.
 C. Nondurables (except agricultural).
 V. *Channels of Distribution for Services*
 A. Business and government services.
 B. Personal services.

In developing the discussion under each subgrouping, it is assumed that the reader has been exposed to the wealth of detail on commodity marketing presented in the better basic marketing textbooks. It is further assumed that he has been exposed to diagrammatic materials which exist for the various commodity and industry channels. With these assumptions in mind, the discussion under each heading will present the following pattern of analysis: (1) The underlying conditions of production which are related to channel structure; (2) the commodity characteristics which bear importantly on the channels of distribution; and (3) the factors that explain the importance of wholesale middlemen in the direct, semidirect, and indirect channels. A final section will deal with the factors that influence the choice of individual manufacturing units for their particular products.

CHANNELS OF DISTRIBUTION—
RAW MATERIALS, AGRICULTURAL PRODUCTS

Characteristics of Production

Agriculture is a series of industries involved in producing a wide range of edible and inedible products which have, in turn, wide variations in physical characteristics, in volume moving to market, in value characteristics, and in conditions of production. Some of the geographic conditions of production have been indicated in Chapter 4. In terms of producing units, the number of farms in the United States in 1950 totaled 5.4 million, with an average size of only 215 acres. All but one third of these are unimportant as commercial producers; nevertheless, the less important units do contribute variable quantities of agricultural products into the marketing channels. Because of locational dependence upon natural production factors —soil, climate, topography—many farms are at considerable geographic distances from consuming markets. Thus, transportation and storage are of even greater significance than for most manufacturing industries.

Conditions of production range from rudimentary dependency upon manual labor for some crops to a revolutionary increase in the use of machinery at the production and harvesting phases. Fertilizers, medicines, and insecticides, together with various forms of botanical experimentation, have increased sharply the yields of crops per acre and of animals. Yet, the time cycle of production remains relatively rigid, ranging from a few weeks, relatively speaking, for certain truck crops to a period of perhaps 5 years before a citrus fruit tree may reach the maturity period of commercial yield.

It must be emphasized in a discussion of this kind that agricultural production, in a collective sense, is essentially speculative. This is so because of the relative unpredictability of weather conditions (despite recent improvements in forecasting techniques) and, similarly, of such related environmental factors as the presence of plant-destroying insects, and the like. This uncertainty affects both the quality of the crop and animal production involved. Obviously, the shorter the period of harvest, the greater the impact of the risk.

These variables have some very marked effects on the channel structure. For one, a great deal of emphasis must be placed upon the necessity of providing agricultural producers with a variety of alternatives so far as liquidation of output for cash and transfers of ownership are concerned. Structurally, the middlemen in the channel must be attuned especially to the phases of concentration and equalization processes within their respective channel positions. Also, a great deal of specialization must be manifested by these middlemen in the price-determining and risk-bearing aspects of the channel structure. Grading and packaging aspects become magnified in importance, also, as compared with factory production.

Commodity Characteristics

The raw-material agricultural products are divided into foods, fibres, and other groupings. The food group has crops and animals as its initial subdivision. The food crops are mainly as follows: The grains (wheat, corn, oats, barley, rye); fruits and vegetables for canning, preserving, and fast freezing; cane and beet sugar; and the vegetable oils—soybeans, cottonseed, etc. The food animals are the livestock group (cattle, calves, hogs, and sheep); and the poultry group (chickens, turkeys, ducks, etc.). In the fibre group are included both animal and vegetable—cotton, wool, hemp. Finally, the "other" category includes the inedible derivatives from livestock, the industrial uses of grains and soybeans; the production of seed crops and breeding animals; and tobacco.

These raw materials have several characteristics which affect the existing channel structures. They vary widely as to the quantities available to be marketed, as to relative perishability, as to susceptibility to grading and standardization, as to the length of the marketing period, as to the variety of producing conditions, and, finally, as to the stage of development of the manufacturing utilization of raw materials. In general, they vary also as to the need which exists for the utilization in the channel of organized as against nonorganized local and central market facilities.

Factors Explaining the Variable Importance of Wholesale Middlemen

From preceding discussions, the following aspects of the role of whole-sale middlemen in the marketing of raw-material agricultural products will have been noted: (1) The existence of certain types of assemblers, such as the grain elevators, local buyers, cooperative shipping associations, which facilitate the performance of the various components of the concentration process; (2) the decision of many agricultural producers to maintain owner-ship control of their products while using specialists—mainly agent middle-men—to carry on the remaining marketing functions through the channel; (3) the existence of organized central commodity markets which, by virtue of their location relative to agricultural producers, require various types of wholesale middlemen who, as members, represent these producers or repre-sent buyers; (4) the existence of other organized markets with such restric-tive membership requirements that more frequently than not wholesale middlemen specialists will be needed; and (5) wholesale middlemen who represent buyers while moving from one agricultural producing area to another.

The resultant of the operation of these forces is a complex mixture of direct, semidirect, and indirect channel arrangements for the same class of raw materials. For the highly perishable raw materials, the role of the nonintegrated wholesale middleman is likely to be at a minimum level because of the necessary close proximity of processing facilities to produc-ing areas. For products such as livestock, there has been an increasing pro-portion of the output moving through direct channels, but there is a very considerable volume moving through semidirect and indirect channels. In these latter cases, the commission agent, the broker, the cooperative market-ing associations, and merchant wholesalers (especially the regular whole-saler) emerge to positions of greatest importance. For export and import trade movements, such wholesale middlemen as exporters, importers, export agents, and import agents assume increased importance. For those com-modities sold on the speculative exchanges, the buying and selling brokers assume considerable importance.

Based on the 1954 Census data, it is apparent that, of the total 1954 wholesale sales of raw-material agricultural products, the agent-broker group was most important with 42.7 per cent of the total, duplicated sales volume. The merchant wholesalers group accounted for 34.3 per cent, and the assemblers for the remainder 22.9 per cent. Such integrated middlemen of importance as are found are the cooperative marketing and shipping associations included in the agent-broker and assembler groups. These data do not reflect, of course, the activities of those buyers employed by manufacturers who do not operate separate places of business.

CHANNELS OF DISTRIBUTION— EDIBLE AGRICULTURAL PRODUCTS

Production Characteristics

The production characteristics for these commodities are identical with those listed above for the raw-material category. This is especially so for those types of edible products also classified as raw-material types of products.

Commodity Characteristics

Most of these edible products are, by physical nature, extremely perishable. At the same time, the variable-equality characteristics, noted above, place a very high premium on sales by inspection. The channel structure must provide, accordingly, for rapid physical flows while still permitting such sales by inspection to take place at any transaction center within the channel.

Highly variable relationships exist as to the length of the marketing season for each category of product. Some fresh fruits such as strawberries may be available for only a few weeks of the year, depending, in part, upon the accessibility of a given market to the sources of supply. Other commodities, by virtue of both their growing seasons and the diversity of producing areas together with their ability to be stored for long periods, may be available in "fresh" condition during every week of the year. Examples of such commodities are potatoes, onions, and apples. There are, of course, several gradations between these two extremes.

The fresh, edible products vary according to weight-value relationships. At one extreme are the bulky products of corresponding heavy weights, such as potatoes and cabbage. Generally, but not always, these have the lower relative prices per pound. At the opposite extreme are the fancy fruits and vegetables, relatively lighter in basic selling weights, and usually commanding relatively higher prices, especially when the first shipments of the season take place. These are, of course, only average tendencies, and there are many exceptions.

These categories of commodities vary widely in susceptibility to packaging. Where the products tend to be of very uniform quality and can be assorted by sizes without affecting quality, packaging may enhance the products' value and facilitate movement through the channel. On the other hand, basic physical characteristics together with highly variable runs of sizes and low unit values may make packaging unsuccessful. As the quality and ingenuity of packages and packaging materials continue to improve, and as the demands of self-service marketing continue to require more and more prepackaging, a larger proportion of these products will appear in some form of packaging, including the use of bindings as for bananas and for some forms of lettuce.

Related to the commodity characteristics as they affect the channel structure are certain demand characteristics. First to be noticed is the existence of an important institutional demand as well as ultimate consumer demand. The nature of the institutional demand stemming from restaurants, hotels, dining cars, hospitals, and the like requires a completely different channel structure than do the movements to ultimate consumers either through retail agencies or by means of direct channels. These institutional buyers have different quality and unit purchase requirements than do ultimate consumers. Obviously, the channel will have less need to provide prepackaging for these customers than for ultimate consumers.

Ultimate consumers, as of the present period, have variable reactions to the purchase of fresh products as against utilizing fast-frozen products. With the design of the modern refrigerator and the use of deep-freeze cabinets, many households prefer to stock fast-frozen products in preference to more frequent purchases of the fresh products. As a result, many ultimate consumers have highly fluctuating demands for the fresh products, and this places considerable stress, in turn, on the various types of food stores handling the perishable produce. There is, of course, some underlying foundation by virtue of the fact that some fruits and vegetables do not have any fast-frozen equivalents.

Factors Explaining the Variable Importance of Wholesale Middlemen

There are some conditions which are favorable to the marketing of fresh, edible products through direct channel arrangements, but these are relatively unimportant. Quality considerations, freshness, and the availability of specialized farmers' market facilities are among the reasons why direct channels exist and will be used. But, in view of the varying quantities and varieties of the products to be marketed and the widespread geographical distribution of users, such channel arrangements can do only a fraction of the marketing job.

Accordingly, the bulk of these products must move through considerably more complicated semidirect and indirect channels. The wholesale middlemen tend to be classed in the following functional-process positions in the channel.

1. The *assemblers* group, consisting mainly of those middlemen close to the producers, who conform to the marketing pattern of arranging for partial or complete aspects of the process of concentration. Thus, they may be producer-oriented, as in the case of cooperative shipping associations; or they may be wholesale-market-oriented, as local representatives of central market wholesalers; or they may be representatives of the large-scale retailers, as the corporate chain buyers. They may be used to facilitate the producers' continuous control of legal ownership; or they may provide him with the earliest channel opportunity for liquidation of harvestings for cash while providing for the transfer of ownership.

2. The *central market middlemen* group consisting, on the one hand, of the agent middlemen representing the producers. Of these, depending upon the product and whether or not physical possession of inventories is necessary to the channel structure, the more important would be the auction companies, brokers, commission agents, and cooperative marketing agencies. A second group consists of the orthodox wholesalers, the voluntary chain representatives, and related types, all of whom own the fresh products offered for sale. A third group represents, on either an agent or merchant middleman basis, the larger institutional buyers noted above. And a fourth group of wholesaler merchants, especially the orthodox wholesaler and the truck distributor, supply the assortment needed by the non-integrated or semi-integrated food stores. These middlemen are involved, collectively, in the equalization process and the beginnings of the dispersion process.

3. The final set of middlemen, completing the dispersion process, consists of the various forms of retail and service agencies who sell the products directly to the ultimate consumers or who use the products in the preparation of meals to be served to these consumers.

On a combined basis, the distribution of 1954 sales of edible farm products was as follows: By merchant wholesalers, 49.1 per cent; by assemblers, 21.7 per cent; by agents and brokers, 17.0 per cent; and by manufacturers' sales branches and sales offices, 12.2 per cent. The gross sales value of the products handled was $12.4 billion.

CHANNELS OF DISTRIBUTION—
OTHER EXTRACTIVE INDUSTRY PRODUCTS

Production Characteristics

The main categories of products to be considered are petroleum, lumber and forest products, ferrous and nonferrous ores, and coal and coke. Except for the lumber group, the products involved are all located in mines, or their equivalents, below the surface of the earth or of bodies of water. These deposits are not replaceable, as is the case for lumber. And, as already noted for agricultural products, the quality of the raw-material deposits is not controllable to any extent for the commercial market by human beings. As to where these raw materials are located has a considerable bearing upon where the commercial users will locate.

The extraction of these products, including lumber, involves increasingly the use of machinery; and, because of the depletion factor, considerable attention must be devoted to the extraction of all usable deposits of every commercial gradation so far as quality is concerned. In the case of petroleum, very expensive efforts must be made to uncover the deposits wherever they may be in the world. As a result, increasing percentages of our domestic petroleum requirements are being derived from foreign deposits.

Commodity Characteristics

The greater part of these commodities are very bulky and heavy in relation to their values. Thus, the channel must provide a wide range of middlemen devices which reduce the number of times the product must be handled physically. Grading must be done systematically because of the importance of such specifications in the use by various classes and because of the small degree of usefulness these commodities serve in the commercial flows.

Practically all of the categories have experienced distinctly widening varieties of intermediate and final uses, thus increasing sharply the varieties of initial and intermediate users of and customers for the raw materials. Thus, the destructive distillation of lumber yields an increasing number of synthetic-product end uses. In addition to the widening varieties of use for fuel, petroleum, by means of the ever developing petro-chemical industries, is also offering an ever-widening range of uses. Coal, too, in addition to its established use as a fuel, is becoming an important raw-material source for many synthetics. Finally, the metallic ores are becoming the initial ingredients in ever-widening lists of industrial and manufactured consumers' goods products.

Factors Explaining the Variable Importance of Wholesale Middlemen

For such basic raw materials as petroleum and the metallic ores, the largest initial movements of the raw materials are likely to be controlled by those plants which are part of the integrated manufacturer structure. In such cases, the movements are between units of the same business empire, and the pricing process becomes a matter of internal accounting. For products such as coal and lumber, a wider variety of channel alternatives is available. Although large integrated companies may control the forests, and their sales branches and sales offices may control, in part, the initial flows of lumber, these meet only a fraction of the channel needs.

As a result of the diverse intermediate and end uses, wholesale middlemen are necessary who can: (a) locate and maintain contact on a continuous basis with all classes of users and (b) maintain inventories—in addition to those at the forest lumber mill points—from which size, shape, and quality inventory adaptations can be made. Because of weight and transportation cost factors, much intermediate handling is reduced to a minimum by using drop shippers, sales offices, brokers, and manufacturers and sales agents.

In the case of coal, there are somewhat the same channel considerations as for lumber, but the industrial uses of the product are far more important than lumber. As a result, the mining companies have their own sales branches and sales offices which assume considerably greater levels of importance than for lumber. The broker and sales agents, in addition, assume increased importance.

Based upon 1954 data, the types-of-operation groups handling petroleum and petroleum products were petroleum bulk stations, et al., 89 per cent; merchant wholesalers, 7.9 per cent; and agents and brokers, 3.1 per cent. For the lumber and forest products, the division was as follows: Merchant wholesalers, 72.9 per cent; agents and brokers, 15.9 per cent; and sales branches and sales offices, 11.3 per cent. Finally, for coal and coke, the distribution was: Merchant wholesalers, 40.9 per cent; agents and brokers, 30.1 per cent; and sales branches and sales offices, 29 per cent.

CHANNELS OF DISTRIBUTION— MANUFACTURED INDUSTRIAL GOODS

Production Characteristics

Data pertaining to the distribution of establishments, employees, and value added by manufacture, as well as by kinds of manufacturing activity and by geographic divisions, have been presented in Chapter 4. From these data, it was apparent that there are wide ranges of importance depending on the types of products produced and on the difference between the highly geographically concentrated industries and those which are dispersed in location. Furthermore, the manufacturing units range from large numbers of small-size units to such integrated giants as the automobile and steel-producing companies.

In addition, there are wide ranges from those companies producing few products of a relatively homogeneous nature to those producing wide varieties of products classified under more than one category. The products produced have wide ranges of end uses as well, and many have both industrial goods and manufactured consumers' goods characteristics. Manufacturing establishments may concentrate on highly technical products made to complex specifications, as in the case of the missile program; or they may produce highly standardized products, as in the case of electric bulbs; or they may produce varying combinations of both.

Commodity Characteristics

The manufactured industrial goods category involves a wide assortment of products. The most useful classification is to distinguish between two categories: (1) those goods which enter directly into, and can be identified in the actual products produced, and (2) those which either facilitate such production or are needed by the various types of institutional customers. In the first category, apart from the primary and secondary raw materials already discussed, would be included the wide array of semiprocessed and fully processed components, ranging in value from a few cents each to thousands of dollars or more; packaging materials which become part of the final products; and directly related services.

In the second category would be included the following: The basic major equipment (or capital goods) and buildings used for the manufacturing, construction, or similar activities; such accessory equipment as small tools, jigs, dies, which are employed in conjunction with the basic major equipment, but which are used up in considerably shorter periods of time; the office equipment needed by any business, government, educational, or other profit and nonprofit units; various kinds of supplies (lubricating, etc.) needed in both the production and the nonproduction aspects of customer activities; such process materials as bleaching chemicals, enzymes, catalytic chemicals; transportation and storage services; shipping containers; stationery, office supplies, etc.; and all types of accounting and statistical machines, including computers.

These commodities may be, as noted, highly standardized, or they may involve manufacturer, buyer, or other specifications. They may be highly technical in nature, requiring salesmen with scientific and engineering training, or they may be of such general nature as to require no such specialized knowledge for selling and servicing. They may be durable and last for decades, as in the case of buildings and railroad equipment, or they may be completely used up by each application. As a result, each category has highly varying periods of customer reordering as compared with other categories. Because of these characteristics, sales negotiations may be of very routine nature, or they may involve, on the other hand, key executives as the negotiating agents and months and even years of negotiation. Technical servicing requirements may range from none to very highly skilled arrangements. Many products are covered by intricate patent and/or cross-licensing agreements, while other types have no such protection. Wide varieties of packaging characteristics are to be noted, together with wide ranges of susceptibility to manufacturer brand identification. Obviously, many products lose their brand identification by being components of other final products.

Factors Explaining the Variable Importance of Wholesale Middlemen

Generally, the following factors will be of some help in understanding the high significance of direct channels: (1) The small number of potential users for certain types of industrial goods, requiring very close and continuous contact by the manufacturer if no potential or actual sales opportunities are to be overlooked; (2) a large average unit sale which requires long periods of time for completion of negotiations;[9] (3) concentration of actual and potential customers in very compact geographic areas, thus permitting intensive use of a relatively small sales force; (4) the need for considerable technical advice and assistance in making the initial sales, and in the continuous postsales servicing period; (5) the need for providing key executives on the selling side to match the organizational levels of the buyers; (6) the impact of reciprocity in making industrial goods sales; (7) the impact of the greater incidence of integration among industrial goods sellers and buyers; and (8) the length of time required to introduce buyers either to new uses of existing products, or to revolutionary types of new products (such as electronic computers).

On the other hand, there are many factors which underlie the use of many types of merchant and/or agent middlemen in semidirect and indirect channels:

1. The need for specialized knowledge of and contact with specific markets on a widely distributed geographical basis, thus involving a relatively large force of marketing representatives.
2. The inability of many manufacturers, because of financial and manpower reasons, to perform any or all of the marketing task for their product line.

[9] Visualize, for example, the time periods involved in the sale of jet planes to airline companies, or complete, streamlined trains to the railroads.

3. The frequent need for guaranteeing products which originate from relatively unknown manufacturing sources.

4. The existence of a "thin" market in the geographic and sales sense. In order to spread the costs of the channel under such conditions, the use of wholesale middlemen handling competing and/or non-competing lines of products may well be the only satisfactory solution.

5. The existence of a large, widespread market in which customers place frequent orders consisting of many items needing rapid delivery service.

6. The existence of well-known, standardized products requiring less technical and intensive sales arrangements.

7. The existence of large numbers of small buyers who frequently require financial assistance in making purchases.

As a result of the diversity of characteristics and factors affecting the channel structure for manufactured industrial goods, it is true, undoubtedly, that the relative importance of the direct channels has been overstated. Data for 1954 show that the merchant wholesalers group accounted for better than $2 out of every $5 of total gross sales, and that the wholesalers and agent-broker groups combined were just about equal in importance to the manufacturers' sales branches and sales offices group.

For individual kinds of business, however, much wider variations are apparent. Thus, within the limits of census data, sales branches and sales offices apparently accounted for the distribution of all textile mill products (excluding consumers' goods), instruments and related products (excluding tires and tubes), and leather and leather products. They also accounted for above-average percentages in the chemical and metal products groups. On the other hand, the merchant wholesalers' group was very important in the wholesale sales of scrap and waste material, plumbing-heating equipment and supplies, and farm supplies. In addition, they had above-average importance for the machinery equipment and supplies, millwork and construction materials, and paper and allied products kinds of business.

CHANNELS OF DISTRIBUTION—
MANUFACTURED CONSUMERS' GOODS

Production Characteristics

It is in this commodity category of channel structure that one finds the greatest diversity of manufacturing units—size ranges, geographical patterns, variety of output, value added, and other measures considered. The producing units range all the way from the numerous individualistic garment manufacturers, with unstable financial structures, unknown brand names, and variable marketing output, to the large, integrated giants. The range of products produced in a single manufacturing plant may consist of one or two to as many as hundreds, especially if the variations in brand names and packages also are considered. The time period of production may range from highly concentrated seasonal periods to an annual cycle.

As to location, the plants producing manufactured consumers' goods range from production-point clusterings, as in the case of meat-slaughtering establishments, to ultimate consumer market orientation, as in the illustrations of bread and bakery products, ice cream, and soft drinks. Every gradation of locational preference is likely to be found, and, once again, the marketing channel structure must reflect an adaptation to these wide ranges. The geographical, chronological, and communication gaps between producers and ultimate consumers create very complex problems for marketing organization.

Commodity Characteristics

The variety of manufactured consumers' goods moving through marketing channels is staggering. No matter which classification scheme is used, it is not difficult to detect sharp increases in the last decade or so in: (a) varieties of products within existing classification categories; (b) identification (brand) names used; (c) varieties of packages for existing categories; and (d) new classification categories. Among other effects, for example, the impact of the foreign automobiles has been the cause to multiply, suddenly and substantially, the buying alternatives. Similarly, the manufacturing of filter-tip cigarettes, together with standard versus king size, and changes in types of packaging are illustrative of explosions in the variety of existing products. On the other hand, the synthetic-fibre and stereophonic-sound-equipment products are examples of new categories which extend existing categories.

In terms of durability, manufactured consumers' goods have a wide range from very perishable to very durable. To many consumers, a loaf of bread has a life of only one to two days, despite the fact that the product may be placed in a deep-freeze unit for use at later dates. On the other hand, a suite of furniture or a rug may last for two or more decades, especially with proper maintenance. Items such as pharmaceuticals may have dosages prescribed which use up the entire amount of the product within a day or a few days. For the various types of durables, there is no comparable notion of dosage.

So far as units of sale are concerned, there exists, once again, a very wide range. Some products are purchased one at a time, whereas others may be purchased by the dozen, bushel, gross, or some similar measure of quantity. Physcially, the unit may vary in weight from a single ounce or less to several thousand pounds. The channel structure receives highly unequal impacts from such variations even so far as the delivery function itself is concerned.

Again, extremely wide ranges in unit product values are apparent. Manufactured consumers' goods range in price from fractional cents per unit to thousands of dollars (as in the case of automobiles, motor boats, or jewelry). Even within the same category of product use, sharp variations in unit values are apparent, e.g., perfumes, women's apparel, and jewelry.

Increasingly, the impact of the channel itself is to magnify the importance of packaging for manufactured consumers' goods. Because of over-all physical size some products, such as automobiles, cannot be packaged. In such cases, it is questionable anyway whether or not the package would have any marketing significance. But, in some cases, startling innovations in packaging materials have led, in turn, to startling innovations in prepackaged products. Two examples may be given: the transparent wrappings for meats and certain other manufactured foods, and the cellophane wrappings for men's white shirts which facilitate self-service retailing.

Closely related to, and affected by, the variations in durability noted above is the characteristic of frequency of purchase. Some products, because they are used up physically in the consumption process, have high rates of frequency of purchase, e.g., meats, toothpaste. Other products, as noted, may last for decades. In one case, accordingly, the channel and the middlemen therein devote considerable marketing efforts to maintain their shares or to increase their shares of existing consumption. They attempt, also, to develop new users. In the furniture case, the channel must devote most of its time in selling those persons involved in the formation of new households while the replacement market assumes reduced importance.

Among the more important characteristics affecting channel structure is the factor of relative weight and bulkiness. Manufactured consumers' goods range in physical size and bulk from the very small sewing needle or tablet of medicine to very bulky items such as refrigerators, certain items of furniture, and automobiles. As a result, once again variable combinations will be found of wholesale middlemen selling with and without inventories of merchandise physically present.

Finally, wide ranges are found in the elasticity of demand for manufactured consumers' goods and in the availability of substitutes. The consumers' goods range all the way from vital necessities to complete luxuries, with corresponding effects on the elasticities of demands. In terms of substitutability, the products range from conditions of having hundreds of brands of direct or semidirect substitutes to conditions of no substitutes, as in the case of a rare gem.

Factors Explaining the Variable Importance of Wholesale Middlemen

The complexities of the channel structure for manufactured consumers' goods almost rival those already described for agricultural products. With the exception of the assemblers group, opportunities exist for the use of all types of merchant wholesalers and agent middlemen. All forms of channels from the most simple and direct to the most complicated indirect patterns characterize the flow of manufactured consumers' goods.

The importance of direct channels is limited, relatively, to a few cases of specialty items and to such marketing arrangements as the various types of "of-the-month" clubs. In the case of the specialties, the basis for the direct channel is found in the unique nature of the merchandise coupled, as in the case of Fuller brushes, with a desire to control the complete channel. In the case of the "of-the-month" clubs, in addition to the factor of unique merchandise, there may be offered the features of low prices and the expert advice of a board in selecting each monthly choice.

Of much greater importance are the semidirect channels. These channels have two distinct structural patterns. The first consists of those manufacturer-controlled channels where, because of the unique nature of the product, of the variety of goods produced, of service, or because of financial considerations, the manufacturers use sales branches and/or sales offices in selling to the various classes of retail customers. In the second form, the retailers, by virtue of backward vertical integration, contact manufacturers directly.

But by far the most important segment of these channel structures consists of the indirect channels. The explanation lies, in part, in the fact that the marketing task to be performed matches very closely the analysis given in explaining the funnel concept of wholesaling and its strategic importance in marketing. This would include the need of many small manufacturers for brokers or selling agents (or their equivalent) in contacting the orthodox wholesaler and other types of merchant wholesalers. Another aspect is to be found, once again, in the close relationship of this particular problem and the importance of the basic marketing processes. A final explanation lies in the complexity of the geographical distribution of retail and ultimate consumers to be reached.

Data exist showing the relative importance of the three types-of-operation groups. On an over-all basis for selected manufactured consumers' goods, the merchant wholesalers had 52 per cent of the gross wholesale sales, whereas the sale branches and sales offices had nearly twice as much of the remaining compared with the agents and brokers group. The merchant wholesalers were very much of above-average importance in the following kinds of business: gift and art goods; jewelry; hardware; beer, wine, distilled spirits; amusements, sporting goods, toys; and tobacco. The kinds of business in which the manufacturers' sales branches and sales offices had above-average sales were: automotive; drugs; electrical appliances, radios, TV sets; books, magazines, newspapers; and tobacco. Finally, the agents and brokers were relatively most important for the dry-goods and apparel groups, and the groceries-confectionery-meats groups.

CHANNELS OF DISTRIBUTION—SERVICES

A discussion of channels of distribution for services opens a field of discussion which has been hardly touched upon in the existing literature.[10] Many of the personal services are either marketed through direct channels from source to user, as in the case of medical, dental, and legal services, or simply involve the use of a retail-type establishment, as in the case of the apparel cleaning, shoe repairing, and barber and beauty shop kinds of business. Some personal services such as motion pictures and baseball require expensive, highly specialized types of establishments. But the discussion here is concerned mainly with other types of channels which involve a much wider range of channel considerations.

Production Characteristics

Most of the types of services being considered here have no concept of production in the ordinary sense in which the term is used for the manufacture of tangible goods. The closest parallel exists in the case of utilities services where there are plants which generate electricity. In most cases, however, the creation of the service is inherent in the professional, semi-professional, skilled, and unskilled talents of one or more persons. In this sense, also, most of the services cannot be produced in advance of use and stored. The locational aspects of most services becomes, again, a considerably different geographical problem than the location of manufacturing industries.

Commodity Characteristics

Although many services are intangible in and of themselves, they become intertwined, nevertheless, in a particular physical environment. Ex-

---

[10] There are, of course, estimates of expenditures for selected services in the national income statistics and data for selected services in the *Census of Business.*

amples are the institutional aspects of the modern commercial and savings banks, the plush offices of advertising agencies and management consulting firms, and the elaborate facilities of storage and transportation agencies. Most services are highly perishable in the sense that the originator cannot, in most instances, store them until they can be marketed. Grading and standardization specifications are nonexistent, and knowledge of quality must depend to a great extent, accordingly, on word-of-mouth promotion. Packaging, at least in the tangible-commodity meaning, is also nonexistent. Pricing and price determination assume far different aspects because of the haziness of what costs are, in most cases, and because of the absence of any systematic price-determining markets.

Factors Explaining the Variable Importance of Wholesale Middlemen

Because of some of the characteristics noted above, it would be expected that the more professional the type of service considered, the greater would be the impact of direct channels of distribution. This is true, however, only where the marketing area is limited or where codes of ethics prevent any widespread use of advertising, as in the legal and medical professions. But in the case of many types of entertainment, various types of management or booking office services exist to establish contracts with the entertainment places used, to publicize the event, to arrange for transportation of the entertainers, and to handle the financial aspects. In the marketing of securities, there do exist organized stock exchanges which rival the organized commodity markets in structure; and within these exchanges there are the important buying and selling brokers.

For the travel industry, including the hotels as well as the transportation agencies, increasing use is being made of travel agents, as well as of the agencies' own controlled sales office, in reaching the wide array of business, government, institutional, and ultimate consumer customers. For such specialized financial problems as one finds in the textile industry, there exist special middlemen known as *factors* who have had a long history of use both in Europe and the United States.[11]

Many services, however, are based either upon individual proprietorship or upon partnership forms of organizations. In such cases, the business must depend upon the ability of its principals to build up a wide, personal acquaintanceship with potential users. This is true, for example, of many corporation lawyers, public accounting firms, advertising agencies, and man-

---

[11] The modern factors, such as the Walter Heller Company in Chicago, not only purchase a concern's accounts receivables but frequently offer a quality of professional managerial advice rivaling that of the consulting firms. See the bibliography for appropriate references.

agement consulting firms. Advertising, except for the strict limitations noted in the professional services, may be used. Great dependency must be placed upon so servicing customers that a very important word-of-mouth reputation is created. Where these agencies are organized on either partnership or corporate bases, the withdrawal of an execution may involve a considerable diversion of business from the existing firm to a newly created firm.

MIDDLEMEN'S SALES, BY CLASS OF CUSTOMER

While available census data permit detailed analyses to be made of each type-of-operations group's sales, by class of customers for the most important kinds of business, only summary information can be presented. Table 19 presents the available data for the 1935, 1939, 1948, and 1954 Census periods. In using these data, it must be remembered that they represent the averages for a wide range found among various kinds of business.

For merchant wholesalers, the main trends have been: (1) A sharp reduction in the percentage of sales made to retailers from 59 per cent in 1935 to 45 per cent in 1954; (2) a sharp rise in the proportion moving to industrial users from 25 to 32 per cent; and (3) increased sales made to other types of wholesale middlemen. For agents and brokers, sales to industrial users and to other types of middlemen account for most of their business. Sales to industrial users have increased steadily since 1935, whereas those made to other types of wholesale middlemen have had irregular movements.

Because of the rise of the fast-frozen food industry, the new and expanded uses of soy beans, and related factors, sales from assemblers of farm products to industrial users have outstripped sales to other types of wholesale middlemen since 1935. Sales to industrial users have risen from 29.5 to 45 per cent, while sales to other types of wholesale middlemen have declined from 55.8 per cent in 1939 to 34.6 per cent in 1954. Reduced proportions of sales to retailers from 13.5 per cent in 1939 to 6.8 per cent in 1954 have been offset by an increase in sales direct to consumers from 4 per cent in 1929 to 11 per cent in 1954, with most of this increase registered between 1948 and 1954.

Data for manufacturers' sales offices and sales branches and for the petroleum group were available on a combined basis only for 1935, 1939, and 1948. For the sales branches and sales offices, sales during this period direct to industrial users have displaced sales to retailers as the most significant. There have been increases, also, in the importance of sales to other wholesale middlemen and for export. Because of the rise of the petrochemical industry, there has been a sharp increase in the proportion of sales

T A B L E   11.1

SALES, BY CLASS OF CUSTOMER: UNITED STATES 1954, 1948, 1939, AND 1935

Type of Operation and Census Year	Total		Percentage Distribution—Reporting Establishment					
	Establishments	Sales ($1,000)	Total ($1,000)	to Retailers	to Industrial Users (including Gov't.)	to Wholesale	to Consumers and Farm	for Export
Merchant wholesalers								
1954	165,153	101,100,941	87,235,929	45.2	32.0	15.1	2.8	4.9
1948	146,518	79,766,589	75,838,020	46.9	31.8	13.7	1.6	6.0
1939	101,627	23,641,924	21,972,974	58.9	23.6	11.6	1.9	4.0
1935	88,931	17,661,691	15,905,271	59.2	24.9	10.2	1.9	3.8
Merchandise agents and brokers								
1954	22,131	39,250,509	33,729,858	13.8	43.7	37.1	2.1	3.4
1948	24,361	34,610,092	28,691,265	16.1	41.8	36.5	0.4	5.2
1939	20,903	11,201,035	9,839,969	16.8	35.8	40.6	0.7	6.1
1935	18,147	8,903,076	6,697,013	21.0	34.9	39.4	0.1	4.6
Assemblers of farm products								
1954	13,255	9,050,816	6,488,377	6.8	45.1	34.6	10.9	2.5
1948	19,268	10,957,893	10,053,170	9.4	32.6	51.8	5.3	0.9
1939	29,122	3,088,571	2,698,058	13.5	21.3	55.8	6.2	3.2
1935	26,515	2,463,011	1,773,011	12.7	29.5	50.0	4.1	3.7
Manufacturers' sales branches, sales offices								
1954	23,768	52,738,577	N.A.	N.A.	N.A.	N.A.	N.A.	N.A.
1948	17,926	14,253,609	51,154,221	31.3	42.7	23.0	0.4	2.6
1939	15,830	11,066,088	12,628,980	31.6	43.2	23.1	0.4	1.7
1935			9,110,062	41.5	37.8	19.4	0.3	1.0
Petroleum bulk stations, terminals								
1954	29,451	9,000,370	N.A.	N.A.	N.A.	N.A.	N.A.	N.A.
1948	30,825	2,942,982	56,522,646	64.1	35.9	[a]	[b]	[a]
1939	27,333	2,704,047	1,903,472	74.0	26.0	[a]	[b]	[a]
1935			1,379,520	73.3	9.9	8.4	8.0	0.4

Source: U. S. Bureau of the Census, U. S. Census of Business—1954, Vol. III, p. 18, Table N.

[a] Included in "to retailers."
[b] Included in "to industrial users."

made to industrial users at the expense of sales of gasoline and oil to filling stations. This has taken place despite the sharp increase in the use of the automobile.

FACTORS EXPLAINING THE USE OF PARTICULAR CHANNELS BY INDIVIDUAL MANUFACTURERS

Finally, a summary explanation needs to be given of the factors which help to explain the use of particular channels of distribution by individual manufacturers for their products. These factors are divided into basic external considerations and selective internal considerations peculiar to the individual manufacturer. The division, however, is not a hard and fast one, but is meant to be merely suggestive.

Basic External Considerations

These considerations may be subdivided into volume of sales, order, market, product, and channel subclassifications. Volume of sales considerations bring into the channel discussion a marketing research approach: the estimation of total sales potentialities for the product or products to be marketed; the percentage of this estimated total sales which the individual manufacturer can expect to realize, subdivided by product lines and geographic units; and the productivity of various individual channel alternatives in realizing these estimates.

The order characteristics summarize the variables which have been discussed for the various channel patterns. These involve, among other things, the influence of the dollar amount of the average sales order, the relative frequency of ordering, the regularity with which orders are placed, the number of separate product items in each order, and the extent to which solicitation by salesmen may or may not be necessary for repeat sales.

Under market considerations are included all of the pertinent factors explaining the composition of the manufacturers' customers. Included are such factors as: Who are the customers? How many are there? What is the geographical distribution? What are their product dislikes and preferences? What type of person influences the purchase? What is the density of distribution? Is it necessary to have personal acquaintanceships in order to make sales?

The product characteristics include the following: (1) Is the product relatively new in the channel or has it an established marketing position? (2) how rapidly does product style or design change? (3) the relative value of the product; (4) the product's weight in relation to such value; (5) the need for promptness in delivery; (6) whether or not technical knowledge is needed for the sale and in installing and servicing the product; (7) the nature and extent of the repair service required, if any; (8) whether or not the product is standardized; and (9) the type of product involved—industrial or consumers' goods.

Finally, increasing attention must be given by the manufacturer to channel characteristics. Pertinent to this analysis is the use of analytical tools and techniques to determine channel costs relative to the functions performed; the effect of channel alternatives on profits; and the attitude of the middlemen in the channel alternatives towards the manufacturer's product or product line.

Internal Considerations

There are, finally, certain selective internal management considerations. One of these considerations involves whether or not the industry, of which the manufacturer is a member, uses orthodox or traditional channel arrangements. If the answer is in the affirmative, then the individual manufacturer must decide whether or not to conform with the industry pattern. In making this decision, he must be guided, in part, by an evaluation of the success achieved by competitors in using nonorthodox channels and, in part, by some of the external considerations.

The manufacturer must consider, also, what functions he needs from the channel; how well his financial and manpower resources will permit him to exercise the degree of channel control he desires; the extent and type of cooperation desired from middlemen in the channel; a critical evaluation of the significant channel trends taking place; and, finally, whether or not there are executive channel preferences or prejudices.

12

Non-price competition at the department-store level

Perry Bliss

Prior to the early 1930's price competition received the lion's share of attention from theorists who were interested in the economics of the firm. As long as the purely competitive model was the conceptual apparatus with which reality was analyzed there appeared to be little or nothing the entrepreneur could do with respect to the impersonal market forces. Demand was assumed to be a datum to which the firm merely adjusted. With the growth of the economic literature on imperfect competition, however, stemming from the works of E. H. Chamberlin and Joan Robinson in the thirties, the business environment was acknowledged by theorists to be a little "looser" and the scope of the entrepreneur greater. With the gradual recognition that the market place contained significant areas of oligopoly the conceptual models admitted almost any pattern of market strategy vis-a-vis a rival. Price competition, methodologically neater, still received considerable at-

From *Journal of Marketing*, national quarterly publication of the American Marketing Association, XVII (April, 1953), pp. 357–365. Reprinted by permission.

The writer wishes to express his indebtedness to Professor Edmund D. McGarry for reading the manuscript and making helpful suggestions and criticisms.

tention but a multitude of non-price factors were seriously considered and where possible woven into the analysis. The present article is concerned with the relation of price to non-price competition in the case of a multi-product firm (the large-scale department store) where several thousand articles have interrelated demands and where price and non-price competition seem to be almost inextricably related.

Interrelationship of Price and Non-Price Competition

In treating the subject of non-price competition in the large-scale department store the distinction between price competition and non-price competition must be closely examined. Some authors indicate the character of non-price competition by a catalog of various business practices.

It has been pointed out . . . that there are hundreds of other grounds upon which sellers may choose to compete, such as the offer of better quality, more convenient terms of payment, chromium plating, neon lights, cellophane wrappings, better radio programs, etc. Reference has been made to the probability that the relative importance of all these latter devices for winning business, which may be collectively designated "non-price competition," has increased materially during the past generation, while emphasis on the price aspect of competition has correspondingly declined.[1]

Wilcox simply lumps non-price competition into ". . . competition in quality, in service, in style and in advertising and salesmanship."[2] Further considerations are offered by Burns and Chamberlin. "A more satisfactory basis of distinction between price and non-price competition is suggested by the separation of costs into production and selling costs, selling costs being those costs which alter the demand curve and production costs those which do not."[3] Chamberlin had earlier made this same point: "Costs of selling increase the demand for the product on which they are expended; costs of production increase the supply."[4]

The latter approach places emphasis on the manner in which a par-

---

[1] S. Nelson and others, *Price Behavior and Business Policy*, Temporary National Economic Committee, Monograph No. 1 (Washington: U.S. Government Printing Office, 1940), p. 154.

[2] C. Wilcox, *Competition and Monopoly in American Industry*, Temporary National Economic Committee, Monograph No. 21 (Washington: U.S. Government Printing Office, 1940), p. 4.

[3] A. R. Burns, *Decline of Competition* (New York: McGraw-Hill Book Co., Inc., 1936), p. 373.

[4] E. H. Chamberlin, *The Theory of Monopolistic Competition*, 3rd ed.; "Harvard Economic Studies," (Cambridge: Harvard University Press, 1939), Vol. XXXVIII, pp. 125–6.

ticular competitive practice affects the demand curve and suggests the distinction made in economic theory between market demand and schedule demand. Price competition is an attempt to alter the amount demanded by changing price. Traditionally this is demand in the market sense. Non-price competition is an attempt to alter the amount demanded without changing price. Traditionally this is demand in the schedule sense. In price competition the movement is along a given demand curve; in non-price competition the movement is a shift in the curve itself.

Specific examples of department store practices illustrate the difficulty of separating price competition from non-price competition in retailing a "mix" of goods and services. On the one hand the use of institutional advertising is quite clearly a form of non-price competition. On the other hand, it is more difficult to classify the practice of "leader pricing." The direct effect of dropping the price on a "leader" is to increase the amount taken. This is a movement down a demand curve and qualifies as price competition. However, the planned effect and the likely result in practice of the use of leader pricing is to increase not only the sales of the leader but also the sale of other products at their usual prices. This is a shift in their demand curves to the right and by definition is non-price competition. This apparent contradiction is explained by the fact that the reasoning shifts from single product analysis to multiple product analysis. The interrelation of the individual demands which exists when a "mix" of consumer goods is offered for sale makes a sharp distinction between price and non-price competition very difficult.

The Interrelation of Demand

In traditional single firm, single product analysis a lowering of price on marginal items involves a drop in the price of all units offered for sale. The exception would be in markets permitting price discrimination. However, in selling units of retail service (which are associated with the sale of units of physical merchandise) it is possible to lower the price of some units of service without lowering the price on all. Assuming a constant cost of merchandise, a cut in the price of a leader item represents a lowering of the retail margin, i.e., a drop in the charge for the unit of retail service performed in the selling of each unit of the leader item. However, the prices of all other goods on display may remain unchanged, i.e., the markups or prices of the units of retail service are not altered. Now, if more units of all goods, leader items plus other items in stock, are sold because of the increased traffic induced by the "pull" of the special bargain of the leader item, this results in the sale of more units of retail service without a price reduction on all units. The necessity to raise other prices because a leader item is lowered in price is a popular misconception. The increased volume of business on other merchandise at normal prices, which it is expected will result from the "pull" of the leader item or items, is what is significant. The fixed factors of the store are more fully exploited and the total volume of sales is profitable.

This concern with total receipts is always present in the thinking of a merchant who handles a variety of goods. The demand for any single item of the several goods in stock is never isolated in the eyes of the decision maker. Not only are the decisions affecting prices centered on this interdependence of demand, but also the decisions which affect non-price competition.

Factors Affecting Non-Price Decisions

The department store executive in choosing a competitive weapon whereby he can increase his sales either in absolute figures or in relation to a particular competitor or group of competitors is quite likely to view sales volume not only as a function of price but also as a function of several factors of a non-price nature. The decision maker knows that for particular items, for particular departments and for the store itself, sales are affected by changes in location, display, personal selling effort, advertising, timing, credit terms, "special events," and so on. Without wishing to burden the word "elasticity" it could be said that the department head or merchandise manager thinks of the sensitivity of sales to changes in location or display or personal selling effort just as quickly as he thinks of the sensitivity of sales to changes in price. Sales are "location elastic" or "display elastic" or "selling effort elastic." This does not mean that the decision maker, in an attempt to increase sales, feels that he can in all cases substitute a change in location or display for a change in price. Rather it means that the decision maker knows that just as different goods have different price elasticities they also have different location elasticities or display elasticities. For example, on many items a sharp drop in price would not overcome an inconvenient or uncongenial location.

Before turning to a description of the competitive practices which the decision maker may utilize to increase sales other than lowering price, it should be pointed out that the executive is "looking out" and estimating the impact of his actions on consumer buying habits and motives. However, "looking in," the decision maker would recognize the costs incident to non-price practices.[5] For example, the outlays in advertising may quickly run

---

[5] The concepts "looking in" and "looking out" were explained in my previous article "Price Determination at the Department Store Level," JOURNAL OF MARKETING, Vol. XVII, No. 1, July, 1952, p. 37.

into decreasing returns and additional expenditures increase costs faster than they increase revenues. More favorable credit terms, expensive displays, extremely lenient return privileges, etc., will also have cost considerations of a like nature. While in some cases a courteous and pleasant selling force may be had as the result of careful selection of personnel, also it is often the result of purchasing better quality sales people at higher wages. Thus, while the point of view of the decision maker "looking out" is the main concern of what follows, the costs associated with types of competitive behavior set limits to their use.

NON-PRICE METHODS OF COMPETING

Location

The decision maker in a department store sees a close relationship between floor location and department sales.[6] This is true both of the absolute location of the entire department as well as the location relative to other departments. It is also true of the location of specific items within the stocks of a single department. The shifting of departments with relation to absolute location as well as location relative to the several other departments and also the shifting of lines of goods and specific items in lines within a department is, of course, carried on in an attempt to get the most profitable

[6] At the Second Marketing Theory Seminar held at the University of Colorado, August, 1952, "location elasticity" was illustrated graphically by Professor Edmund D. McGarry:

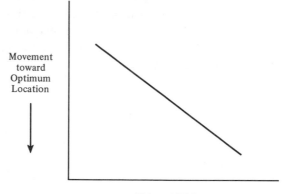

Volume of Sales

(Holding all other things equal, including price, sales volume will vary as goods are moved relative to the optimum location point.)

arrangement. In this respect it is not unlike similar activities carried out in the industrial field. Plant layouts and assembly line procedures are also attempts to get the most profitable arrangement of resources. However, there is this difference: in industry the aim is to reduce costs; in retailing the aim is in part to increase revenue. Also the results of manufacturing are more amenable to objective measurement, i.e., time and motion studies, material savings, and so on. The results in department store operations are much more difficult to determine. People's buying habits and motives are the determining factors and these are not as readily measurable. Nevertheless the department head is aware that for the hundreds of items in his stocks there is, in a rather loosely defined way, an "optimum" interrelation of his goods as they are placed on the selling floor at any given time.

However, this "best" layout shifts constantly with the seasons of the year as well as with "special" sales events, national holidays, and so on. For example, in the sporting goods department the sale of baseball items may be increased without a proportional loss in sales of other items by prominent display on a traffic aisle in the spring of the year. The location might be shifted shortly after midsummer to a slightly less conspicuous spot to make way for the more seasonal fall lines of football and hunting. The entire line of baseball items may be removed from the floor or a small display of key items moved to the back of the department for the remaining interval between fall and spring. However, in many cases, a more forward location may be used during the Christmas season on the theory that baseball items are gift items. This pattern of location obviously will vary greatly depending on the section of the country, the importance of the line to the area, and so on.

Also the exact timing of the changes of location is of crucial importance for sales, and will be taken up later. The important point for non-price competition is that before price is determined at any specific time the relation of location to sales will be considered. For example, if the goods are to be reduced in price at the close of the season the location of the display is selected at the same time. The expected increase in sales due to the seasonal "close-out" price is expected only if a favorable selling spot is selected, with due regard to the opportunity cost of the location.

The sensitivity of sales to floor location is closely related to buying habits of the customers. Convenience goods and impulse items, usually low in price and of a standardized nature, must be located near the main flows of traffic. Consumers generally wish to purchase notions, razor blades, cigarettes, and so on, with a minimum of inconvenience and effort. Such merchandise often responds to location more than to price.

At the other extreme are "big ticket" goods of high unit value and whose price is usually the subject of "bargaining." Such prices may be called "negotiated prices" as the terms of sale generally call for trade-in allowances, credit negotiations, etc. Refrigerators, stoves, vacuum cleaners, and the like are in this category. Whereas impulse and convenience goods must be located on the main floor or close to traffic aisles and entrances, these "big ticket" items may be on upper floors or in the rear of the departments for the consumer is willing to take the time and effort to look them up.

Illustrations could be multiplied of the relationship of sales to location when selling a variety of goods to consumers who have varied shopping habits and patterns, but the above examples indicate sufficiently that if sales are falling off the department manager may often think first of increasing the demand not by a drop in price but by a change in location.

Display

The main purpose of displays is to make the presentation as vivid as possible and stimulate the imagination. They are also used to suggest other articles of a complementary or related nature. The need for proper display is too obvious to need spelling out. It is important in non price competition for two reasons. First, it affords an opportunity for the store to differentiate itself in the eyes of the public. This is also true of advertising, product selection and other competitive practices, but it is especially true in display work. And second, it sets the tone and general character of the store. Display in this sense has strong emotional appeals for which price changes are often rather ineffective substitutes.

With regard to the first point, displays are capable of great individuality. They can be constantly changed and adjusted. Unique, one-time displays can be used to differentiate a store from its competitors and thus in some degree remove it from direct competition. A competitor may readily match your prices, but not so readily your over-all display. Secondly, display in this over-all sense represents not only the show cases and shelf space but also the wall ornaments, the type of flooring, the lighting, the general arrangement of all fixtures, and so on. The general impression customers receive when patronizing a store is the direct result of this total display pattern. To a large extent whether a store is considered modern, friendly, attractive, exclusive or ordinary is determined by the display policy. The store character thus created has a strong emotional appeal and in many competitive cases emotional appeals must be met in kind. For example, if a competitor in the department store field modernizes his lighting, puts soft carpets on the floors of some departments or introduces new display fixtures, the only effective competitive action may well be to do likewise. A price reduction, unless of a drastic nature, may not be an effective answer to a competitor's emotional appeal.

Advertising

The role of advertising has been treated so extensively that it is of little advantage to develop it in detail here. However, for the department store competitive advertising is of particular urgency. With the stocks of merchandise constantly changing and with the use of leader pricing, much selling effort is centered in letting people know just what is offered at what prices. Also, the character of the advertising determines in part the nature of the store in the eyes of the consumer. By featuring a high-fashion dress, omitting any reference to price or price changes, and emphasizing an exclusive atmosphere of presentation, the store can set a "prestige" appeal. On the other hand, by the selection of a popular item and the use of "regular" and "sale" prices, a "bargain" appeal can be established. In the former case non-price elements are used exclusively; in the latter case the appeal is to price competition.

Personal Selling Effort

The importance of the selling effort put forth by the sales people is of particular importance in competitive strategy because it can be used to increase the sales of items not currently affected by other types of promotional activities. For example, items which have not been advertised can be suggested to customers who have been attracted to the store by some "special" item which has been advertised. Likewise, if a price reduction has been made on Item A with a resulting increase in its sales a complementary good B can be suggested with each sale of Item A. Or again, if a "novelty" item is used to attract trade or if a special display is used to induce more purchases, personal selling effort can be used to "tie in" regular stock items or goods from normal displays with the sale of the faster selling items.

Likewise, the use of personal selling effort to "up trade" is very common. By putting special effort to sell quarts instead of pints, or two rather than one, or a higher price line rather than a low price line, the total revenue to the store is increased. The direction which this selling effort will take will depend on many considerations and, in deciding which items to single out to be suggested or "sold" by the selling force, the department head looks at the problem much as he would look at a price problem. Not all items respond to price reduction, nor do all items respond to selling effort. Items with "hidden qualities" need to be explained or demonstrated; on the other hand, items with "face value" tend to sell themselves or, more precisely, explanation, suggestion, etc., have little effect in increasing sales.

Inasmuch as there is a limit to the amount of selling effort each sales person can perform, and inasmuch as Item B can not be given attention if

Item A is chosen as the product to be "pushed," the optimum use of personal selling effort is difficult to determine. However, the use of persuasion, suggestion, cajolery, and so on, is considered by the retailer as having an effect not unlike a price reduction, or a change of location or display. The demand curve for many items can be shifted to the right by applying selling effort. In fact, selling effort may be the only means of increasing the sales of an item with a highly inelastic price demand and the total department sales may be maximized by dropping prices on goods with price elastic demands while at the same time applying selling effort to those items having inelastic price demand. This is often the rationale of a department store "promotion" or "special event."

Product

Perhaps the first thing which comes to the mind of a retail merchant in seeking ways to increase revenue is to make changes in the product. That is, to seek sales by product competition primarily rather than by price competition. This may mean (1) changing the quality or quantity of the "product" retail service, or (2) changing the goods in stock.

With regard to the first point, in attempting to compete on a non-price basis, the retailer may alter the quality or quantity of the retail service itself. Consumers, in their endeavor to maximize satisfaction, in reality purchase a "bundle" of utilities and may often associate in their minds the retail service with the actual goods purchased. Air conditioning, credit, delivery, rest rooms, lunch counters, and so on, are all parts of the unit of retail service and by adding to this "mix" sales may be more profitably increased, within the limits set by the costs of such services, than by lowering the price, i.e., markup on the existing service.

With regard to the second point, if we look at the department store field in general we will see why product competition in its usual sense of altering and changing actual items of merchandise is always present. The large-scale department store has several hundred sources or manufacturers whose products it sells. Hence the store is, in a sense, a funnel through which flows the collective product of all its suppliers. Thus, whether or not a department store makes any changes in the quality or quantity of its own product (units of retail service), it will, nevertheless, be handling the changes in product of all its sources. In short, by the very nature of the case, product variation plays an important competitive role. Furthermore, the clustering of large department stores in the shopping area and the resulting oligopolistic nature of the competition imposes a fear in the mind of the retailer that his competitor will be first with some new product or novel adaption of an old product. He knows that one of the most powerful "pulls" for any store is the monopoly position which comes with exclusive possession of a new and popular item which, in the short run at least, is not available to competitors.

Another consideration in product competition is the effect of variety on the general demand for the services of a store. People are attracted by complete lines and by full assortments within the lines. Sales of all goods may often be increased by carrying an inclusive inventory when price cuts on a narrow inventory would not induce trade.

Also, when handling a large number of goods, it is possible to substitute a combination of product and price competition for direct price competition. For example, if Store A drops price on a standard grade of white shirts of a kind also handled by Store B, it may not be necessary for Store B to drop the price also even though Store A is a close competitor, Store B may retaliate not by offering shirts at all but rather by featuring nylon stockings at a reduced price. This puts the consumer in the position of having to decide which is the better purchase and neither store is embarrassed by the necessity of suffering a direct price comparison on a homogeneous product. Nor is this the limit to such use of product competition. Store B's answer to Store A's price cut on white shirts may often be merely the "promotion" of a new or novel product which is not in the stocks of Store A. This new product may carry no price reduction whatever, its novelty being sufficient attraction in itself.

Timing

In discussing the previous factors of display, advertising and product competition we were in effect dealing with what to sell and how to sell it. However, in the department store field the matter of when to sell is often of vital importance. The essence of style is time and in the merchandising of style goods the volume of sales is as much a function of correct timing as any other competitive factor. If merchandise is offered for sale later than a competitor, for example, the lost sales can not be made up by inducing customers via price reductions.[7]

---

[7] Hall and Hitch, in their study of an English manufacturer of style merchandise, found that "the demand for its good was a peculiar one, the price itself being regarded as one of the properties of the commodity, and sales being often higher at a high price than at a low one. Thus it was necessary to discover the 'right' price, which might not be related to the cost at all; cost was the bottom limit of price." R. L. Hall and C. J. Hitch, *Price Theory and Business Behavior*, "Oxford Economic Papers No. 2" (Oxford: Oxford University Press, 1939). In this "prestige" or "snob" merchandise, price cuts may often indicate either poor quality, inferior style or that the style is "going out," which is a dimension of time with respect to the style cycle.

See also, for a general consideration of the time element, R. Cassady, Jr., "The Time Element and Demand Analysis," *Theory in Marketing*, ed. by Reavis Cox and Wroe Alderson (Chicago: Richard D. Irwin, Inc., 1950).

Not only is timing important in high fashion merchandise but it is also important in seasonal goods of all varieties. The decision maker is aware that while the demand for retail service itself is not a constant one, fluctuating irregularly over the year with an extreme demand at Christmas, the demand for particular merchandise is extremely seasonal. In such items as straw hats, bathing suits, canning equipment, and overshoes, the demand is concentrated into a few days or weeks. The sales of such goods are thought of in relation to correct timing as much as to price or location or display.

The Special Event

All of the foregoing non-price practices find their greatest effectiveness in combination with each other and to a large extent department store competition has centered around this fact. Some stores more than others, but all to some extent, use the "special event" or "promotion" to increase demand. The demand for the services and goods of any particular store is felt to be extremely elastic. The decision maker is generally aware that the aim of his competitive strategy is primarily to increase his sales at the expense of other stores, and only secondarily to enlarge the total demand for the market by drawing from a wider area. The rationale of pricing, display, product, location, advertising, timing and personal selling effort policies is to divert demand to the individual store.

The special event or promotion of a large scale department store is the use of special products, special displays, special prices, and the like, to disturb the normal competitive pattern and turn the customer's attention, by means of some special consideration such as a holiday, a unique event or an historical practice, to the attractiveness of the store itself. Thus stores bring in new items of merchandise, rearrange locations, adopt unusual advertising and display techniques and time the event to coincide with Thanksgiving or Easter or Christmas, or with the date of the founding of the store, or the start of the school season, or housecleaning time. January White Sales and Pre-Inventory Sales are also of this nature. There is some reason to question whether these special events actually add to the yearly volume of a store's business or whether what would be sold in any case is not merely concentrated in these special periods. However, from the point of view of any particular store, it can not avoid doing what its competitors do in this respect.

This practice of periodic promotions may be what Chamberlin had in mind when he stated that ". . . in some kinds of business, the long time market may be made up in large part of a series of short time bargain sales."[8] The normal or usual pattern of competition in the department store

---

[8] E. H. Chamberlin, *op. cit.*, p. 139.

field is this constant attempt to increase the volume of business in the store by the technique of special offerings. By bringing to the attention of the buying public in a more or less spectacular and dramatic manner the fact that special merchandise or special prices are available, the store hopes to induce people to come and shop. Traffic, the flow of people through a store, is the lifeblood of department store business and the main reason for the close attention paid to non-price factors. The apparent habit of people to buy other goods when they are convenient, the latent wants that become evident upon seeing thousands of items of merchandise, and the inclination to purchase suggested complementary and related goods tend to make the demand for all items in the store shift to the right when exposed to increasing numbers of potential buyers. Thus, the use of special events is the result of the knowledge that demand, in a schedule sense, is "traffic elastic," i.e., that more will tend to be sold at all prices when exposed to more people.

It is by the persistent and systematic development of the various types of non-price competition that department stores seek to attain a distinctive character, thus removing themselves from the bargain or "price" stores and segmenting the market in their favor. Price competition is not absent but is subordinated to non-price factors. When customers insist on the Lord & Taylor or Marshall Field label, and the prestige that goes with it, the store itself has become a "commodity." Non-price competition can not go much further.

SUMMARY

The foregoing analysis of non-price competition has been an attempt (a) to indicate that in a multi-product firm, such as the large scale department store, demands are so interrelated that reductions in price have the effect of shifting the over-all demand to the right, selling more units at normal prices; (b) to indicate that in competitive strategy the decision maker views the sales of his merchandise as being a function not only of price but also of location, display, advertising, personal selling effort, product, timing and the like; and (c) to show that the systematic use of all non-price devices in combination is the most effective means of segmenting the market and developing the store itself into a differentiated commodity.

SELECTED READINGS

BOOKS

Ralph Cassady, Jr., *Competition and Price Making in Food Retailing: The Anatomy of Supermarket Operations* (New York: Ronald, 1962).

Edward H. Chamberlin, *The Theory of Monopolistic Competition* (8th ed., Cambridge: Harvard University Press, 1962).

Edward H. Chamberlin, *Towards a More General Theory of Value*
    Part II, "Non-price Competition," (New York: Oxford University Press,
    1957).
Richard M. Clewett (ed.), *Marketing Channels for Manufactured Products*
    (Homewood, Ill.: Irwin, 1954).
Douglas J. Dalrymple and Donald L. Thompson, *Retailing: An Economic
    View* (New York: Free Press, 1969).
Bruce E. Mallen (ed.), *The Marketing Channel: A Conceptual Viewpoint*
    (New York: Wiley, 1967).
John C. Narver and Ronald Savitt, *The Marketing Economy: An
    Analytical Approach* (New York: Holt, Rinehart and Winston, 1971),
    especially Chapters 5-7 and 10-13.
David A. Revzan, *Wholesaling in Marketing Organization* (New York:
    Wiley, 1961).
Louis W. Stern, *Distribution Channels: Behavioral Dimensions* (Boston:
    Houghton Mifflin, 1969).
Roland S. Vaile, E. T. Grether, and Reavis Cox, *Marketing in the American
    Economy* (New York: Ronald, 1952).

ARTICLES

Helmy H. Baligh, "A Theoretical Framework for Channel Choice," in
    P. D. Bennett (ed.) *Economic Growth, Competition and World
    Markets* (Chicago: American Marketing Association, 1965),
    pp. 631–654.
Louis P. Bucklin, "The Economic Structure of Channels of Distribution,"
    in Martin L. Bell (ed.), *Marketing: A Maturing Discipline* (Chicago:
    American Marketing Association, 1960), pp. 379–385.
———, "Postponement, Speculation, and the Structure of Distribution
    Channels," *Journal of Marketing Research* 2 (February, 1965),
    pp. 26–31.
E. R. Hawkins, "Marketing and the Theory of Monopolistic Competition,"
    Journal of Marketing, April 1940.
Jack Hirschleifer, "The Exchange Between Quantity and Quality," *Quarterly
    Journal of Economics*, November 1955.
Robert F. Lanzillotti, "Pricing Objectives in Large Companies," *American
    Economic Review*, December 1958.
Paul J. McNulty, "Economic Theory and the Meaning of Competition,"
    Quarterly Journal of Economics, November 1968.
George J. Stigler, "The Division of Labor Is Limited by the Extent of
    the Market," *Journal of Political Economy*, June 1951.
——— "Price and Non-Price Competition," *Journal of Political
    Economy*, Jan.–Feb., 1968.

III   Buyer structure and behavior

The three selections in Part III are not intended to be a cross-section introduction to buyer structure and behavior. The selections have been specifically limited to one area, namely, buyer learning. However, the works listed in Suggested Readings extend the present analysis and should be consulted so that the vastness of the buyer structure and behavior literature may be fully appreciated. Note that the word "buyer" is used instead of "consumer." This more inclusive term permits extension of the analysis to all purchasing situations—ultimate consumers, business organizations, governmental agencies, and so on.

Buyer behavior is a function of buyer structure, where structure means the elements taken into consideration in making a buying decision. Thus, by definition, structural elements affect behavior through the decision process. The major elements of buyer structure are generalized in terms of tastes (social-psychological aspects), purchasing power (economic aspects), and the number of current and potential buyers and sellers in the market. Specific structural elements for the individual, with identifiable counterparts for the firm or organization, are: (1) economic resources and considerations,

217

(2) psychological characteristics, (3) sociological characteristics, (4) life cycle and family status, and (5) demographic characteristics.

Buyer behavior emanates from the recognition of needs—physical, psychological or social conditions which require satisfaction. As needs are perceived and coupled with purchasing power, they become wants. James A. Bayton in the first article discusses the manner in which behavior is aroused. Motivation arises out of tension in the system. As the buyer becomes aware of this condition, he is driven to engage in some type of action to eliminate the tension. This can range in complexity from the individual who perceives thirst and proceeds to purchase a soft drink, to the purchasing agent of a large corporation who is informed of the need for additional operating materials. Of great importance is the fact that what buyers perceive and the means by which they proceed to satisfy wants are functions of their structure, part of which is learned from past experience.

Buyer behavior in the most general form is a process of four sequential steps. The four steps are: (1) problem recognition—the perception of needs; (2) search—examination of internal and external sources for possible want-satisfying items; (3) choice; and (4) postdecision evaluation. As buyers confront wants, they attempt to satisfy them by choice of product class, brand, and supplier. The dynamics of this process are developed in "A Theory of Buyer Behavior" by John A. Howard and Jagdish N. Sheth. The theory put forth by these authors shows how the various structural elements affect purchase behavior at a number of points in the buying process. For example, they examine various structural conditions—high price brand and time pressure on buyer, to name only two—which affect the steps of the process as well as the final selection.

Some important conceptual aspects and emperical evidence of buyer behavior as learning are presented in the article by Alfred Kuehn. As buyers have positive experiences with products that satisfy wants, they continue to purchase the same item every time that want arises. Learning essentially means brand loyalty. This phenomenon is expressed by the learning curve which shows that, with a greater number of trials, there is a high probability —though never certainty—that given the same want the same response will be made. The fact that a buyer may reject a brand even though he has been brand loyal is known as brand switching, which takes place as structural elements change. For example, a housewife may regularly buy brand A of toothpaste but suddenly switch to brand B because of increased advertising, lowering of price, belief that brand B is better for her family, or other structural changes.

13

Motivation, cognition, learning— basic factors in consumer behavior

James A. Bayton

MOTIVATION, COGNITION, LEARNING

The analysis of consumer behavior presented here is derived from diverse concepts of several schools of psychology—from psychoanalysis to reinforcement theory.

Human behavior can be grouped into three categories—motivation, cognition, and learning. Motivation refers to the drives, urges, wishes, or desires which initiate the sequence of events known as "behavior." Cognition is the area in which all of the mental phenomena (perception, memory, judging, thinking, etc.) are grouped. Learning refers to those changes in behavior which occur through time relative to external stimulus conditions.

From *Journal of Marketing*, national quarterly publication of the American Marketing Association, 28 (January, 1958), pp. 282–289. Reprinted by permission.

About the Author. James A. Bayton received his B.S. and M.S. from Howard University and his Ph.D. from the University of Pennsylvania. Professor of Psychology at Howard, he was for several years associated with the Department of Agriculture. He received one of the Department's Superior Service Awards and an award from the District of Columbia Chapter of the American Marketing Association for an outstanding contribution by government personnel to problems of marketing. Dr. Bayton has been on leave-of-absence from Howard University, serving as Projects Manager with National Analysts, Inc. of Philadelphia.

Each broad area is pertinent to particular problems of consumer behavior. All three together are pertinent to a comprehensive understanding of consumer behavior.

MOTIVATION

Human Needs

Behavior is initiated through needs. Some psychologists claim that words such as "motives," "needs," "urges," "wishes," and "drives" should not be used as synonyms; others are content to use them interchangeably. There is one virtue in the term "drive" in that it carries the connotation of a force pushing the individual into action.

Motivation arises out of tension-systems which create a state of disequilibrium for the individual. This triggers a sequence of psychological events directed toward the selection of a goal which the individual *anticipates* will bring about release from the tensions and the selection of patterns of action which he *anticipates* will bring him to the goal.

One problem in motivation theory is deriving a basic list of the human needs. Psychologists agree that needs fall into two general categories—those arising from tension-systems physiological in nature (biogenic needs such as hunger, thirst, and sex), and those based upon tension-systems existing in the individual's subjective psychological state and in his relations with others (psychogenic needs).

Although there is not much disagreement as to the list of specific biogenic needs, there is considerable difference of opinion as to the list of specific psychogenic needs. However, the various lists of psychogenic needs can be grouped into three broad categories:

1. *Affectional needs*—the needs to form and maintain warm, harmonious, and emotionally satisfying relations with others.
2. *Ego-bolstering needs*—the needs to enhance or promote the personality; to achieve; to gain prestige and recognition; to satisfy the ego through domination of others.
3. *Ego-defensive needs*—the needs to protect the personality; to avoid physical and psychological harm; to avoid ridicule and "loss of face"; to prevent loss of prestige; to avoid or to obtain relief from anxiety.

One pitfall in the analysis of motivation is the assumption that a particular situation involves just one specific need. In most instances the individual is driven by a combination of needs. It seems likely that "love" brings into play a combination of affectional, ego-bolstering, and ego-defensive needs as well as biogenic needs. Within the combination some needs will be relatively strong, others relatively weak. The strongest need within the combination can be called the "prepotent" need. A given consumer product can be defined in terms of the specific need-combination involved and the relative strengths of these needs.

Another pitfall is the assumption that identical behaviors have identical motivational backgrounds. This pitfall is present whether we are thinking of two different individuals or the same individual at two different points in time. John and Harry can be different in the motivational patterns leading to the purchase of their suits. Each could have one motivational pattern influencing such a purchase at age twenty and another at age forty.

Ego-Involvement

One important dimension of motivation is the degree of ego-involvement. The various specific need-patterns are not equal in significance to the individual. Some are superficial in meaning; others represent (for the individual) tremendous challenges to the very essence of existence. There is some evidence that one of the positive correlates of degree of ego-involvement is the amount of cognitive activity (judging, thinking, etc.) involved. This means that consumer goods which tap low degrees of ego-involvement will be purchased with a relatively lower degree of conscious decision-making activity than goods which tap higher degrees of ego-involvement. Such a factor must be considered when decisions are made on advertising and marketing tactics.

At times the ego-involvement factor is a source of conflict between client and researcher. This can occur when research reveals that the product taps a low degree of ego-involvement within consumers. The result is difficult for a client to accept; because *he is* ego involved and, therefore, cognitively active about his product, consumers must certainly be also. It is hard for such a client to believe that consumers simply do not engage in a great deal of cognitive activity when they make purchases within his product class. One way to ease this particular client-researcher conflict would be for the researcher to point out this implication of the ego-involvement dimension.

"True" and Rationalized Motives

A particular difficulty in the study of motivation is the possibility that there can be a difference between "true" motives and rationalized motives. Individuals sometimes are unaware of the exact nature of drives initiating their behavior patterns. When this occurs, they attempt to account for their behavior through "rationalization" by assigning motivations to their behavior which are acceptable to their personality structures. They may do this with no awareness that they are rationalizing. There can be other instances, however, in which individuals are keenly aware of their motivations, but feel it would be harmful or socially unacceptable to reveal them. When this is the case, they deliberately conceal their motivations.

These possibilities create a problem for the researcher. Must he assume that every behavior pattern is based upon unconscious motivation? If not, what criteria are to be used in deciding whether to be alert to unconscious motivation for this behavior pattern and not that one? What is the relative importance of unconscious motives, if present, and rationalized motives? Should rationalized motives be ignored? After all, rationalized motives have a certain validity for the individual—they are the "real" motives insofar as he is aware of the situation.

The situation is even more complicated than this—what about the dissembler? When the individual actually is dissembling, the researcher must attempt to determine the true motives. But, how shall we determine whether we are faced with a situation where the respondent is rationalizing or dissembling? In a given case, did a projective technique reveal an unconscious motive or the true motive of a dissembler? Conceptually, rationalized motives and dissembled motives are not equal in psychological implication; but it is rare, if ever, that one finds attempts to segregate the two in consumer research directed toward the analysis of motivation. This failure is understandable, to some extent, because of the lack of valid criteria upon which to base the distinction.

COGNITION

Need-Arousal

Motivation, thus, refers to a state of need-arousal—a condition exerting "push" on the individual to engage in those activities which he anticipates will have the highest probability of bringing him gratification of a particular need-pattern. Whether gratification actually will be attained or not is a matter of future events. Central to the psychological activities which now must be considered in the sequence are the complex of "mental" operations and forces known as the cognitive processes. We can view these cognitive processes as being *purposive* in that they serve the individual in his attempts to achieve satisfaction of his needs. These cognitive processes are *regulatory* in that they determine in large measure the direction and particular steps taken in his attempt to attain satisfaction of the initiating needs.

The Ego-Superego Concept

The ego-superego concept is pertinent to a discussion of cognitive activities which have been triggered by needs. Discussions of the ego-superego concept usually come under the heading of motivation as an aspect of personality. It is our feeling that motivation and the consequences of motivation should be kept systematically "clean." In the broadest sense, ego and superego are mental entities in that they involve memory, perceiving, judging, and thinking.

The Ego

The ego is the "executive," determining how the individual shall seek satisfaction of his needs. Through perception, memory, judging, and thinking the ego attempts to integrate the needs, on the one hand, and the conditions of the external world, on the other, in such manner that needs can be satisfied without danger or harm to the individual. Often this means that gratification must be postponed until a situation has developed, or has been encountered, which does not contain harm or danger. The turnpike driver who does not exceed the speed limit because he sees signs saying there are radar checks is under the influence of the ego. So is the driver who sees no cars on a straight stretch and takes the opportunity to drive at excessive speed.

The Superego

The superego involves the ego-ideal and conscience. The ego-ideal represents the positive standards of ethical and moral conduct the individual has developed for himself. Conscience is, in a sense, the "judge," evaluating the ethics and morality of behavior and, through guilt-feelings, administering punishment when these are violated. If a driver obeys the speed limit because he would feel guilty in doing otherwise, he is under the influence of the superego. (The first driver above is under the influence of the ego because he is avoiding a fine, not guilt feelings.)

Specific Examples

Credit is a form of economic behavior based to some extent upon ego-superego considerations. It is generally felt that one cause of consumer-credit expansion has been a shift away from the superego's role in attitudes toward credit. The past ego-ideal was to build savings; debt was immoral —something to feel guilty about, to avoid, to hide. These two superego influences restrained the use of credit. For some cultural reason, credit and debt have shifted away from superego dominance and are now more under the control of the ego—the primary concern now seems to be how much of it can be used without risking financial danger.

The purchasing of specific consumer goods can be considered from the point of view of these two influences. Certain goods (necessities, perhaps) carry little superego influence, and the individual is psychologically free to try to maximize the probability of obtaining satisfaction of his needs while minimizing the probability of encountering harm in so doing. Other goods, however, tap the superego. When a product represents an aspect of the ego-ideal there is a strong positive force to possess it. Conversely, when a product involves violation of the conscience, a strong negative force is generated against its purchase.

Let us assume that, when the need-push asserts itself, a variety of goal-objects come into awareness as potential sources of gratification. In consumer behavior these goal-objects may be different brand names. The fact that a particular set of goal-objects come into awareness indicates the generic character of this stage in the cognitive process—a class of goal-objects is seen as containing the possible satisfier. What the class of goal-objects and the specific goal-objects within the class "promise" in terms of gratification are known as "expectations."

There are, then, two orders of expectation: generic expectancies, and object-expectancies. Suppose the needs were such that the individual "thought" of brands of frozen orange juice. Some of the generic expectations for frozen orange juice are a certain taste, quality, source of vitamin C, protection against colds, and ease of preparation. The particular brands carry expectations specifically associated with one brand as against another. The expectation might be that brand A has a more refreshing taste than brand B.

In many instances, cognitive competition occurs between two or more generic categories before it does between goal-objects within a generic category. Much consumer-behavior research is directed toward the investigation of generic categories—tires, automobiles, appliances, etc. But perhaps not enough attention has been given to the psychological analysis of cognitive competition between generic categories. An example of a problem being studied is the competition between television viewing, movie going, and magazine reading. For a particular producer, cognitive competition within the pertinent generic category is usually of more concern than cognitive competition between his generic category and others. The producer usually wants only an intensive analysis of consumer psychology with respect to the particular generic category of which his product is a member.

Let us now assume that under need-push four alternative goal-objects (brands A, B, C, and D) came into awareness. Why these particular brands and not others? Why are brands E and F absent? An obvious reason for brand E's absence might be that the individual had never been exposed to the fact that brand E exists. He had been exposed to brand F, however. Why is it absent? The problem here is one of memory—a key cognitive process. The producers of brands E and F obviously are faced with different problems.

Two sets of circumstances contain the independent variables that determine whether a given item will be remembered. One is the nature of the experience resulting from actual consumption or utilization of the goal-object. This will be discussed later when we come to the reinforcement theory of learning. The other is the circumstances present on what might be called vicarious exposures to the goal-object—vicarious in that at the time of exposure actual consumption or utilization of the goal-object does not occur. The most obvious example would be an advertisement of the goal-object. Of course, the essential purpose of an advertisement is to expose the individual to the goal-object in such a manner that at some subsequent time it will be remembered readily. The search for the most effective methods of doing this by manipulation of the physical aspects of the advertisement and the appeals used in it is a continuing effort in consumer-behavior research. Finally, for many consumers these two sets of circumstances will be jointly operative. Experiences with the goal-object and subsequent vicarious exposures can coalesce to heighten the memory potential for an item.

Making a Choice

With, say, four brands in awareness, the individual must now make a choice. What psychological factors underlie this choice? The four brands could be in awareness due to the memory factor because they are immediately present in the environment; or some because they are in the environment, and the others because of memory.

The first problem is the extent to which the items are differentiated. The various goal-objects have attributes which permit the individual to differentiate between them. The brand name is one attribute; package another; design still another. These differentiating attributes (from the point of view of the consumer's perceptions) can be called signs or cues. All such signs are not equally important in consumer decisions. Certain of them are depended upon much more than others. For example, in a study of how housewives select fresh oranges, the critical or key signs were thickness of skin, color of skin, firmness of the orange, and presence or absence of "spots" on the skin.

The signs have expectancies associated with them. Package (a sign) can carry the expectancy of quality. Thin-skin oranges carry the expectancy of juice; spots carry the expectancy of poor taste quality and insufficient amount of juice. Often sign-expectancies determined through consumer research are irrelevant or invalid. Signs are irrelevant when they do not represent a critical differentiating attribute of a goal-object. Certain discolorations on oranges have nothing to do with their intrinsic quality. Expectancies are invalid when they refer to qualities that do not in fact exist in association with a particular sign.

The different goal-objects in awareness can be assessed in terms of the extent to which they arouse similar expectancies. This phenomenon of similarity of expectations within a set of different goal-objects is known as generalization. One goal-object (brand A, perhaps), because of its associated expectancies, can be assumed to have maximum appeal within the set of alternative goal-objects. The alternates then can be ordered in terms of how their associated expectancies approximate those of brand A. Is this ordering and the psychological distances between the items of the nature of:

Brand A   Brand A
Brand B
                        or
                                           Brand B
Brand C   Brand C

These differences in ordering and psychological distance are referred to as generalization gradients. In the first case, the expectancies associated with brand B are quite similar to those for brand A, but are not quite as powerful in appeal. Brand C has relatively little of this. In the second case, the generalization gradient is of a different form, showing that brand B offers relatively little psychological competition to brand A. (There will also be generalization gradients with respect to cognitive competition between generic categories.) In addition to the individual producer being concerned about the memory potential of his particular brand, he needs to determine the nature of the generalization gradient for his product and the products of his competitors. Mere ordering is not enough—the "psychological distances" between positions must be determined, also, and the factor determining these distances is similarity of expectancy.

The discussion above was concerned with cognitive processes as they relate to mental representation of goal-objects under the instigation of need-arousal. The items brought into awareness, the differentiating sign-expectancies, and the generalization gradient are the central factors in the particular cognitive field aroused under a given "need-push." One important dimension has not yet been mentioned—instrumental acts. These are acts necessary in obtaining the goal-object and the acts involved in consuming or utilizing it. Examples are: "going downtown" to get to a department store, squeezing the orange to get its juice, ease of entry into service stations, and the operations involved in do-it-yourself house painting.

Instrumental acts can have positive or negative value for the individual. One who makes fewer shopping trips to downtown stores because of traffic and parking conditions displays an instrumental act with negative value. Frozen foods are products for which much of the appeal lies in the area of instrumental acts. The development of automatic transmissions and of power-steering in automobiles are examples of product changes concerned with instrumental acts. The point is that concentration upon cognitive reactions to the goal-object, *per se*, could be masking critical aspects of the situation based upon cognitive reactions to the instrumental acts involved in obtaining or utilizing the goal-object.

LEARNING

Goal-Object

Starting with need-arousal, continuing under the influence of cognitive processes, and engaging in the necessary action, the individual arrives at consumption or utilization of a goal-object. Using our consumer-behavior illustration, let us say that the consumer bought brand A and is now in the process of consuming or utilizing it. We have now arrived at one of the most critical aspects of the entire psychological sequence. It is with use of the goal-object that degree of gratification of the initial needs will occur.

Reinforcement

When consumption or utilization of the goal-object leads to gratification of the initiating needs there is "reinforcement." If at some later date the same needs are aroused, the individual will tend to repeat the process of selecting and getting to the same goal-object. If brand A yields a high degree of gratification, then at some subsequent time, when the same needs arise, the consumer will have an increased tendency to select brand A once again. Each succeeding time that brand A brings gratification, further reinforcement occurs, thus further increasing the likelihood that in the future, with the given needs, brand A will be selected.

This type of behavioral change—increasing likelihood that an act will be repeated—is learning; and reinforcement is necessary for learning to take place. Continued reinforcement will influence the cognitive processes. Memory of the goal-object will be increasingly enhanced; particular sign-expectancies will be more and more firmly established and the generalization gradient will be changed in that the psychological distance on this gradient between brand A and the competing brands will be increased.

Habit

One of the most important consequences of continued reinforcement is the influence this has on the extent to which cognitive processes enter the picture at the times of subsequent need-arousal. With continued reinforcement, the amount of cognitive activity decreases; the individual engages less and less in decision-making mental activities. This can continue until, upon need-arousal, the goal-obtaining activities are practically automatic. At this stage there is a habit.

Note this use of the term "habit." One frequently hears that a person does certain things by "*force* of habit," that habit is an initiator of behavioral sequences. Actually habits are not initiating forces in themselves; habits are repeated response patterns accompanied by a minimum of cognitive activity. There must be some condition of need-arousal before the habit-type response occurs. This has serious implications in the field of consumer behavior. The promotional and marketing problems faced by a competitor of brand A will be of one type if purchase behavior for brand A is habitual, of another if this is not true. If the purchase is largely a habit, there is little cognitive activity available for the competitor to "work on."

Frequency of repeating a response is not a valid criterion for determining whether or not a habit exists. An act repeated once a week can be just as much a habit as one repeated several times a day. The frequency of a response is but an index of the frequency with which the particular need-patterns are aroused. Frequency of response also is often used as a measure of the *strength* of a habit. The test of the strength of a habit is the extent to which an individual will persist in an act after it has ceased providing need gratification. The greater this persistence, the stronger was the habit in the first place.

PROBLEM—CONCEPT—RESEARCH

The above views integrate concepts in contemporary psychology which seem necessary for a comprehensive explanation of human behavior, and apply these concepts to the analysis of consumer behavior. Each psychological process touched upon contains areas for further analysis and specification.

Some type of comprehensive theory of human behavior is necessary as a *working tool* to avoid a lack of discipline in attacking problems in consumer behavior. Too frequently a client with a practical problem approaches a researcher with an indication that all that is needed is a certain methodology—depth interviewing, scaling, or projective devices, for example.

The first step should be to take the practical problem and translate it into his pertinent conceptual entities. This phase of the problem raises the question of motivations. Here is a question involving relevance and validity of sign-expectancies. There is a question dealing with a generalization gradient, etc. Once the pertinent conceptual entities have been identified, and only then, we arrive at the stage of hypothesis formulation. Within each conceptual entity, a relationship between independent and dependent variables is established as a hypothesis to be tested.

Often the relation between conceptual entities must be investigated.

For example, what is the effect of continuing reinforcement on a specific generalization gradient? Within the same research project, one psychological entity can be a dependent variable at one phase of the research and an independent variable at another. At one time we might be concerned with establishing the factors associated with differential memory of sign-expectancies. At another time we could be concerned with the influence of remembered sign-expectancies upon subsequent purchase-behavior.

Discipline requires that one turn to methodology only when the pertinent conceptual entities have been identified and the relationships between independent and dependent variables have been expressed in the form of hypotheses. Fundamentally this sequence in the analysis of a problem serves to delimit the methodological possibilities. On any event, the methodologies demanded are those which will produce unambiguous tests of each particular hypothesis put forth. Finally, the results must be translated into the terms of the original practical problem.

We have used the term "discipline" in this phase of our discussion. The researcher must discipline himself to follow the above steps. Some find this a difficult thing to do and inevitably their data become ambiguous. They must resort to improvisation in order to make sense of the results *after* the project is completed. A research project is truly a work of art when the conceptual analysis, the determination of the hypotheses, and the methodologies have been developed in such an "air-tight" sequence that practically all that is necessary is to let the facts speak for themselves.

14

A theory
of
buyer behavior

John A. Howard and Jagdish N. Sheth

The usual purpose of a theory is to explain empirical phenomena. The empirical phenomenon which we want to explain is the buying behavior of individuals over a period of time. More specifically, our theory is an attempt to explain the *brand choice* behavior of the buyer. We assume that brand choice is not random but systematic, and the task we have undertaken in developing this theory is to formulate a structure that enables us to view it as a system.

To elaborate on our assumption: First, we assume that buying behavior is rational in the sense that it is within the buyer's "bounded rationality" (March and Simon, 1958); that is, his behavior is rational within the limits of his cognitive and learning capacities and within the constraint of limited information. Second, we are attempting to build a positive theory and not a normative theory. Third, if brand choice behavior is assumed to be systematic, then it can be observed in certain standard ways. Later on, we describe a series of measures of the buyer's buying behavior generally labeled purchase behavior, attitude toward a brand, comprehension of the brand, attention to impinging stimuli, and intention to buy a brand. Fourth, if behavior is systematic, it is caused by some event—a stimulus—either in the buyer or in the buyer's environment. This event or stimulus is the input to the system, and purchase behavior is the output. What we must describe then, is what goes on between the input and the output.

A SUMMARY OF THE THEORY

Much buying behavior is more or less repetitive, and the buyer establishes purchase cycles for various products which determine how often he will buy. For some products, such as durable appliances, this cycle is lengthy and purchase is infrequent. For many other products, such as food and personal-care items, the purchase cycle is short and purchase is frequent. Confronted by repetitive brand-choice decisions, the consumer simplifies his task by storing relevant information and establishing a routine in his decision process. Therefore our theory must identify the elements of his decision process, observe the changes that occur in them over time as a result of their repetitive nature, and show how a combination of decision elements affects search processes and the incorporation of information from the buyer's commercial and social environment.

The elements of a buyer's brand-choice decision are (1) a set of motives, (2) several alternative courses of action, and (3) decision mediators by which the motives are matched with the alternatives. Motives are specific to a product class, and reflect the underlying needs of the buyer. The alternatives are the various brands that have the potential of satisfying the buyer's motives.

There are three important notions involved in the definition of alternatives as brands. First, the several brands which become alternatives to the buyer need not belong to the same product class *as defined by the industry*. For example, a person may see Sanka coffee, Ovaltine, and Tetley's tea as three alternatives to satisfy his motives related to beverage consumption. He also may see only two alternatives, such as coffee and beer, both belonging to physically dissimilar product classes. Second, the brands which are alternatives of the buyer's choice decision are generally small in number, collectively called his "evoked set." The evoked set is only a fraction of the brands he is aware of, and a still smaller fraction of the total number of brands actually on the market. Third, any two consumers may have quite different alternatives in their evoked sets.

Decision mediators are the set of rules that the buyer employs to match his motives and his means of satisfying those motives. They serve the function of ordering and structuring the buyer's motives, and then ordering and structuring the various brands based on their potential to satisfy these ordered motives. Decision mediators develop by the buyer's process of learning about the buying situation. They are therefore influenced by information from the buyer's environment, and even more importantly by the actual experience of purchasing and consuming the brand.

When the buyer is just beginning to purchase a product class, he lacks experience; he does not have a set of decision mediators for that product class. To develop them, he *actively seeks information* from his commercial and social environments. The information he actively seeks, or accidentally receives, is subjected to perceptual processes, which not only limit his intake of information (magnitude of information is affected) but modify it to suit his frame of reference (quality of information is affected). These modifications are significant in that they distort the neat "marketing-stimulus consumer-response" relation.

Along with his active search for information, the buyer may to some extent generalize from similar past experience. Such generalization may be due to the physical similarity of a new product class to an old product class. For example, during initial purchases of whisky, a buyer may generalize from his experiences in buying gin. Generalization can also occur when two product classes are physically dissimilar, but have a common meaning deriving from a company brand name. For example, a buyer might generalize from his experience in buying a refrigerator or range to his first purchase of a dishwasher.

Whatever the source, the buyer develops sufficient decision mediators to enable him to choose a brand which seems to have the best potential for satisfying his motives. If the brand proves satisfactory, the potential of that brand to satisfy his motives for subsequent purchases is increased, and the probability of his buying that brand again is likewise increased. With repeated satisfactory purchases of one or more brands, the buyer is likely to manifest a routine decision process in which the sequential steps in buying are so well structured that an event which triggers the process may also complete it. Routine purchasing implies that decision mediators are well established, and that the buyer has strong brand preferences.

The phase of repetitive decision making in which the buyer reduces the complexity of a buying situation with the help of information and experience is called "the psychology of simplification." The more the buyer simplifies his environment, the less is his tendency to engage in active search behavior. The environmental stimuli related to the purchase situation become more meaningful and less ambiguous. Furthermore, the buyer establishes more cognitive consistency among brands as he moves toward routine response, and the incoming information is then screened with regard to its magnitude and quality. He becomes less attentive to stimuli which do not fit his cognitive structure, and he distorts these stimuli when they are forced upon him. These implied mechanisms explain a phenomenon for which there is growing evidence (cf. the work of John Dollard of Yale University): people can be exposed to a television commercial but not perceive it.

A surprising phenomenon occurs in the case of frequently purchased products, such as food and personal-care items. The buyer, after establishing a routine decision process, may begin to feel bored with such repetitive decision making. He may also become satiated, even with a preferred brand. In both cases, he may feel that all existing alternatives—including the preferred brand—are unacceptable, which generates a desire to *complicate* the buying situation by considering new brands. This process can be called "the psychology of complication." Ultimately the buyer identifies a new brand, and begins again to simplify. Thus the continuing process of buying frequently purchased items develops a cycle of information seeking that goes from simplification to complication and back again.

Determining the intensity of a buyer's information-seeking effort at a point in time is obviously important to the marketing manager. For example, if he knows that a substantial group of buyers are at a level of routine decision making where they feel satiated or bored, he can introduce a new brand or innovation which might provide the needed source of change. Similarly, if buyers are engaged in extensive brand-choice problem solving, they are likely to actively seek information. The mass media may therefore prove very effective in communicating information about a brand.

Any theory of human behavior must account for individual differences. However, in order to identify the invariant relations of human behavior, at least under field conditions, it is often necessary to hold interpersonal variability constant by taking into account mediating variables and so classify individuals into homogeneous subgroups. The marketing manager is also interested in differentiated masses of buyers. He wants to understand and separate individual differences so that he can classify or segment the total market in terms of these differences. If we can understand the psychology of the individual buyer, we may achieve this classification.

Depending on the internal state of the buyer, a given stimulus may result in a given response. For example, one buyer who urgently needs a product may respond to an ad for a brand in that product class by buying it; another buyer who does not need the product may simply notice the ad and store the information; a third buyer may ignore the ad altogether. A construct such as "level of motivation" will then explain divergent reactions to the same stimulus. Alternatively, two buyers may both urgently need a product, but they buy two different brands. This can be explained by another construct: "predisposition toward a brand."

ELEMENTS OF THE THEORY

Figure 14.1 represents our theory of buyer behavior. The central rectangular box isolates the various internal variables and processes which, taken together, show the state of the buyer. The inputs to the rectangular box are stimuli from the marketing and social environments. The outputs are a variety of responses which the buyer is likely to manifest, based on the interaction between the stimuli and his internal state.

Besides the inputs and outputs, there are a set of seven influences which affect the variables in the rectangular box.[1] These variables appear at the top of the diagram and are labeled "exogenous" variables. Their function is to provide a means of adjusting for the interpersonal differences discussed above.

The variables within the rectangular box are hypothetical constructs, which serve the role of endogenous variables in the sense that changes in them are explained, but they are something less than endogenous variables in that they are not well defined and are not observable. Their values are inferred from relations among the output intervening variables.

Several of the exogenous variables such as personality, social class, and culture have traditionally been treated as endogenous variables. We believe that they affect more specific variables, and that, by conceiving their effect via the hypothetical constructs, we can better understand their role.

Our theory of buyer behavior has four major components: stimulus variables, response variables, hypothetical constructs, and exogenous variables. We will elaborate on each of these components below, in terms of both their substance and their interrelationships.

Stimulus Input Variables

At any point in time, the hypothetical constructs which reflect the buyer's internal state are affected by numerous stimuli from his environ-

---

[1] Terminology is difficult in a problem area that cuts across both economics and psychology, because each discipline has often defined its terms differently from the other. We find the economist's definitions of "exogenous," vs. "endogenous," and "theory" vs. "model" more useful than those of the psychologist. The psychologist's distinction of hypothetical constructs and intervening variables, however, provides a helpful breakdown of endogenous variables. Finally, for the sake of exposition, we have often not clearly distinguished here between the theory and its empirical counterparts. Although this practice encourages certain ambiguities, and we lay ourselves open to the charge of reifying our theory, we believe that it simplifies the exposition.

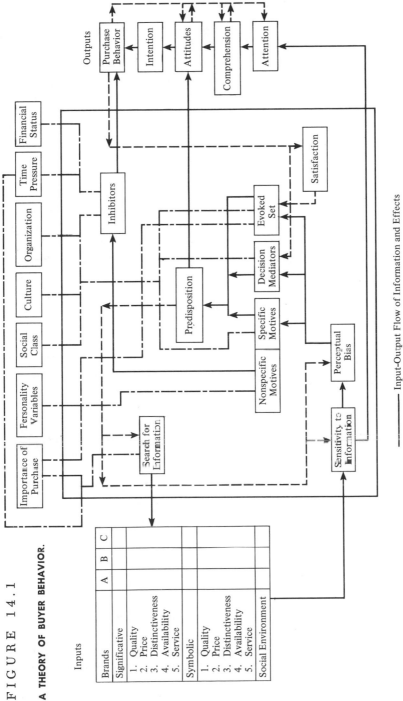

FIGURE 14.1

A THEORY OF BUYER BEHAVIOR.

Inputs

Outputs

——— Input-Output Flow of Information and Effects

- - - - Feedback Effects

—·—·— Influence of Exogenous Variables

Brands	A	B	C
Significative			
1. Quality			
2. Price			
3. Distinctiveness			
4. Availability			
5. Service			
Symbolic			
1. Quality			
2. Price			
3. Distinctiveness			
4. Availability			
5. Service			
Social Environment			

Importance of Purchase · Personality Variables · Social Class · Culture · Organization · Time Pressure · Financial Status

Search for Information · Inhibitors

Nonspecific Motives · Specific Motives · Predisposition · Decision Mediators · Evoked Set

Sensitivity to Information · Perceptual Bias · Satisfaction

Purchase Behavior · Intention · Attitudes · Comprehension · Attention

ment. This environment is classified as either commercial or social. The commercial environment consists of the marketing activities of various firms, by which they attempt to communicate to the buyer. From the buyer's point of view, these communications basically come via either the brand objects themselves or some linguistic or pictorial representation of brand attributes. If brand elements such as price, quality, service, distinctiveness, or availability are communicated through brand objects (significates), the stimuli are defined and classified as *significative* stimuli. If, on the other hand, brand attributes represented by linguistic or pictorial symbols are communicated via mass media, billboards, catalogs, salesmen, etc., the stimuli from these commercial sources are classified as *symbolic* stimuli. We view the marketing mix as the optimum allocation of funds between the two major channels of communication to the buyer—significative and symbolic.

Each commercial input variable is hypothesized to be multivariate. The five major dimensions of a brand—price, quality, distinctiveness, availability, and service—probably summarize the various attributes. The same dimensions are present in both the significative and symbolic communication that becomes the input stimuli for the buyer. However, certain dimensions may be more appropriately conveyed by significative rather than symbolic communication, and vice versa. For example, price is easily communicated by both channels; shape may best be communicated by two-dimensional pictures rather than verbal communication. Finally, size may not be easily communicated by any symbolic representation: the physical product (significate) may be necessary.

The third stimulus input variable is the information that the buyer's social environment provides for a purchase decision. The most obvious example is word-of-mouth communication.

The inputs to the buyer's mental state from the three major categories of stimuli are processed and stored through their interaction with a series of hypothetical constructs. The buyer may react to these stimuli immediately, or later.

Hypothetical Constructs

Our hypothetical constructs and their interrelationships are the result of an integration of Hull's (1943, 1952) learning theory, Osgood's (1957[a,b]) cognitive theory, and Berlyne's (1963) theory of exploratory behavior, along with other ideas.

These constructs fall into two classes: (1) those having to do with perception, and (2) those having to do with learning. Perceptual constructs serve the function of information processing; learning constructs serve the function of concept formation. It is interesting that, after years of experience in advertising, Reeves (1961) arrived at a very similar classification, his "penetration" is analogous to perceptual variables, and his "unique selling propositions" are analogous to learning variables. We will first describe learning constructs, since they are the major components of decision making; the perceptual constructs which serve the important role of obtaining and processing information are more complex, and will be described later.

Learning Constructs

The learning constructs are labeled (1) motives—specific and non-specific, (2) brand-potential of the evoked set, (3) decision mediators, (4) predisposition toward brands, (5) inhibitors, and (6) satisfaction with the purchase of a brand.

Motive is impetus to action. The buyer is motivated by expectation or anticipation, based on learning from the outcome of past purchase of a brand in his evoked set. Motives or goals may be thought of as constituting a means-end chain, and hence as being general or specific, depending upon their position in the chain.

The specific motives—lower level motives in the means-end chain—are very closely anchored to the attributes of a product class; in this way they become purchase criteria. Examples of specific motives are those for buying a dietary product—low calories, nutrition, taste, and value. Similarly, the specific motives in buying an air conditioner might be durability, quietness, cooling power, and design.

Very often, several specific motives are nothing more than indicators of some underlying, more general motive; that is, some motive that is higher in the means-end chain. In the foregoing example, the specific motives of nutrition and low calories might be indicators of the common motive of good health.

Motives also serve the important function of raising the buyer's general motivational state, thereby rousing him to pay attention to environmental stimuli. Probable examples of nonspecific motives are anxiety and fear, the personality variables of authoritarianism, exhibitionism, and aggressiveness, and the social motives of power, status, and prestige. Although they are non-specific, they are not innate but learned, mostly as a result of acculturation. The nonspecific motives also possess a hierarchy within themselves. For example, anxiety is considered to be the source of another motive, that of the need for money (Brown, 1961).

Brand potential of the evoked set is a second learning construct. A buyer who is familiar with a product class has an evoked set of alternatives to satisfy his motives. The elements of his evoked set are some of the brands that make up the product class. This concept is important because the brands in a buyer's evoked set constitute competition for the seller.

A brand is, of course, a class concept, like many other objects or things. The buyer attaches a *word* to this concept—a label or brand name. The brand name conveys certain meanings, including its potential to satisfy his motives. In an advanced economy with relatively careful quality controls, the buyer in generally assured that any one brand object is like another. If quality controls are not adequate, the buyer will probably not summarize the potential of a brand in one word or label, but instead divide it into subclasses.

Various brands in the buyer's evoked set will generally satisfy his goal structure differently. One brand may possess such strong potential that it is an ideal brand for the buyer. Another brand may satisfy his motives barely enough to be part of his evoked set. Through a learning process, the buyer obtains and stores knowledge of each brand's potential, and then ranks them in order of their potential to satisfy his wants. The evoked set, in short, is a set of alternatives to be evaluated. Predisposition represents the buyer's preference ranking of them.

Decision mediators, a third learning construct, are the buyer's mental rules for matching alternatives with motives and ranking them in terms of their want-satisfying capacity. As mental rules, they exhibit reasoning, wherein the cognitive elements related to alternatives and motives are structured. In addition, decision mediators also contain a set of criteria by which the buyer denotatively discriminates between the brands he views as being in a product class, and those brands that are not. The words he uses to describe these criteria are the words he thinks with and finds easy to remember. These criteria are important to the manufacturer, because if he knows them he can deliberately build into his product and its promotion those characteristics which will differentiate his brand from competing brands.

Decision mediators thus represent enduring cognitive rules established by the process of learning, and their function is to establish meaningful and congruent relations among brands, so that the buyer can manifest goal-directed behavior. In view of the fact that decision mediators are learned, principles of learning become crucial in understanding their development and change over time.

There are two broad sources of learning: (1) actual experience, and (2) information. Actual experience can be with either the *same* buying situation in the past, or with a *similar* buying situation. The latter is generally labeled "generalization." Similarly, information as a source of learning can come from either the buyer's commercial or his social environment. Later, we will elaborate on each of these sources of learning.

Predisposition, a fourth construct, is the summary effect of the previous three constructs. It refers to the buyer's preference toward brands in his evoked set. It is, in fact, an aggregate index expressed in attitudes, which in turn can be measured by attitude scales. It might be visualized as the "place" where brands in the evoked set are compared with the mediator's choice criteria, to yield a judgment on the relative contribution of the brands to the buyer's motives. This judgment includes not only an estimate of the value of the brand, but also an estimate of the confidence with which the buyer holds that position. This uncertainty aspect of predisposition can be called "brand ambiguity," in that the more confidently he holds it, the less ambiguous the connotative meaning of the brand is to him and the more likely he is to buy it (G. S. Day, 1967).

Inhibitors, the fifth learning construct, are forces in the environment which create important disruptive influences on the actual purchase of a brand, even when the buyer has reasoned out that that brand will best satisfy his motives. In other words, when the buyer is motivated to buy the product class and is predisposed to buy a particular brand, he may not buy it because certain environmental forces inhibit the purchase act and prevent him from satisfying his preferences.

We postulate at least four types of inhibitors. They are (1) a high price for the brand, (2) lack of availability of the brand, (3) time pressure on the buyer, and (4) the buyer's financial status. The first two are part of the environmental stimuli, and therefore they are part of the input system. The last two come from the two exogenous variables of the same name. Temporary barriers to the purchase of a brand may also be created by social constraints emanating from other exogenous variables.

An essential feature of all inhibitors is that they are *not internalized* by the buyer, because their occurrence is random and strictly situational. However, for a given buyer, some inhibitors may persist systematically over time. If they persist long enough, the buyer is likely to incorporate them as part of his decision mediators, thus permitting them to affect the mental structure of his alternatives and motives. An example of such internalization might be the consequences of the constant time pressure a housewife faces because she has taken a job. Continuation of the time pressure may alter her evoked set as well as her motive structure. Convenience and time saving become important motives, and her evoked set may come to include time-saving brands, such as instant coffee. Similarly, a brand may be withdrawn by a company because of its stage in the product life cycle. The permanent unavailability of that brand will be learned and internalized by buyers, and they will remove that brand from their evoked sets.

Satisfaction, the last of the learning constructs, refers to the degree of congruence between the actual consequences of purchase and consumption of a brand, and what was expected from it by the buyer at the time of purchase. If the actual outcomes are judged by the buyer to be *better than or equal to* the expected, the buyer will feel satisfied; that is,

$$\text{actual consequences} \geqq \text{expected consequences.}$$

If, on the other hand, the actual outcomes are judged to be *less than* what he expected, the buyer will feel dissatisfied; that is,

$$\text{actual consequences} < \text{expected consequences.}$$

Satisfaction or dissatisfaction with a brand can be with any one of its different attributes. If the brand proves to be more satisfactory than the buyer expected, the attractiveness of the brand will be enhanced. If it proves less satisfactory than he expected, its attractiveness will diminish. Satisfaction, therefore, affects the ranking of brands in the evoked set for the next buying decision.

We also think that, if a brand purchase proves completely unsatisfactory, the buyer will *remove* the brand from his evoked set. In other words, he will not consider it for future purchases. If the brand has proved extremely satisfactory, the buyer will retain *only* the purchased brand in his evoked set; other brands will have close to zero probability of consideration. In short, *extreme* outcomes are likely to affect the *number* of brands in the evoked set, and reasonable discrepancies between actual and expected outcomes will affect the *ranking* of the brands in the evoked set.

Relations Among Learning Constructs

Several important notions underlie the concept of predisposition toward a brand and its related variables. The simplest way to describe them is to state that we may classify a decision process as either "extensive problem solving," "limited problem solving," or "routine response behavior," depending on the strength of predisposition toward brands. In the early phases of buying, the buyer does not yet have well-developed decision mediators; specifically, his product-class concept is not well formed and his predisposition is low. As he acquires information and gains experience in buying and consuming a brand, his decision mediators become firm and his predisposition toward that brand is generally high.

In extensive problem solving, predisposition toward a brand is low. None of the brands are sufficiently discriminated on the basis of their decision-mediator criteria for the buyer to show preference for any one brand. At this stage of decision making, brand ambiguity is high, and the buyer actively seeks information from his environment. The more extensive the search for information, the greater is *latency of response*—the time interval between initiation of a decision and its completion. Similarly, deliberation or reasoning is high, since the buyer lacks a well-defined product-class concept—the denotative aspect of his decision mediators. He is also likely to consider many brands as part of his evoked set, and stimuli coming from the commercial environment are less likely to trigger an immediate purchase reaction.

When predisposition toward brands is moderate, the buyer's decision process is one of limited problem solving. Brand ambiguity still exists, since he is not able to discriminate and compare brands to develop a preference for one brand over others. He is likely to seek information, but not to the extent he does for extensive problem solving. More importantly, he seeks information to compare and discriminate various brands more on a relative basis than to compare them absolutely. He thinks and deliberates, since his predispositions are only tentatively defined. His evoked set consists of a small number of brands, and he has about the same degree of preference for each of them.

In routine response behavior, the buyer has accumulated sufficient experience and information to eliminate brand ambiguity, and he has a high level of predisposition toward one or two brands in his evoked set. He is unlikely to actively seek information from the environment, since such information is not needed. Also, insofar as he does admit information it will tend to be that which supports his current choice. Very often, this congruent information will act as a "triggering cue" to motivate him to manifest purchase behavior.

Much impulse purchase behavior is really the outcome of a strong predisposition and a facilitating commercial stimulus, such as a store display. The buyer's evoked set consists of a few brands, toward which he is highly predisposed. However, he will have greater preference toward one or two brands in his evoked set than toward the others.

As mentioned earlier, predisposition is an aggregate index of how well a brand conforms to the choice criteria contained in a decision mediator. Thus, any changes in these criteria as a result of learning from experience or information imply some change in predisposition. The greater the learning, the stronger is predisposition toward brands in the evoked set. The exact nature of learning will be described later, when we discuss the dynamics of buying behavior. However, there are two other issues which need some attention here.

First, although our focus is on brand choice behavior, the buyer also simplifies the total sequence of behavior necessary to make a purchase— i.e., going to the store, looking at products, paying at the counter, etc.—by reducing the number of steps and ordering them in a definite sequence. The greater is his predisposition, the more will be his simplification of total buying behavior, and therefore the more routine will be his purchase behavior.

Second, if the purchase cycle is very long, as is the case for automobiles and other durable appliances, the buyer may develop firm decision mediators and yet manifest exploratory behavior to a marked degree at each purchase decision, because (1) market conditions invariably change and the buyer may find past experience insufficient, and (2) his decision mediators have become fuzzy, through lack of use and the resultant forgetting.

Perceptual Constructs

Another set of constructs serves the function of procuring and processing information relevant to a purchase decision. As mentioned earlier, information can come from any one of the three stimulus inputs—significative commercial stimuli, symbolic commercial stimuli, and social stimuli. Here we will describe only the constructs; their use by the buyer will be explained when we discuss the dynamics of buying behavior. The perceptual constructs in Figure 14.1 are (1) sensitivity to information, (2) perceptual bias, and (3) search for information.

A perceptual phenomenon implies either ignoring a physical event which could be a stimulus, seeing it attentively, or sometimes imagining what is not present in reality. All perceptual phenomena create some change in the quantity or quality of objective information.

Sensitivity to information refers to the opening and closing of sensory receptors which control the intake of information. The manifestation of this phenomenon is generally called "perceptual vigilance" (paying attention) or "perceptual defense" (ignoring information). Sensitivity to information therefore serves primarily as a gatekeeper for information entering the buyer's nervous system, thus controlling the quantity of information input.

Sensitivity to information is a function of two variables, according to Berlyne (1963). One is the degree of stimulus ambiguity. If a stimulus to which the buyer is exposed is very familiar or too simple, its ambiguity is low and the buyer will not pay attention—unless he is predisposed to such information from past learning. Furthermore, if stimulus ambiguity continues to be low, the buyer feels a sense of monotony and actively seeks other information—he can be said to *complicate* his environment. If the stimulus is so complex and ambiguous that the buyer finds it hard to comprehend, he will ignore it by resorting to perceptual defense. Only if the stimulus is moderately ambiguous will the buyer be motivated to pay attention and freely absorb objective information about the brand under consideration.

In response to a single communication, the buyer at first may find the information complex and ambiguous and tend to ignore it. As the information continues to enter his nervous system, he may find it really to be at the medium level of ambiguity, and pay attention. As the process of communication progresses and he pays continuing attention, he may find the information too simple and look for more complex information.

The second variable which governs sensitivity to information is the buyer's predisposition toward the brand which is the subject of that information. The buyer learns to attach connotative meanings to a brand and to the symbols which stand for the brand. Thus, both the *source* of communication and the *content* of communication, as well as the brand itself, can come to have meaning for him. For example, he may have learned in the past to associate *low* credibility with commercial sources and *high* credibility with social sources. Similarly, he may attach connotations of quality to certain attributes of the brand, such as package, color, flavor, and taste. These connotations are part of his predisposition toward the brand.

Predisposition thus acts as a feedback in Figure 14.1, governing sensitivity to information, and, in turn, the intake of further information. This feedback is his degree of interest. The more pertinent to the brand is the information, the more likely the buyer is to open up his receptors and pay attention to it. Similarly, the more pertinent the source, the greater the attention the buyer is likely to give the communication.

Perceptual bias is the second perceptual construct. The buyer not only selectively attends to information, but he may actually distort it, once it enters his nervous system. In other words, the quality of information can be altered by the buyer. He may distort the cognitive elements contained in information to make them congruent with his own frame of reference, as determined by the amount of information he has already stored. Theories of cognitive consistency have been developed (Feldman, 1966; Fishbein, 1967) to explain how this congruency is established and what its consequences are, in terms of the distortion of information that might be expected. Most qualitative change in information occurs as a result of feedback from various decision components, such as motives, the evoked set, and decision mediators. These relations are too complex, however, to describe in this summary.

The perceptual phenomena described above are likely to be less operative if information is received from the buyer's social environment. This is so because (1) the source of social information (such as a friend) is likely to be favorably regarded by the buyer, and (2) the information itself is modified by the social environment (the friend) so that it conforms to the needs of the buyer; therefore, distorted reception and further modification is less likely.

Search for information is the third perceptual construct. During the total buying phase, which extends over time and involves several repeat purchases of a product class, there are times when the buyer *actively* seeks information. It is very important to distinguish times when he passively receives information from occasions when he actively seeks it. We believe that perceptual bias is less operative in the latter instance, and that a commercial communication at that stage has, therefore, a high probability of influencing the buyer.

Active seeking of information occurs when the buyer senses ambiguity of brand meaning in his evoked set. As we saw earlier, this happens in the extensive problem-solving and limited problem-solving phases of the decision process. Ambiguity of brand meaning exists because the buyer is not certain of the purchase outcome of each brand. In other words, he has not yet learned enough about alternatives to establish an expectancy of brand potential that will satisfy his motives. This type of brand ambiguity is generally confined to initial buying of that brand.

However, ambiguity may exist despite knowledge of relative brand potential. This ambiguity rests in the buyer's inability to discriminate between alternatives. The buyer may be unable to discriminate because his motives are not well structured; he does not know how to order them. He may then seek information to resolve conflict among goals—a resolution implied in his learning of the appropriate product-class aspect of decision mediators, as discussed earlier.

There is yet another stage of buying behavior in which the buyer is likely to seek information. It is when the buyer has established a routine decision process, but he is so familiar and satiated with repeat buying that he feels bored. Then all the existing alternatives in his evoked set, including the more preferred brand, become unacceptable to him. He seeks change or variety in that buying situation. In order to obtain this change, he actively searches for information on other alternatives (brands) that he never considered before. At this stage, he is particularly receptive to any information about new brands. This explains large advertising budgets in a highly stable industry, a phenomenon which has long baffled both the critics and defenders of advertising. New products on the market and buyer forgetfulness are not plausible explanations.

Response Variables

The complexity of buyer behavior extends beyond our hypothetical constructs. Just as there is a variety of inputs, there is also a variety of buyer responses, which become relevant for different areas of marketing strategy. The wide variety of consumer responses can be easily appreciated in the diversity of measures used to evaluate advertising effectiveness. We have attempted to classify and order this diversity of buyer responses in terms of output variables. Most of our output variables are directly related to some, but not other constructs. Each output variable serves different purposes, both in marketing practice and in fundamental research.

Attention

Attention is related to sensitivity to information. It is a buyer response that indicates the magnitude of his information intake. Attention is measured continuously during the time interval that the buyer is receiving information. There are several psycho-physiological methods of quantifying the degree of attention a buyer pays to a message. Awareness is not an appropriate measure, because it is a stock concept, not a flow concept.

Comprehension

Comprehension refers to the store of knowledge about a brand that the buyer possesses at any point in time. This knowledge can vary from simple awareness of a single brand's existence, to a complete description of the attributes of a brand. It reflects the denotative meaning of the brand. In that sense it is strictly cognitive, and not included in the motivational aspects of behavior. Simply stated, it is a description of the common denotative elements of the brand in words with which the buyer communicates, thinks, and remembers. Some of the standard measures of advertising effectiveness such as awareness, aided or unaided recall, and recognition may capture different aspects of the buyer's knowledge of a brand.

Attitude Toward a Brand

Attitude toward a brand is the buyer's evaluation of the brand's potential to satisfy his motives. It therefore includes the connotative aspects of the brand concept; it contains those aspects of the brand which are relevant to the buyer's goals. Attitude is directly related to predisposition, consisting of both the evaluation of a brand in terms of the decision-mediator criteria of choice, and the confidence with which that evaluation is held.

Intention to Buy

Intention to buy is the buyer's forecast of which brand he will buy. It includes not only the buyer's predisposition toward a brand, but also a forecast of inhibitors. Intention to buy has been used extensively in predicting the purchases of durable goods, with some recent refinements in terms of the buyer's confidence in his own forecast; however, these studies are in terms of broadly defined product classes (Juster, 1964). We may characterize intention to buy as a response short of actual purchase behavior.

Purchase Behavior

Purchase behavior is the overt manifestation of the buyer's predisposition, in conjunction with any inhibitors that may be present. It differs from attitude to the extent that inhibitors are taken into consideration; and it differs from intention to the extent that it is actual behavior, which the buyer only forecasted in his intention.

What becomes a part of a company's sales, or what the consumer records in a diary as a panel member, is only the terminal act in the sequence of shopping and buying. Very often, it is useful to observe the complete movement of the buyer from his home to the store and his purchase in the store. Yoell (1965), for example, presents several case histories showing that time-and-motion study of consumer purchase behavior has useful marketing implications.

We think that, at times, it may be helpful to go so far as to incorporate the act of consumption into the definition of purchase behavior. We have, for example, used a technique for investigating decision making in which the buyer verbally describes the sequential pattern of his purchase and consumption behavior in a given buying situation. Out of this description, we have obtained a "flow chart" of sequential decision making which reveals the number and structure of the decision rules the buyer employs.

Several characteristics of purchase behavior become useful if we observe the buyer in a repetitive buying situation. These include the incidence of buying a brand, the quantity bought, and the purchase cycle. Several stochastic models of brand loyalty, for example, have been developed (Sheth, 1967; this book). Similarly, we could take the magnitude purchased and compare light buyers with heavy buyers to determine if heavy buyers are more loyal buyers.

The Interrelationships of Response Variables

In Figure 14.1 the five response variables are ordered to create a hierarchy, similar to the variety of hierarchies used in practice, such as AIDA (attention, interest, desire, and action); to the Lavidge and Steiner (1961) hierarchy of advertising effectiveness; as well as to the different mental states a person is alleged by anthropologists and sociologists to pass through when he adopts an innovation (Rogers, 1962[b]). There are, however, some important differences which we believe will clarify certain conceptual and methodological issues raised by Palda (1966) and others.

First, a response variable called "attention" has been added, which is crucial because it indicates whether or not a communication is received by the buyer. Second, several different aspects of the cognitive realm of behavior, such as awareness, recall, and recognition, are lumped into one category called "comprehension," to suggest that they are all varying indicators of the buyer's storage of information about a brand. In this way we obtain leverage for understanding buyer innovation. Third, attitude is defined to include its affective and conative aspects, since any attempt to establish causal relations between attitude and behavior must take into account the motivational aspects of attitude. Furthermore, the perceptual and the preference maps of the buyer with respect to brands are separated into "comprehension" and "attitude," respectively. Fourth, another variable, "intention to buy," is added, because properly defined and measured intentions for several product classes in both durable and semidurable goods have proved useful. To the extent that intention incorporates a buyer's forecast of his inhibitors, it might form a basis for marketing strategy designed to remove the inhibitors before actual purchase behavior is manifested.

Finally, and most important, we have incorporated several feedback effects which were described when the hypothetical constructs were discussed. We will now show the relations as direct connections among response variables—although these "outside" relations are merely the reflection of relations among the hypothetical constructs. For example, purchase behavior via satisfaction involves consequences that affect decision mediators and brand potential in the evoked set; any change in mediators and brand potential constitutes a change in predisposition. Attitude is related to predisposition, and therefore it can change in the period from pre-purchase to post-purchase. By incorporating this feedback, we are opening the way to resolving the question of whether attitude causes purchase behavior, or purchase behavior causes attitude. Over a period of time the relation is interdependent, each affecting the other. Similarly, we have a feedback from "attitude" to "comprehension" and "attention," the rationale for which was given when perceptual constructs were described.

THE DYNAMICS OF BUYING BEHAVIOR

We will now explain the changes in hypothetical constructs which occur as a result of learning. Learning constructs are, of course, directly involved in the change that we label "learning." Since some learning constructs indirectly govern perceptual constructs by way of feedback, there is also an indirect effect on the learning constructs themselves. As mentioned earlier, decision mediators, which structure motives and the evoked set, can be learned from two broad sources, (1) past experience, and (2) information. Past experience can be further classified as deriving from buying a specified product or buying a similar product. Similarly, information can come from the buyer's commercial environment or his social environment; if the source is commercial, the information may be significative or symbolic.

We will look at development and change in learning constructs as due to (1) generalization from similar buying situations, (2) repeat buying of the same product class, and (3) information.

Generalization from Similar Purchase Situations

Some decision mediators are often similar across product classes because many motives are common to a wide variety of purchasing activities. For example, a buyer may satisfy his health motive by buying many different product classes. Similarly, he may buy many product classes at the same place; this very often leads to spatial or contiguous generalization. The capacity to generalize allows the buyer to exercise great flexibility in adapting his purchase behavior to the myriad of varying market conditions he faces.

Generalization refers to the transfer of responses from past situations to new situations which are similar, based on the relevance of stimuli. It saves the buyer time and effort otherwise spent in seeking information to resolve the uncertainty inevitable in a new situation. Generalization can occur at any one of the several levels of purchase activity, but we are primarily interested in the generalization of those decision mediators which involve only *brand-choice* behavior, in contrast to choice of store or choice of time and day for shopping.

Two kinds of brand generalization should be distinguished. First, there is *stimulus generalization*, in which the buyer—who has associated a brand purchase with a decision mediator (product class)—associates with the same decision mediator a new brand similar to the old one. For example, suppose a buyer has a decision mediator which calls for the purchase of *double-edged* shaving blades. His purchase response may then be transferred to a new brand of *stainless steel* double-edged blades via the same decision mediator. He may further refine his decision mediator to associate his purchase behavior with only one brand of new stainless steel blades, rather than with all.

Stimulus generalization can occur, not only when two brands are physically similar, but also when two brands are physically dissimilar but possess the same meaning. This is called *semantic generalization.* It is likely to occur when a radically new product is introduced by a company with which the buyer has had satisfactory past experience. The buyer can generalize via the company image. This is especially true of durable appliances, where a brand name is common to different products.

Second, there is *response generalization*, in which the buyer generalizes an *old response* to a *new response*, given the *same stimulus*. It can occur when the buyer, after reading an ad for brand A, goes to the store to buy it, but finds brand B, which is similar to brand A, and switches. In the same fashion, a buyer may "move up" the quality ladder for a particular make of automobile. Finally, he might buy *larger* packages of the same brand product.

Just as we find semantic *stimulus* generalization, we also find semantic *response* generalization. For example, a buyer who is motivated to purchase low-calorie food may generalize his response from skim milk to diet cola.

Repeat Purchase Experiences

Another source of change in learning constructs is the repeated purchase of the same product class over a period of time. In Figure 14.1 the purchase of a brand involves two types of feedback, one affecting decision mediators and the other affecting brand potential of the evoked set. First, the experience of buying, with all its cognitive aspects of memory, reasoning, etc., has a learning effect on decision mediators. This occurs irrespective of which specific brand the buyer chooses in any one purchase decision, because decision mediators, like motives, are product-specific and not limited to any one brand. Hence, every purchase has an incremental effect in more firmly establishing decision mediators. This is easy to visualize if we remember that buying behavior is a series of mental and motor steps; the actual choice is only its terminal act.

Purchase of a brand creates certain satisfactions for the buyer which he compares with his evaluation of the brand's potential. If the buyer is satisfied, the potential of the brand is enhanced, increasing the probability of repeat purchase. If he is dissatisfied, the potential of the brand is diminished, and the probability of repeat purchase is reduced. Hence the second feedback, from purchase behavior to satisfaction, changes the attractiveness of the brand purchased.

If there are no inhibitory forces influencing the buyer, he will continue to buy a brand which proves satisfactory. In the initial stages of decision making, he may show some tendency to oscillate between brands in order to formulate his decision mediators. In other words, he may learn by trial-and-error at first, then settle on a brand, and thereafter buy it with such regularity as to suggest that he is brand loyal. However, unless a product involves high purchase risk, there is a time limit on this brand loyality: he may become bored with his preferred brand and look for something new.

Information as a Source of Learning

The third major means by which learning constructs are changed is information received from (1) the buyer's commercial environment, consisting of advertising, promotion, salesmanship, and retail shelf display; and (2) his social environment, consisting of his family, friends, reference groups, and social class.

We will first describe the influence of information as if perceptual constructs were absent. In other words, we will assume that the buyer receives information with perfect fidelity, as it exists in the environment.

Also, we will discuss separately information received from commercial and social environments.

The Commercial Environment

A company communicates its offerings to buyers either by the physical brand itself (significates), or by symbols (pictorial or linguistic) which represent the brand. Significative and symbolic communication are the two major means of interaction between sellers and buyers.

Figure 14.1 shows the influence of information on motives, decision mediators, the evoked set, and inhibitors. We believe that the influence of commercial information on motives (specific and nonspecific) is limited. The main effect is primarily to *intensify* whatever motives the buyer has, rather than to create new ones. For example, a physical display of the brand may intensify his notives above the threshold level, which, combined with strong predisposition, can result in impulse (unplanned) purchase. A similar reaction is possible when an ad creates sufficient intensity of motive to provide an impetus for the buyer to go to the store. A second way to influence motives is to show the *perceived instrumentality* of the brand, and thereby make it a part of the buyer's defined set of alternatives.

Finally, to a very limited extent, marketing stimuli may change the *content of motives*. This, we believe, is rare. The general conception among both marketing men and laymen is that marketing stimuli do change the buyer's motives. However, on a closer examination it would appear that what is changed is the *intensity* of those motives already provided by the buyer's social environment. Many dormant or latent motives may become stimulated. The secret of success very often lies in identifying the change in motives created by social change and intensifying them, as seems to be the case in the advertising projection of youthfulness for many buying situations.

Marketing stimuli are important in determining and changing the buyer's evoked set. Commercial information tells him of the existence of brands (awareness), their identifying characteristics (comprehension plus brand name), and their relevance to the satisfaction of his needs (decision mediator).

Marketing stimuli are also important in creating and changing the buyer's decision mediators. They become important sources for *creating* (learning) decision mediators when the buyer has no prior experience to rely upon. In other words, when he is in the extensive-problem-solving (EPS) stage, it is marketing and social stimuli which are his important sources of learning. Similarly, when the buyer actively seeks information because all existing alternatives are unacceptable to him, marketing stimuli become important in *changing* his decision mediators.

Finally, marketing stimuli can unwittingly create inhibitors. For example, a company's efforts to emphasize a price-quality association may result in a high-price inhibition in the mind of the buyer. Similarly, in emphasizing the details of usage and consumption of a product, marketing communication might perhaps create inhibition related to time pressure.

The Social Environment

The social environment of the buyer—family, friends, and reference groups—is another major source of information influencing his buying behavior. Most social input is likely to be symbolic (linguistic), although at times a friend may show the physical product to the buyer.

Information from the social environment also affects the four learning constructs: motives, decision mediators, the evoked set, and inhibitors. However, the effect on these constructs is different than that of the commercial environment. First, information about brands is considerably modified by the social environment before it reaches the buyer. Most of the modifications are likely to be in adding connotative meanings to brands and their attributes, and in the effects of such perceptual variables as sensitivity to information and perceptual bias.

Second, the buyer's social environment will probably strongly influence the content of his motives, and his ordering of them to establish a goal structure. Several research studies have concentrated on such influences (Bourne, 1957, this book; Bush and London, 1960; Gruen, 1960; Laird, 1950; Katz and Lazarsfeld, 1955).

Third, the buyer's social environment may also affect his evoked set. This is particularly true when he lacks experience. Furthermore, if the product class is important to the buyer, and he is not technically competent or he is uncertain in evaluating the consequences of the brand for his needs, he may rely more on the social than on the marketing environment for information. This is well documented by several studies using the perceived risk hypothesis (Bauer, 1960 and this book, 1961; Bauer and Wortzel, 1966; Cox, 1962; S. M. Cunningham, 1966; Arndt, 1967[a]).

Information-Processing Effects

As we have said, distortion of stimuli by the perceptual constructs—sensitivity to information, perceptual bias, and search for information—is likely to be much greater for marketing stimuli than for social stimuli. This is so essentially because the buyer attaches greater credibility—competence and trust—to social sources, and because of the ease of two-way communication in social situations. Similarly, the buyer may more actively seek information from his social environment, particularly evaluative information.

Thus, the foregoing discussion of the commercial and social environments must be qualified by the perceptual effects inevitable in any information processing.

EXOGENOUS VARIABLES

As mentioned earlier, there are several influences operating on the buyer's decisions which we treat as exogenous; that is, we do not explain their formation and change. Many of these influences come from the buyer's social environment, and we wish to separate those effects of his environment which have occurred in the past and are not related to a specific decision, from those which are current and do directly affect the decisions that occur while the buyer is being observed. The inputs that occur during the observation period provide information to the buyer to help his current decision making. Past influences are already embedded in the values of the perceptual and learning constructs. These exogenous variables are particularly appropriate as market-segmenting variables, because they are causally linked to purchase.

Strictly speaking, there is no need for exogenous variables, since in the social sciences these forces are traditionally left to *ceteris paribus*. We will bring them out explicitly, however, for the sake of research design, so that a researcher may control or take into account the individual differences among buyers that are due to past influence. Incorporating the effects of these exogenous variables reduces the unexplained variance, or error in estimation, which it is particularly essential to control under field conditions. Figure 14.1 presents a set of exogenous variables which we believe provide the control essential to obtaining satisfactory predictive relations between the inputs and outputs of the system.

Importance of purchase refers to differential degrees of ego-involvement in or commitment to different product classes. It is therefore an entity which must be carefully examined in inter-product studies. Importance of purchase will influence the size of the evoked set and the magnitude of the search for information. For example, the more important the product class, the larger is the evoked set (Howard and Moore, 1963).

Time pressure is a current exogenous variable and therefore specific to a decision situation. When a buyer feels pressed for time, because of any of several environmental influences, he must allocate his time among alternative uses. In this process a reallocation unfavorable to purchasing activity can occur. Time pressure will create inhibition, as mentioned earlier. It will also unfavorably affect the search for information.

Financial status refers to the constraint a buyer may feel because he lacks financial resources. This can affect his purchase behavior by creating a barrier (inhibitor) to purchasing the most preferred brand. For example, a buyer may want to purchase an expensive foreign car, but lacking sufficient financial resource, he will settle for a low-priced American model.

Personality traits are such variables as self-confidence, self-esteem, authoritarianism, and anxiety, which have been researched to identify individual differences. These individual differences are "topic free" and therefore supposedly exert their effect across product classes. We believe their effect is felt on (1) nonspecific motives and (2) the evoked set. For example, the more anxious a person, the greater his motivational arousal; dominant personalities are more likely (by a small margin) to buy a Ford instead of a Chevrolet; the more authoritarian a person, the narrower the category width of his evoked set.

Social and organizational setting involves the group, a higher level of social organization than the individual. It includes informal social organization, such as family and reference groups, which is relevant for *consumer behavior*; and formal organization, which constitutes much of the environment for *industrial purchasing*. Organizational variables are those of small group interaction, such as power, status, and authority. We believe that the underlying processes of intergroup conflict in both industrial and consumer buying behavior are in principle very similar, and that the differences are largely due to the formal nature of industrial activity. Organization, both formal and social, is a crucial variable because it influences most of the learning constructs.

Social class involves a still higher level of social organization, the social aggregate. Several indices are available to classify people socially. Perhaps the most common index is Warner's classification (see Ch 5, this book). Social class mediates the relation between input and output by influencing (1) specific motives, (2) decision mediators, (3) the evoked set, and (4) inhibitors. The latter influence is important, particularly in the adoption of innovations.

Culture provides a more comprehensive social framework than social class. It consists of patterns of behavior, symbols, ideas, and their attached values. Culture will influence motives, decision mediators, and inhibitors.

CONCLUSIONS

In the preceding pages we have summarized a theory of buyer brand choice. It is complex, but we strongly believe that complexity is essential to an adequate description of buying behavior.

We hope that our theory will provide new insights into past empirical data, and guide future research by instilling coherence and unity into current research, which now tends to be atomistic and unrelated. Models can be constructed of the relations between the output intervening variables, and a splendid beginning along these lines has been carried out by Day (1967). Also, as the hypothetical constructs are explored, elements of the constructs will be broken out and better defined, so that these elements can be invested with the operational status of intervening variables. McClelland's work with achievement, for example, has shown how this transformation can occur with motive. In this way our theory suggests specific programs of research.

We are vigorously pursuing a large research program aimed at testing the validity of this theory. The research was designed in terms of the variables specified by the theory, and our preliminary results lead us to believe that it was fruitful to use the theory in this way. Because it specifies a number of relationships, it has clearly been useful in interpreting preliminary findings. Above all, it is a great aid in communication among the researchers and with the companies involved.

Finally, a number of new ideas are set forth in the theory, but we would like to call attention to three in particular. The concept of evoked set provides a means of reducing the noise in many analyses of buying behavior. The product class concept offers a new dimension for incorporating many of the complexities of innovation, and especially for integrating systematically the idea of innovation into a framework of psychological constructs. Anthropologists and sociologists have been generally content to deal with peripheral variables and to omit the psychological constructs which link the peripheral variables to behavior. The habit-perception cycle in which perception and habit respond inversely offers hope for explaining, to a great extent, the phenomenon which has long baffled both critics and defenders of advertising: large advertising expenditures in a stable market, where, on the surface, it would seem that buyers are already sated with information.

15

Consumer brand choice as a learning process[1]

Alfred A. Kuehn

The phenomenon of consumer brand shifting is a central element underlying the dynamics of the marketplace. To understand and describe market trends adequately, we must first establish the nature of the influences on consumer

[1] The research underlying this paper has been supported by grants from the Graduate School of Industrial Administration and the Market Research Corporation of America. The paper is based in part on lectures presented at the Ford Foundation Faculty Seminar in Marketing, conducted by the University of Chicago at Williamstown, Mass., in August 1961.

From *Journal of Advertising Research*, 2 (December, 1962), pp. 10–17, © 1962, Advertising Research Foundation. Reprinted by permission.
    Alfred A. Kuehn is an assistant professor in the Graduate School of Industrial Administration at the Carnegie Institute of Technology, as well as a consultant to the Market Research Corporation of America and to major merchandisers of packaged grocery and drug products. He received a B.S. in 1952, an M.S. in 1954, and a Ph.D. in 1960, all from Carnegie Tech. The present article appears in a book coedited by Dr. Kuehn (with Ronald E. Frank and William F. Massy), *Quantitative Techniques in Marketing Analysis*, just published by Richard D. Irwin.

choice with respect to products and brands. Research directed at establishing the conditions under which consumers will shift from one brand to another offers hope of providing a framework within which to evaluate the influence of price, advertising, distribution and shelf space, and various types of sales promotion.

What do we know about brand choice? What behavioral mechanisms appear to underlie this phenomenon? Is such behavior habitual? Is learning involved? Does repeated purchasing of a brand reinforce the brand choice response? What is the relationship between consumer purchase frequencies and brand shifting behavior? These questions will be discussed in the light of available empirical data and a model which appears to describe them.

A MODEL OF CONSUMER BRAND SHIFTING

A model equivalent to a generalized form of the Estes (1954) and Bush-Mosteller (1955) stochastic (probabilistic) learning models appears to describe consumer brand shifting quite well. To illustrate how this brand shifting model describes changes in the consumer's probability of purchasing any given brand as a result of his purchases of that brand (e.g., Brand A) and competing brands (e.g., Brand X), let us examine the effect of the four-purchase sequence XAAX on a consumer with initial probability $P_{A,1}$ (see Figure 15.1).

The model is described or defined in terms of four parameters, namely, the intercepts and slopes of the two lines referred to in Figure 15.1 as the Purchase Operator and the Rejection Operator. If the brand in question is purchased by the consumer on a given buying occasion, the consumer's probability of again buying the same brand the next time that type of product is purchased is read from the Purchase Operator. If the brand is rejected by the consumer on a given buying occasion, the consumer's probability of buying that brand when he next buys that type of product is read from the Rejection Operator. Thus in Figure 15.1 our hypothetical consumer begins on trial 1 with the probability $P_{A,1}$ of buying Brand A. The consumer chooses some other brand (X) on trial 1, however, and thus his probability of buying Brand A on trial 2 ($P_{A,2}$) is obtained from the Rejection Operator, resulting in a slight reduction in the probability of purchasing A on the next trial. On trial 2, however, the consumer does purchase Brand A and thus increases the likelihood of his again buying the brand on the next occasion (trial 3) to $P_{A,3}$. Continuing in this fashion, the consumer again buys A on trial 3, thereby increasing his probability of purchasing Brand A on trial 4 to $P_{A,4}$. He again rejects A on trial 4, however, decreasing his probability of buying A on trial 5 to $P_{A,5}$.

FIGURE   15.1

STOCHASTIC (PROBABILISTIC) BRAND SHIFTING MODEL

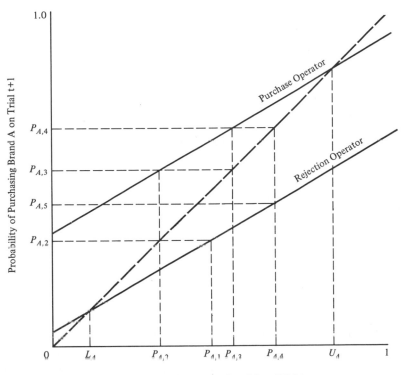

Probability of Purchasing Brand A on Trial t

Two characteristics of the model should be noted: 1) the probability $P_{A,t}$ approaches but never exceeds the upper limit U_A with repeated purchasing of the brand, and 2) the probability $P_{A,t}$ approaches but never drops below the lower limit L_A with continued rejection of the brand. Using Bush and Mosteller's terminology, this would be referred to as an incomplete learning, incomplete extinction model insofar as U_A is less than one and L_A is greater than zero. This is equivalent to saying that consumers will generally not develop such strong brand loyalties (or buying habits) as to insure either the rejection or purchase of a given brand.

It should also be pointed out that the Purchase and Rejection Operators are functions of the time elapsed between the consumer's t^{th} and $t + 1^{st}$

purchases and of the merchandising activities of competitors. The time effect can be illustrated by the three sets of operators shown for high, medium, and very low frequency purchasers of a rapidly consumed, nondurable consumer product (see Figure 15.2). Note that the Purchase and Rejection Operators decrease in slope and that the upper and lower limits approach each other as the time between purchases increases.

FIGURE 15.2

EFFECT OF TIME BETWEEN PURCHASES UPON PURCHASE AND REJECTION OPERATORS

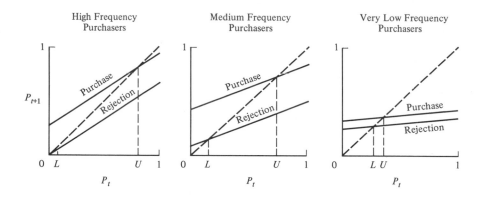

At the one limit (time between purchases approaching zero) the Purchase and Rejection Operators approach the diagonal, L approaches zero, and U approaches one. At the other limit (time between purchases approaching infinity), L and U approach each other and the Purchase and Rejection Operators approach a slope equal to zero.

The main problem that remains in making use of the model is then the estimation of the four parameters defining the Purchase and Rejection Operators as a function of the time between purchases. If this could be done a priori, the model might be of value to marketing management for use in forecasting. At present, however, the model's primary use is in evaluating the effects of past and current competitive marketing activity. Thus the parameters of the model are estimated for short time periods and related to the actions of all competitors in the market. Since the path of aggregate consumer purchasing behavior could be established for any given set of parameter values, it follows that the parameter estimates obtained from fitting the model can provide a means for evaluating the influence of the market conditions prevailing during the period that the sequential purchase data were collected.

An efficient method has been developed to estimate these brand shifting parameters (maximum likelihood estimates) on the basis of sequences of two to four purchases. The method makes it feasible to relate this model to consumer purchasing behavior observed during relatively short periods of time. This is a must if the technique is to be useful, since merchandising conditions do not remain constant for long periods of time—products are modified, advertising themes and budgets are altered, special promotions are generally temporary in nature, and price levels may change from time to time. The technique used to estimate the brand shifting parameters will be outlined in the near future as a working paper in the Research in Marketing Project series of the Graduate School of Industrial Administration, Carnegie Institute of Technology. The Bush-Mosteller approach to estimating the parameters of their stochastic learning model cannot, in its current state of development, be applied to the brand shifting model since 1) techniques have not been developed to estimate simultaneously the four basic parameters of the model, and 2) the methods outlined require a long history or record of trials (and, therefore, data collected over a long period of time during which there is stability in merchandising activity) from which to develop parameter estimates.

EMPIRICAL BRAND SHIFTING RESEARCH

What evidence is there in support of the model? Three types of empirical studies have led to the formulation and continued development of the above model:

1. Analysis of three-, four-, five-, and six-purchase sequences of consumer brand purchases (Kuehn, 1958),
2. Analysis of effects of time between consumer purchases on a consumer's probability of purchasing individual brands of product (Kuehn, 1958), and
3. Simulation of consumer brand choice behavior.

Each of these three studies is discussed briefly below.

Analysis of Brand Purchase Sequences

Sequential purchase data can provide some insight into consumer brand switching. The data analyzed below represent the frozen orange juice purchases of approximately 600 Chicago families in the three years 1950 to

1952, covering more than 15,000 individual purchases collected in monthly diaries by the Chicago Tribune Consumer Panel. The data were analyzed as sequences of five purchases by means of a factorial analysis to determine the influence of the consumer's first four sequential brand choices on his choice of a brand on the fifth buying occasion. The data and analysis prepared for Snow Crop brand are summarized in Table 15.1.

In column 1, the letter "S" is used to represent a purchase of the Snow Crop brand, the letter "O" to represent the purchase of any *other* brand of frozen orange juice. Thus SSSS indicates a sequence of four purchases of Snow Crop. The sequence OSSS represents one purchase of some other brand followed by three purchases of Snow Crop.

T A B L E   1 5 . 1

COMPARISON OF OBSERVED AND PREDICTED PROBABILITY OF PURCHASING SNOW CROP GIVEN THE FOUR PREVIOUS BRAND PURCHASES

Previous Purchase Pattern (1)	Sample Size (2)	Observed Probability of Purchase (3)	Predicted Probability of Purchase* (4)	Deviation of Predictions (5)
SSSS	1047	.806	.832	+.026
OSSS	277	.690	.691	+.001
SOSS	206	.665	.705	+.040
SSOS	222	.595	.634	+.039
SSSO	296	.486	.511	+.025
OOSS	248	.552	.564	+.012
SOOS	138	.565	.507	−.058
OSOS	149	.497	.493	−.004
SOSO	163	.405	.384	−.021
OSSO	181	.414	.370	−.044
SSOO	256	.305	.313	+.008
OOOS	500	.330	.366	+.033
OOSO	404	.191	.243	+.052
OSOO	433	.129	.172	+.043
SOOO	557	.154	.186	+.032
OOOO	8442	.048	.045	−.003

* To illustrate the computation of the values in column 4, the probability of a Snow Crop purchase given the history SOOO is .045 (the probability of purchase given OOOO) plus .141, or .186; the probability given SOOS is .045 + .141 + .321 = .507; and the predicted probability given OSSS is .045 + .127 + .198 + .321 = .691.

Column 2 tabulates the sample sizes from which were calculated the observed and predicted probabilities of purchasing Snow Crop on the subsequent (fifth) purchase in the sequence.

Column 3 is computed on the basis of the observed frequencies of the five-purchase sequences. Thus, there were 296 sequences exhibiting the pattern SSSO in the first four positions of the sequence. Snow Crop was purchased on the fifth buying occasion in 144 of these sequences. The best estimate of the observed probability of buying Snow Crop given the past purchase record of SSSO is therefore $144/296 = .486$.

The predicted column is based on the results of the factorial analysis of past purchase effects. Each of the four past brand purchases was examined with respect to its individual (primary) effect and the effect of its interactions with the other purchases. The individual effects of the past four purchase positions were highly significant but the interaction effects were not significantly different from zero at the five per cent level of significance; that is, there was greater than five per cent probability of results as extreme as those observed arising by chance if there were in fact no interaction effects.

There is close agreement between the observed and predicted probabilities, in view of the limited sample size. The predicted values, however, appear to deviate systematically on the high side when Snow Crop is purchased either one or three times on the last four buying occasions; also, predictions are generally low given two purchases. Subsequent analysis indicated that these systematic deviations were reduced or eliminated when a record of the fifth past brand purchase was included in the analysis.

Casual inspection of Table 15.1 suggests that the most recent purchase of the consumer is not the only one influencing his brand choice. This finding raises some question about the uses currently being made of purchase-to-purchase Markov chain analyses which assume that only the most recent purchase of the consumer is influential. The analysis of "primary" effects referred to above showed that the purchase of Snow Crop on the most recent buying occasion added .321 to the probability of the consumer's buying Snow Crop on his next purchase. Similarly, the second most recent purchase added .198, the third .127, and the fourth .141 (see footnote, Table 15.1).

Note that the first three purchase effects decline roughly exponentially. That is, the ratio of the importance of the first purchase to that of the second is approximately equal to the ratio of the second to the third. The fourth, however, increases rather than decreases! This reversal occurs because past purchases beyond the fourth most recent purchase were excluded from the analysis. The increased importance attached to the fourth most recent purchase for prediction purposes reflects its high correlation with the fifth and earlier past purchases not incorporated in the study. When these same data were reanalyzed using six-purchase sequences, the exponential relationship of declining primary purchase effects fits the first through fourth past purchases. As would be expected, however, the fifth past purchase effect was larger than the fourth because of its higher correlation with the consumer's sixth and even earlier past purchases.

Observation of the exponentially declining effects of past purchases led to the testing of the brand shifting model outlined in Figure 15.1, since that model has the characteristic of weighting the influence of past brand choices exponentially when the slopes of the Purchase and Rejection Operators are identical. Subsequent research with products other than frozen orange juice has tended to confirm the predictive value of exponential weighting of past brand purchases by consumers. The exponential weights vary substantially, however, among product classes. Products such as toilet soaps, cereals, and toothpaste were found to have substantially lower rates of decline in weights as one goes back into the purchase history, as a result of the tendency of purchasing families to use some mix of brands on a routine basis so as to satisfy different uses, desires for variety, and differences in preference of individual family members. To be sure, this brand-mix effect is operative even in the case of frozen orange juice, but for quite a different reason. Many families use a mix of brands of frozen orange juice because of the unavailability of specific brands in all the stores among which the consumer shifts in the course of his week-to-week shopping trips.

Effect of Consumer Purchase Frequencies

Let us consider the effect of time between purchases on the consumer's probability of repurchasing the same brand. In Figure 15.3 we observe that the probability of a consumer's buying the same brand on two consecutive purchases of the product decreases to that brand's share of market as time between purchases increases. Whenever a great amount of time has elapsed since the consumer's last purchase of the product, the brand he last bought has little influence on his choice of a brand—the probability of his buying any given brand in this case is approximately equal to the share of market of that brand. Note that the probability of repurchase decreases at a constant rate with the passing of time; this characteristic, which we shall refer to as the "time rate of decay of purchase probability," provides a simple framework for incorporating the effects of time into a procedure for forecasting consumer purchase probabilities.

Let us now expand our view of the effects of time on repurchase probability in terms of the time period required for the consumer to make N individual purchases of frozen orange juice concentrate. Note that the curve in Figure 15.4 labelled $N = 1$ is the same curve as in Figure 15.3. Observe also that the probability of repurchasing the same brand at any given time in the future, without regard to the brands chosen in the interim, increases as we go up from $N = 1$ to $N = 3$, $N = 10$, and $N = 50$. Thus on the average a consumer who makes his fiftieth purchase of frozen orange juice 300 days after some arbitrary purchase of a given brand has a much higher probability of again choosing that brand than does the consumer who makes only 1, 3, or 10 purchases in that interval of time.

FIGURE   15.3

THE PROBABILITY OF A CONSUMER'S BUYING THE SAME BRAND ON TWO CONSECUTIVE PURCHASES OF FROZEN ORANGE JUICE DECREASES EXPONENTIALLY WITH AN INCREASE IN TIME BETWEEN THOSE PURCHASES

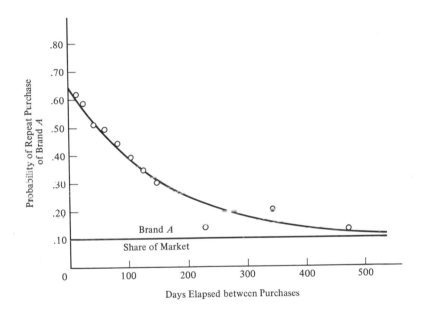

Figure 15.5 illustrates the relationship between the rates of decay of purchase probability associated with the curves in Figure 15.4 and the average time elapsed between purchases. The rate of decay of $N = 1$ in Figure 15.4 is .01298 per day. The rate of decay of $N = 50$ is .00282. Here again we find a relationship which, because of its simplicity, can after some manipulation be conveniently incorporated into a model forecasting consumer brand choice probabilities. The rate of decay increases linearly with

an increase in the average time between purchases. The data points plotted in Figure 15.5 represent the rates of decay computed for ten values of N, four of which were illustrated by the curves in Figure 15.4.

FIGURE 15.4

CONSUMERS BUYING FROZEN ORANGE JUICE WITH GREATEST FREQUENCY HAVE THE HIGHEST PROBABILITY OF CONTINUING TO BUY THE SAME BRAND

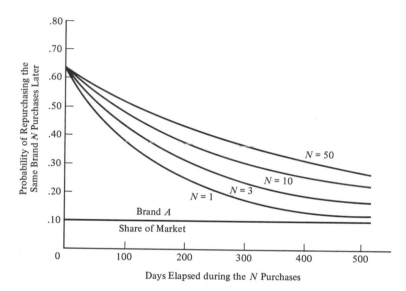

Simulation of Consumer Brand Choice

The brand shifting model outlined in Figure 15.1 has been tested by computing the predicted purchase probabilities of consumers on each of approximately 13,000 occasions of purchase of frozen orange juice, and comparing aggregates of these predictions with recorded brand purchases. The procedure followed was first to divide the probability space, zero to one, into 76 probability ranges. Then, whenever the computer-programed model predicted a certain probability of a given family's buying a particular brand on a given buying occasion, the results of that purchase were recorded in the computer storage location representing the corresponding probability range. Thus it was possible within each of the 76 probability cells to compare the average predicted probability of purchasing individual brands with the observed proportion of trials on which the brand was in fact purchased. The predicted probabilities and observed proportions of purchases were then compared individually and simultaneously for all 76 cells with respect to the binomial and chi square distributions that would be expected if the model were perfect. The 76 normal deviates, referred to here by "t," computed for the individual cells with respect to the Snow Crop predictions, were approximately normally distributed, 50 lying within one standard deviation, 71 lying within two standard deviations, and 76 falling within three standard deviations. The chi square value indicated no significant deviation at the 10 per cent level. Similar results were obtained in an analysis of predictions for the Minute Maid brand, 53 "t" values lying within one standard deviation, 70 lying within two standard deviations, and all 76 cases falling within three standard deviations.

The above results suggest that the model offers promise for use in describing consumer behavior in probabilistic terms. The model was not tested with respect to individual families, the number of purchases made by most individual families providing too small a sample to yield a reasonably powerful test of the predictions from the model. In other words, since rejection is unlikely with a small sample size per family, acceptance does not carry much weight with respect to an evaluation of the model. In the aggregate, the model stood up surprisingly well, given the overall test sample size of approximately 13,000 purchase predictions. Of course, if the sample size were to be increased substantially, significant deviations would be obtained, since the model is not a perfect representation of the brand purchase sequences of consumers.

The predictions of the model were also used to obtain a frequency distribution of consumers throughout the three year time period according to their probability of buying specific brands of product. Figure 15.0 provides a comparison of the smoothed profiles for Libby and Minute Maid frozen orange juice. As might be expected, most consumers have a low probability of buying any specific brand. Those consumers who have a high probability of buying one brand must necessarily have a low probability of buying several other brands. Minute Maid was in the enviable position of having a small group of customers with a very high probability of buying the brand. Libby did not have such a following. Minute Maid developed frozen orange juice and was the first brand available to consumers; these facts probably helped develop the group of loyal (or habitual) customers, a sizable portion of whom were retained in the face of growing competition. As the innovator of frozen orange juice, Minute Maid also developed a preeminent market position in terms of retail availability, a factor which undoubtedly helped the firm maintain a sales advantage relative to competition.

FIGURE 15.5

RELATIONSHIP OF DECAY RATES TO TIME BETWEEN PURCHASES

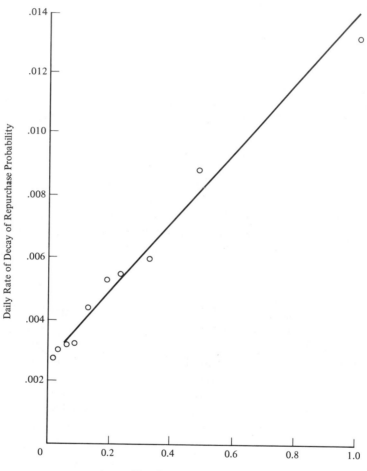

Average Time Elapsed between Purchases $(1/N)$

ADAPTIVE BEHAVIOR OR SPURIOUS RESULTS?

In a paper titled "Brand Choice as a Probability Process," Ronald Frank (1962) reported that certain results concerning repeat purchase probabilities as a function of a brand's run length appear similar to what would be expected with associative learning under conditions of reward. He then observed in a footnote that my data (Kuehn, 1961) also seem to suggest this interpretation, a point on which there is agreement. The balance of Frank's article is then directed at demonstrating that:

1. purchase sequence data generated by families for a given brand using a Monte Carlo approach, on the assumption that each family's probability of purchasing the brand remained constant throughout the time period, produced repeat purchase probabilities as a function of run length which closely approximated in the aggregate the actual observed probabilities, and

2. the number of runs observed for *most* families is consistent with what might be expected under the assumption that each family's probability of purchasing any given brand remained constant throughout the time period.

As a result of his success in generating a relationship that has the appearance of actual data, Frank states, "These results cast suspicion on the use of a 'learning' model to describe the observations." In view of this statement, which bears directly on the work outlined here, in my thesis, and elsewhere, some defense appears to be in order.

Frank's observations in no way invalidate the findings outlined earlier in this paper. He has shown that it is inappropriate to attribute to learning *all* the increase in repeat purchase probability associated with increases in run length, an error probably made by more than a few researchers. This, however, is not the approach outlined here or in my thesis. The approach used in my thesis could be applied to Frank's coffee data to test whether the probabilities are in fact constant and, if this is not the case, to estimate the appropriate weightings. If consumers were to have a constant probability of brand choice from trial to trial, the most recent purchase positions would not have a greater primary effect on the predicted purchase probabilities than would any other purchase position—all the primary effects would be identical except for sampling variations. Similarly, if the probabilities of brand choice were constant from trial to trial, the Purchase and Rejection Operators in the adaptive brand shifting model would be superimposed on the diagonal (see Figure 15.1). In other words, the special case considered by Frank can be treated successfully by both of the analytic techniques used in my studies and discussed in this paper. Frank is correct when he states

FIGURE 15.6

PROBABILITY OF PURCHASING SPECIFIC BRANDS

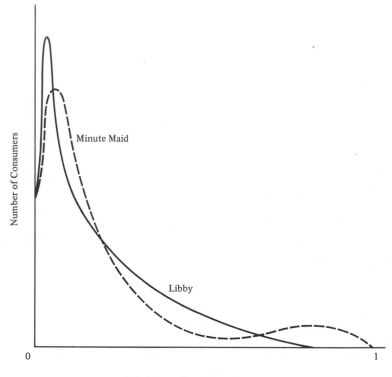

Probability of Purchasing on Any Given Trial

that much of what might appear to be a learning effect on the basis of repeat purchase probabilities as a function of run length is due to the aggregation of consumers with different probabilities (at the start of the run). But this is no problem when one takes into account the effect of all past purchases which have a significant impact on the consumer's purchase probability; such an approach does not disregard the information contained in purchases prior to the current run—an important consideration when the run is very short. Since past purchases will, except in highly unusual cases, have decreasing effects (as one goes back in time) on the consumer's subsequent purchase probability, taking into account all significant past purchases does not generally require the availability of an unduly long record of the consumer's purchase history.

The second point that Frank makes—namely, that most consumers behave as though they had constant purchase probabilities—would appear to represent a misinterpretation of statistical results. Frank sets up his hypothesis, tests it at some level of significance for each of a large number of cases (families), and then interprets the results as though all cases not shown to deviate statistically on an individual basis are consistent with the hypothesis. Actually, the hypothesis was that consumers have a constant probability of purchase, and the results indicated that a larger number of the individual cases tested lay outside the confidence limits than is consistent with the hypothesis, thereby rejecting the hypothesis *in toto!*

To be sure, the hypothesis of constant probability is, in effect, a straw man. It is generally recognized that consumers do change their buying behavior over time. Whether such behavior is called adjustment, adaptation, or learning is unimportant. It should be noted, however, that even though the overall market for coffee was quite stable in the period studied by Frank, and the sample sizes were limited to 14 months of purchase by each family, the hypothesis was in fact rejected on an overall basis, the only appropriate way in which to interpret the results of the test. Perhaps, as Frank suggests, some consumers do have constant probabilities of choosing individual brands during certain periods of time. Such a hypothesis cannot be tested, however, unless a procedure independent of the test is available for identifying these consumers and the relevant time periods.

SUMMARY

A model describing brand shifting behavior as a probabilistic process and incorporating the effects of past purchases and time elapsed between purchases has been outlined. A defense of this approach to the study of mechanisms underlying consumer brand choice has also been presented. What has not been discussed is the way in which such merchandising factors as price, advertising, product characteristics, retail availability, and promotions (price off, coupons, merchandise packs, etc.) influence the parameters of the model and the extensions of the model that might be required to incorporate such effects. Some earlier results of research on the influence of these variables have been incorporated into an aggregate "expected value" form of the model presented here (Kuehn, 1961). Much work, however, remains to be done.

REFERENCES

Bush, Robert R., and Frederick Mosteller. *Stochastic Models for Learning.* New York: John Wiley, 1955.

Estes, William K. Individual Behavior in Uncertain Situations: An Interpretation in Terms of Statistical Association Theory. In Thrall, R. M., C. H. Coombs, and R. L. Davis (Eds.), *Decision Processes.* New York: John Wiley, 1954.

Frank, Ronald E. Brand Choice as a Probability Process. *Journal of Business*, Vol. 35, No. 1, January 1962, pp. 43–56.

Kuehn, Alfred A. An Analysis of the Dynamics of Consumer Behavior and Its Implications for Marketing Management. Unpublished doctoral dissertation. Graduate School of Industrial Administration, Carnegie Institute of Technology, 1958.

Kuehn, Alfred A. A Model for Budgeting Advertising. In Bass, Frank M., et al. (Eds.), *Mathematical Models and Methods in Marketing.* Homewood, Ill.: Richard D. Irwin, 1961.

SELECTED READINGS

BOOKS

Harper W. Boyd, Jr. and Sidney J. Levy, *Promotion: A Behavioral View* (Prentice-Hall, 1967).

Francis Bourne (ed.), *Group Influence in Marketing and Public Relations* (Foundation for Research on Human Behavior, 1956).

Kalman J. Cohen and Richard M. Cyert, *Theory of the Firm: Resource Allocation in a Market Economy* (Prentice-Hall, 1965).

James F. Engel, David F. Kollat, and Roger D. Blackwell, *Consumer Behavior* (Holt, Rinehart and Winston, 1968).

John A. Howard, *Marketing Management: Analysis and Planning* (rev. ed., Irwin, 1963).

George Katona and Eva Mueller, *Consumer Responses to Income Changes* (The Brookings Institution, 1968).

John C. Narver and Ronald Savitt, *The Marketing Economy: An Analytical Approach* (Holt, Rinehart and Winston, 1971), Chapters 8 and 9.

Francesco M. Nicosia, *Consumer Decision Processes: Marketing and Advertising Implications* (Prentice-Hall, 1966).

ARTICLES

Richard P. Coleman, "The Significance of Social Stratification in Selling," in Martin L. Bell (ed.), *Proceedings of the 43rd National Conference of the American Marketing Association*, 1960.

Tamatsu Shibutani, "Reference Groups as Perspectives," *American Journal of Sociology* (May, 1955).

IV Social perspectives of the marketing economy

The selections in this part of the anthology are divided into three groups. This has been done because of the diverse nature of the topics, even though each has the common thread of social value. Each section has its own preface.

A

Marketing
and public
policy

Public policy in marketing is any governmental policy at the federal, state, or local level which in any way affects the supply of or demand for goods and services. In that virtually each one affects either supply or demand, every governmental economic policy is essentially a public policy in marketing. The two articles which follow, Walter Adams' "Public Policy in a Free Enterprise Economy," and David R. Kamerschen's "A Critique of the Status Quo Approach to Public Policy," are concerned primarily with antitrust. Antitrust is a set of policies at the Federal level, and in many states as well, designed to maintain competition, that is, to promote rivalry among sellers and among buyers. In particular, maintaining competition means diffusing economic power, thereby encouraging independent actions by firms and increased alternatives and value to consumers. Economic regulation, unlike antitrust, is the explicit control of specific activities of firms. Examples of regulated industries are utilities such as electricity and appliance gas; ground, sea, and air transportation; radio and television broadcasting; and commercial banking and insurance. In general, regulated industries are exempt from the antitrust laws though the rationale for regulation and antitrust exemption is increasingly being reappraised.

Other important policies in marketing are: (1) consumer protection, which attempts to assist the consumer in buying and using products; (2) government procurement policies; (3) direct and indirect governmental subsidization of firms and industries; (4) international and interregional trade policies; and (5) monetary and fiscal policy, such as changes in interest rates and tax structures affecting disposable income and its use. The list of public policies in marketing could easily be continued to include, for example, policies such as those of the Post Office Department, which by regulating selling and buying through the mails also affects geographic markets; the Agriculture Department, which inspects and grades various commodities; the local building code and zoning authorities, whose policies obviously affect the sale of construction materials, the geographical distribution of businesses and houses, and the sale of real property. All of these and more are included in public policy in marketing. The reader is encouraged to consider the many additional public policies in marketing; and we challenge the reader to think of major government economic policies that do *not* in some way affect marketing.

16

Public policy
in a
free enterprise economy

Walter Adams

When Congress passed the Sherman Act of 1890 it created what was then—
and what has remained to this day—a uniquely American institution. Her-
alded as a magna carta of economic freedom, the Sherman Act sought to
preserve competitive free enterprise by imposing legal prohibitions on
monopoly and restraint of trade. The objective of the Act, according to
Judge Learned Hand, was not to condone *good* trusts or condemn *bad* trusts,
but to forbid *all* trusts. Its basic philosophy and principal purpose was "to
perpetuate and preserve, for its own sake and in spite of possible cost, an
organization of industry in small units which can effectively compete with
each other."[1]

[1] *U. S.* v. *Aluminum Company of America*, 148 F.2d 416 (C.C.A. 2d, 1945). In elaborat-
ing on the goals of the Sherman Act, Judge Hand stated: "Many people believe that
possession of unchallenged economic power deadens initiative, discourages thrift and

Reprinted with permission of the Macmillan Company from *The Structure of
American Industry*, Walter Adams (ed.), (New York: The Macmillan Company,
1954), pp. 510–543. Copyright 1950 by the Macmillan Company.

THE ANTIMONOPOLY LAWS

Specifically, the Sherman Act outlawed two major types of interference with free enterprise, viz. collusion and monopolization. Section 1 of the act, dealing with collusion, stated: "Every contract, combination . . . or conspiracy, in restraint of trade or commerce among the several States, or with foreign nations, is hereby declared illegal." As interpreted by the courts, this section made it unlawful for businessmen to engage in such collusive action as agreements to fix prices; agreements to restrict output or productive capacity; agreements to divide markets or allocate customers; agreements to exclude competitors by systematic resort to oppressive tactics and discriminatory policies—in short, any joint action by competitors to influence the market. Thus Section 1 was, in a sense, a response to Adam Smith's warning that "people of the same trade seldom meet together even for merriment and diversion, but the conversation ends in a conspiracy against the public, or on some contrivance to raise prices."[2]

Section 2 of the Sherman Act, dealing with monopolization, provided: "Every person who shall monopolize or attempt to monopolize, or combine or conspire with any other person or persons to monopolize any part of the trade or commerce among the several States, or with foreign nations, shall be deemed guilty of a misdemeanor, and . . . punished." This meant that businessmen were deprived of an important freedom, the freedom to mo-

---

depresses energy; that immunity from competition is a narcotic, and rivalry is a stimulant, to industrial progress; that the spur of constant stress is necessary to counteract an inevitable disposition to let well enough alone. Such people believe that competitors, versed in the craft as no consumer can be, will be quick to detect opportunities for saving and new shifts in production, and be eager to profit by them. . . . True, it might have been thought adequate to condemn only those monopolies which could not show that they had exercised the highest possible ingenuity, had adopted every possible economy, had anticipated every conceivable improvement, stimulated every possible demand. . . . Be that as it may, that was not the way that Congress chose; it did not condone "good" trusts and condemn "bad" ones; it forbade all. Moreover, in so doing it was not necessarily actuated by economic motives alone. It is possible, because of its indirect social or moral effect, to prefer a system of small producers, each dependent for his success upon his own skill and character, to one in which the great mass of those engaged must accept the direction of a few. These considerations, which we have suggested only as possible purposes of the Act, we think the decisions prove to have been in fact its purposes." (*Ibid.*)

[2] *The Wealth of Nations*, Book 1, Chapter 10. Here it should be pointed out that businessmen engage in trade restraints and organize monopolies not because of any vicious and anti-social motives, but rather because of a desire to increase personal profits. As George Comer, the chief economist of the Antitrust Division, recently observed, monopolies are formed "not because business-men are criminals, but because the reports from the bookkeeping department indicate, in the short run at least, that monopoly and restraints of trade will pay if you can get away with it. It will pay a large corporation

nopolize. Section 2 made it unlawful for anyone to obtain a stranglehold on the market either by forcing rivals out of business or by absorbing them. It forbade a single firm (or a group of firms acting jointly) to gain a substantially exclusive domination of an industry or a market area. Positively stated, Section 2 attempted to encourage an industry structure in which there are enough independent competitors to assure bona fide and effective market rivalry.

As is obvious from even a cursory examination of the Sherman Act, its provisions were general, perhaps even vague, and essentially negative. Directed primarily against *existing* monopolies and *existing* trade restraints, the Sherman Act could not cope with specific practices which were, and could be, used to effectuate the unlawful results. Armed with the power to dissolve existing monopolies, the enforcement authorities could not, under the Sherman Act, attack the *growth* of monopoly. They could not nip it in the bud. For this reason Congress passed, in 1914, supplementary legislation "to arrest the creation of trusts, conspiracies and monopolies *in their incipiency and before consummation.*"[3] In the Federal Trade Commission Act of 1914, Congress set up an independent regulatory commission to police the industrial field against "all unfair methods of competition." In the Clayton Act of the same year Congress singled out four specific practices which past experience had shown to be favorite weapons of the would-be monopolist, viz. 1) price discrimination, i.e. local price cutting and cut-throat competition; 2) tying contracts and exclusive dealer arrangements; 3) the acquisition of stock in competing companies; and 4) the formation of interlocking directorates between competing corporations. These practices were to be unlawful whenever their effect was to substantially lessen competition or to create tendencies toward monopoly. Thus price discrimination, for example, was not made illegal per se; it was to be illegal only if used as a systematic device for destroying competition—in a manner typical of the old Standard Oil and American Tobacco trusts.[4] The emphasis throughout

---

to agree with its competitors on price fixing. It pays to operate a basing-point or zone-price system. If patent pools can be organized, especially with hundreds or thousands of patents covering a whole industry, the profits will be enormous. If an international cartel can be formed which really works, the very peak of stabilization and rationalism is reached. If the management of all the large units in an industry can get together with the labor unions in the industry, a number of birds can be killed with one stone. And finally, if the government can be persuaded to legalize the restrictive practices, the theory of 'enlightened competition' is complete." ("The Outlook for Effective Competition," *American Economic Review, Papers and Proceedings*, May, 1946, pp. 154–55.)

[3] Senate Report No. 695, 63rd Congress, 2d Session, 1914, p. 1 (italics supplied).

[4] A Congressional Committee explained the background of the price discrimination provision of the Clayton Act as follows: "In the past it has been a most common practice

was to be on prevention rather than cure. The hope was that—given the provisions of the 1914 laws to supplement the provisions of the Sherman Act—the antitrust authorities could effectively eliminate the economic evils against which the antitrust laws were directed.

THE CHARGES AGAINST MONOPOLY

What those evils were has never been clearly stated, and perhaps never been clearly conceived, by the sponsors of antitrust legislation. In general, however, the objections to monopoly and trade restraints—found in literally tons of antitrust literature—can be summarized as follows:[5]

1) *Monopoly affords the consumer little protection against exorbitant prices.* As Adam Smith put it, "the price of monopoly is, upon every occasion, the highest which can be got. The natural price, or the price of free competition, on the contrary is the lowest which can be taken, not upon every occasion indeed, but for any considerable time taken together. The one is upon every occasion the highest which can be squeezed out of the buyers, or which, it is supposed, they will consent to give; the other is the lowest which the sellers can commonly afford to take, and at the same time continue their business."[6] The consumer is, under these conditions, open prey to extortion and exploitation—protected only by such tenuous self-restraint as the monopolist may choose to exercise because of benevolence,

---

of great and powerful combinations engaged in commerce—notably the Standard Oil Co., and the American Tobacco Co., and others of less notoriety, but of great influence—to lower prices of their commodities, oftentimes below the cost of production in certain communities and sections where they had competition, with the intent to destroy and make unprofitable the business of their competitors, and with the ultimate purpose in view of thereby acquiring a monopoly in the particular locality or section in which the discriminating price is made.

"Every concern that engages in this evil practice must of necessity recoup its losses in the particular communities or sections where their commodities are sold below cost or without a fair profit by raising the price of this same class of commodities above their fair market value in other sections or communities.

"Such a system or practice is so manifestly unfair and unjust, not only to competitors who are directly injured thereby but to the general public, that your committee is strongly of the opinion that the present antitrust laws ought to be supplemented by making this particular form of discrimination a specific offense under the law when practiced by those engaged in commerce." (House Report No. 627, 63d Congress, 2d Session, 1914, pp. 8–9.)

[5] For a good summary of the charges against monopoly as well as the claims made in support of monopoly, see C. Wilcox, *Competition and Monopoly in the American Economy*, T.N.E.C. Monograph No. 21, 1941, pp. 15–18.

[6] Smith, *op. cit.*, Book 1, Chapter 7.

FIGURE 16.1

PRICEFIXING

Which is the American Way?

(*Source:* Thurman W. Arnold, *Cartels or Free Enterprise?* Public Affairs Pamphlet No. 103, 1945; reproduced by courtesy of Public Affairs Committee, Inc.)

irrationality, concern over government reprisals, or fear of potential competition.

The monopolist can generally charge all the traffic will bear, simply because the consumer has no alternative sources of supply. The consumer is forced to pay the monopolist's price, turn to a less desirable substitute, or go without. His freedom is impaired, because his range of choice is artificially limited.

An example, while admittedly extreme, serves to illustrate this point. It involves tungsten carbide, a hard-metal composition of considerable importance in such industrial uses as cutting tools, dies, etc. In 1927, tungsten carbide sold in the United States at $50 per pound; but after a world monopoly was established by the General Electric Company and Friedrich Krupp A. G. of Germany, under which G. E. was granted the right to set prices in the American market, the price promptly rose to a maximum of $453 per pound. During most of the 1930's the price fluctuated between $225 and $453 per pound, and not until 1942—when an indictment was issued under the antitrust laws—did the price come down. Thereafter, it fluctuated between $27 and $45 per pound.[7]

2) *Monopoly causes a restriction of economic opportunity and a misallocation of productive resources.* Under free competition, it is the consumer who—through his dollar votes in the market place—decides how society's land, labor and capital are to be used. Consumer tastes generally determine whether more cotton and less wool, more cigarettes and less pipe tobacco, more aluminum and less steel shall be produced. Under free competition the consumer is in this strategic position because businessmen must, if they want to make profits, do as the consumer demands. Since a businessman, under competition, is free to enter any field and to produce any type and quantity of goods he desires, the tendency will be for him to do those things which the consuming public (in its wisdom or ignorance) deems most valuable. In short, under a truly competitive system, the businessman can improve himself only by serving others. He can earn profits only by obeying the wishes of the community as expressed in the market.

Under monopoly, by contrast, the individual businessman finds his freedom of enterprise limited. He cannot do as he pleases, because the monopolist has the power of excluding newcomers or stipulating the terms under which newcomers are permitted to survive in an industry. The monopolist can interfere with a consumer-oriented allocation of resources. He, instead of the market, can determine the type and quantity of goods that shall be produced. He, and not the forces of supply and demand, can

---

[7] See C. D. Edwards, *Economic and Political Aspects of International Cartels*, Monograph No. 1, Senate Committee on Military Affairs, 78th Congress, 2d Session, 1946, pp. 12–13.

decree who shall produce what, for whom, and at what price. In the absence of competition, it is the monopolist who decides what *other* businessmen shall be allowed to do and what benefits the consuming public shall be allowed to receive.

A good illustration of this is the Hartford-Empire Company which, until recently, was an undisputed monopolist in the glass bottle industry. Through its patent control over glass bottling machinery, Hartford-Empire held life-and-death power both over the producers already in the industry and those attempting to enter it. As one observer described the situation,[8] Hartford had become benevolent despot to the glass container. Only by its leave could a firm come into the industry; the ticket of admission was to be had only upon its terms; and from its studied decision there was no appeal. The candidate had to subscribe to Hartford's articles of faith; he could not be a price-cutter or a trouble-maker. He could not venture beyond his assigned bailiwick or undermine the market of his partners in the conspiracy. Each concern had to accept the restrictions and limitations imposed by Hartford. Thus the Buck Glass Company was authorized to manufacture wine bottles for sacramental purposes only. The Sayre Glass Works were restricted to producing "such bottles, jugs, and demijohns as are used for vinegar, ciders, sirups, bleaching fluids, hair tonics, barber supplies and fluid extracts." Knox Glass Bottle Company was allowed to make only amber colored ginger ale bottles. Mary Card Glass Company could not make products weighing more than 82 ounces. Baurens Glass Works Inc. was licensed to provide bottles for castor oil and turpentine, but none to exceed 4 ounces in capacity. Here indeed was a shackling of free enterprise and a usurpation of the market—a private government more powerful than that of many states. Here indeed was a tight little island, where the law of the monopolist was supreme and unchallenged. Only through antitrust prosecution were the channels of trade reopened, and the Hartford dictatorship dissipated.[9]

3) *Monopoly often restrains technological advances and thus impedes economic progress.* As Clair Wilcox points out, "the monopolist may engage in research and invent new materials, methods, and machines, but he will be reluctant to make use of these inventions if they would compel him to scrap existing equipment or if he believes that their ultimate profitability is in doubt. He may introduce innovations and cut costs, but instead of moving goods by price reduction he is prone to spend large sums on alternative methods of promoting sales; his refusal to cut prices deprives the community of any gain. The monopolist may voluntarily improve the quality of

[8] See W. H. Hamilton, *Patents and Free Enterprise*, T.N.E.C. Monograph No. 31, 1941, pp. 109–15.
[9] See *U. S. v. Hartford-Empire Co. et al.*, 323 U.S. 386 (1945).

his product and reduce its price, but no threat of competition compels him to do so."[10]

Our experience with the hydrogenation and synthetic rubber processes is a case in point. This, one of the less illustrious chapters in our industrial history, dates back to 1926 when I.G. Farben of Germany developed the hydrogenation process for making oil out of coal—a development which obviously threatened the entrenched position of the major international oil companies. Soon after this process was patented, Standard Oil Company of New Jersey concluded an agreement with I.G. Farben, under which Farben promised to stay out of the world's oil business (except inside Germany) and Standard agreed to stay out of the world's chemical business. "By this agreement, control of the hydrogenation process for making oil outside Germany was transferred to the Standard Oil Co. in order that Standard's petroleum investment might be fully protected. In the United States, Standard licensed only the large oil companies which had no interest in exploiting hydrogenation. Outside the United States, Standard . . . proceeded to limit use of the process so far as the threat of competing processes and governmental interest [of foreign countries] permitted."[11] As a result this revolutionary process was almost completely suppressed except in Germany where it became an effective tool for promoting the military ambitions of the Nazi government.

The development of synthetic rubber production in the United States was similarly retarded by the I.G.-Standard marriage of 1928. Since Buna rubber, under the agreement of 1928, was considered a chemical process, it came under the exclusive control of I.G. Farben—both in- and outside Germany. Farben, however, was not interested in promoting the manufacture of synthetic rubber anywhere except in Germany, and proceeded therefore—both for commercial (i.e. monopolistic) and nationalistic reasons—to forestall its development in the United States. In this purpose, Farben had at least the tacit support of its American partner. As a result the outbreak of World War II found the United States without production experience or know-how in the vital synthetic rubber field. In fact, when the Goodrich and Goodyear tire companies attempted to embark on synthetic rubber production, the former was sued for patent infringement and the latter formally threatened with such a suit by Standard Oil Company (acting under the authority of the Farben patents). This happened in November, 1941, one month before Pearl Harbor. Not until after our formal entry into World War II was the Farben-Standard alliance broken under the impact

[10] Wilcox, op. cit., pp. 16–17.

[11] Edwards, op. cit., p. 36. For a popular discussion of the I.G.-Standard marriage, see also G. W. Stocking and M. W. Watkins, Cartels in Action, New York: Twentieth Century Fund, 1946, Chapter 11, especially pp. 491–505.

of antitrust prosecution, and the production of vital synthetic rubber started in the United States. Here, as in the case of hydrogenation, monopolistic control over technology had serious implications not only for the nation's economic progress but also its military security.[12]

4) *Monopoly contributes to the inequality in the distribution of income, because the monopolist is not compelled to pass on to consumers, suppliers, or laborers (in the absence of strong unions) the gains of improved technology.* Moreover, monopoly profits are not widely distributed, since the ownership of all corporate stock (in competitive as well as monopolistic companies) is highly concentrated, and since corporate dividends go mainly to the upper income groups. In 1929, according to one source, over 83 per cent of all dividends paid to individuals went to the top 3.28 per cent of the population filing income tax returns; 78 per cent of such dividends went to the top three-tenths of one per cent.[13] According to another source, 64.7 per cent of all dividends paid to individuals between 1919 and 1938 went to the top one per cent of the nation's income recipients.[14] While this distribution is gradually becoming less unequal over time, it is still true that the great bulk of all dividend payments goes to a relatively small percentage of the total population.

Since there is little reason to suppose that the dividends derived from "monopolistic" enterprises are any more widely distributed than the dividends of *all* corporations taken together, monopoly thus makes for economic inequality. As Wilcox puts it, "the laborers whose incomes may be limited by the monopolist's failure to pay wages equal to their productivity are numerous. The producers of materials whose incomes are depressed by the low prices that the monopolist sometimes pays may also be numerous. The consumers whose real incomes are reduced by the high prices that the monopolist charges are likewise numerous. The stockholders who share the unnecessarily high profits that the monopolist thus obtains are few in number. A more nearly perfect mechanism for making the poor poorer and the rich richer could scarcely be devised."[15]

5) *Monopoly threatens not only the existence of a free economy, but*

---

[12] See W. Berge, *Cartels: Challenge to a Free World*, Washington: Public Affairs Press, 1944, pp. 210–14; G. W. Stocking and M. W. Watkins, *Cartels or Competition*, New York: Twentieth Century Fund, 1948, pp. 114–17; J. Borkin and C. A. Welsh, *Germany's Master Plan*, New York: Duell, Sloan & Pearce, 1943.

[13] Wilcox, *op. cit.*, p. 17.

[14] S. Kuznets, *Shares of Upper Income Groups in Income and Saving*, New York: National Bureau of Economic Research, 1950, pp. 9 and 34 ff.

[15] Wilcox, *op. cit.*, pp. 17–18. It is because of this accentuation of inequality in the distribution of income by monopoly that some economists consider monopoly to be one of the causal factors in the occurrence of depressions. The scientific evidence on this point, however, is rather meager.

also the survival chances of free political institutions. Enterprise which is not competitive cannot for long remain free, and a community which refuses to accept the discipline of competition inevitably exposes itself to the discipline of absolute authority. As Mutual Security Administrator Harold Stassen recently observed, "world economic history has shown that nationalization and socialization have come when there has been complete consolidation and combination of industry, not when enterprise is manifold and small in its units. . . . We must not permit major political power to be added to the other great powers that are accumulated by big business units. Excessive concentration of power is a threat to the individual freedoms and liberties of men, whether that excessive power is in the hands of government or of capital or of labor."[16] The enemy of democracy is monopoly in all its forms, and political liberty can survive only within an effective competitive system. If concentrated power is tolerated, giant pressure groups will ultimately gain control of the government or the government will institute direct regulation of organized pressure groups. In either event, free enterprise will then have to make way for collectivism, and democracy will be superseded by some form of authoritarianism.

This objection to monopoly, this fear of concentrated economic power, is deeply rooted in American traditions—the tradition of federalism, the separation of church and state, the tripartite organization of our governmental machinery. It is the expression of a socio-political philosophy which believes in the decentralization of power, a broad base for the class structure of society, and the economic freedom and opportunity for new men, new ideas, and new organizations to spearhead the forces of progress. It stands in stark contrast to the European varieties of free enterprise which involve merely curbs on governmental powers without similar checks on excessive private power.[17]

---

[16] Address reprinted in *Congressional Record*, February 12, 1947, p. A545. See also H. C. Simons, *Economic Policy for a Free Society*, Chicago: University of Chicago Press, 1948; F. A. Hayek, *The Road to Serfdom*, Chicago: University of Chicago Press, 1945; R. A. Brady, *Business as a System of Power*, New York: Columbia University Press, 1943; G. W. Stocking, "Saving Free Enterprise from Its Friends," *Southern Economic Journal*, April 1953, pp. 431–44. Also relevant in this connection are the repeated warnings by the Federal Trade Commission to the effect that "the capitalist system of free initiative is not immortal, but is capable of dying and dragging down with it the system of democratic government. Monopoly constitutes the death of capitalism and the genesis of authoritarian government." (*The Basing Point Problem*, T.N.E.C. Monograph No. 42, 1941, p. 9.)

[17] This point was well made by Senator Cummins in 1914, when he pressed for adoption of the Federal Trade Commission Act and the Clayton Act. Senator Cummins' statement is as true today as it was in 1914. Said the Senator: "We have adopted in this country the policy of competition. We are trying to preserve competition as a living, real force in our

By way of illustrating this charge against monopoly some students contend that the rise of Hitler in Germany was facilitated by the pervasive cartelization of the German economy—by the absence of competitive freedom in German business and the lack of democratic freedom in German government. Similarly, they point out that unregulated private monopoly was the breeding ground for Italian fascism and Japanese totalitarianism. Whether or not these correlations are scientifically valid is difficult to determine. Certainly, the seriousness of a danger is not easy to evaluate. "Who can say whether any particular warning is due to overcautiousness, timidity or even superstition or, on the other hand, to prudence and foresight? . . . It is, of course, possible that 'monopoly' is merely a bugbear frightening the believers in free enterprise and free society; but it is equally possible that we have underestimated the danger and have allowed the situation to deteriorate to such a degree that only a very radical effort can still save our social and political system."[18]

THE EXTENT OF CONCENTRATION

Despite a recognition of monopolistic evils; despite the antitrust laws which were enacted to combat them, we find that American industry today

---

industrial life; that is to say, we are endeavoring to maintain among our business people that honorable rivalry which will prevent one from exacting undue profits from those who may deal with him. . . . We are practically alone, however, in this policy. , , , England long ago became indifferent to it; and while that great country has not specifically adjusted her laws so as to permit monopoly they are so administered as to practically eliminate competition when the trade affected so desires. France has pursued a like course.

"Austria, Italy, Spain, Norway, Sweden, as well as Belgium, have all pursued the course of permitting combinations and relations which practically annihilate competition, and Germany, our most formidable rival, so far as commerce is concerned, not only authorizes by her law the formation of monopolies, the creation of combinations which restrain trade and which destroy competition, but oftentimes compels her people to enter into combinations which are in effect monopolies. We are, therefore, pursuing a course which rather distinguishes us from the remainder of the commercial world.

"I pause here to say, and I say it emphatically and earnestly, that I believe in our course; I believe in the preservation of competition, I believe in the maintenance of the rule that opens the channels of trade fairly and fully to all comers. I believe it because it seems to me obvious that any other course must inevitably lead us into complete State socialism. The only monopoly which civilized mankind will ever permanently endure is the monopoly of all the people represented in the Government itself." (*Congressional Record*, June 30, 1914, p. 11379.)

[18] F. Machlup, *The Political Economy of Monopoly*, Baltimore: Johns Hopkins Press, 1952, pp. 77–78.

is highly concentrated. No monistic explanation of this concentration pattern is possible, for many forces coalesced to bring it about. Suffice it to say, that the dominance of giant firms in many industries is primarily attributable to 1) modern technology which required, in the interests of efficiency, substantial capital investments in large-scale production, distribution, and research facilities; 2) the structure of the capital market which made funds more easily and cheaply available to large and established firms; 3) the efforts of financial interests to collect handsome promoter's fees and monopoly profits by organizing giant consolidations; and 4) the failure of government to promote competition vigorously and imaginatively,[19] i.e. the failure, by and large, to make antitrust more than a policeman looking the other way.

It is noteworthy that economists are by no means agreed on the direction or interpretation of the "concentration movement." Some believe that since 1890 concentration has, on the whole, increased. Others vigorously deny this.[20] All are agreed, however, that the present *degree* of concentration—regardless of its implications—is substantial. The T.N.E.C., for example, found that as of 1937 one-third of the total value of all manufactured goods was produced under conditions where the leading four producers of each individual product turned out from 75 to 100 per cent of the value of the product. Similarly, the Federal Trade Commission found that, as of 1947, the 113 largest manufacturing corporations (with assets in excess of $100,000,000 each) owned approximately 46 per cent of all net capital assets (both corporate and noncorporate) engaged in manufacturing.[21]

In classifying 26 selected industries according to their degree of con-

---

[19] Many students of the concentration movement, including the distinguished historian Charles A. Beard, feel that monopoly is to a considerable extent the creature of government action and inaction. Professor Beard explained his position to a Congressional Committee as follows: "I should like to emphasize the fact that our state and national governments have a responsibility for the corporate abuses and economic distress in which we now flounder. It is a matter of common knowledge that corporations are not natural persons. They are artificial persons. They are the creatures of government. Only with the sanction of government can they perform any acts, good or bad. The corporate abuses which have occurred, the concentration of wealth which has come about under their operations, all can be laid directly and immediately at the door of government. The states of the American Union and the Congress of the United States, by their actions and their inaction, have made possible the situation and the calamities in which we now find ourselves." (*Hearings before a Subcommittee on the Judiciary*, 75th Congress, 1st Session, 1937, Part I, p. 72.)

[20] For conflicting views on the extent of concentration in the American economy, see M. A. Adelman, "The Measurement of Industrial Concentration," *Review of Economics and Statistics*, November, 1951; and J. M. Blair, "The Measurement of Industrial Concentration: A Reply," *Review of Economics and Statistics*, November, 1952.

[21] Federal Trade Commission, *The Concentration of Productive Facilities, 1947*, p. 14.

centration in 1947, the commission listed the following as "extremely concentrated" (because in these industries the largest three producers own 60 per cent or more of the net capital assets):[22]

T A B L E   1 6 . 1

"EXTREMELY" CONCENTRATED INDUSTRIES

Industry	Per Cent of Net Capital Assets Held by 3 Largest Companies
Aluminum	100.0
Tin cans & other tinware	95.3
Linoleum	92.1
Copper smelting & refining	88.5
Cigarettes	77.6
Distilled liquors	72.4
Plumbing equipment & supplies	71.3
Rubber tires & tubes	70.3
Office and store machines & devices	69.5
Motor vehicles	68.7
Biscuits, crackers, & pretzels	67.7
Agricultural machinery	66.6
Meat products	64.0

Industries in which 60 per cent control was attained by the largest *five* or *six* companies were considered to have "high (though not extreme)" concentration. Industries in this category, together with the percentage control of the largest six companies, were: glass and glassware (69.9 per cent); carpets and rugs (00.3 per cent); dairy products (66.3 per cent); primary steel (63.4 per cent); industrial chemicals (62.7 per cent); and aircraft and parts (60.4 per cent).[23]

Industries in which approximately 60 per cent control was attained by the largest *eleven* to *fifteen* companies were considered in the "moderate" concentration group, and included the following: electrical machinery (60.1 per cent); grain mill products (56.6 per cent); drugs and medicines (53.8 per cent); canning and preserving (59.2 per cent); and footwear except rubber (57.5 per cent).[24]

Finally, industries where the *fifteen* largest companies controlled substantially *less* than 60 per cent of net capital assets were considered to have

22 *Ibid.*, p. 17.
23 *Ibid.*, p. 19.
24 *Ibid.*, p. 19.

relatively "low" concentration. This category included bakery products and woolen and worsted goods.[25]

Certain caveats are recommended to guard against unwarranted conclusions based on the above figures. *First,* it is difficult to define an "industry," and high concentration in one industry may not be very significant if its product competes actively with that of another industry (i.e. where the cross-elasticity of demand is high). For example, concentration in the field of textile fibers taken as a whole may, for public policy purposes, be more relevant than concentration in silk, wool, cotton, rayon, nylon, orlon, acrilan, dynel, dacron, etc. taken separately. *Second,* some giant firms are listed as members of one industry, although their capital assets are spread over a number of other industries. General Motors, for example, is listed as an automobile producer, although some of its capital investment lies in such fields as diesel engines, electric appliances, refrigerators, etc.—a fact which results in partial overstatement of the degree of concentration in the automobile industry. *Third,* concentration must not be confused with monopoly. The mere fact that an industry is highly cencentrated is not positive proof that the industry is monopolized or that its firms are in active collusion. Under extreme circumstances, it is even conceivable that as few as two companies are enough to provide effective competition in an industry. As Dexter Keezer, vice-president of the McGraw-Hill Company, points out: "If the heads of the two surviving firms were the hard-driving, fiercely independent type of businessman who has played such a large part in the industrial development of the U.S.A., two of them would be enough to create a ruggedly competitive situation. But," Dr. Keezer adds, "if the two were of the genteel, clubby and take-it-easy type which is also known in the high reaches of American business, two companies might get together and tend to sleep together indefinitely. When the number of firms involved is small, the chances of having the industry animated by vigorously competitive leadership also seem to me to be small."[26]

In view of the many controversial aspects of present-day concentration, this much perhaps can be asserted with some measure of confidence: there is substantial concentration in the American economy, especially in such segments as manufacturing, transportation, public utilities, and some areas of finance. Many industries—some of them basic industries—are concentrated in the sense that the Big Three, Big Four, Big Five, or Big Six control the lion's share of their output. Many firms are, in absolute terms, of gigantic size and possess, therefore, considerable economic and political power (both actual and potential). Many of these firms control vast indus-

[25] *Ibid.,* p. 19.

[26] "Antitrust Symposium." *American Economic Review,* June, 1949, p. 718.

trial empires, extending over several industries, and are sometimes joined into informal interest groups encompassing large segments of economic activity.[27] The significance of all this is still the subject of violent controversy, and all we can say—as Machlup suggests—is that economists regard the current degree of concentration either as a) desirable and avoidable; b) desirable and unavoidable; c) undesirable and avoidable; or d) undesirable and unavoidable.

PUBLIC POLICY ALTERNATIVES

Depending on which of these views is accepted, economists will then recommend one of the following policy alternatives with respect to concentrated industries: 1) maintenance of the status quo which, by and large, is regarded as satisfactory; 2) imposition of public regulation or public ownership; or 3) rejection of both private and public monopoly, and the promotion of vigorous competition under the antitrust laws. It is these policy alternatives which shall now be examined in greater detail.

THE STATUS QUO

The defenders of the status quo generally advocate a policy of non-interference with respect to our concentrated industries. They seem satisfied with the prevailing industrial structure, either because they believe that bigness and concentration are now controlled by the "right" people or because they refuse to regard concentration as indicative of pervasive monopolization.

Three distinct, though related, facets of this position are discernible. One is the belief that the business leader of today is a far cry from the

---

[27] In 1935, the National Resources Committee found that there were eight major interest groups of large corporations closely knit together by interlocking directorships, stock ownership, family ties, joint financing, and other associations. These interest groups, which allegedly occupy a dominant role in American industry, were listed as the Morgan-First National group, the Rockefeller group, the Mellon group, the du Pont group, the Kuhn-Loeb group, the Chicago group, the Boston group, and the Cleveland group. In 1935, the largest of these (Morgan-First National) included 13 industrial corporations (headed by U. S. Steel), 12 utility corporations (headed by A. T. & T.), 37 electric generating companies, 11 major railroads, and several important financial institutions. (National Resources Committee, *The Structure of the American Economy*, 1939, Part I, pp. 160–63.) For the capital assets controlled by these interest groups, before World War II, see Smaller War Plants Corporation, *Economic Concentration and World War II*, Senate Document No. 206, 79th Congress, 2d Session, pp. 353–56.

robber baron of yesterday; the belief that industrial statesmanship, social
responsibility, enlightened self-restraint, and progressive labor, customer,
and supplier relations have replaced the exploitative behavior, the sharpshooting competitive practices, and the "public-be-damned" attitude of a
bygone age; in short, the belief that the present managers of giant corporate enterprise have demonstrated their capacity for exercising industrial
stewardship.[28]

The second facet of the status quo position is the "workable competition" thesis.[29] Its supporters hold that bigness and concentration are no
cause for alarm, because competition is present and *working* in an economy
such as ours where constant technological progress is reflected in ever-
increasing output, lower prices, and new and improved products. They urge
that the effectiveness of competition be judged not in terms of market structure (i.e. the degree of concentration in particular industries) but rather
by market results (i.e. performance in the public interest). They suggest
that an industry is "workably competitive"—regardless of the fewness of
sellers in it—if it shows, among other things, "a progressive technology, the
passing on to consumers of the results of this progressiveness in the form
of lower prices, larger output, improved products, etc."[30] The emphasis here
is on performance and results rather than on structural organization which
compels such performance and results.

[28] David E. Lilienthal, in his recent book *Big Business: A New Era* (New York: Harper
& Brothers, 1953), argues that the antitrust philosophy is no longer applicable and that
the antitrust laws are, in fact, crippling America. He feels that the newer type of
American big businessman is in little need of the restraints imposed by the antitrust laws.
In contrast to Mr. Lilienthal's position, it is interesting to note that a distinguished Wall
Street attorney, General William J. Donovan, disagrees. Mr. Donovan's warning, sounded
in 1936, is still relevant today: "Those who would remove the inhibitions of existing law
must recognize that the alternative is not between the Sherman Act on the one hand and
the regulation of industry on the other. The alternative is between the continuance of
the competitive system as a proper safeguard to the public, and the closest supervision
and control of industry by the government. The self-interest of business in such matters
would often be antagonistic to the interest of the public as a whole. The recent experience
under the NRA shows the abuses that may arise by vesting in business the power of
self-regulation without at the same time providing for adequate and capable supervision
and control by a governmental agency." (Address before the American Bar Association,
1936, quoted in V. A. Mund, *Government and Business*, New York: Harper and
Brothers, 1950, pp. 628–29.)

[29] See primarily J. M. Clark, "Toward a Concept of Workable Competition," *American
Economic Review*, June, 1940.

[30] E. S. Mason, "Antitrust Symposium," *op. cit.*, p. 713. See also C. E. Griffin, *An
Economic Approach to Antitrust Problems*, New York: American Enterprise Association,
1951.

The believers in workable competition usually buttress their position with the suggestion that "old-fashioned" competition—i.e. competition among sellers and among buyers *within* an industry—be replaced with a more dynamic concept of *inter*-industry or technological competition. Their argument is this: classical, intra-industry competition tends to promote maximum output, minimum prices, and optimum utilization of capacity; in short, it stimulates efficiency. But this efficiency is static and unprogressive in character. It makes no allowance for the research, development, and innovation required for economic growth. While it prevents concentration, it stifles progress. To have progress we need more, not less, concentration. Only bigness can provide the sizable funds necessary for technological experimentation and innovation in the industrial milieu of the twentieth century. Only monopoly earnings can provide the bait that lures capital to untried trails. While progress may thus require high power concentrations in many industries, this need not be a source of concern to society at large. Technological development will serve as an offset against any short-run position of entrenchment which may be established. The monopoly of glass bottles will be subverted by the introduction of the tin can; and the dominance of the latter will, in turn, be undermined by the introduction of the paper container. The consumer need not rely, therefore, on the static competition between large numbers of small firms as protection against exploitation. In the long run, he can find greater safety—and better things for better living to boot—in the technological competition of a small number of large firms who, through research and innovation, eventually destroy any position of market control which may be established.[31]

The third facet of the status quo position is the recently promulgated "countervailing power" thesis which concedes the pervasiveness of concentration and monopoly, but maintains that the dangers of exploitation are minimized by certain built-in safeguards in our economy.[32] According to this thesis, the actual or real restraints on a firm's market power are vested not in its competitors, but in its customers and suppliers. These restraints are imposed not from the same side of the market (as under classical competition), but from the opposite side. Thus "private economic power is held in check by the countervailing power of those subject to it. The first begets the second."[33] A monopoly on one side of the market offers an inducement

---

[31] See J. A. Schumpeter, *Capitalism, Socialism, and Democracy*, New York: Harper & Brothers, 1943, p. 79 ff.

[32] See J. K. Galbraith, *American Capitalism: The Concept of Countervailing Power*, Boston: Houghton Mifflin Company, 1952.

[33] *Ibid.*, p. 118.

to both suppliers and customers to develop the power with which they can defend themselves against exploitation. For example, concentration in the steel industry will stimulate concentration among the industry's customers (automobile manufacturers) as well as among its suppliers (steel workers). The result will be, so the argument runs, a balance of power within the economy—the creation of almost automatic checks and balances requiring a minimum of interference or "tampering."

The foregoing arguments in defense of the status quo are subject to a number of criticisms. As to the beneficence of industrial stewardship and workable competition, we should note that "results alone throw no light on the really significant question: have these results been *compelled* by the system—by *competition*—or do they represent simply the dispensations of managements which, with a wide latitude of policy choices at their disposal, happened for the moment to be benevolent or smart?"[34] In other words, what assurance do we have that the workable competition of today will not be transformed into the abusive monopoly or oppressive conspiracy of tomorrow? How, in the absence of competition or constant and detailed supervision, can we ever determine whether the performance of industrial giants does, in fact, serve the public interest and will continue to do so in the future? By what concrete yardsticks do we measure the workability of competition?

Secondly, with regard to the countervailing power thesis, it can be argued 1) that countervailing power is often undermined by vertical integration and top level financial control which blend the opposing sides of the market into one; 2) that the bilateral monopolies created through the countervailance process often conclude bargains prejudicial to the consumer interest (witness, for example, wage increases for the C.I.O. Steelworkers followed by price increases for the steel industry); 3) that the countervailing influence of technological or inter-industry competition is often subverted by a combination of the potential competitors (witness, for example, the merger between motion picture houses and television networks); 4) that any countervailance through government action is often undermined by unduly intimate affiliation between regulator and regulatee (witness, for example, the I.C.C. which seems to have degenerated into a lobby on behalf of railroad interests); and finally 5) that the whole thesis rests on the dubious assumption that industrial giantism is inevitable under modern technological conditions—an assumption which still awaits scientific validation.[35]

---

[34] Ben W. Lewis, "Antitrust Symposium," *op. cit.*, p. 707.

[35] For a more comprehensive critique of the countervailing power thesis, see W. Adams, "Competition, Monopoly and Countervailing Power," *Quarterly Journal of Economics*, November, 1953.

PUBLIC REGULATION OR PUBLIC OWNERSHIP

The advocates of public regulation or public ownership hope simultaneously to insure industrial efficiency and to avoid the abuses of private monopoly—not by the dissolution of monopoly but by its social control. Their argument runs along these lines: Competition in many basic industries is a thing of the past and has been replaced by trade agreements and price fixing, cartels and monopolies. While legislation to eliminate specific abuses of monopoly power can do some good, it cannot compel a return to competition in industries where it would be wasteful and undesirable. The facts of life are that efficient organization in mass production and mass distribution fields requires unification, coordination, and rationalization. Only monopoly can bring this about. But private monopoly is no guarantee of efficiency. By fixing prices, allocating production, imposing levies on the efficient to keep the inefficient in production, the general level of prices is kept high, and incentives to modernization may be lacking. Hence, if monopoly is inevitable, it is preferable that such monopoly be publicly supervised or publicly owned.[36]

Basic to this argument is the assumption that monopoly, or at least cooperation on a comprehensive scale, is necessary in many industries—the assumption that monopoly is inevitable under modern industrial conditions. It is this belief in the inevitability of monopoly which has led men of such distinguished position, unimpeachable integrity, and obvious sincerity as Judge Gary (former president of the U. S. Steel Corporation) to advocate a public-utility-type regulation for concentrated industries. Thus Judge Gary, as long ago as 1911, offered the following testimony to a Congressional committee investigating the steel industry:

'I realize as fully, I think, as this committee that it is very important to consider how the people shall be protected against imposition or oppression as the possible result of great aggregations of capital, whether in the possession of corporations or individuals. I believe that is a very important question, and personally I believe that the Sherman Act does not meet and will never fully prevent that. I believe we must come to enforced publicity and governmental control, even as to prices, and, so far as I am concerned, speaking for our company, so far as I have the right, I would be very glad if we had some place where we could go, to a responsible governmental authority, and say to them, 'Here are our facts and figures, here is our property, here our cost of production; now you tell us what we have the right to do and what

[36] For this formulation of the argument, see the work of the British socialist, E. Davies, *National Enterprise*, London: Victor Gollancz Ltd., 1946, p. 16.

prices we have the right to charge.' I know this is a very extreme view, and I know that the railroads objected to it for a long time; but whether the standpoint of making the most money is concerned or not, whether it is the wise thing, I believe it is the necessary thing, and it seems to me corporations have no right to disregard these public questions and these public interests."

"Your idea then," said Congressman Littleton of the committee, "is that cooperation is bound to take the place of competition and that cooperation requires strict governmental supervision?"

"That is a very good statement," replied the Judge.[37]

Unfortunately, Judge Gary's faith in independent regulatory commissions has, in the light of American experience, not proved justified. These commissions—the Interstate Commerce Commission,[38] the Civil Aeronautics Board,[39] the Federal Power Commission,[40] the Federal Communications Commission[41]—have at times failed to regulate their respective industries in the public interest. Often these commissions adopted regulatory techniques which did little to promote operational efficiency and innovative progress; which were ineffective, costly and debilitating; and which suffered from administrative incompetence, unimaginativeness, and dishonesty. Moreover, no satisfactory solution seems yet to have been found for the vexing problem of watching the watchers. (*Quis custodiet ipsos custodies?*) As ex-Senator Wheeler once sadly observed, "It seems to invariably happen, that when Congress attempts to regulate some group, the intended regulatees wind up doing the regulating."[42]

Dissatisfied with the past record of regulatory commissions, some groups have gone further and advocated the nationalization, i.e. outright government ownership, of concentrated industries. Typical of these groups is the

---

[37] Special Committee to Investigate the United States Steel Corporation, House Report No. 1127, 62d Congress, 2d Session, 1911, quoted in W. Adams and L. E. Traywick, *Readings in Economics*, New York: The Macmillan Company, 1948, p. 223.

[38] See, for example, S. P. Huntington, "The Marasmus of the I.C.C.," *Yale Law Journal*, April, 1952.

[39] See Chapter XII above; also Senate Small Business Committee, *Report on Role of Irregular Airlines in United States Air Transportation Industry*, Report No. 540, 82d Congress, 1st Session, 1951.

[40] See, for example, Federal Power Commission, *In the Matter of the Phillips Petroleum Company*, Opinion No. 217, Docket No. G-1148, August 16, 1951.

[41] See, for example, Federal Communications Commission, *In the Matter of American Broadcasting Company Inc. and United Paramount Theatres, Inc.*, Docket No. 10046, 1953.

[42] Quoted in B. Bolles, *How to Get Rich in Washington*, New York: Dell Publishing Company, p. 23.

British Labour Party which, in 1948, demanded nationalization of the steel industry on the grounds that the public supervision of private monopoly is unworkable. Said the Labour Party:[43]

> A board controlling a private monopoly must in the long run be ineffective. Its activities must be negative. It can, for example, refuse to recommend a price increase, but it cannot force the industry to take steps to cheapen production. It has no power to make the monopoly spend money on new plant or scrap old plant. A supervised private monopoly can be prevented from doing the wrong things, but it cannot be forced to do the right things. In the future, the control of steel must be dynamic and purposeful, not negative and preventive. . . . There is no hope, then, in a supervised monopoly. The only answer is that steel must be made a public enterprise.

According to the socialist, then, nationalization is preferable both to public regulation and to private monopoly. It is better than public regulation, because the latter has proved generally ineffective. It is better than private monopoly, because the power to control basic industries, and hence the economy, must be "democratized."[44] Such power must, according to the socialist, be held by the many and not as hitherto concentrated—without corresponding responsibility—in the hands of a few. There must be assurance that monopoly—a system which can be used for good or evil—will be used in the public interest. According to the socialist, a nationalized industry affords such assurance, simply because its management will be motivated by considerations of public service and not private profit.

The disadvantages of public ownership are fairly obvious: administrators in nationalized industries may easily succumb to the disease of security, conservatism, procrastination, and bureaucracy. Their enterprises, as a result of supercentralization and lack of competitive incentives, may come to suffer from inflexibility and inelasticity. Moreover, the public enterprise may develop a tendency of using its monopoly power as a cloak for inefficient operation by resorting to the ready device of raising prices to meet increased costs, and thus avoid showing a deficit. Finally, there is the distinct possibility that the very people in whose interest a particular industry may originally have been nationalized will eventually lose control of it. This result is probable for two reasons: 1) general elections are no substitute for the market as an agency of social control (because people cannot indicate their dissatisfaction with a *particular* public enterprise by means of the ballot);

---

[43] *British Steel at Britain's Service*, London, 1948, p. 15; quoted in Mund, *op. cit.*, p. 548.
[44] See Ben W. Lewis, *British Planning and Nationalization*, New York: Twentieth Century Fund, 1952, pp. 43–45.

and 2) the public enterprise, if it is to operate efficiently, must be "taken out of politics" and put in the hands of an autonomous body—again with the result of removing such enterprise from the direct control of the electorate.[45]

In summary, public regulation and public ownership suffer from the same basic drawback as private monopoly, viz, the concentration of power in the hands of a few. Such power may be used benignly or dangerously, depending on the men who possess and control it. They may be good men, benevolent men, and socially minded men; but society still confronts the danger of which Lord Acton so eloquently warned: power corrupts, and absolute power corrupts absolutely.

THE PROMOTION OF EFFECTIVE COMPETITION

The advocates of promoting greater competition through vigorous antitrust enforcement reject both the Scylla of private monopoly and the Charybdis of public ownership. Believing that the preservation of competitive free enterprise is both desirable and possible, they point out that this does not mean a return to the horse-and-buggy age, nor a strict adherence to the textbook thories of "perfect" or "pure" competition. What they advocate

---

[45] See F. A. Hayek, *The Road to Serfdom*, Chicago: University of Chicago Press, 1945; L. Von Mises, *Planned Chaos*, New York: Foundation for Economic Education, 1947; C. E. Griffin, *Britain: A Case Study for Americans*, Ann Arbor: University of Michigan Press, 1950. These criticisms of public ownership are confirmed by the distinguished British scholar, W. Arthur Lewis. In his "Recent British Experience of Nationalization as an Alternative to Monopoly Control" (a paper presented to the International Economic Association in 1951), Professor Lewis makes the following comments on Britain's experiment in socialism: "The appointment of public directors to manage an undertaking is not sufficient public control." "Parliament is handicapped in controlling corporations by its lack of time. . . . Neither have Members of Parliament the competence to supervise these great industries. . . . Parliament is further handicapped . . . by paucity of information . . . for example, less information is now published about the railways than was available before they were nationalized." "Except in the case of transport, the British government resisted proposals that public corporations should be treated in the same way [as private monopolies], with the result that the consumer is formally less well protected vis-à-vis public corporations than he was vis-à-vis private firms operating public utilities." "The [public] corporation's Board, though publicly appointed, has many loyalties in addition to its loyalty to the public. It has also a loyalty to itself, and to its own staff, which may well conflict with the interests of the consumer." "Public corporations have not found it easy to dismiss redundant workers, or even to close down inefficient units or to expand more efficient units in some other place (e.g. railways, mines). It may well turn out that public corporations are less able to promote this kind of efficiency than are private corporations, in the British atmosphere of tenderness towards established sources of income." (Quoted in Machlup, *op. cit.*, p. 50)

is a structural arrangement in private industry characterized by decentralized decision-making and "effective" competition.

Among the ingredients necessary for effective competition, the following are considered of primary importance:[46] 1) an appreciable number of sellers and buyers for substantially the same product, so that both sellers and buyers have meaningful alternatives of choice; 2) the economic, as well as legal, freedom to enter the market and gain access to essential raw materials; 3) the absence of tacit or open collusion between rivals in the market; 4) the absence of explicit or implicit coercion of rivals by a dominant firm or a group of dominant firms; 5) the absence of "substantial preferential status within the market for any important trader or group of traders on the basis of law, politics, or commercial alliances";[47] 6) the absence of diversification, subsidization and political motivation to an extent where giant firms may escape the commercial discipline of a *particular* market or a *particular* operation.

Some economists feel that the maintenance of this type of competition may, under modern conditions, be difficult if not impossible. They contend that antitrusters are faced with the dilemma of choosing between "1) firms of the most efficient size but operating under conditions where there is inadequate pressure to compel firms to continue to be efficient and pass on to the consumer the benefits of efficiency, and 2) a system in which the firms are numerous enough to be competitive but too small to be efficient."[48] According to this view our choice is between monopoly and efficiency, on the one hand, and competition and relative inefficiency, on the other.

The supporters of vigorous antitrust enforcement deny that such a choice is necessary, at least in many of our highly concentrated industries. The following reasons are usually given for rejecting the ostensible conflict between competition and efficiency. *First,* large firms, while technologically imperative in many industries, need not assume the Brobdignagian proportions of some present-day giants. The unit of technological efficiency is the plant and not the firm. This means that, while there are undisputed advantages in the large-scale integrated steel operations at Gary or Pittsburgh or Birmingham, there seems little technological justification for combining these functionally separate plant units into a single administrative giant. *Second,* it seems significant that many of our colossal firms were not formed to gain the technical advantages of scale, but organized instead to achieve monopolistic control over the market and to reap profits from the

---

[46] See C. D. Edwards, *Maintaining Competition,* New York: McGraw-Hill Book Co., 1949, pp. 9–10.

[47] *Ibid.,* p. 10.

[48] A. R. Burns, "Antitrust Symposium," *op. cit.,* p. 603.

sale of inflated securities. Giantism in industry today is not unrelated to the investment banker's inclination of yesteryear to merge and combine competing companies for the sake of promoter's profits.

Finally, to the extent that profit figures are valid as measures of comparative efficiency, it seems that in a number of cases medium-sized and small firms outperform their giant rivals. Moreover, a breaking down of huge firms does not necessarily have fatal effects on efficiency *or* profitability. In the public utility field, for example, the comprehensive dissolution program carried out under the Public Utility Holding Company Act of 1935 has resulted in increased efficiency and profitability among the successor companies. This was demonstrated in the above average appreciation in the security values of the successor companies which occurred despite declining utility rates, higher costs, and the inevitably higher taxes.[49] On the basis of experience, therefore, it may not be unreasonable to suggest, as *Fortune* does, that there are areas in American industry where an unmerging process among the giants can contribute both to increased efficiency and more vigorous competition.[50]

If such an unmerging process were to be accomplished through antitrust action, three types of market structure would have to be identified and dealt with, viz, horizontal, vertical, and conglomerate integration. The horizontal size of *some* firms would have to be reduced, if competition is to be promoted, because an oligopolistic industry structure often results in conscious or unconscious parallelism among the giant firms.[51] Price leadership, live-and-let-live policies, nonprice competition, etc.—in short, the type of gentlemanly behavior which imposes higher and more inflexible prices on the consumer—are common among firms of oligopolistic size, because each fears retaliation by its large rivals as punishment for independence and nonconformity. 2) Vertically integrated size would, in some cases, have to be reduced because the large integrated concern can apply the squeeze—both on prices and supplies—to its smaller rivals who are both its customers and competitors.[52] A case in point here would be a fully integrated aluminum firm which simultaneously supplies independent fabricators with aluminum ingot and then competes with them in the market for fabricated

---

[49] See W. Adams, "The Dilemma of Antitrust Aims: A Reply," *American Economic Review*, December, 1952.

[50] See editorials in *Fortune*, March and April, 1938.

[51] See E. H. Chamberlin, *The Theory of Monopolistic Competition*, Cambridge: Harvard University Press, 1946, pp. 46–55.

[52] Senate Small Business Committee, *Monopolistic Practices and Small Business*, 82d Congress, 2d Session, 1952, pp. 21–55; also, *The Distribution of Steel Consumption, 1949–50*, 82d Congress, 2d Session, 1952.

products.[53] 3) Conglomerate integration would pose a problem, because the widely diversified giant can exercise undue power as a buyer of materials, energy, transportation, credit, and labor; and also because such a concern often enjoys special advantages in litigation, politics, public relations, and finance.[54]

In launching a comprehensive program against these forms of integration a case-by-case approach seems preferable to any absolute prohibition on size per se. Moreover, to avoid any major conflicts with vested interests, enforcement might at first be confined to new industries where the problem of concentration is not yet extreme and where structural arrangements have not yet been solidified. This may have significant results, since ours is a dynamic economy in which new industries—if they remain competitive—can substantially curb the power of older and more entrenched interests. Finally, to forestall any possible interference with industrial efficiency, antitrust prosecution might be confined to cases where the goals of competition and efficiency are not in conflict. Toward that end, the antitrust laws can be amended to provide that "any corporation whose size and power are such as to substantially lessen competition and tend to create a monopoly in any line of commerce shall be dissolved into its component parts, *unless* such corporation can demonstrate that its present size is necessary for the maintenance of efficiency."[55] Given a provision of this sort, the dilemma of antitrust may be resolved and our twin goals of competition and efficiency actively promoted.

Antitrust enforcement along the above lines, however, is not enough if competitive free enterprise is to be maintained. Competition must become the core of an integrated national economic policy.[56] It must be positively promoted, rather than negatively preserved.[57] It must have an environment which provides opportunity for new men, and is receptive to new ideas. To create such an environment, a number of recommendations merit consideration:

[53] See *U. S.* v. *Aluminum Company of America*, 148 F. 2d 416 (C.C.A. 2d, 1945).

[54] See Edwards, *Maintaining Competition, op. cit.*, pp. 99–108.

[55] Cp. Monopoly Subcommittee of the House Judiciary Committee, *Hearings*, Part 2-B, 81st Congress, 1st Session, 1949, pp. 1311–39, 1600–25.

[56] See House Small Business Committee, *United States versus Economic Concentration and Monopoly*, 79th Congress, 2d Session, 1947.

[57] As Vernon Mund observes, "a policy of individual enterprise and price competition is a highly elaborate and complex plan for organizing the conduct of economic activity. It is a plan, however, which is not self-enforcing. When the policy of competition is accepted, it must be implemented by positive measures to provide for its creation, maintenance, and preservation. Competition is a form of human behavior; and like other

1) Defense contracts, accelerated amortization privileges, and other wartime bonanzas coming down the government pike should not be restricted to a favored few, but distributed to many firms so as to assure the nation of a broad industrial base for future defense efforts.[58]

2) In the disposal of government property—whether war surplus, synthetic rubber plants, or atomic energy installations—to private industry, sales should be made in a manner calculated to encourage competitive newcomers rather than to rigidify existing patterns of industrial control.

3) The corporate tax structure should be overhauled so as to remove present penalties on the growth and expansion of small business.[59]

4) Government financing of small business should be more than polite encouragement for prospective hot-dog stands and gasoline stations.

5) The patent laws should be revised so as to prevent monopolistic abuse of the patent grant without destroying the incentives for invention. This may entail compulsory licensing of patents on a *royalty-free* basis in cases involving violations of the antitrust laws; compulsory licensing of patents on a *reasonable-royalty* basis in cases of patent suppression and nonuse; and outright prohibition of restrictive and exclusive licensing provisions in private patent agreements. In any event, an invention made as a result of government financing or subsidy should become part of the public domain and not allowed

---

behavior it should be conducted according to good manners and morals. The big mistake which government has made with respect to economic regulation is in thinking that in the absence of direct price control (as in the case of public utilities) government intervention is not necessary. The lessons of history clearly show that we cannot have fair competition unless positive measures are taken to create and maintain it." (Mund, *op. cit.*, p. 642.)

[58] See, for example, Senate Small Business Committee, *Concentration of Defense Contracts*, Report No. 551, 82d Congress, 1st Session, 1951; House Committee on Expenditures in the Executive Departments, *Inquiry into the Procurement of Automotive Spare Parts by the United States Government*, 82d Congress, 2d Session, House Report No. 1811, 1952; Attorney General, *Report Prepared Pursuant to Section 708(e) of the Defense Production Act of 1950*, 1950; Joint Committee on Defense Production, *Hearings on Tax Amortization*, 82d Congress, 1st Session, 1951.

[59] See Senate Small Business Committee, *Tax Problems of Small Business*, Report No. 442, 83d Congress, 1st Session, 1953; J. K. Butters and J. Lintner, *Effect of Federal Taxes on Growing Enterprises*, Boston: Harvard Business School, 1945; J. K. Butters, J. Lintner, and W. Carey, *Effects of Taxation: Corporate Mergers*, Boston: Harvard Business School, 1951.

to accrue as private property to the corporation doing the contract research.[60]

6) Any further exemptions from the antitrust laws should be discouraged, and some existing exceptions re-examined.[61] We must stop what Leverett S. Lyon has called the "growing tendency in the United States for special groups to identify their limited good with the national good and to ask government for subsidy, support, or special protection rather than for laws which increase competitive opportunity."[62] Such laws as the Webb-Pomerene Act, for example,

---

[60] In this connection the Attorney General has recommended that "where patentable inventions are made in the course of performing a Government-financed contract for research and development, the public interest requires that all rights to such inventions be assigned to the Government and not left to the private ownership of the contractor. Public control will assure free and equal availability of the inventions to American industry and science; will eliminate any competitive advantage to the contractor chosen to perform the research work; will avoid undue concentration of economic power in the hands of a few large corporations; will tend to increase and diversify available research facilities within the United States to the advantage of the Government and of the national economy; and will thus strengthen our American system of free, competitive enterprise." (*Investigation of Government Patent Practices and Policies*, 1947, Vol. I, p. 4). Obviously, it makes little sense to permit—as in the past—"publicly-financed technology to be suppressed, used restrictively, or made the bases of an exaction from the public to serve private interests." (*Ibid.*, p. 2.)

[61] The problem of exemptions from the antitrust laws is well illustrated in the following story about a Polish ghetto, told by Congressman Celler: "The rabbi of the synagogue said: 'There is a very poor family on the other end of the ghetto. They have not raiment, they have not food, and they have not shelter. You are too poor yourselves'—he said to his congregation—'to help them, but I have an idea. . . . On the Sabbath eve when you praise the Lord for the fruitage of the earth, and you praise him by drinking a glass of wine, do not drink the full glass of wine. Drink a half a glass of wine, and the next morning when you come to the temple, I will have a barrel, and as you all come in, you will pour the half glass of wine that you left from the night before in the barrel. The Lord will not mind being blessed by the drinking of half a glass of wine, and at a given time the barrel will be filled. I will sell the barrel of wine and give the proceeds to this poor family. You will not be hurt; nobody will be harmed, and even the good Lord will bless you for it.' At a given time the barrel was opened and lo and behold, it was all water, and the rabbi reprimanded every member of the congregation, and they all had this answer: 'We figured what difference would a half glass of water make in a full barrel of wine.' . . . That is what is happening here. If we keep whittling away, and whittling away, and everybody asks to be exempted, everybody asks to put the half a glass of water in the full barrel of wine, we will have a barrel of water, and we will have no antitrust laws left." (Subcommittee on the Study of Monopoly Power, *Hearings*, 81st Congress, 1st Session, Serial No. 14, Part I, 1949, pp. 267–68.)

[62] "Government and American Economic Life," *Journal of Business*, April, 1949, pp. 89–90.

which exempts foreign trade associations from the Sherman Act, should be drastically revised or altogether repealed.[63]

7) Protective tariffs which serve to shield highly concentrated industries from the potential inroads of foreign competition should be reduced or repealed.

8) Incorporation and licensing laws should not be made a front for monopolistic privilege and restrictive practices.

9) The advisability of a progressive tax on advertising—with a generous exemption of, say, $3,000,000—should be examined, in an effort to prevent excessive advertising expenditures from acting as an obstacle to free entry in some concentrated industries.[64]

Such steps as these—and the list is by no means complete—may serve to stimulate an environment favorable to genuine free enterprise. The task is not easy, for we must strike a delicate balance between the businessman's search for profit and economic security, and society's insistence on freedom and opportunity for the newcomer. But while the task is difficult, it is not insuperable. Given a comprehensive and imaginative economic policy, it is likely that competition can be maintained (or revived), for the record shows that free enterprise in our generation has not failed; it has never been tried.

A hard look at the choice before us is indicated because, in the absence of positive action, we can expect little but aimless drifting and a gradual erosion of our traditional values. As Stocking and Watkins point out, "either the people must call a halt to the concentration—whether in governmental or private hands—of economic power, or they must be prepared to give up a competitive economy, bit by bit, year by year, until it is beyond recall. They will then be obliged to accept some collective alternative that may give more short-run basic security but in the long run will almost certainly provide less freedom, less opportunity for experiment, less variety, less economic progress, and less total abundance."[65]

---

[63] Committee on the Webb-Pomerene Act, American Economic Association, "The Webb-Pomerene Law: A Consensus Report," *American Economic Review*, December, 1947, pp. 848–63.

[64] See W. H. Nicholls, *Pricing Policies in the Cigarette Industry*, Nashville: Vanderbilt University Press, 1951, pp. 412–15.

[65] G. W. Stocking and M. W. Watkins, *Monopoly and Free Enterprise*, New York: Twentieth Century Fund, 1952, p. 526. We might profit from British experience which the conservative London *Economist* has summarized as follows: "The fact is that British industrialists, under the deliberate leadership of the Tory Party in its Baldwin-Chamberlain era, have become distinguishable from British Socialists only by the fact that they still believe in private profits. Both believe in 'organising' industry; both believe in protecting it, when organized, against any competition, either from foreigners or from native newcomers; both believe in standard prices for what they sell; both unite in condemning competition, the one as 'wasteful,' the other as 'destructive.' If free, competitive, private-

FIGURE 16.2

PUBLIC POLICY ALTERNATIVES

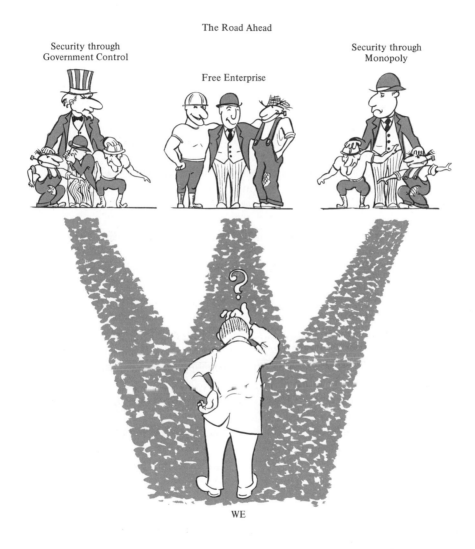

(*Source:* Thurman W. Arnold, *Cartels or Free Enterprise?* Public Affairs Pamphlet No. 103, 1945; reproduced by courtesy of the Public Affairs Committee, Inc.)

SUGGESTED READINGS

Books and Pamphlets

American Economic Association, *Readings in the Social Control of Industry*, Philadelphia: Blakiston Press, 1942.

J. B. Dirlam and A. E. Kahn, *The Law and Economics of Fair Competition: An Appraisal of Antitrust Policy*, Ithaca: Cornell University Press, 1954.

P. F. Drucker, *Concept of the Corporation*, New York: John Day Co., 1946.

C. D. Edwards, *Maintaining Competition*, New York: McGraw-Hill Book Co., 1949.

W. Fellner, *Competition among the Few*, New York: Alfred Knopf, 1949.

J. K. Galbraith, *American Capitalism: The Concept of Countervailing Power*, Boston: Houghton Mifflin Co., 1952.

C. E. Griffin, *An Economic Approach to Antitrust Problems*, New York: American Enterprise Association, 1951.

D. E. Lilienthal, *Big Business: A New Era*, New York: Harper & Brothers, 1952.

F. Machlup, *The Political Economy of Monopoly*, Baltimore: Johns Hopkins Press, 1952.

V. A. Mund, *Government and Business*, New York: Harper & Brothers, 1950.

H. L. Purdy, M. L. Lindahl, and W. A. Carter, *Corporate Concentration and Public Policy*, New York: Prentice-Hall, Inc., 1942.

J. A. Schumpeter, *Capitalism, Socialism and Democracy*, New York: Harper & Brothers, 1942.

H. C. Simons, *Economic Policy for a Free Society*, Chicago: University of Chicago Press, 1948.

G. W. Stocking and M. W. Watkins, *Cartels in Action*, New York: Twentieth Century Fund, 1946.

G. W. Stocking and M. W. Watkins, *Cartels or Competition?* New York: Twentieth Century Fund, 1948.

G. W. Stocking and M. W. Watkins, *Monopoly and Free Enterprise*, New York: Twentieth Century Fund, 1951.

Government Publications

Business Advisory Council, Secretary of Commerce, *Effective Competition*, Washington, 1952.

---

enterprise capitalism is to continue to exist, not throughout the national economy, but in any part of it, then it needs rescuing from the capitalists fully as much as from the Socialists." (*The Economist*, London, June 29, 1946, p. 22. Copyright *The Economist*. Reprinted by permission of the publishers.)

W. H. Hamilton, *Antitrust in Action*, Temporary National Economic Committee, Monograph No. 16, Washington, 1940.

Hearings before the Subcommittee on the Study of Monopoly Power, House Judiciary Committee, *Study of Monopoly Power*, Serial 14, Parts 1, 2-A, 2-B, 81st Congress, 1st Session, 1949.

S. Nelson and W. Keim, *Price Behavior and Business Policy*, Temporary National Economic Committee, Monograph No. 1, Washington, 1940.

C. Wilcox, *Competition and Monopoly in American Industry*, Temporary National Economic Committee, Monograph No. 21, Washington, 1940.

Journal and Magazine Articles

W. Adams, "Competition, Monopoly and Countervailing Power," *Quarterly Journal of Economics*, Vol. LXVII, November, 1953.

W. Adams, "Dissolution, Divorcement, Divestiture: The Pyrrhic Victories of Antitrust," *Indiana Law Journal*, Vol. 27, Fall, 1951.

M. A. Adelman, "Integration and Antitrust Policy," *Harvard Law Review*, Vol. 63, November, 1949.

R. Heflebower, "Economics of Size," *Journal of Business of the University of Chicago*, Vol. 24, April, 1951.

C. Kaysen, "Collusion under the Sherman Act," *Quarterly Journal of Economics*, Vol. LXV, May, 1951.

D. Keezer (ed.), "The Antitrust Laws: A Symposium," *American Economic Review*, Vol. XXXIX, June, 1949.

E. S. Mason, "Current Status of the Monopoly Problem," *Harvard Law Review*, Vol. 62, June, 1949.

G. J. Stigler, "The Case Against Big Business," *Fortune*, May, 1952.

G. W. Stocking, "Saving Free Enterprise from Its Friends," *Southern Economic Journal*, Vol. XIX, April, 1953.

C. Wilcox, "On the Alleged Ubiquity of Monopoly," *American Economic Review*, May, 1950.

17

A critique
of the status quo approach
to public policy

David R. Kamerschen

> Unless we can establish the prop-
> osition that the upper limit to the
> size of the firm is increasing, there
> is no need for a more vigorous
> program of antitrust policy than
> we have already.[1]

I. INTRODUCTION

The opinion cited above follows what has been called the *status quo* approach to public policy. In addition to this group, which is satisfied with the structure and performance of American industry and on occasion even

[1]David Schwartzman, "The Economics of Antitrust Policy," *Antitrust Bulletin*, Vol. VI, No. 3, May–June, 1961, p. 242.

From *The Antitrust Bulletin*, 9 (1965), pp. 747–760. Reprinted by permission. [The author is] Assistant Professor of Economics, Washington University, St. Louis, Mo.

suggest some relaxation of antitrust enforcement, there are those who would like either to increase the public regulation and ownership of industry or restore effective competition through a vigorous antitrust policy.[2]

Although we personally feel that the final proposal would be the most effective and/or feasible of the latter two alternatives, this question is of secondary importance here. More importantly we would like to suggest that the first approach should be rejected. We shall base our argument mainly upon the fact that the magnitude of the "welfare" loss emanating from monopoly positions is too large to be neglected.

The proponents of this *status quo* approach seem to have been singularly effective in getting their point across to both the economics profession and the general public. Indeed, the famous Keynes quotation, at the close of his controversial classic concerning the underrating of the power of ideas of economists and political philosophers, is no better illustrated than in a recent Chase Manhattan Bank Survey of college and university economists (November-December, 1963) in which one of the questions and its tabulated reply was the following:

Does Monopoly on the part of the U. S. Business now constitute:

A minor problem 70%
A major problem 23%
No problem at all 7%

To be sure, there are some economists who favor dissolving leading firms if various economic tests suggest monopoly power—W. Adams,[3] J. S. Bain,[4] C. Kaysen and D. Turner,[5] W. N. Nicholls[6] and A. G. Papandreou[7] to name a few. Nonetheless, the consensus appears to be that the problems of economic growth, balances of payment, unemployment, inflation, etc., are Brobdingnagian in proportion to the monopoly problem. The purpose of this paper is to indicate that the empirical evidence does not support such a position. However, before we look at this information, let us first briefly review the three general positions on public policy.

[2] Walter Adams (ed.), *The Structure of American Industry*, Third Edition, New York, 1961, Chap. 15.

[3] *Ibid.*, 554–561; and Walter Adams and Horace M. Gray, *Monopoly in America*, New York, 1955, p. 10.

[4] *Industrial Organization*, New York, 1959, pp. 609–610.

[5] *Antitrust Policy*, Cambridge, Mass., 1959, pp. 44–99.

[6] "The Tobacco Case of 1946," *American Economic Review*, 39, May, 1949, p. 296.

[7] Andreas G. Papandreou and John T. Wheeler, *Competition and Its Regulation*, New York, 1954, p. 487.

II. PUBLIC POLICY ALTERNATIVES

The defenders of the *status quo* generally advocate a policy of non-interference with respect to concentrated industries based on the following arguments: (a) Nonprice competition, interproduct competition, counter-vailing power, potential competition, fear of government regulation, techno-logical advance and the competition of all products for the dollar all render "workable competition" in industries where large-numbers competition does not prevail.[8] (b) The social responsibility of our "new" business leaders will counter the abuses of monopoly power. The robber baron, "public-be-damned," sharpshooting, exploitative business leader of yesterday has been replaced by the industrial statesman or industrial steward.[9] (c) The most significant and most sounded claim for the preservation of the *status quo* is based on the doctrine of technological determinism, i.e., the realization that the effective use of productive resources which modern technology makes possible depends upon the existence of monopolistic giants. A return to large-numbers, small-producers competition, it is claimed, would mean foregoing economics of scale and gaining economic inefficiency. Of course, Schumpeter[10] is responsible for the classic argument on technology.

The advocates of public regulation or public ownership hope to insure industrial efficiency and to avoid the abuses of private monopoly by social control. Their argument rests on three points: (a) The *status quo* arguments are not valid—monopolist self-restraint, workable competition, counter-vailing power, etc., are either myths or riddled with exceptions. (b) Modern technology dictates that monopoly power is necessary to achieve and main-tain productive efficiency. But *private* monopoly is no guarantee of efficiency. (c) Present antitrust laws are too weak to prevent the abuses of monopoly power; yet, if tightened up and rigorously enforced such laws would mean the loss of modern technology's productive efficiency.

Of course, the independent regulatory commissions, e.g., the Interstate Commerce Commission, the Civil Aeronautics Board, the Federal Power Commission, the Federal Communication Commission, have not always regulated their respective industries, willy-nilly, for the social good. And the who will watch the watchers (*Quis custodiet ipsos custodies?*) problem remains in any set-up of this type. Similarly, the nationalization argument has its flaws. Not the least of which may be founded on Britain's historian

[8] John M. Clark, "Toward a Concept of Workable Competition," *American Economic Review*, June, 1940, 241–246; John K. Galbraith, *American Capitalism: The Concept of Countervailing Power*, Boston, 1952; C. E. Griffin, *An Economic Approach to Economic Problems*, New York, 1951; and Edward S. Mason, "Antitrust Symposium," *American Economic Review*, June, 1949, p. 713.

[9] David E. Lilienthal, *Big Business: A New Era*, New York, 1953.

[10] Joseph A. Schumpeter, *Capitalism, Socialism and Democracy*, New York, 1943, p. 79 ff.

C. Northcote Parkinson's third and fourth socioeconomic laws (the first two are "Work expands to fill the time available;" "Expenditures rise to meet income;" viz., "Expansion means complexity, and complexity decay," and "Nationalized industries have built-in trends toward bankruptcy." Although the scientific evidence on these two points is rather meager, they are suggestive.

> In summary, public regulation and public ownership suffer from the same basic drawback as private monopoly, viz., the concentration of power in the hands of a few. Such power may be used benignly or dangerously, depending on the men who possess and control it. They may be good men, benevolent men, and socially minded men; but society still confronts the danger of which Lord Acton so eloquently warned: power corrupts, and absolute power corrupts absolutely.[11]

The advocates of promoting or restoring "effective" competition through stiff antitrust enforcement reject both "the Scylla of private monopoly and the Charybdis of public ownership."[12] Although the establishment of "pure" competition may be institutionally unattainable and perhaps even economically undesirable, "effective" competition—large numbers, no collusion, no entry barriers—is sought.

Since this "effective" competition is felt to be realistic, attainable and highly desirable, the *status quo* or public ownership approaches are viewed as intolerable, firstly, because the forces of "workable competition," countervailing power, etc. are weak or nonexistent, and secondly, because they reject the ostensible conflict between competition and efficiency. For in most cases, we find either that the growth of big business monopolies has far exceeded that necessary for the attainment of all the economies of scale which modern technology allows or that the growth was not an inevitable result of spontaneous generation or natural selection, but often the end product of governmental or investment banker action. Finally, for the reasons mentioned above, it is felt that the public regulation of monopoly has not been, nor can be expected to be, effective.

Of course, strengthened and vigorously enforced antitrust laws are only a *necessary*, but not *sufficient* condition for the maintenance of an effective and dynamic economy. It is felt that what is needed is an integrated national economic policy that positively promotes rather than negatively preserves competition. After eliminating all exceptions to the antitrust laws, legislation and policies which promote the growth of monopoly, patent laws, protective tariffs, expenditure and taxation laws, must be either modified or eliminated.

---

[11] Adams, *op. cit.*, 554.
[12] *Ibid.*

Thus, in summary, we can say that one of above three general alternatives is the usual response to what is the most desirable path for public policy to follow in the future. To be sure, there is also a host of hybrid views on this important question. However, these refinements are not important for the purpose at hand. Our goal here is to point out that although the analytical arguments against the *satus quo* approach are felt to be generally valid, if somewhat speculative, the final conclusions must be grounded on the facts, i.e., the empirical evidence. And, in our opinion, the relevant empirical questions to be answered are: 1) Is the American economy substantially monopolistic? 2) Are most monopoly positions necessary to obtain the scale economics of modern technology? 3) Even if the answers to 1) and 2) suggest monopoly is both important and undesirable, is the general order of magnitude of the resulting "welfare" loss sufficiently high to be worth bothering about?

It is important to remember that the answers to these questions are more relevant to the hypothesis that the *status quo* approach is intolerable than to the next problem as to which of the remaining two approaches is the more desirable. However, in our brief review of these approaches, we indicated some of the reasons we feel the restoration of vigorous competition is more sensible.

III. ANALYSIS OF SOME EMPIRICAL EVIDENCE

In deciding whether or not monopoly power is substantial in our economy, the usual approach, and the one we shall employ, is to look at concentration ratios (CR). Of course, not all economists agree on the *direction* or *interpretation* of the concentration movement. For instance, some deny that concentration has increased since, say, 1890 (for conflicting views see 3.7).

There are conflicting views on even the present evidence on CR. Schwartzman,[13] basing his position mainly upon Bain[14] and more or less rejecting, because of the arbitrariness of the criteria, the findings of Adelman,[15] Kaysen and Turner,[16] and Nutter,[17] says: "Thus a basic premise in

[13] David Schwartzman, *op. cit.*, p. 239.

[14] Joe S. Bain, "Relation of Profit Rate to Industry Concentration," *Quarterly Journal of Economics*, 65, August, 1951, 294–296.

[15] Morris A. Adelman, "The Measurement of Industrial Concentration," *Review of Economics and Statistics*, 33, November, 1952, p. 291.

[16] Carl Kaysen and Donald F. Turner, *Antitrust Policy*, Cambridge, Mass., 1959.

[17] G. Warner Nutter, *The Extent of Enterprise Monopoly in the United States, 1899–1939*, Chicago, 1951, p. 21.

the argument for revamping the antitrust laws is unfounded. The monopolistic sector does not appear to be large." Clearly, however, Schwartzman is in the minority on this question. Adams goes so far as to say "*All* are agreed . . . that the present *degree* of concentration—regardless of its implications —is substantial."[18] In addition to the above mentioned sources, the T.N.E.C., the Federal Trade Commission,[19] Rosenbluth[20] and the Subcommittee on Antitrust and Monopoly[21] all concur with this latter opinion.

Of course, it may be argued[22] that the CR are unreliable since (a) it is difficult to define an industry, and inter-industry and inter-product competition make high concentration in an industry questionable anyway; (b) the CR overstate the degree of concentration when giant firms such as General Motors, are listed in one industry—automobile production—when their capital assets are spread over a number of industries—diesel engines, refrigerators, electric appliances, etc., and (c) high concentration is not positive proof that the industry is monopolized or collusive.

We decided to look at this question for ourselves using the comprehensive *Concentration in American Manufacturing, 1958* report[23] which shows four-digit manufacturing CR based on the percentage of value-added (VA) and employment (E) accounted for by the 4, 8, 20, and 50 largest firms in each industry ($N = 443$ for E, 446 for VA). Since the rest of our results, discussed below were in two-digit form, we estimated these by averaging the CR for the four-digit industries and using their VA or E as weights. There are some problems, connected with this approach, such as the fact that the estimation procedure will overestimate the correct CR whenever the four-digit industries are highly competitive with one another, which we must neglect here, but are discussed in Stigler.[24]

Although, we make no adjustment for local, regional or national markets, we find that 15 (VA) and 13 (E) of the 20 two-digit manufacturing industries met the Kaysen and Turner[25] criteria of oligopoly—if the 8 largest firms account for roughly one-third or better of the total VA or N provided in the industry. The other criteria involving the 4, 20 or 50 largest were also

[18] Adams, *op. cit.*, p. 544; first italics supplied.

[19] Federal Trade Commission, *The Concentration of Productive Facilities*, 1947, p. 14.

[20] Gideon Rosenbluth, "The Trend in Concentration and Its Implications for Small Business," *Law and Contemporary Problems*, Winter, 1959, 194–195.

[21] *Concentration in American Industry*, 85th Congress, 1st Sess., 1957, Table 44 for 1954.

[22] Adams, *op. cit.*, pp. 545–546.

[23] Subcommittee on Antitrust and Monopoly, Senate Judiciary Committee, 1958, Parts I and II, Washington, 1963, 1962.

[24] George J. Stigler, *Capital and Rates of Return in Manufacturing Industries*, New York, 1963, Appendix C, pp. 206–215.

[25] *Op. cit.*, p. 27.

on the relatively concentrated side. If the reader feels the four-digit data are vastly superior, he will find similar results on this level.

While not in itself convincing, these findings support the opinion of *most* economists that there is substantial concentration in the American economy—especially, in such sectors as manufacturing, transportation, public utilities and some areas of finance. In fact, Harberger,[26] Kaplan,[27] Schwartzman[28] and Weston[29] are the only specific economists, that we know of, that are even suggestive that monopoly is not important in our economy. Incidentally, the results of the survey mentioned above, in which over two-thirds of the sampled economists felt monopoly is a minor problem, are not incompatible with our statement that most economists feel concentration is substantial in our economy. For it is possible to feel that while concentration is high, the resultant "welfare" losses are rather insignificant in comparison to, say, our national income. Alternatively, it could be argued that concentration and monopoly are not synonymous. This first proposition we shall examine below; the second, we neglect on the grounds that almost all correlations of CR with various indices of *adjusted* profit rates have discovered a significant relationship.

We ask the second question concerning economies of scale, since even if it is agreed that concentration is high, it may be argued that *status quo* is still best since the existing concentration in American industry can be explained in terms of technological imperatives. Indeed, since Schumpeter[30] this has been the classic comeback.

Unfortunately, there are considerable difficulties involved in any investigation of scale economies. The "empty economic box" is still largely empty. There are some industries, for example, electric power production, where it is possible to get a pretty good idea of the effects of economies of scale. However, for the bulk of industries it would be difficult to measure the effect on average costs of scale taken by itself.

However, such work that has been done, directly or indirectly, on this

[26] Arnold C. Harberger, "Monopoly and Resource Allocation," *American Economic Review*, 44, May, 1954, 77–87.

[27] A. M. D. Kaplan, *Big Enterprise in a Competitive System*, Washington, 1954.

[28] David Schwartzman, *op. cit.*; and "Monopoly and Wages," *Canadian Journal of Economic and Political Science*, 26, August, 1960, 428–438; "The Effect of Monopoly on Price," *Journal of Political Economy*, 67, August, 1959, 627–630; "A Correction," *Journal of Political Economy*, 69, October, 1961, 494.

[29] J. Fred Weston, *The Role of Mergers in the Growth of Large Firms*, Berkeley, 1963.

[30] *Op. cit.*, p. 79 ff.

question by Bain,[31] Kaysen and Turner,[32] Stigler,[33] Saving,[34] and Weiss[35] hardly support the technological determinism argument. In fact, we do not know of a single instance of *empirical support* of the scale argument. Part of the reason the data may be so difficult to come by may stem from firm uncertainty as to the existence of any such economies of scale. An interesting approach to this problem is suggested by Kaysen and Turner[36] who would require the firms, in the event they were questioned as to their monopoly power, to prove their power was "reasonable," i.e., based on valid patents, economies of large-scale production, or the introduction of a new process or product. Firm archives should become much more available under such a proposition!

Finally, we get to what in our minds constitutes the most important consideration of all, viz., if monopoly is both ubiquitous and undesirable, in what general order of magnitude are the ensuing welfare losses? Are they a big splash or but a secondary ripple in our annual aggregate income?

Actually, the question is loaded in the sense that either a large or small order of magnitude may be interpreted as implying that monopoly is important. If the results are large, by definition, monopoly is important. However, even if the welfare losses are small, it can be argued that monopoly is important.

No one knows the amount of welfare loss that would be found if all the appropriate modifications could be carried through. Perhaps it would come to only $2,000,000 a year for every economist. Whatever it may be, we may still properly devote much attention to monopoly. *The loss would be much larger if we were less diligent in combating monopoly, and the cumulative effects of widespread cartelization would eventually move the losses into a new order of magnitude.*[37]

Of course, the first result is unambiguous in the sense that if "welfare" losses are large, the problem is important and hardly befitting a *status quo* approach. The second result can be viewed as being inconclusive or a

[31] *Barriers to New Competition*, Cambridge, Mass., 1956, pp. 73, 85 ff.

[32] *Op. cit.*, pp. 44–99, 117.

[33] George J. Stigler, "The Economies of Scale," *Journal of Law and Economics*, October, 1958, 61–67.

[34] Thomas R. Saving, "Estimation of Optimum Size of Plant by the 'Survivor Technique,'" *Quarterly Journal of Economics*, November, 1961, 569–607.

[35] Leonard W. Weiss, "The Survival Technique and the Extent of Suboptimal Capacity," *Journal of Political Economy*, LXXII, June, 1964, 246–261.

[36] *Op. cit.*, 44–99, 114.

[37] George J. Stigler, "The Statistics of Monopoly and Merger," *Journal of Political Economy*, 44, February, 1956, p. 35.

contradiction of the monopoly-is-important hypothesis. Fortunately, we can justify our position on the basis of the first result.

In estimating the "welfare" losses from monopoly, we use an approach similar to the one employed by Schwartzman[38] and more especially Harberger.[39] This latter approach looks at the rates of return on capital to determine the places where resources are misallocated. Those industries which are returning higher than average rates have too few resources; and those with lower than average returns have too many resources. The "welfare" loss produced by monopolistic misallocation of resources is then estimated as follows: given the distribution of income, society would be better off if resources were shifted from competitive to monopolistic industries, since firms in the latter restrict production below the optimum level in order to maximize profits, and exactly how much better off depends upon the elasticity of demand for the products.

In the previous studies, they found the "allocative" loss (the possible undesirable impact on the distribution of income was neglected) from monopolies quite small—less than one-tenth of one per cent of national income. However, the studies were based on manufacturing corporations only—in one case on 1924–28 data. It has also been suggested that they employed some "heroic" assumptions and questionable statistical procedures. We continued the work started by these men by extending the scope. We use not only manufacturing corporations but all sectors of the economy and all types of business establishments, partnerships, proprietorships and corporations—(the detail), adjusting the accounting profit rates to allow for the hidden "quasi-monopoly" elements in advertising expenditures, royalties and intangible assets and estimating industry-by-industry elasticities rather than assuming unity elasticity for each industry. As for the timing, we use roughly two-digit data from the *IRS Statistics of Income* for the five-year period 1956–57 to 1960–61 for the analysis.

Our results were strikingly different from the miniscule loss estimated by these other men. Although we found a number of different estimates, depending upon whether we used total capital or equity as our capital base, before-or-after-tax income, etc., the most realistic estimate based on after-tax income, using a total capital base yielded an estimated loss of better than $25 *billion* (compared to the previous estimates of from $200–$400 *million*) or about 6 per cent of national income (compared to one-tenth of one per cent to one per cent of national income), with "welfare" losses of this magnitude, the *status quo* position is clearly tenuous.

[38] See footnote 28.
[39] *Op. cit.*

IV. SUMMARY AND CONCLUSIONS

In conclusion, we feel that the monopoly problem takes on a rather different perspective in the light of the present study. The problem of monopoly acquires aggregative significance in addition to its importance in studying particular industries. In short, monopoly does affect aggregative "welfare" in a significant way through its effect on resource allocation. This suggests, from a public policy point of view, that we might do well in the U. S. to view the monopoly problem in the same light as we do, say, the balance of payments or economic growth problem. For contrary to the poll cited above, monopoly is a *major* problem in the U. S. and as such, a *status quo* position is singularly inappropriate. Alternatively, we feel the proposal of public control is intolerable. However, the goal of effective competition, working primarily the 3 D's of antitrust—Dissolution, Divorcement and Divestiture—, is realistic, attainable and highly desirable. However, as Stigler[40] points out:

> The dissolution of big business is only part of the program necessary to increase the support for a private, competitive enterprise economy, and reverse the drift toward Government control. But it is an essential part of this program, and the place for courage and imagination. *Those conservatives who cling to the status quo do not realize that the status quo is a state of change, and the changes are coming fast.* If these changes were to include the dissolution of a few score of our giant companies, however, we shall have done much to preserve private enterprise and the liberal-individualistic society of which it is an integral part.

REFERENCES

Walter Adams (ed.), *The Structure of American Industry*, Third Edition, New York, 1961.
Walter Adams and Horace M. Gray, *Monopoly in America*, New York, 1955.
Morris A. Adelman, "The Measurement of Industrial Concentration," *Review of Economics and Statistics*, 33, November, 1952, 269–296. Rejoinders May, 1952, 174–178 and November, 1952, 356–364.
Joe S. Bain, *Industrial Organization*, New York, 1959.
———, "Relation of Profit Rate to Industry Concentration," *Quarterly Journal of Economics*, 65, August, 1951, 293–294.

[40] George J. Stigler, "The Case Against Big Business," *Fortune*, May, 1952.

————, *Barriers to New Competition*, Cambridge, 1956.

John M. Blair, "The Measurement of Industrial Concentration: A Reply," *Review of Economics and Statistics*, 33, November, 1952, 343–355.

John M. Clark, "Toward a Concept of Workable Competition," *American Economic Review*, June, 1940, 241–256.

Federal Trade Commission, *The Concentration of Productive Facilities*, 1947.

John K. Galbraith, *American Capitalism: The Concept of Countervailing Power*, Boston, 1952.

C. E. Griffin, *An Economic Approach to Economic Problems*, New York, 1951.

Arnold C. Harberger, "Monopoly and Resource Allocation," *American Economic Review*, 44, May, 1954, 77–87.

A. M. D. Kaplan, *Big Enterprise in a Competitive System*, Washington, 1954.

Carl Kaysen and Donald F. Turner, *Antitrust Policy*, Cambridge, Mass., 1959.

David E. Lilienthal, *Big Business: A New Era*, New York, 1953.

Edward S. Mason, "Antitrust Symposium," *American Economic Review*, June, 1949.

William M. Nicholls, "The Tobacco Case of 1946," *American Economic Review*, 39, May, 1949, 284–296.

G. Warner Nutter, *The Extent of Enterprise Monopoly in the United States, 1899–1939*, Chicago, 1951.

Andreas G. Papandreou and John T. Wheeler, *Competition and Its Regulation*, New York, 1954.

Gideon Rosenbluth, "The Trend in Concentration and Its Implications for Small Business," *Law and Contemporary Problems*, Winter, 1959, 194–195.

Thomas R. Saving, "Estimation of Optimum Size of Plant by the Survivor Technique," *Quarterly Journal of Economics*, November, 1961, 569–607.

Joseph A. Schumpeter, *Capitalism, Socialism and Democracy*, New York, 1943.

David Schwartzman, "Monopoly and Wages," *Canadian Journal of Economic and Political Science*, 26, August, 1960, 428–438.

————, "The Effect of Monopoly on Price," *Journal of Political Economy*, 67, August, 1959, 352–362.

————, "The Burden of Monopoly on Price," *Journal of Political Economy*, 67, August, 1959, 627–630.

————, "A Correction," *Journal of Political Economy*, 69, October, 1961, 494.

————, "The Economics of Antitrust Policy," *Antitrust Bulletin*, Vol. VI, No. 3, May–June, 1961, 235–243.

George J. Stigler, "The Case Against Big Business," *Fortune*, May, 1952.

————, "The Statistics of Monopoly and Merger," *Journal of Political Economy*, 44, February, 1956, 33–40.

————, "The Economies of Scale," *Journal of Law and Economics*, October, 1958, 61–67.

————, *Capital and Rates of Return in Manufacturing Industries*, New York, 1963.

Subcommittee on Antitrust and Monopoly, Senate Judiciary Committee, *Concentration in American Industry*, 85th Congress, 1st Sess., 1957.

Subcommittee on Antitrust and Monopoly, Senate Judiciary Committee, *Concentration in Manufacturing Industry*, 1958, Parts I and II, Washington, 1963, 1962.

Leonard W. Weiss, "The Survival Technique and the Extent of Suboptimal Capacity," *Journal of Political Economy*, LXXII, June, 1964, 246–261.

J.Fred Weston, *The Role of Mergers in the Growth of Large Firms*, Berkeley, 1963.

SUGGESTED READINGS

Joe S. Bain, *Industrial Organization* (New York: Wiley, 1959).

E. T. Grether, *Marketing and Public Policy* (Englewood Cliffs, N.J.: Prentice-Hall, 1966).

Carl Kaysen and Donald F. Turner, *Antitrust Policy: An Economic and Legal Analysis* (Cambridge: Harvard University Press, 1959).

Sumner Marcus, *Competition and the Law* (Belmont, Calif.: Wadsworth, 1967).

Lee E. Preston, *Social Issues in Marketing* (Glenview, Ill.: Scott, Foresman, 1968).

Eugene M. Singer, *Antitrust Economics: Selected Legal Cases and Economic Models* (Englewood Cliffs, N.J.: Prentice-Hall, 1968).

J. Fred Weston and Sam Peltzman, *Public Policy Toward Mergers* (Goodyear, 1969).

B

Marketing performance: productivity and efficiency

Assessing the productivity and efficiency of industrial activity is difficult at best, but is most complex with respect to marketing. It is possible to argue that the marketing system could be more efficient than it is—if we had some notion of the Platonic or ideal system. It is not especially illuminating to compare our level of efficiency with that of other economies, for no other has either the same goals, scale, production functions, or structures. In the first selection in this section, Stanley C. Hollander points out the major complexities in evaluating marketing productivity. He indicates some of the basic problems in measuring the inputs and outputs of marketing.

We can and do make distinctions between various firms and industries. In his statement, F. M. Scherer points out that one industry or firm may use less input for its output than others or that one has greater technological change, but this too is very misleading unless we specify exactly the technological relationships between the firms and industries. It is of little value to say that the data-processing industry is more efficient than the food-services industry, because both have different combinations of labor and capital as well as other structural differences. It can be misleading to say that a large integrated food-service firm is more "efficient" than the family-run café somewhere on a side street in a large city. There are certain almost nonquantifiable values, such as the ability to enter, operate, and leave an industry, as well as consumer convenience which must be included in efficiency. Scherer also compares small and large firms in regard to inventions and technological change.

Carefully approached, comparisons of efficiency can be meaningful. The Federal Trade Commission's *Economic Report on the Structure and Competitive Behavior of Food Retailing* compares and contrasts similar-sized firms in the same industry with respect to technological efficiency, after certain differences in structures are taken into account. Even if extreme technological inefficiency exists—as may be the case with the small corner grocery store—consumers may be willing to pay for the inefficiency in return for the shopping convenience. One need only consider the (relative) pleasure of being able to walk to a corner drugstore in the midst of winter to purchase aspirin or other medicines, rather than having to travel a long distance for the same items. The corner store may be technologically inefficient by the standards of the chain drugstore, but net consumer satisfaction is socially a more important test.

18

Measuring the
cost and value
of marketing[1]

Stanley C. Hollander

When did marketing begin? When were the first criticisms of marketing voiced? We do not know the answer to either question, but we can be certain of two things. One is that the function of marketing, that is, trade and exchange, has been part of the human economic system for many thousands of years. The other is that criticisms and defenses of trading activities are almost as old as trade itself. In 1776, these criticisms provoked a thundering answer from Adam Smith:

> The statute of Edward VI, therefore, by prohibiting as much as possible any middleman from coming in between the grower and the consumer, endeavoured to annihilate a trade, of which the free exercise is not only the best palliative of the inconveniences of a dearth, but the best preventative of that calamity: after the trade of the farmer,

[1] The author wishes to acknowledge his debt to a former teacher, Professor Reavis Cox of the University of Pennsylvania, whose work and lectures have shaped many of the thoughts expressed herein.

From *MSU Business Topics*, Summer 1961, pp. 17–27. Reprinted by permission of the publisher, the Bureau of Business and Economic Research, Division of Research, Graduate School of Business Administration, Michigan State University.

no trade contributing so much to the growing of corn as that of the corn merchant.[2]

Smith declared: "The popular fear of engrossing and forestalling [buying for resale] may be compared to the popular terrors and suspicions of witchcraft."[3] Today the fear of witchcraft seems to have abated; it has been many years since books attacking witches made the best-seller lists. But the persistent popularity of books attacking marketing suggests that the fear of engrossers and forestallers has not vanished. The attacks have, of course, aroused a ready response, and the marketing journals have been filled with criticisms of the critics, interspersed with a modicum of self-criticism.

As is true of most such debates, the discussions have tended to generate considerably more heat than light. Only in fairly recent years have we had any really serious attempts to measure both the costs and the benefits of marketing in our society. The dearth of such studies is not the fault of the many serious and well-intentioned people who have debated the value of marketing. It is simply an indication of the complexity and magnitude of the problem.

A PRODUCTIVITY ANALOGY

The difficulty of measuring marketing productivity may be illustrated by attacking a comparable problem: attempting to measure the productivity of a magazine article. An examination of the silent post-mortem in which you will indulge after finishing this or any other article will suggest some of the difficulties we face when we try to evaluate the marketing system.

In either case, we are trying to determine a ratio. On the one hand, we have the inputs into the system—the social and individual contributions to the product or process, and on the other hand, we have the outputs—the social and individual benefits. If the benefits are high in proportion to the inputs, we describe the article, the product, or the system in question as *highly productive*. But if the ratio is low, then the system is not very productive. The concept is simple to state: the real problems apply when we attempt to apply it.

Types of Input

The reading experiences that provide the final tests of a magazine article's value result from two major categories of inputs. One group con-

[2] *The Wealth of Nations* (Modern Library edition). New York: Random House, 1937, p. 499. Emphasis supplied.

[3] *Ibid.*, p. 500.

sists of those supplied by the publisher and the people and firms associated with him. These include the work of paper and ink manufacturers, printers and production craftsmen, the postal service and the newsdealers, editorial employees, illustrators, and even authors. Supposedly the value of these services is measured by the prices and wages these contributors receive during the process of assembling the magazine. But this supposition involves a number of assumptions to which we will want to return shortly. Magazines, like every other product and service, present a number of unique problems in social cost measurement. For example, publications that derive much of their revenue from advertising may incur heavy production and promotional expenses so as to attract the readership that will attract advertising which in turn may, in various ways, affect the prices and the sales of the commodities advertised. Under such circumstances it is often difficult to determine the exact inputs provided by each participant. A similar quandry arises out of the eternal debate between the publishers and the postmasters-general over the relationship of postal charges to the costs of furnishing postal services.

Another group of inputs is extremely important and many of these are often overlooked. These are provided by the readers, and include their time and effort as well as whatever they may pay, directly or indirectly, for the publication. These inputs are analogous to the time, effort and money expended by consumers in both the shopping and the consumption process. And, from the standpoint of the individual consumer, these are the personal costs that must be balanced against the personal benefits.

Simple Evaluation

Let us start with the simplest version of this problem; the individual judgment each one of you will make after finishing this article or this issue of *Business Topics*. Undoubtedly, you will ask yourself whether it has been worth reading or not. Not *how* worthwhile, or *how* it compares with other things you might have read instead, but simply: am I pleased or not that I decided to take the time to read this article? This is the sort of judgment that we all make frequently. Yet notice how often our reactions are ambivalent. We say of some experience or book or lecture, "I guess it was worthwhile," or "I don't know—it wasn't too bad," or "I'm rather glad I read it, and yet maybe I could have used the time more profitably."

Now it is no wonder that our judgments are sometimes vague. To decide that reading a particular article, or engaging in any other activity, is worthwhile involves a very complex accounting process. Very few of us have enough time to do all the things we would like to do, or to read all the things that we would like to read. The segments of time that we invest in reading a particular article may be especially precious segments, on a busy day or when there are many alternative activities clamoring for our attention. Then again, the time may consist of minutes spent in the dentist's anteroom, when there is little else that we can do and when we really only want a little intellectual anaesthesia before climbing into the chair. The article may demand considerable attention and intellectual effort, which we may consider as output, as a source of enjoyment (witness the pleasure many people derive from solving puzzles) or, under other circumstances and at other times, we may consider as input, as an unwarranted drain on our energies. The benefits of our reading are elusive and subtle. We may obtain intellectual exercise, new insight, stimulation and entertainment. Or our reading may prove stultifying, boring, or misleading. All of this we have to balance in some rough and ready fashion before we can say whether the magazine was, or was not, worthwhile.

Complexities of Evaluation

However, this is still at the kindergarten level in productivity evaluation. Let us look at two more problems of greater complexity. One arises out of the fact that such rough balance sheets are really inadequate for comparative purposes or for social appraisals. Suppose, in the course of a year, that each of us reads two hundred magazine issues. Each issue consumes its own combination of time, money and energy; each yields its own patterns of information, insight and entertainment. How can we compare these two hundred: can we rank them in an ordinal line, and will our judgments be consistent each time that we express them? How can we add these two hundred patterns into a composite figure if we want to compare this year's reading with last year's, or with the magazines we read ten years ago? How can we make comparisons between, say, the magazines published in the U. S. and those published in other countries, or between publications issued under various auspices? What measures can we use to quantify either the inputs or the outputs, and how do we relate them to each other? It is perfectly apparent that these considerations are frivolous and frustrating, yet this is exactly the sort of problem we face when we try to make comparative judgments about the productivity of marketing.

But the problem is still more complex. Magazine articles are written in the hope of reaching large audiences. Each member of that audience is an individual. Each has his own standards, each has his own alternative ways of spending his time, each seeks his own particular satisfactions and ends. None is a replica of the others. In evaluating the effectiveness of an article, how can we add all of their tastes, inclinations and judgments into a single composite whole? Shall we regard one person's intense pleasure as the equivalent of several people's mild displeasure? Shall we allow extra, or reduced, weight in our calculus to the connoisseurs, to those who are the most sensitive to small differences, or to those whose swings on the manic-depressive axis are the widest?

WEIGHING THE COSTS

Conceptualizing and evaluating are equally difficult in any attempt to aggregate all of the inputs and outputs of a complex economic system. Given certain assumptions and conditions, it is relatively easy to measure the physical results of highly specific, small operations. For example, it is not too hard to determine which of two machines is more efficient at punching out sardine cans. This may involve some judgments about the relative cost of labor, capital and raw materials in the future. For example, one machine may be more efficient at low levels of output and the other at high levels, so some judgments have to be made about the nature and future demand for sardine cans. But practical, workable estimates can be made, and some of these judgments work out fairly well. Similarly, we can compare two different methods of putting those sardine cans on the supermarket shelves, subject to some assumptions as to the total number of cans to be stacked, the cost of labor, and the alternative uses for the stockmen's time in the store. But the only available measure, aside from miscellaneous hunches, guesses and opinions, of whether the whole operation is worthwhile is whether enough people buy those sardines to warrant allocating the social energies necessary to produce canned sardines instead of something else.

There seem to be only two measures by which we can evaluate the total inputs into the total marketing system. One is hours of labor, the other is monetary costs. Both have their limitations.

Labor as a Measure

Labor hours are not all homogenous, and hence we have a problem if we try to use number of hours worked in marketing as the measure of marketing cost. How can we properly equate an hour of time worked by an unskilled laborer with an hour of time spent by a highly trained engineer or architect? They are both human beings. Moreover, the job that is assigned to the laborer may be far more burdensome than the work performed by the professional. But each hour of the skilled man's time represents an expenditure of the human capital invested in training, and so, in a sense, constitutes a higher cost than does an hour of common labor. The problem can be resolved through evaluating each hour of labor at its actual wage or salary rate, but this approach leads into the monetary problems we will face in a moment. Another difficulty, of somewhat less significance, bothers the statisticians who try to compute labor productivity figures. They argue whether it is more accurate to use actual hours worked as the labor investment, or whether paid vacations, holidays and sick leaves should be added. The issue is often described as the question of hours worked versus hours paid for. (Although it would drive the statisticians crazy, conceptually one might be justified in including some portion of the future hours to be spent in paid retirement as part of this year's "labor paid for.")

Another problem is more difficult. The number of hours invested in marketing measures, at any one moment, only a portion of the total cost of the system. Our economy also draws upon natural resources and upon the capital that the past has produced. We can only equate units of capital and units of labor by converting them to a common factor—their monetary value. This again leads us to the problems inherent in applying monetary measures to marketing input.

Money as a Measure

Some of these problems are technical in nature. For example, should we evaluate the capital equipment used in any one year on the basis of its original cost, original cost minus depreciation (and if so, at what rate), cost to reproduce, or cost to replace with modern equipment? How shall we measure the labor of unpaid family workers? What shall we do about deferred compensation? More basic problems center around two major assumptions that underlie the use of monetary costs as a measure of input. When we use monetary costs expended in the private sector as our measure, we are, in effect, assuming that the government's contribution to marketing, which is considerable, is roughly equal to the net tax burden (also considerable), that is levied upon marketing. If the contribution and the taxes are unequal, then one party is, in a sense, contributing more to the bargain than it derives from the other. Our other assumption is that the costs represent free market values, that each dollar earned represents equal sacrifices, that each dollar spent obtains equal pleasure, and that there has been no exploitation of any of the participants in the system.

But there is an even more fundamental problem. The U.S. Census uses a monetary concept, "the value added by manufacturing," to measure the output of the manufacturing industry. The value-added figure is obtained by subtracting the total cost of the materials (and some services) that manufacturing industry purchases from the total amount of its sales. Many writers now advocate using a similar concept in marketing. A moment's reflection, however, shows that this concept of output is roughly equivalent to a monetary cost measure of input. Profits are usually a relatively small portion of the total figure and certainly are, at least in part, the price of certain managerial and entrepreneurial services. So, under this accounting, input and output will always be roughly equal.

Consumer Satisfaction

The most difficult part of the whole business is to measure the real output of marketing. In spite of all talk about motivation research, hidden persuaders and the like, we really seem to know very little about what people want from the marketing system. An example from retail distribution may help to illustrate this point.

One school of thought holds that most people look upon stores very largely as places in which they can obtain merchandise. According to this point of view, people consider shopping as a nuisance, and are most satisfied when they can obtain their purchases with minimum expenditures of time, money, and effort. Some interesting experiments with shopping games and with records of consumer behavior tend to substantiate this view, although the results are by no means conclusive.[4] On the other hand, there is the view advanced by many motivational researchers and by some very successful merchants, that people like to shop. The advocates of this position maintain that shopping is an end in itself, apart from the goods that are purchased, and that the retail system should be designed to maximize the pleasures of shopping.[5] Now, of course, no hard and fast election can be made between these two approaches. Much depends upon the customer, the products being purchased, the place and the time. Some people seem to react to shopping differently than others.[6] Most people will display one attitude when buying antiques, and another when purchasing a tube of toothpaste. Some people, who normally try to rush in and out of the supermarket, will be willing, when traveling, to spend hours in the quaint native market place, probably much to the annoyance of the natives. If we have only ten minutes in which to catch a plane, we want the airport newsstand to have our favorite magazine readily accessible; if we have two hours to kill between planes we like the airport bookstore that permits uninterrupted browsing. But even after allowing for all of these differences, we find that a fundamental question for both managerial strategy and social evaluation in retailing has been answered only indifferently and on an *ad hoc* basis. The devices for identifying and measuring consumer satisfaction in any

[4] Wroe Alderson, *Marketing Behavior and Executive Action.* Homewood, Illinois: Richard D. Irwin, Inc., 1957, p. 183.

[5] See, for example, Pierre Martineau, *Motivation in Advertising*, Chap. XV, "A Store is More Than a Store." New York: McGraw-Hill Book Company, 1957, pp. 173–85.

[6] An interesting classification of shoppers appears in Gregory P. Stone, "City Shoppers and Urban Identification," *American Journal of Sociology*, July 1954, pp. 36–45.

general sense are limited to votes in the market place, which is probably the most significant single argument for a free market place.

COST RESEARCH

A few unusually dedicated analysts have attempted to measure the cost of marketing in our society, in the face of all the difficulties we have noted and in spite of a number of technical obstacles we have not considered. In general, these people have been well aware of the problems and limitations inherent in their work. But they have felt that even a rough approximation of the actual figures would be ample reward for the herculean labors involved in such a task.

Stewart and Dewhurst

By far the best known single study of this sort is *Does Distribution Cost Too Much?* (New York: Twentieth Century Fund, 1938), a study conducted by Professors Paul W. Stewart and J. Frederic Dewhurst under the sponsorship of the Fund. Stewart and Dewhurst worked with census figures on purchases and sales, and other data, to trace the 1929 flow of commodities in this country from original sources (agriculture, importation, and extractive industries) to final buyers (consumers, institutions, public utilities, and export) via such intermediate levels as manufacturing and trade. Increases in value resulting from transportation and from wholesale and retail trade were assigned as costs of marketing, increases at the manufacturing level were apportioned between marketing and processing. Stewart and Dewhurst estimated that, in 1929, final buyers absorbed $65.6 billion worth of finished tangible goods, of which three-fourths, or $49 billion, went to individual ultimate family consumers. These figures do not include the consumption of services, such as haircuts, medical attention or personal transportation. Total marketing costs for this $65 billion worth of goods were estimated at $38.5 billion.

In other words, according to this analysis, retailing, wholesaling, transportation, advertising, selling and other marketing activities took 59¢ out of every consumption dollar spent on goods or tangible commodities. This figure, which as we shall see has been subjected to some very serious criticism, included marketing and transportation expenses at all levels. Thus, it embraced practically all of the selling and distribution expenses involved in transferring cotton to the yarn spinner, in transferring cotton yarn to the fabric weaver, and in transferring fabric to the shirt manufacturer, as well as the marketing costs involved in moving finished shirts to the consumer. Stewart and Dewhurst were careful to point out that their figure, 59¢, was meaningless unless it was compared with what distribution did in return for its compensation. They also were careful to point out that a more efficient manufacturing system, turning out large quantities and obtaining economies of scale, would necessitate a more complex marketing system. Nevertheless, in reading their report one can sense a sort of physiocratic bias, a feeling that changes in form utility ought to be relatively more costly than changes in time, place and possession utility.

Barger Study

In 1955, Harold Barger, relying on the vast data collections assembled by the National Bureau of Economic Research, published his study *Distribution's Place in the American Economy since 1869* (Princeton: Princeton University Press, 1955). This is generally regarded as the most authoritative work yet published on the subject. Barger limited his analysis to wholesale and retail trade, and did not include manufacturers' marketing costs, as did Stewart and Dewhurst.

Barger was not overly impressed with distribution's performance in some respects. He concluded, for example, that labor productivity per man hour increased in commodity production at an annual rate of 2.6 percent per year from 1869 to 1949. Contrasted with this, he found that productivity in distribution went up only about 1 percent per year. The analysis is somewhat limited, since the measure used, total volume handled, does not allow for changes in functions performed. However, probably most of the difference is due to the greater relative application of machinery and other forms of capital in manufacturing than in trade.

However, he did find that wholesaling and retailing accounted for only about 35–36¢ out of the consumer's dollar in 1929. Since he was working with only a portion of the total distributive activity for that year, rather than with the whole, we should expect his figure to be smaller than the Stewart and Dewhurst 59¢. However most analysts, including Barger, believe that part of the discrepancy is really a correction of the old figure, that would reduce it by an indeterminate amount, perhaps 8 or 9¢.

Cox Study

For the last several years Reavis Cox and some of his associates at the University of Pennsylvania have been conducting an investigation of marketing costs to serve as a companion to, or as a revision of, the Stewart and Dewhurst study. Their work has not yet been published, although it should be released in the near future. Cox gave an advance presentation of some of their findings at the 1960 meeting of the American Statistical Association. There he disclosed that an analysis of the Bureau of Labor Statistics' massive input-output table for the U. S. economy in 1947 revealed that ultimate consumers that year took $96 billion worth of goods, of which $41 billion, or about 43 percent, went for distribution *activities*. This figure included the marketing expenses incurred by manufacturing firms, as well as the marketing activities of the distributive industries, i.e. wholesalers, retailers, transportation agencies and advertising agencies. The distributive industries themselves accounted for about 31.1 percent of the final value of all consumption goods, and a considerably smaller portion of the total final value of consumer services.[7]

Department of Agriculture

In addition to these three studies and many smaller scale attempts there has been the massive work of the U. S. Department of Agriculture in measuring what it calls "marketing margins" for agricultural products. Unfortunately for our purposes, the Department uses the word "marketing" to embrace almost everything that can happen to agricultural products once they leave the farm. It determines its so-called marketing margin for consumer food products by subtracting the farm value of raw foodstuffs and by-products from the final retail value of agricultural foods. This margin thus includes, for example, both the cost of grinding wheat into flour and the cost of baking bread. The procedure is somewhat analogous to saying that the cost of manufacturing Ford cars is part of the cost of marketing iron ore.[8]

The economists who prepare the USDA marketing margin reports are always extremely careful in explicitly stating just what is included in their figures, although the same cannot always be said for the people who use those figures in political debate. But the agricultural definition yields results which simply are not comparable to the marketing cost studies we have examined, however useful the Department's work may be for other purposes. In 1939, for example, the Department said that 63 percent of

---

[7] 1960 *Proceedings of the Business and Economics Section, ASA.* Washington: American Statistical Association, 1961, pp. 319–22.

[8] The Department does usually make one reasonable but inconsistent adjustment in these figures. Consumer expenditures for restaurant meals are adjusted down to the retail store value of equivalent foodstuffs. The work of a restaurant chef is not treated as marketing, but the work of a cook in a frozen food plant is. In this connection though, it is only fair to say that increases in the sales of prepared food, the so-called "built-in maid service," fall short of explaining all of the recent changes in farm marketing and processing margins. Finally, we may note that in a recent unofficial study, two leading USDA economists added farmer's cost for machinery and purchased supplies into the total marketing margin reported for farm food products. Frederick V. Waugh and Kenneth E. Ogren, "An Interpretation of Changes in Agricultural Marketing Costs," *American Economic Review*, May 1961, pp. 213-27.

the consumer's farm food dollar was absorbed by marketing costs, a slightly higher figure than has been reported for the last several years. Professors Beckman and Buzzell of Ohio State University reanalyzed the 1939 figures and found that just about one-third of the total 63 percent was the cost of processing prepared and semi-manufactured foods. The true marketing cost was about 41 percent, a figure much closer to those reported in the Barger and Cox studies for consumer goods in general.[9]

THE ACTUAL OUTPUT

But even the most accurate marketing cost figure is relatively meaningless until it is compared with the work performed by marketing. Much of that work, as we have noted, consists of intangibles that resist quantification, and so we do not have an output figure to set against the cost percentage. But it is an inescapable fact that a dynamic, high level economy involves a very considerable amount of marketing work. Even the Soviets, who have not been outspoken admirers of our marketing system, are beginning to pay us the compliment of imitation as their own economies emerge from the subsistence level. The western world is just beginning to notice such communist developments as a conference on advertising methods held in Prague in 1958, and attended by delegates from the Soviet Union, East Germany, Albania, Bulgaria, Poland, Czechoslovakia, Hungary, Rumania, Yugoslavia, China, Mongolia, North Korea and Vietnam.[10]

Dr. E. D. McGarry, of the University of Buffalo, has provided the best statement of what constitutes the actual output of marketing.[11] He lists six major functions of marketing which may be summarized as follows.

Six Functions of Marketing

The contactual function: the searching out of buyers and sellers. This is a not inconsiderable task. A typical supermarket may carry five to six thousand items produced by hundreds of different

[9] T. N. Beckman and R. D. Buzzell "What Is the Marketing Margin for Agricultural Products?" *Journal of Marketing*, October 1955, pp. 166–68.

[10] Lazlo Sonkodi, "Advertising in a Socialist Economy," *Cartel*, July 1959, pp. 78–79. Sonkodi's source is, interestingly enough, a publication called *Magyar Reklam*, i.e., *Hungarian Advertising*. For a discussion of other Russian marketing developments, see Marshall Goldman, "Marketing—A Lesson for Marx," *Harvard Business Review*, January-February 1960, pp. 79–86.

[11] "Some Functions of Marketing Reconsidered," in Reavis Cox and Wroe Alderson, editors, *Theory in Marketing*. Chicago: Richard D. Irwin, Inc., 1950, pp. 263–79.

processors.[12] One study of twelve representative drug stores found each carried an average of 1,300 proprietary items (minerals, vitamins, patent medicines, etc.) alone, out of a selection of perhaps 20,000 or 30,000 such items produced for distribution through drug stores.[13] The American consumer draws upon a selection of literally tens, perhaps hundreds, of thousands of items. An elaborate and often unnoticed mechanism is needed to maintain contact between all of the people who use and produce both these items and their components, supplies and equipment.

The pricing function: in our society, the principal device for allocating our supply of scarce resources.

The merchandising function: the work of gathering information about consumer desires and translating it in to practicable product designs.

The propaganda function: "the conditioning of the buyers or of the sellers to a favorable attitude toward the product or its sponsor." This is the most criticized of all the marketing functions. But probably few will dispute the need for some activity of this sort to support an economy in which consumption rises above subsistence and in which the advantages of scale are obtained through mass production in advance of sale.

Physical distribution: the brute job of transporting and storing goods to create time and place utility.

The termination function: something of a catch-all category, that includes both the process of reaching agreement in the case of fully negotiated transactions, and all of the contingent liabilities that remain with the seller after delivery takes place.

Since many of these functions are concerned with intangibles, facile evaluation of marketing performance seems unlikely, and perhaps impossible, even for the future. Probably room will always exist for debate concerning both the objectives of marketing and the means used to achieve these objectives. We may be certain that our present methods are not perfect. We may well anticipate the development of new and better techniques for the performance of many marketing tasks. Nevertheless, even though their work resists quantification, marketers need not apologize for their share of the consumer's dollar.

[12] "The Dillon Study," *Progressive Grocer*, May 1960, p. D18.

[13] Burley, Fisher and Cox, *Drug Store Operating Costs and Profits*. New York: McGraw-Hill Book Company, Inc., 1956, p. 263.

19

Technology
and
innovation

F. M. Scherer

I appreciate this opportunity to appear before the subcommittee in connection with your important inquiry. The central issue, as I see it, can be put very tersely: What industrial structure provides the most favorable environment for the invention and innovation upon which our Nation's prosperity and growth depend? Today I intend to focus on one aspect of this question: the relationship between firm size and innovation. My evidence will be drawn from 19 detailed case studies of weapon systems and commercial research and development programs compiled between 1958 and 1960 by members of the Harvard University weapons acquisition research project, and from a statistical study of U.S. research and development employment and patenting which I executed during the past year.

As I am sure the committee already knows, one can find arguments both for and against bigness as a favorable climate for technological progress. Proponents of bigness assert that economies of scale in research

From *Economic Concentration,* Hearings before the Subcommittee on Antitrust and Monopoly of the Committee on the Judiciary, United States Senate, Part 3 (Washington, D. C.: United States Government Printing Office, 1965), pp. 1188–1200.

are important; that is, only large corporations may be able to hire scientists and engineers specializing in all the many disciplines relevant to a complex technical problem, or to invest in the most elaborate scientific apparatus. A big firm can support a diversified portfolio of research projects, hedging against the risk of failure in one or a few. An innovation which reduces costs by a given percentage margin will yield larger absolute savings to the firm with high sales than to the firm with modest sales. And big firms are generally able to acquire capital funds for investment in research on more favorable terms than small firms. On the other hand, critics claim that the more elaborate organization and procedures common to large firms inhibit creativity and the response of top management to new technical possibilities. And as the recent proliferation of small research-based new enterprises founded by big firm refugees testifies, this more formalistic environment may also be less attractive to the most creative scientists and engineers.

Obviously, with such a welter of conflicting theories, we must turn to the facts for guidance. First, however, an important distinction must be drawn. Some of the arguments relate to incentives for investing company funds in new technology, while others relate to the physical and organizational environment within which R. & D. takes place. The physical and organizational aspects are relevant to all types of R. & D. activity, and so I shall discuss them first. But conventional financial incentives have little meaning in the 60 or so percent of the Nation's industrial research and development effort supported under Government contracts. Whether a defense or space specialist carries out a substantial research and development program depends more upon the types of contracts it succeeds in acquiring than upon its own risk-bearing decisions. My statistical study, to be discussed in the second half of this statement, was concerned primarily with the quite different world of privately supported R. & D.

ECONOMIES OF SCALE

Let us begin with the question of economies of scale. This is a subject on which considerable confusion has been propagated by scholars. No one would suggest that the least average total cost scales for a broadwoven-cotton mill and a steel mill are the same. But there is a tendency to overlook the fact that research and development operations can be just as diverse. Some R. & D. is eminently suited for conduct on a small scale, while other R. & D. is not.

Consider initially the field of fundamental research and scientific discovery. Many of the basic discoveries and inventions leading to the dramatic weapons innovations of World War II and more recent times seem to have emerged from either individuals or small groups. Teams of two persons were, for example, responsible for the discovery of nuclear fission, the first work showing that an atomic bomb of feasibly small size could be built, and the invention of the resonant cavity magnetron tube, which opened up new horizons in radar. Similarly, the transistor, the maser, the laser, and radio command guidance were conceived either by individuals or groups of not more than a dozen persons. There are of course exceptions—research projects requiring equipment which only an affluent or liberally endowed organization can afford. Current experimental research in high-energy nuclear physics is the best example. And the "typical" basic research project has probably tended to become larger over the past three decades. Still the great majority of all basic research projects currently underway in academic, government, and industrial laboratories appear to involve only a few individuals with modest annual budgets.

For reasons related more to the nature of its outputs than its scale requirements, basic research has not been the forte of U.S. industry. About 78 percent of U.S. industrial R. & D. expenditures are devoted to development, and 96 percent to development plus applied research, as defined by the National Science Foundation. Here again the most notable scale characteristic is diversity. At one extreme are the major systems developments— ballistic missile systems, communications satellites, electronic telephone switching systems, etc. An organization of substantial scale may well be required in order to bring together the numerous skills needed for such projects. At the other extreme are the thousands of components, instruments, chemical compounds, and simple mechanical and electromechanical devices which can be invented by one ingenious person and developed by a small team possessing a modest range of skills. To illustrate, I am familiar with a Massachusetts firm employing some 40 persons which developed and now produces a crucial precision component for ballistic missile guidance systems. So skilled was this firm in its narrow art that a giant prime contractor was unable to duplicate the product, despite substantial expenditures of technical manpower and Government funds in the attempt. Between these extremes lies a continuous spectrum of research and development challenges, placing intermediate demands upon the R. & D. organizations involved.

Because such a diversity of technical challenges exists, small firms are by no means precluded from research and development work simply because they are small. They must only choose wisely those projects which are within their capabilities. Medium-sized firms can gain the further advantages of risk spreading if they wish by authorizing a portfolio of small research projects. If large firms have an overall advantage in terms of straightforward research project scale economies, it is only because both modest and massive projects lie within their potential grasp.

Two qualifications to this conclusion must be articulated. First, I have referred up to this point only to scale economies at the level of an individual project. It is conceivable that particular projects, however large or small, may benefit from the fact that the conducting research establishment is large in overall scale. Only a large organization may be able to hold in reserve a staff of specialists able to jump in on a moment's notice and help individual project members solve especially difficult problems. Benefits from the cross-fertilization of ideas among different project groups may also be secured. But the evidence I have seen through our case studies suggests that these economies of scale above the project level are modest. This is so partly because many research and development projects call for only a narrow range of skills attainable by even small organizations, and also because specialists from university faculties and private research institutes can be brought in for consultation on exceptional technical problems. Supra-project scale economies are therefore not likely greatly to restrict the choice of projects open to small firms. They may simply induce research-oriented firms to locate in geographic areas with a vigorous academic research climate —an inclination well known to Congressmen from areas lacking this advantage. . . .

My second qualification concerns the peculiarities of Government con-tracting. Especially in the military and space fields, a systems development project is often much bigger than the organization which accepts responsi-bility for integrating and managing the effort. In a reconnaissance satellite program, for instance, one firm may develop the booster, another the orbital injection rockets, a third the guidance system, a fourth the instrumentation, and still another firm (the systems manager) the orbital and reentry vehicles. We must also not overlook the hundreds of firms supplying minor components and subsystems. Bringing all of these elements together into a system which functions effectively poses significant interfirm coordination problems, especially when the systems manager competes with subsystem suppliers in other lines. Some economies of coordination may be achieved by consolidating subsystem development tasks into the firm responsible for systems management, which may thereby grow to a scale encompassing the whole development task. Still the economies realizable in this way do not appear very impressive, partly because weapons and space system makers have over the years developed effective procedures for minimizing coordina-tion breakdowns. And offsetting the benefits of smoother coordination can be a serious loss of advantages stemming from specialization. Notably, a systems manager receptive to subcontracting is able to choose the sub-systems and components best suited to the technical job at hand, and is not limited psychologically to the ideas favored by its own captive development teams.

Even though consolidation of systems development tasks into a single organization is in general undesirable on balance, there has in fact been some tendency toward consolidation, stimulated by the desire of old-line aerospace firms to hedge against technical obsolescence by diversifying into subsystem and component technologies. This they achieve in the context of systems development contracts by performing development tasks in-house which otherwise might be subcontracted out to smaller specialist firms capable of accomplishing the tasks with greater internal efficiency. The result is a restriction of Government research and development opportunities for small firms. Government procurement agencies have tried to check this propensity by instituting elaborate "buy versus make" reviews. But systems contractors normally have the upper hand in bargaining over subcontracting decisions, since Government contracting personnel suffer from an inferior understanding of the technical problems at hand, and therefore are unable to refute contractor claims that coordination will be excessively difficult in border-line cases.

In my opinion, this contract-financed growth by diversification of big defense contractors at the expense of smaller specialist firms is a serious policy problem. As a corrective to this and other dilemmas in the present system of weapons contracting I have proposed an approach to contract awards which would relate the growth of major defense vendors to the quality of their performance in past programs.[1]

However, this proposal has been received unenthusiastically in defense circles, mainly because of the difficulties involved in evaluating the performance of research and development organizations.

THE ORGANIZATIONAL ENVIRONMENT

Let us consider now the environment for research and development provided by large as opposed to small firms. It is often alleged that the greater bureaucracy and more detailed controls typical in larger firms stifle creativity and frustrate the exploitation of inventions already made. This is an attractive enough hypothesis. Yet the issue is singularly resistant to conclusive proof. One can cite many examples of extreme resistance to change on the part of large firms. The big steel companies, for instance, showed little interest in developing a new stainless steel sheet to meet the Atlas ICBM's needs, largely because they saw no prospect for high volume production in the project. A smaller firm was found to do the job. Similarly, the top management of a leading aircraft company gave only faint support

[1] F. M. Scherer, "The Weapons Acquisition Process: Economics Incentives" (Boston, 1964), especially pp. 327–362.

to its small missile and space development group during the 1950's until shocked by the departure of a key executive. Still the mere listing of examples is futile, for all sorts of counterexamples—cases in which big firms pioneered new technologies—can also be found. Only a quantitative analysis of big firms' inventive and innovative contributions relative to their size can yield more positive interpretations. And such analyses (like the one which will be reported shortly) cannot disentangle the influences of bureaucracy and rigid controls from other factors which affect the output of inventions and innovations. Therefore, the most I can say is that big firms have certain environmental characteristics which seem, on a priori grounds, likely to discourage technological progressiveness.

It is important in this connection to distinguish the advantages of smallness from the advantages of newness. Most new firms are small, but most small firms are not new. One of the chief barriers to innovation is a commitment to technical approaches which have served the organization well in the past. Both big firms and well-established small firms have such commitments, and so both are apt to resist certain technical changes. The commitments may be overcome, but the existence of favorable conditions is not assured.[2] New firms on the other hand typically lack commitments to past technical concepts, and so we should not be surprised if industrial newcomers accounted for a disproportionate number of innovations. The implication is clear: barriers to the entry of new firms should be kept as low as possible if maximum innovation is to be encouraged.

One further environmental characteristic deserves mention. Cost consciousness is a difficult thing to achieve in research and development, especially for large organizations operating under Government contracts. Engineers and scientists naturally seek perfection of the products or processes on which they are working. In this quest for perfection, there is virtually no end to the number of steps which can be taken. Perfection is of course an impossible goal, and the quest for it must be limited by cost constraints. But scientists and engineers are as a rule not very enamored of budgetary matters, while the representatives of management concerned with controlling costs usually have too limited an understanding of the technical problems in a development project to set meaningful efficiency standards. The result is a bias toward overmanning of R. & D. projects. This tendency seems to be stronger in large organizations than in small for two main reasons. First, the organizational separation between persons concerned with costs and the R. & D. staff is greater, and the communication between these groups less effective, in large organizations than in small. Second, at any moment in time large R. & D. organizations are more likely to have

[2] Ibid., pp. 22–26.

some "organizational slack"—i.e., free personnel who can be assigned to an ongoing project. And once engineers are so assigned, they can always find things to do—even if the activities will not repay their cost.[3] This second problem is aggravated in defense contracting by the nature of the contract award process, which leads company executives to ask not "How much can we do with the R. & D. staff we have?" but "How can we keep our R. & D. staff busy with the limited number of contracts in hand?"[4] Overmanning of research and development projects follows, especially in large firms with considerable organizational slack. This in turn means inefficient utilization of the Nation's technical manpower.

SUMMARY

To sum up, small firms are not barred from performing research and development in the less complex areas of industrial technology by the existence of scale economies, and small firms may have an advantage over large firms in terms of originality and efficient technical resource utilization. From these findings it seems clear that a substantial role exists for both small and large firms in Government research and development programs, even though efforts by major prime contractors to diversify by retaining new work in their own laboratories may prevent small firms from achieving their maximum potential. For privately supported research and development the question is more complicated, since large firms may possess greater financial power, stronger monetary incentive to invest in R. & D., and are better able to spread risks over a balanced portfolio of projects, perhaps offsetting their creative and cost-control deficiencies. The net effect of these partly conflicting influences in the private sphere can best be assessed by analyzing statistics on R. & D. spending, employment, and patenting. The second half of my presentation will follow this more quantitative line.

[3] As Dr. R. B. Kershner observed in an article arguing that the average defense R. & D. project employs three times the optimum number of personnel, "If you add an engineer and assign him an area of responsibility, he will proceed to engineer something. You simply do not get faced with the problem of an engineer coming back and saying, 'Look, I don't have to be assigned to this area because there is nothing to do.' He would consider such a statement as evidence of a failure of imagination on his part." "The Size of Research and Engineering Teams." "IRE Transactions on Engineering Management," June 1958, p. 36. See also M. J. Peck and F. M. Scherer, "The Weapons Acquisition Process: An Economic Analysis" (Boston, 1962), pp. 467–478 and 492–501.

[4] The dynamics of this problem are examined in Scherer, "The Weapons Acquisition Process: Economic Incentives," pp. 315–320 and 339–345.

BROAD PATTERN IN R. & D. EXPENDITURES

Statistics collected by the Census Bureau for the National Science Foundation lend preliminary support to the case for big business. In 1958, for instance, firms with 5,000 or more employees were responsible for 88 percent of all research and development expenditures, both federally supported and privately supported, and 81 percent of all privately financed R. & D. outlays by manufacturing companies, but only about 41 percent of manufacturing employment and 47 percent of manufacturing sales.[5] The same large firms employed about 80 percent of all full-time-equivalent research and development scientists and engineers.[6] Thus we see that firms with 5,000 or more employees accounted for a share of formal R. & D. activity considerably greater than their share of economic activity in general —a conclusion which holds throughout the 8-year period on which National Science Foundation data have been published. This suggests that big business enjoys conditions favorable to the conduct and support of research and development.

Still these data only whet one's appetite for more detailed information. Employment of 5,000 persons is a rather low threshold, as bigness in business goes. In 1958 General Motors had 100 times that number of employees, and more than 75 manufacturing firms employed at least 25,000 persons. We should like to probe deeper into the structure of R. & D. activity among the 300 to 400 industrial firms surpassing the 5,000-employee mark.

MORE DETAILED RESULTS

On this question National Science Foundation publications afford little insight. To carry the analysis further, I sought data on two measures of inventive activity: persons employed in research and development during 1955, as an index of inputs, and U.S. invention patents assigned to firms in 1959, as an index of inventive outputs. The patent data covered 448 corporations (after consolidation of 15 disappearances due to mergers) on Fortune's list of the 500 largest industrials for 1955, and the R. & D. employment data covered a subsample of 352 firms from this list. The choice of 1955 as a base year was made partly because government support of industrial R. & D. was not as widespread then as it is now, and so the data reflect private

[5] National Science Foundation, "Industrial R. & D. Funds in Relation to Other Variables" (NSF 64–25), pp. 49–55.

[6] National Science Foundation, "Funds for Research and Development in Industry, 1959" (NSF 62–3), p. 76.

incentives more effectively, and partly to permit an analysis (not reported here) of how R. & D. affects firms' subsequent profits. The 4-year lag between measured R. & D. employment inputs and patent outputs reflects the time required for corporate counsel and the Patent Office to process an average invention patent application.

One methodological problem must be identified immediately. We are interested in the relationship between firm size and inventive activity. But how should we measure firm size—by employment, value added, sales, or assets? The results, it turns out, differ somewhat from measure to measure, the use of employment being most favorable to the case for big business and assets being least favorable.[7] I use sales here partly as a compromise, but mainly because it is the variable considered most frequently by company executives in their actual research and development program budget decisions.[8]

Table 19.1 shows the concentration of research and development employment and Table 19.2 the concentration of patents among the firms in my samples, ranked in order of 1955 sales volume. It is readily apparent that sales are more concentrated among the largest firms than either research and development employment or invention patents received.[9] For instance, the largest 30 firms by sales volume (corresponding roughly to those with $1 billion or more sales in 1955) accounted for 49 percent of the sales of all 352 corporations on which comparable data were available, but only 45 percent of the R. & D. employment and 43 percent of the patents. This relationship holds for nearly every rank group. The implication is that among firms big enough to appear on Fortune's 1955 list, the largest firms supported inventive and innovative activity less intensively relative to their size than did the smaller firms.

[7] F. M. Scherer, "Size of Firm, Oligopoly, and Research: A Comment," Canadian Journal of Economics and Political Science, May 1965.

[8] U.S. National Science Foundation, "Science and Engineering in American Industry: Final Report on a 1953–54 Survey" (USF 56–61), pp. 46 and 47.

[9] This finding may surprise those familiar with the concentration data presented in National Science Foundation publications, showing that the largest 4, 8, 20, etc., companies ranked by research and development performance account for a much higher proportion of all R. & D. performance than of all sales. Cf. National Science Foundation, "Research and Development in Industry: 1961" (NSF 64–9), pp. 23 and 24. The reason for this disparity is a difference in ranking assumptions: The NSF ranked firms on the basis of R. & D. performance, while I ranked them on the basis of sales. When one is concerned with a causal chain running from firm size to R. & D., it is more appropriate to use the presumed causal variable—firm size—as the basis for ranking. My data reveal a pattern similar to the NSF pattern when firms are ranked on the basis of patents or R. & D. employment, since firms leading the pack in patenting and R. & D. are often far from the top in terms of sales.

TABLE 19.1

CONCENTRATION OF SALES, PATENTS, AND R. & D. EMPLOYMENT IN A SAMPLE OF 352 CORPORATIONS

Number of firms included ranked by 1955 sales	Percentage of total for all 352 firms		
	1955 sales	1959 patents	1955 R. + D. employment
1st 4	19.9	10.4	9.7
1st 8	27.5	16.8	16.4
1st 12	32.8	24.9	25.9
1st 20	41.5	32.9	36.7
1st 30	49.0	42.9	44.7
1st 40	55.0	45.0	50.4
1st 50	59.9	50.8	57.8
1st 75	69.3	64.5	68.1
1st 100	75.9	71.0	71.9
1st 150	84.9	81.3	81.7
1st 200	90.8	89.4	90.0
1st 250	94.9	94.2	94.8
1st 300	97.7	97.6	97.8
All 352	100.0	100.0	100.0

TABLE 19.2

CONCENTRATION OF SALES AND PATENTS IN A SAMPLE OF 448 CORPORATIONS

Number of firms included, ranked by 1955 sales	Percentage of total for all 448 firms	
	1955 sales	1959 patents
1st 4	18.2	9.9
1st 8	25.2	15.9
1st 12	30.1	23.6
1st 20	38.1	31.2
1st 30	44.9	40.7
1st 40	50.4	42.6
1st 50	54.9	48.2
1st 75	63.8	59.0
1st 100	70.1	67.9
1st 150	79.0	76.7
1st 200	85.3	84.6
1st 250	89.9	89.5
1st 300	93.3	93.3
1st 350	96.0	95.9
1st 400	98.2	99.0
All 448	100.0	100.0

A similar conclusion emerges when we study average patenting and average R. & D. employment per billion dollars of sales, as in Figures 19.1 and 19.2 and Table 19.3. . . . The sample of corporations was broken down into four technology groups, each group including only industries with roughly the same average level of inventive activity relative to sales.[10] The four technology groups were then subdivided into five size classes: sales of less than $100 million, $100 to $199 million, $200 to $499 million, $500 to $999 million, and $1 billion and over. Examining the charts, we see that in technically least vigorous groups C and D, which include about four-fifths of all sampled firms, there is a pronounced tendency for patenting and R. & D. employment per billion dollars of sales to fall as firm size increases beyond the $200 million level.[11] Results for the most vigorous electrical industry group are more irregular, although the highest patents-to-sales and R. & D.-to-sales ratios occur for firms in the $100 to $199 million range. The basic chemicals and drugs group appears as an exception, displaying a slight but also irregular tendency for inventive activity to arise with firm size. Altogether, in six cases out of eight, the highest average rates of patenting and R. & D. employment per billion dollars of sales are found for firms with 1955 sales of less than $200 million. These patterns persist when two-digit industries are analyzed one by one. The results clearly do not support the hypothesis that bigness per se is especially conducive to technological invention and innovation. If anything, they imply that giant firms are somewhat less progressive relative to size than their smaller brethren.

THE SHARE OF LARGE FIRMS IN INDUSTRIAL PATENTING

Further insight into the structure of American industrial inventive activity can be gained by extending the data presented in Table 19.2. The

[10] Aircraft and rubber products firms were not included in the analysis of R. & D. employment because most of those industries' R. & D. personnel were engaged under Government contracts and because, in the aircraft case, the data appeared to be especially unreliable (even though consistent with the conclusions drawn here). Fourteen firms in the soap, paint, fertilizer, and miscellaneous chemicals fields were excluded from the R. & D. analysis because their average levels of R. & D. employment did not fit well with any of the four groups. If they are included in the basic chemicals and drugs groups, the results are unaltered.

[11] The R. & D. employment averages for these groups must be interpreted with caution, since many of the firms on which R. & D. employment data were unavailable in fact did little or no organized R. & D., and most of these nonreporting firms fell into the smaller size groups. It is not likely, however, that the pattern of Figure 19.1 would be reversed if the full set of data were available. And the patent statistics do not suffer from this limitation.

FIGURE 19.1

AVERAGE 1955 RESEARCH AND DEVELOPMENT EMPLOYMENT PER BILLION DOLLARS OF SALES, BY SIZE AND TECHNOLOGY GROUPS

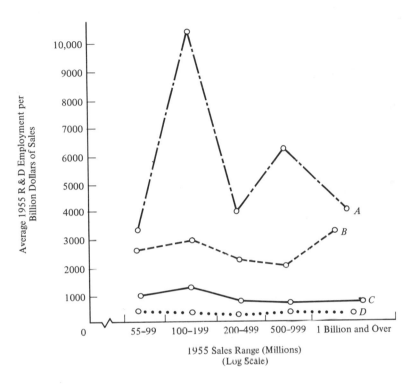

Group A: Electrical Equipment and Communications.
Group B: Basic Chemicals and Drugs.
Group C: Petroleum, Stone-Clay-Glass, Fabricated Metal Products, Machinery, and Transportation Equipment (excluding Aircraft).
Group D: Food, Tobacco, Textiles, Apparel, Paper, and Primary Metals.

448 firms in my complete sample accounted for about 57 percent of the 1955 sales of all U.S. manufacturing corporations, as estimated by the Federal Trade Commission. They received about 56 percent of the invention patents assigned at the time of issue to domestic U.S. manufacturing corporations in 1959, as estimated from Patent Office data and a count of patents assigned to nonmanufacturing corporations. Thus, these 448 of the Nation's 500 largest industrial corporations apparently did not generate a disproportionate share of inventive outputs, as measured by invention patents issued,

FIGURE 19.2

AVERAGE 1959 PATENTS PER BILLION DOLLARS OF SALES, BY SIZE AND TECHNOLOGY GROUPS

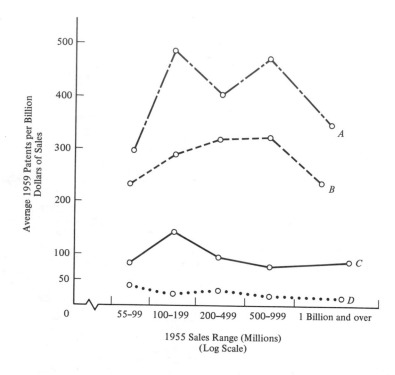

1955 Sales Range (Millions)
(Log Scale)

Group A: Electrical Equipment and Communications.
Group B: Basic Chemicals and Drugs.
Group C: Petroleum, Rubber, Stone-Clay-Glass, Fabricated Metal Products, Machinery, and Transportation Equipment (including Aircraft).
Group D: Food, Tobacco, Textiles, Apparel, Paper, and Primary Metals.

even though they did contribute a share of research and development inputs (e.g., R. & D. expenditures and employment) substantially exceeding their share of sales and total employment.

This initially surprising result could have several explanations. First, it is likely that many firms too small to appear among Fortune's 500 generate patentable inventions through activities not organized as formal research and development sections, as defined by the National Science Foundation. While one might question whether such inventions are comparable to the

TABLE 19.3

**AVERAGE RESEARCH AND DEVELOPMENT EMPLOYMENT AND
PATENTS PER BILLION DOLLARS IN 1955 SALES, BY SIZE AND TECHNOLOGY GROUPS[1]**

Technology group	1955 sales range (millions)				
	$55 to $99	$100 to $199	$200 to $499	$500 to $999	$1,000 and over
	1955 research and development employment/sales (billions)				
Electrical	$3,422	$10,444	$3,988	$6,199	$4,005
	(12)	(4)	(8)	(3)	(4)
Chemicals and drugs	2,593	2,947	2,134	2,064	3,195
	(12)	(13)	(8)	(2)	(2)
Petroleum: stone-clay-glass; fabricated metals; machinery; and transportation equipment (excluding aircraft)	953	1,210	841	818	818
	(39)	(29)	(25)	(10)	(13)
Food, tobacco, textiles, apparel, paper, and primary metals	466	342	280	363	181
	(34)	(33)	(35)	(18)	(6)
	1959 invention patents/sales (billions)				
Electrical	300	488	403	479	354
	(15)	(4)	(9)	(3)	(4)
Chemicals and drugs	235	289	314	318	243
	(12)	(14)	(9)	(1)	(2)
Petroleum, rubber, stone-clay-glass, fabricated metals, machinery, and transportation equipment (excluding aircraft)	84	144	101	85	88
	(66)	(49)	(37)	(20)	(15)
Food, tobacco, textiles, apparel, paper, and primary metals	45	25	30	21	15
	(63)	(50)	(47)	(19)	(6)

[1] Numbers in parentheses below each entry indicate the number of firms included in subgroup.

output of formal R. & D. groups, there exist no indications of substantial qualitative inferiority. Notably, studies by the George Washington University patent research group indicate that small companies utilize commercially a higher proportion of their patented inventions than companies with assets exceeding $100 million and holding more than 100 patents.[12] This suggests that the average quality of small firms' patents may in fact be superior. Second, small firms apparently acquire more patents from outside inventors. The same research group found that small firms acquire by assignment about 8 percent of their patents from outsiders prior to the time of issue, compared to about 4 percent for firms with assets exceeding $100 million and holding more than 100 patents.[13] Third, it is conceivable for reasons outlined earlier in this statement that large firms with organizational slack and/or a mass-engineering bias use more resources on the average to achieve a given technical advance than do small firms. Fourth, small new firms are apt to generate a share of patents exceeding their share of sales because of their lack of commitment to prior technical concepts. Finally, big firms may apply for patent protection on a smaller proportion of their patentable inventions than do small firms, since the patent positions of industrial giants have proved especially vulnerable to antitrust remedies during the past two decades.[14] Here however there are also arguments for the opposite assumption: that big firms have a higher propensity to patent than do small firms. The meager evidence I have examined on this issue indicates that incentives to patent do not in fact vary much on the average between big and little corporations.[15]

SOME CAVEATS

We find then that the available data afford little aid to the case for corporate bigness. Still a completely confident and unqualified verdict would be inappropriate, given the hazards of quantitative analysis in this new and little-explored field. Several caveats are in order.

For one, it is all too easy to be wrong in measuring something as slippery as inventive inputs and outputs. Neither R. & D. employment nor the number of patents issued to firms is a completely satisfactory index of inventive or innovative activity. These two measures were simply the best I could obtain for a broad sample of firms. While perfect measurement can hardly be expected, one hopes that on the average the two indices reflect at least reasonably well the true state of affairs. Some confidence may be de-

[12] B. Sanders, J. Rossman, and L. J. Harris, "Patent Acquisition by Corporations," *Patent, Trademark, and Copyright Journal*, Fall 1959, p. 238.

[13] Ibid., p. 258.

[14] F. M. Scherer, S. E. Herzstein, et al., "Patents and the Corporation" (rev. ed., Boston: 1959), pp. 119–146.

[15] F. M. Scherer, "Firm Size, Market Structure, Opportunity, and the Output of Patented Inventions," "American Economic Review," Dec., 1965, pp. 1097–1125.

rived from the fact that the indices are highly correlated and show consistent patterns (as in Figures 19.1 and 19.2). My results for particular two-digit industries are also consistent with Edwin Mansfield's findings in major innovations and R. & D. spending in several industries,[16] and with William Comanor's analysis of sales-weighted innovations in the drug industry.[17]

Second, my data cover but a single year—1955 for R. & D. employment and 1959 for patenting. It is possible that the structural relationship between firm size and inventive activity has changed since then. I doubt whether major structural changes have actually occurred, partly because the share of firms with 5,000 or more employees in total industrial R. & D. expenditures has, according to the most recent and consistent National Science Foundation estimates, remained quite steady between 1956 and 1961.[18] But, of course, there is no way in which it is possible for us to be certain.

Third, there is the problem of the variable used to measure firm size. If either employment or (to a much less pronounced degree) value added were taken as the size measure, the case for big business would receive somewhat more support, since both are less concentrated than sales. Still a change in scale measures would not turn my results decisively in favor of the bigness hypothesis. If Table 19.1 is recomputed using total employment as the ranking criterion, one finds R. & D. employment somewhat more concentrated than total employment beyond the 30 firm mark, although the difference in no instance amounts to more than 4 percentage points. Patenting remains for the most part less concentrated than total employment.

Fourth, it is conceivable that bigness confers an advantage not in research and development lumped together or in the creation of patented inventions (which seem most closely associated with development activities), but only in undertaking the most risky kinds of scientific effort—for example, basic research. But the available evidence does not support this conjecture. In 1961, for instance, firms with 5,000 or more employees accounted for 85.9 percent of all industrial R. & D. outlays but only 84.6 percent of industrial basic research. Their basic research share was greater than their 80.5-percent share of company-financed R. & D., however. In a more detailed analysis of data from a sample of 123 large firms Mr. Dennis Mueller, a graduate student in economics at Princeton University, found that 1963 basic research expenditures were no more concentrated than either total R. & D. spending

[16] "Size of Firm, Market Structure, and Innovation," Journal of Political Economy, December 1963, pp. 565–568; and "Industrial Research and Development Expenditures," Journal of Political Economy, August 1964, pp. 333–334.

[17] "The Economics of Research and Development in the Pharmaceutical Industry" (unpublished Ph.D. dissertation, Harvard University, 1963).

[18] National Science Foundation, "Research and Development in Industry," 1961 (NSF 64–9), p. ix.

or company-financed R. & D. outlays when the firms were ranked on the basis of sales.

Finally, it is probable, as I have implied earlier, that giant firms do have an advantage in carrying out large-scale systems development efforts, even though they enjoy none in less grandiose inventive activities.

CONCLUSION

In conclusion, the best interpretation I can draw from my research results is that giant firm size is no prerequisite for the most vigorous inventive and innovative activity. There may be a size threshold below which firms are disadvantaged because they cannot reap all R. & D. scale economies, spread risks, or tap sufficiently large markets in exploiting. their research results. But if such a threshold exists, it has probably been surpassed already by the several hundred U.S. firms with sales exceeding $100 million. Bigness beyond this point is apparently no major advantage, and may well be an impediment, to technical progressiveness, although the handicaps of bigness can be overcome by especially effective and forward-looking management.

20

The performance
of food
retailing

Federal Trade Commission

Preceding chapters have dealt with various aspects of the structure and conduct patterns of food retailing. Economic theory and industrial experience teach that market structure and conduct ultimately determine, in part, industrial performance.

Because food retailing is still undergoing marked structural and behavioral changes, it is too early to make a judgment concerning its ultimate performance. However, available data shed some light on certain key aspects of its performance up to the present. Of particular interest are those broad aspects of performance applicable in all industries; namely, "the efficiency of the organization of the industry in terms of the scales of plants and firms, the relation of price to cost as reflected in the profit rate, and the size of selling costs in relation to sales revenue."[1]

In addition to shedding some light on existing industry performance, these factors may also provide meaningful insights into present and future

[1] Joe S. Bain, *Industrial Organization*, p. 341.

From Federal Trade Commission, *Economic Report on the Structure and Competitive Behavior of Food Retailing* (Washington, D.C.: United States Government Printing Office, January 1966), pp. 245–270.

industry structure. For example, if some existing companies are too small to operate efficiently or have relatively low profits, this suggests such companies are disadvantaged relative to large concerns and may have difficulty surviving.

THE EFFICIENCY OF FOOD RETAILING

The Federal Trade Commission staff did not collect any original data concerning the efficiency of food retailing, either in terms of the efficiency of stores or of companies. Therefore, the following analysis of efficiency is devoted primarily to the changing costs, over time, of performing the food retailing function and to certain comparisons of the relative costs of various size retailers.

But before turning to the subject of costs, it is important to recognize that the character of the food retailing function has changed markedly over the past three decades. Looking only at the *costs* of performing this function neglects the quality with which it is performed. Although it is not possible to measure precisely certain qualitative aspects of performance, they are no less important. It is therefore appropriate to contrast briefly the modern food store with its predecessor store.

Qualitative Changes in Food Retailing

The modern supermarket is spacious and attractive and offers a wide variety of alternative food and nonfood products. The typical supermarket opened in 1964 had a total area of 20,000 square feet, 68 percent of which consisted of selling area. Its large size enables the modern supermarket to offer consumers a wide variety of choices. Whereas in 1928 the typical grocery store handled 867 different items, today it offers the consumer about 7,000 items. These include a wide variety of nongrocery as well as grocery products. In 1963 nongrocery products accounted for 15.5 percent of all grocery store sales. These nongrocery items are divided as follows: cosmetics, drugs, etc., 28 percent; tobacco products, 28 percent; alcoholic drinks, 10 percent; all other nongrocery items, 34 percent.

The greatly expanded product line of the modern supermarket is one of its most attractive features. It enables "one-stop shopping."

On the other hand, in certain respects today's supermarket offers consumers fewer services than did its predecessor. The latter extended credit, provided home delivery, and offered more extensive personalized services. Although it is not possible to weigh precisely the relative qualities of alternative methods of retailing, judged by the standard of consumer acceptance, most Americans have expressed a marked preference for the supermarket method of merchandising. Nevertheless, the housewife of today undoubtedly spends a considerable amount of time and money driving to and from the supermarket, as well as performing the shopping function itself. There is no accurate way of determining whether she saves more money this way than under the old system.

Another important qualitative factor of modern retailing is its diversity. In recent years convenience stores and discount supermarkets have appeared in response to the preferences of consumers for the unique services offered by these divergent forms of retailing. Convenience stores offer more services to the consumer who is willing to pay for them; on the other hand, the discount supermarket offers lower prices to those consumers who are willing to settle for fewer services.

In all of the above respects, then, the modern food store represents a qualitatively different and, judging by its success in the market place, a more desired product than its predecessor of decades past.

CHANGES IN GROSS MARGINS OF FOOD RETAILERS—1921–1964

A measure of the efficiency with which firms perform the food retailing function is the "gross profit margin" of food retailers. This margin measures the difference between the cost of merchandise and the price at which it is sold. All other things being equal, the lower the gross margins, the more efficiently the retailer is performing. Precise comparisons over time are hazardous because "other things" do not remain equal.

Over the past four decades, grocery retailing has experienced a number of fundamental technological and structural changes which we could expect to affect gross retail margins. The 1920's might be characterized as the decade of the chains. Most of today's leading chains had achieved a prominent place in food retailing by the end of that decade. By 1929, five chains, each with annual sales of over $100 million, accounted for about 25 percent of all grocery store sales. But this was still a time of small stores; the average store of even the largest chains had annual sales of only $50,000.

The onset of the Great Depression and the introduction of the supermarket by independent operators marked the beginning of two decades of intense price competition and change, slowed only temporarily by World War II. Over the two decades, the number of supermarkets grew from a scant 300 in 1932 to around 15,000 in 1950. During this period, the corporate chains' share of grocery store sales remained rather stable—a decline occurring during World War II having been nearly offset in the immediate postwar years.

The period since about 1948 has been marked by dramatic structural change in three ways. Tens of thousands of stores disappeared as their places were taken by supermarkets owned by chains or independent operators. There occurred a resurgence of corporate chains, expanding significantly their share of food store sales. These changes were accompanied by increased concentration in local and national markets.

What happened to retail gross margins while these changes were occurring? While we have no entirely comparable data on gross profit margins over the past four decades of change, sufficient data are available to permit us to follow the general *trend* in margins. It should be recognized that the available data are not precise estimates of the size of retail gross margins. Companies use a variety of accounting practices so that direct comparisons between or among companies often are not possible. In spite of the admitted shortcomings of all available series on margins, however, the data presented below probably portray accurately the *trend* in margins over the past several decades.

Figure 20.1 shows a number of gross margin series covering various periods during the past four decades. During the 1920's, as the figure shows, there was no marked trend in gross profit margins of large chains (Figure 20.1—series 1). The average for all chains covered was 20.6 percent during 1921–25 and 19.3 percent during 1926–30.[2] Nor were there great differences in margins by size of chains.

The only series which spans the entire period since the late 1920's is one based on published financial data of 3 large corporate food chains.[3] These chains' gross margins averaged around 18 percent in the late 1920's, rose during the depression years of the early 1930's, and then held rather steadily—at around 20 percent—until 1939 (Figure 20.1—series 2). Following 1939, this series declined, and held at around 15 percent for the 6-year period 1947–52. Thereafter it began a steady increase, reaching a peak of 20.7 percent in 1964. Certain changes were made in accounting procedures[4] which prevent this series from depicting the precise levels of margins. However, the series represents quite accurately the general trend in gross margins.[5] Also, it seems significant that the margins of these three chains rather closely paralleled one another over the entire period. Various other series spanning shorter periods generally parallel this long-term series.

[2] Federal Trade Commission, *Chain Stores, Gross Profit and Average Sales per Store of Retail Chains*, 72nd Cong., 2d Sess., U. S. Senate Document No. 178, 1933, p. 22.

[3] These three chains, Safeway, Kroger, and American Stores, were the second, third, and fourth largest chains throughout the period. They accounted for about 23 percent of chain grocery sales in 1929 and about 26 percent in 1964.

[4] The sharp decline in 1948 in the three chain series shown in figure 29 is due to a change in Safeway's accounting procedures beginning in that year.

[5] Wholesale costs apparently are excluded in recent years. If wholesale costs are included, the average margins of these three chains would be about 2 percentage points higher. For

A series covering A&P's gross profit margins shows a somewhat more substantial fall in gross margins over the period 1931 to 1944, from 21.1 percent to 14.2 percent (Figure 20.1—series 3).[6]

A Harvard-Cornell series for the period 1955–64, based on data supplied by members of the National Association of Food Chains, shows an increase from 18.1 percent to 22.5 percentage (Figure 20.1—series 4).

A series derived from Internal Revenue Service data shows that gross margins of large corporate food chains (with assets of over $50 million) declined from 19.0 percent in 1938 to 15.0 percent in the early 1940's; thereafter they followed an irregular course until the early 1950's, when they began a steady upward course (Figure 20.1—series 5).[7]

What may be inferred from these general trends in margins over the past four decades? First, most of the sharp changes in retail margins are associated with drastic swings in farm prices rather than in the absolute size of gross margins as such.[8] This explains entirely the rise in retailers' margins between 1929 and the early 1930's. During this period farm prices dropped drastically.[9] Similarly, between the early 1940's and 1948, farm prices rose much more rapidly than did retail food prices.[10] In some other

---

example, in response to a Federal Trade Commission survey in 1959, these chains reported average gross margins of 18.1 percent in 1954 and 20.9 percent in 1958. These margins, which included warehouse costs, are about 2 percentage points higher than those shown in appendix table 44.

[6] As shown in appendix table 44, A&P's gross profit margins increased from 14.0 percent in 1954 to 18.0 in 1963.

[7] Data developed by Super Market Institute showed "typical" median gross profit margins rising from 17.4 percent to 19.8 percent over the period 1954–63 (appendix table 49). These data include independent supermarket operators as well as large chains. Data from a Federal Trade Commission study showed average margins of all corporate chains rising from 16.8 percent in 1954 to 18.5 percent in 1958. The largest increase occurred among chains with sales exceeding $100 million.

[8] When farm prices rise or fall more rapidly than absolute processing and retailing costs, they affect the percentage of the retail price represented by retail margins even though there is no change in the retailers' absolute margins. An example will illustrate this point: Suppose that in one period farmers receive sixty cents for a particular product, manufacturers receive 20 cents for processing it, and retailers receive 20 cents for distributing it. If farm prices for the product dropped to 40 cents, but processors' and retailers' absolute marketing costs remained the same, retailers' gross margin would increase from 20 to 25 percent. Of course, the reverse would occur during periods when farm prices are rising more rapidly than absolute margins of processing and retailing.

[9] Between 1929 and 1935 the index of all farm prices fell by 56 percent whereas prices of food for home consumption fell by only 24 percent.

[10] Between 1941 and 1948 farm prices rose by about 130 percent whereas retail food prices rose by about 100 percent.

periods, however, the changes in retail margins appear to have been due primarily to real changes in the cost of performing the retail functions. One such period was between 1935 and 1940 when retail margins of large chains declined from 20.4 percent to 18.9 percent.[11] This decline probably reflected the impact of the supermarket on retailers' margins.

FIGURE 20.1

RETAIL GROSS PROFITS OF LARGE FOOD CHAINS, 1921–1964

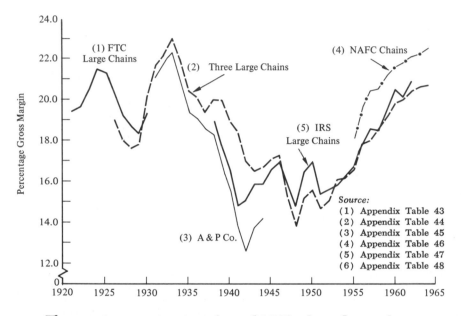

The growing margins since the mid-1950's also reflect real increases in the cost of performing the retailing function.[12]

In summary, after the initial rise in gross profit margins in the early 1930's, margins of large chains followed a downward trend until around 1950. At least part of this decline was due to the impact of supermarket merchandising which slashed margins far below those of existing stores. During the 1930's, many independent supermarket operators had margins of only 10 to 14 percent, while conventional stores had margins exceeding 20 percent.[13] Price competition was keen in many areas and large chains

[11] Between 1935 and 1940 farm prices declined by 9 percent. Therefore, had other things remained unchanged, retailers' margins would have increased over the period.

[12] Since 1955 farm prices have risen only moderately.

[13] Charles F. Phillips, "The Supermarket," *Harvard Business Review*, XVI, No. 2, Winter, 1938, p. 192.

participated vigorously in this price competition as they turned increasingly to supermarkets. By the early 1950's, large chains had replaced most of their small stores with supermarkets. But during the 1950's, margins began to rise, and by the early 1960's gross margins of large chains not only were about 6 percentage points higher than the postwar lows, but they actually were higher than they had been in the 1920's when chains were still operating very small stores.

Variations in Gross Margins Among Various Size Retailers

Harvard-Cornell series

This series is based upon data supplied by members of the National Association of Food Chains, and was prepared by Harvard University and, more recently, Cornell University.

Between 1955 and 1964, the gross margins of NAFC large chains rose 4.7 percentage points—from 18.1 percent to 22.8 percent. Gross margins of NAFC medium-sized chains followed a mixed course between 1955 and 1964, but their gross margins were only slightly higher at the end of the period than they were at the beginning (Figure 20.2). The gross margins of the large chains series were greater than those of the medium chains for every year but the first, and showed a marked increase over the period—from 18.1 percent in 1955 to 22.8 percent in 1964. Over the period, the gap between the margins of small and large chains widened from 0.9 percent to 3.9 percent.

I.R.S. series

Internal Revenue Service data make it possible to estimate gross margins for a longer period than NAFC data. Figure 20.3, which begins with 1953, permits comparisons with margins in the years immediately prior to the substantial growth in margins in the mid-1950's.

In 1953 the gross margins of large chains (assets exceeding $50 million) were well below those of three other size classes shown in Figure 20.3. By 1961, however, gross margins of large chains exceeded those of small chains (assets between $1 million and $10 million) and independents (assets of less than $1 million). Whereas in 1953 the gross margins of medium-sized chains (assets between $10 million and $50 million) were below those of independents and small chains, by 1961 they were above those of both size classes.

Over the period the gap between the large and medium chains narrowed (from about 4 percentage points to 1 percentage point), but the medium chains still had somewhat higher margins than did large chains.

For 1962, gross margin information is available only for the large chains and independents: between 1961 and 1962 large chains' gross margins increased by about 1 percentage point and those of independents increased by about .5 percentage point.

WHICH COSTS HAVE RISEN?

The most comprehensive data of operating costs of large food retailers are those appearing in the "Operating Results of Food Chains," prepared in cooperation with the National Association of Food Chains by Harvard University, from 1955 through 1961, and by Cornell University, from 1962–63 through 1964–65. As we have seen above, these data show a steady increase in gross margins from 18.12 percent in 1955 to 22.48 percent of sales in 1964–65.

Because of changes in accounting methods, it is not possible to make direct comparisons of individual expense items over the entire period.[14]

[14] Prior to 1961 imputed interest was charged to three expense categories: real estate and fixtures, equipment costs, and selected assets. Beginning in 1961 a single charge has been made for imputed interest. This charge is calculated as 6 percent on adjusted capital stock and surplus. (*Operating Results of Food Chains in 1961*, Harvard University, p. 49.) The effect of this change in accounting procedures is responsible for the

FIGURE 20.2

GROSS MARGINS OF FOOD CHAINS, 1955–1964

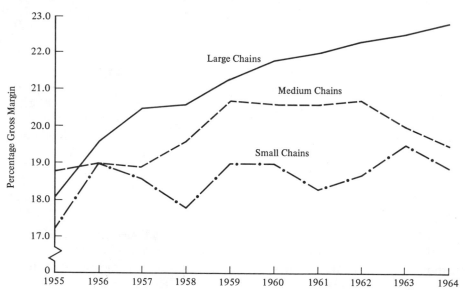

FIGURE 20.3

GROSS MARGINS OF RETAIL FOOD CORPORATIONS, BY ASSETS SIZE, 1953–1962

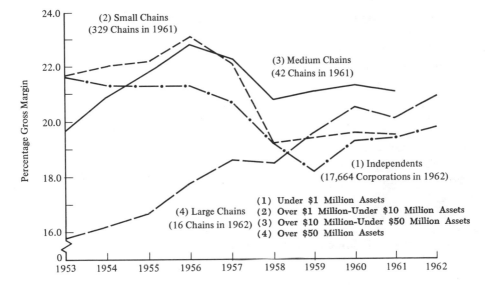

Therefore, the following analysis is divided into periods: 1955 to 1960 and 1961 to 1964.

Analysis of various expense items indicates that for *all* chains covered, costs of advertising and of promotional giveaways, plus costs of trading stamps, increased from 0.83 percent of sales in 1955 to 2.12 percent of sales in 1960.[15] Most of this increase was due to the increasing use of trading stamps. Real estate, fixture and equipment costs, and utilities also went up appreciably, from 3.41 to 4.27 percent. Payroll costs increased from 9.64 to 10.53 percent. The large increases, therefore, were in promotion expenses, trading stamps, occupancy, and payroll.

Figure 20.4 shows the various expense components as a percentage of the increase in gross margins. Together, these 3 items represented 83 percent of the increase over the period.

Profits before taxes of all NAFC chains went up slightly over the period

---

rise of interest costs from 0.32 percent in 1960 to 0.76 percent in 1961. The rate used in computing imputed interest was changed from 4 percent to 6 percent in 1959. (*Operating Results of Food Chains, 1959,* Harvard University, p. 32.) This change was responsible for the increase in "total interest" costs from 0.24 percent in 1958 to 0.33 percent in 1959.

[15] For purposes of convenience only, the place of trading stamps in the increase in gross margins is discussed along with advertising and promotional giveaways.

—from 2.49 percent to 2.74 percent of sales (app. table 52). Net operating profits of large chains also were up slightly, and represented 3.2 percent of the increase in gross margins of large chains.

Between 1961 and 1964, gross margins of all NAFC chains increased by 0.72 percentage points. Again, the largest single increase occurred in trading stamps, advertising and sales promotion, which represented 36.1 percent of the increase (Figure 20.4). Occupancy and payroll costs accounted for most of the remainder, 29.2 percent and 23.6 percent, respectively. Over the period, net income before taxes remained unchanged.

It is possible to measure for all reporting chains the expenses of trading stamps, of services purchased, and of "giveaways" associated with advertising and promotion over the entire period 1955–1964. As shown in Figure 20.5, over the period this cost component rose steadily from .83 percent of sales to 2.42 percent of sales. Expressed as a percent of operating margins, these expenses rose from 4.58 percent in 1955 to 10.76 percent in 1964.

FIGURE 20.4

COMPONENTS CONTRIBUTING TO INCREASE IN GROSS MARGINS OF FOOD CHAINS

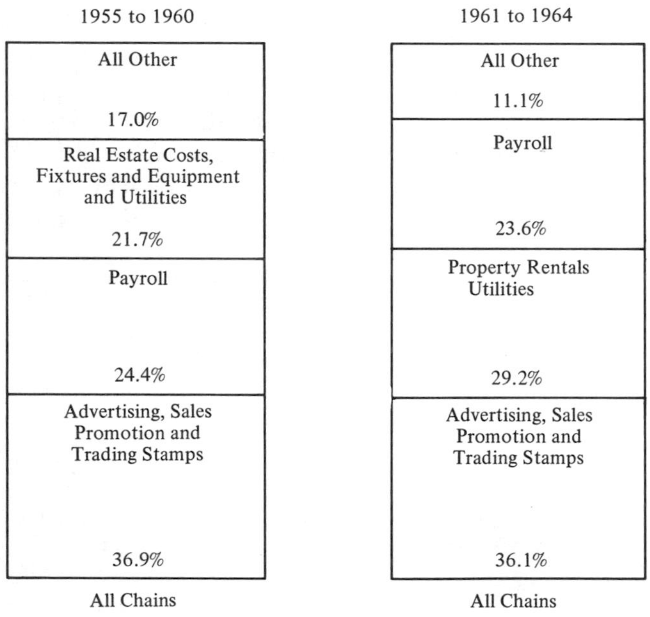

1955 to 1960	1961 to 1964
All Other 17.0%	All Other 11.1%
Real Estate Costs, Fixtures and Equipment and Utilities 21.7%	Payroll 23.6%
Payroll 24.4%	Property Rentals Utilities 29.2%
Advertising, Sales Promotion and Trading Stamps 36.9%	Advertising, Sales Promotion and Trading Stamps 36.1%
All Chains	All Chains

An alternative method of allocating costs is on a responsibility center basis. This accounting method includes all the expenses associated with a given function. When advertising and promotion costs are measured in this way, in 1964 NAFC large chains' trading stamp, advertising, and promotion expenditures of 2.64 percent of sales represented 13 percent of their total operating expenses. Using this method of accounting, trading stamp, advertising, and promotion expenses accounted for nearly 50 percent of the increases in expenses between 1961 and 1964.

Regardless of the method used in analyzing the operating expense data, it is clear that promotional and occupancy costs accounted for over 60 percent of the increases in gross margins over the period. Increasing payroll costs accounted for most of the remainder.

REASONS FOR INCREASING COSTS

The data on operating expense presented above suggest that the single most important factor responsible for increasing retail costs since 1950 has been the rising promotional and related expenditures by food retailers. These expenditures represent an intensification of promotional and related types of competition in food retailing and in food manufacturing.[16]

The hypothesis that these types of competition in retailing tend to push gross margins upward is not a new one. In his analysis of food retailing during the 1920's and 1930's, Dr. A. C. Hoffman reached the following conclusion:

[16] This does not imply that other factors have not played a contributory role. A frequently given explanation is that supermarkets are selling an increasing volume of nonfood items and that markups are higher on these items. While this could be a factor, available information suggests it could have accounted for only a very small part of the increase in recent years, since there has been practically no change in nongrocery sales as a percentage of total supermarket sales since 1956.

Another commonly given explanation for the recent increase is that food items include an increasing amount of "built-in maid service." While this is true, in itself this does not necessarily mean that *retailers'* margins on these items should be greater than on other items. This development may sometimes result in higher margins (e.g., frozen juices have higher margins than canned juices), but it may also result in lower margins (e.g., cake mixes often have lower margins than flour).

A variant of the preceding argument is that the product mix of retailers is changing in favor of high markup items. Retailers always have an incentive to move toward the most profitable items; we would expect, however, that if competition is effective, the gross margins on such "profitable" new items would soon be pushed down to levels competitive with other products, i.e., levels reflecting the relative handling costs and turnover of the item.

FIGURE 20.5

ADVERTISING, PROMOTION, AND RELATED EXPENSE OF FOOD CHAINS, 1955–1964

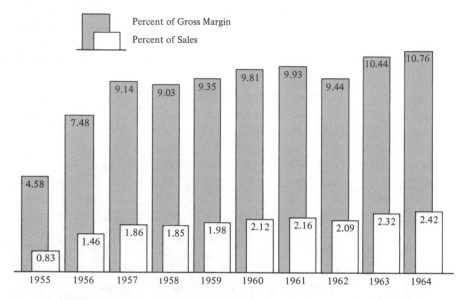

During the period of their rapid expansion, the chains almost without exception had an aggressive price policy calculated to bring new customers into their stores and expand their business. But close observers were able to note late in the decade of the 1920's that the chains were placing less emphasis on the price appeal and were giving less attention than formerly to methods for reducing retail costs. Competition had begun to take the form of institutional advertising and more elegant store buildings and equipment.[17]

The introduction of the supermarket by independent retailers in the early 1930's reversed for nearly two decades the trend observed by Hoffman. Price competition was intensified and margins of large chains apparently fell to an all-time low following World War II.

But beginning shortly after the Korean War, retail margins began a steady upward climb. By then the supermarket was no longer a novelty. The period of "easy" growth—when supermarkets were replacing small stores—was over. The replacement of tens of thousands of small stores with supermarkets and the postwar resurgence of food chains increased market concentration. By the early 1950's, the four or eight largest retailers in most

[17] A. C. Hoffman, *op. cit.*, pp. 102–103.

cities accounted for well over half of all grocery store sales. This oligopolistic market setting encouraged some large retailers to de-emphasize price competition, which had proved so effective with smaller stores. They turned more and more to nonprice rivalry. Some placed increasing emphasis on advertising and other promotional techniques. And nearly all turned to more modern, fancier supermarkets, in-store facilities, and parking lots as a way of attracting customers. Often the result was "overbuilding" of supermarkets and the higher costs resulting from excess capacity.[18] Even some of the increase in labor costs may be associated with the above factors, since each would be reflected ultimately in somewhat higher labor and occupancy costs.

The intensification of promotional competition among large manufacturers of grocery products also seems to have played a role. In their drive to get increased shelf space, grocery manufacturers have created a proliferation of products, promotion deals, cents-off coupons, etc., many of which ultimately spell higher operating costs for retailers. Often, brand proliferation in a product line may cause retailers to increase shelf space without a corresponding increase in total sales.[19]

A retailer participant at a 1959 meeting of the Grocery Manufacturers Association stated:

> There are more deals and promotions available than our ability to handle them . . . I wish there were more deals and promotions that increased total consumption, rather than just a temporary shift from one brand to the other.[20]

With reference to the same problem, Prof. Max Brunk of Cornell University recently observed:

> Certainly most of the proliferation of new items is traceable to food manufacturers who increasingly engage in various forms of non-price competition. A careful examination of the so-called new items handled

[18] In explaining the large jump in operating expense between 1956 and 1957, Professor Wilbur B. England concluded, "Greater advertising expenditures and fixture equipment costs accounted for most of the increase in total expense." Wilbur B. England, *Operating Results of Food Chains in 1957* (Boston: Harvard University, Graduate School of Business Administration, 1958), p. 3.

[19] Cigarettes are only an obvious example. Whereas the leading cigarette companies sold 16 brands in 1954, by 1964 they sold 36 brands. Most retailers very probably carry more brands and devote more shelf space to cigarettes today than 10 years ago. Other areas where we have had a proliferation of brands are soaps and detergents, breakfast cereals, and pet foods.

[20] Panel discussion at the mid-year Conference of the Grocery Manufacturers of America, Inc., June, 1959.

by grocers will reveal that a great many of them are nothing more than deals designed to entice the retailers.[21]

It is indisputable that gross margins of large retail food chains are higher today than they were in the 1920's before they operated supermarkets. It is also true that the chains' gross profit margins are approximately four percentage points higher today than they were *after* supermarket operation became prevalent in the early 1950's. In terms of absolute dollars and cents, this means that if the gross margins of *all* food retailers had increased by a like amount, the 1964 foodstore marketing bill would have been about $2.5 billion larger than if gross margins had not increased!

As already noted, advertising and promotion costs are the chief cause for the recent increases in distribution costs. It is therefore appropriate to estimate the total volume of resources devoted to these purposes.

According to Internal Revenue Service data, total advertising expenses by food retailing corporations have risen both in absolute and relative terms since 1945. Between 1945 and 1950, food retailing corporations spent less than $75 million annually on advertising; these expenditures were equal to 0.5 percent of their sales. After 1953 these expenditures rose rapidly—from $115 million in 1953 to $467 million in 1962.[22] Over the period they rose from 0.5 percent of sales to 1.3 percent of sales (table 20.1).

Internal Revenue Service data understate substantially *total* trading stamp, advertising, and promotion expenditures of food retailers for two reasons.[23] First, some corporations apparently include only the *net* advertising expenditures of food retailing corporations; that is, they exclude the advertising allowances given retailers by their suppliers. Second, not all food retailers report their trading stamp expenditures either separately or

[21] Max E. Brunk, "Discussion of paper by William W. Tongue, 'Competition in the Affluent Society,'" Annual Meeting of the American Farm Economic Association, December 28, 1964. *Supermarket News* reported, April 26, 1965, "Retailers feel they are being 'had' by manufacturers' promotions offered in lieu of legitimate price declines, Joseph Senitt, head grocery buyer for Waldbaum, Inc., told the Grocery Manufacturers' Representatives of New York Monday. Suppliers also are building up discontent with a trend to offering deals which eat into the retailer's profit margin, he stated."

[22] Some of this absolute increase occurred because the number of food retailing corporations increased over the period; however, practically all of this increase involved small corporations. In 1961 the 58 corporations with assets exceeding $10 million accounted for 55 percent of the total advertising expenditures made by the 16,299 retail food corporations.

[23] These reasons explain, in part, the discrepancy in the advertising and promotion expenditures of 1.0 percent reported by large chains to IRS (table 20.1), and the advertising and promotion expenditures of 2.5 percent reported by large chains in the NAFC studies.

among their promotional costs; instead, trading stamp expenditures often are included among the costs of goods sold.

Very probably the *total* advertising expenditures of most large chains amount to about 1.5 percent of sales and trading stamp expenditures, for those making them, amount to an additional 2 percent of sales.[24]

In 1963 food retailers, as a group, spent at least $570 million on total advertising and related expenditures and an additional $600 million on trading stamps.[25]

A substantial portion of the advertising expenditures were used to perform the traditional "informational purposes . . . essential to the effective working of a market system."[26] Trading stamps, of course, were not given for information purposes. Consumers did receive payments in money or merchandise in return for saving trading stamps, however, although it is difficult to estimate the precise value of the merchandise given.[27]

PROFITABILITY OF FOOD RETAILING

Profits play a central role in organizing and allocating economic resources in a free market economy. The prospect of profits, or the fear of losses, performs a key role in integrating and distilling the forces of supply and demand. Profits are the reward of business success, and business enterprise will not survive unless it receives adequate compensation on its invested capital.

The general level of profits in an industry are thus a useful index of its overall performance, and an indicator of the vigor of competition. For when competition is effective, there is a tendency for profits to be pushed toward the *cost* of capital. Noncompetitive profits in an industry suggest that new competitors face entry barriers. In the absence of such barriers, capital

[24] The National Association of Food Chains' figure for all chains includes only *net* advertising expenditures. If advertising allowances of .75 percent of sales received from suppliers are added to chains' net advertising expenses of .83 percent of sales, their total advertising expenses would be 1.58 percent of sales, plus promotional expenses and trading stamps of 1.59 percent of sales.

[25] The estimate on advertising expenditures assumes that all retailers spent an average of 1 percent of sales on advertising. As shown in table 90, in 1962, even very small food retailing corporations made advertising expenditures of 1.3 percent of sales. The estimate of total trading stamp expenditures is made by assuming that for those food retailers giving them, trading stamp expense was 2 percent of sales. In 1963 the total food store sales of stamp users was about $30 billion.

[26] Joe S. Bain, *Industrial Organization, op. cit.*, p. 389.

[27] See chapter IX, pp. 207, 236–240.

would be infused into the industry until its profits were comparable to those earned in alternative uses.

Estimating corporation profit rates is a hazardous procedure at best;[28] however, comparisons over time of profits earned in different industries, or of different groups of firms in the same industry, provide a useful indication of *relative* if not *absolute* profitability. Below we shall measure the profitability of food retailing relative to other industries and the profitability of various size categories of food retailers.

Food Retailing vs. Manufacturing and other Retailing Corporations

Internal Revenue Service data provide a most comprehensive profit series of American corporations. Figure 20.6 compares the profits of food retailing corporations with those of corporations in all manufacturing, all retail trade, and all food and kindred products manufacturing. Profits, after taxes, are expressed as a percentage of stockholders' investment.

Over the entire period 1938–61, the profit rates of the various industries followed a roughly parallel pattern. Not until 1949, however, did food retailing corporations register a higher profit rate than the other groups, and that was the only such instance in the entire span of a decade and a half up to 1953. Since 1953, the showing has been reversed and food retailing corporations have been more profitable than the other three categories in all but one year, 1955. In recent years the difference between the profitability of food retailers and all retail trade appeared to widen, whereas the gap between food retailers and food manufacturers has narrowed.

Food Retailers vs. Other Retail Trade

In recent years, not only have food retailers been more profitable than all other areas of retail trade combined, but they also have been more profitable than the individual fields of retail trade.

Figure 20.7 compares the profitability of food retailers and 6 other areas of retailing. In these comparisons, profits (after taxes) are expressed as a percentage of stockholders' investment.

Prior to 1953, food retailing corporations earned about the same average rate of profit as corporations in other fields of retail trade. Since 1953, however, food retailers have enjoyed a consistently higher profit rate than other areas of retail trade, and it appears that the profit gap is widening. In recent years food retailing corporations had a profit rate about twice as great as that of most other areas of retail trade.

[28] Joe S. Bain, "Profit Rate as a Measure of Monopoly Power," *Quarterly Journal of Economics*, Feb. 1940, pp. 271–293.

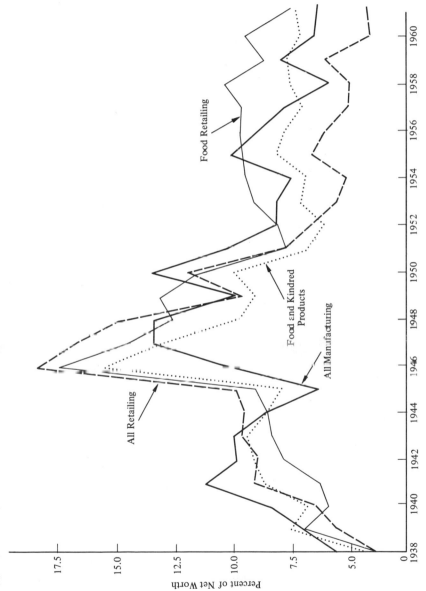

FIGURE 20.6

PROFITS AFTER INCOME TAXES OF MANUFACTURING AND RETAILING CORPORATIONS

TABLE 20.1

SALES, ADVERTISING EXPENDITURES, AND ADVERTISING AS A PERCENT OF SALES OF RETAIL FOOD CORPORATIONS, BY TOTAL ASSETS SIZE, 1945–62

(Dollar figures in millions of dollars)

Year	Total all returns Sales	Total all returns Advertising expenditures[1]	Total all returns Advertising as percent of sales	Under $1,000,000 assets Sales	Under $1,000,000 assets Advertising expenditures	Under $1,000,000 assets Advertising as percent of sales	Over $1,000,000 under $10,000,000 Sales	Over $1,000,000 under $10,000,000 Advertising expenditures	Over $1,000,000 under $10,000,000 Advertising as percent of sales	Over $10,000,000 under $50,000,000 Sales	Over $10,000,000 under $50,000,000 Advertising expenditures	Over $10,000,000 under $50,000,000 Advertising as percent of sales	$50,000,000 and over Sales	$50,000,000 and over Advertising expenditures	$50,000,000 and over Advertising as percent of sales
1945	$5,963	$28	0.5	$1,423	$6	0.4	$1,160	$6	0.5	$1,191	$4	0.4	$2,189	$12	0.6
1946	7,994	35	.4	1,917	8	.4	1,733	8	.5	1,278	4	.3	3,066	15	.5
1947	10,356	49	.5	2,239	11	.5	2,225	11	.5	1,373	6	.4	4,519	21	.5
1948	11,905	56	.5	2,624	14	.5	2,705	15	.6	1,568	6	.4	5,010	21	.4
1949	12,055	65	.5	2,717	18	.6	2,442	15	.6	1,958	8	.4	4,938	24	.5
1950	13,576	74	.6	3,134	21	.7	2,717	17	.6	1,646	7	.4	6,079	29	.5
1951	15,816	86	.6	3,575	23	.6	3,114	21	.7	1,764	7	.4	7,363	35	.5
1952[2]	NA	NA	NA	NA	NA	NA	NA	NA	NA	NA	NA	NA	NA	NA	NA
1953	18,767	115	.6	4,280	34	.8	3,461	27	.8	2,247	13	.6	8,779	41	.5
1954	19,920	135	.7	4,749	42	.9	3,811	31	.8	2,417	16	.7	8,943	46	.5
1955	22,508	172	.8	5,802	56	1.0	4,119	42	1.0	2,404	16	.7	10,183	58	.6
1956	25,078	212	.8	6,158	62	1.0	4,446	51	1.1	2,867	23	.8	11,607	77	.7
1957	27,348	234	.9	7,008	71	1.0	4,448	47	1.1	2,997	30	1.0	12,897	86	.7
1958	26,673	238	.9	6,481	72	1.1	3,698	44	1.2	3,346	34	1.0	13,148	87	.7
1959	28,302	261	.9	10,672	98	1.0	3,837	47	1.2	3,710	45	1.2	10,083	72	.7
1960	30,776	304	1.0	7,675	86	1.1	4,391	56	1.3	4,466	55	1.2	14,244	107	.8
1961	33,634	375	1.1	10,062	114	1.1	4,382	56	1.3	4,257	55	1.3	14,933	150	1.0
1962	35,346	467	1.3	10,636	135	1.3	NA	NA	NA	NA	NA	NA	15,178	206	1.4

Source: *Source Book, Statistics of Income, Corporation Tax Returns,* 1945 to 1962, U.S. Treasury Department, Internal Revenue Service.

1 Advertising first appeared as a separate expense item in the IRS source book in 1945.

2 Source book data was not compiled for 1952.

Food Retailing vs. Food Manufacturing

Figures 20.8 and 20.9 show the profitability of corporations in 10 food manufacturing categories as a percentage of the profitability of food retailing corporations. Profits after taxes as a percent of stockholder equity are used in the comparisons.

Only 3 of the 10 food manufacturing categories enjoyed, in most years, greater profit rates than food retailers. Cereal manufacturers earned substantially greater rates of return in each year during 1950–57, the only years for which cereal manufacturers are given separately.[29] Confectionery corporations enjoyed greater rates of return than food retailers in all but 3 years. The other category to earn consistently higher returns is the N.E.C. (not elsewhere classified) category, which includes firms that are so widely diversified or conglomerated that the I.R.S. does not assign them to a single industry. This category includes several of the largest and most profitable food manufacturing corporations.[30]

Meatpackers and sugar processors consistently earned returns far below those of food retailing corporations.

The above comparisons indicate that since 1950 food retailing corporations as a group have been significantly more profitable than food manufacturing corporations as a group. Of course, this does not imply that all food manufacturing corporations are relatively less profitable than food retailers. In fact, another FTC study shows that large food manufacturing corporations frequently are much more profitable than large food retailers.[31]

Profitability of Food Retailers of Various Sizes

Although food retailing corporations as a group are substantially more profitable than various other industries, there is considerable variation among retailers of various sizes. Figure 20.10 compares the profitability of four size classes of food retail corporations over the period 1938–61.[32] The top grid of the figure uses profits after taxes as a percentage of total assets

[29] Beginning in 1958 cereal manufacturers were combined with grain milling corporations.

[30] In 1961 this category included 120 corporations. The 3 largest corporations had sales of $1,089 million, $168 million, and $115 million, and accounted for 85 percent of the total sales in this category. Internal Revenue Service, *Source Book of Statistics of Income*, 1961–62, Minor Industry, 209, Not Allocable.

[31] Forthcoming report on grocery products manufacturing industries being prepared for the National Commission on Food Marketing by the staff of the Federal Trade Commission.

[32] The number of firms in each size class in 1961 was as follows: large chains (assets over $50 million), 16; medium chains (assets of $10–$50 million), 42; small chains (assets of $1–$10 million), 329; independents (assets under $1 million), 15,192.

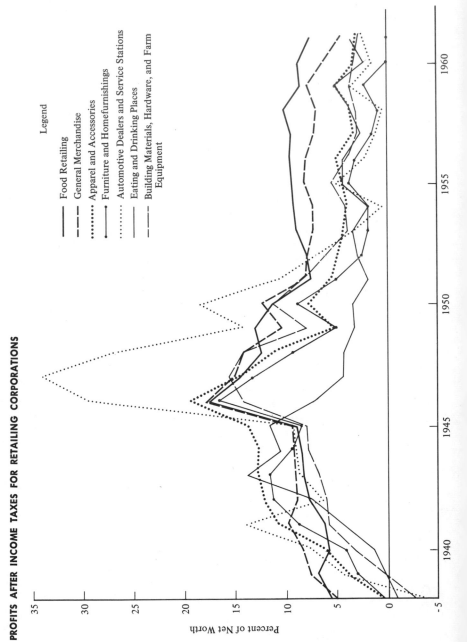

FIGURE 20.7

PROFITS AFTER INCOME TAXES FOR RETAILING CORPORATIONS

Legend

—— Food Retailing
— — General Merchandise
········ Apparel and Accessories
—•— Furniture and Homefurnishings
········ Automotive Dealers and Service Stations
—— Eating and Drinking Places
— — Building Materials, Hardware, and Farm
　　　Equipment

Percent of Net Worth

FIGURE 20.8

**PROFITABILITY OF FOOD MANUFACTURING VS. FOOD RETAILING CORPORATIONS, 1950–1961
(PROFITS AFTER TAXES AS A PERCENT OF STOCKHOLDER EQUITY)**

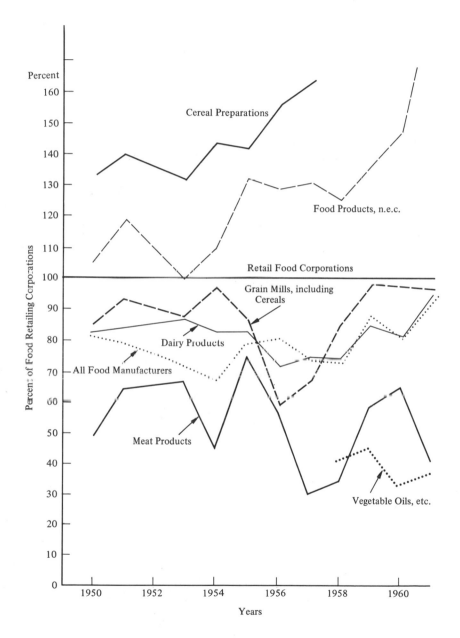

FIGURE 20.9

**PROFITABILITY OF FOOD MANUFACTURING VS. FOOD RETAILING CORPORATIONS, 1950–1961
(PROFITS AFTER TAXES AS A PERCENT OF STOCKHOLDER EQUITY)**

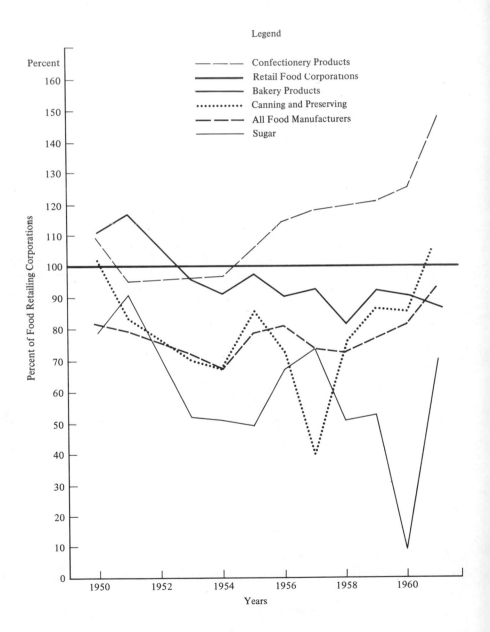

in measuring the pattern of profits.[33] Prior to 1956 the profitability of the four size classes followed a generally parallel pattern, although the "independent" category, retailers with assets below $1 million, was generally below the other categories.

Beginning with 1956 a new pattern of relative profitability began to emerge among the three chain categories. Both the small ($1–$10 million in assets) and medium ($10–$50 million in assets) chain classes declined relative to the large. By 1961 pronounced gaps existed among the three size groups. The largest chains' profit rate was significantly above that of the medium sized chains, about twice that of the small chain class, and about three times that of the independents.

Grids 2 and 3 of Figure 20.10 express profits after taxes as a percentage of stockholder equity and of total sales, respectively. When these measures of relative profitability are used, the same general profit pattern as described above emerges.

Profitability of Retail Food Chains of Various Sizes

Figure 20.11 summarizes the profit experience of 30 chains over the period 1948–64. These chains are divided into three sales size classes.[34]

The top grid of the figure shows, for each group, profits expressed as a percentage of total assets. During the first year covered, small chains had significantly higher profits expressed as a percentage of assets than did medium or large chains. However, in each year since 1957, the profit rate of small chains has been below that of large chains, and after 1959 it fell below that of medium-sized chains. Prior to 1956 the profit rate of medium-sized chains was generally above that of large chains, but thereafter the profit rate of medium chains was consistently below that of large chains.

Grids 2 and 3 of Figure 20.10 show for these three groups of chains their profit expressed as a percentage of net worth and as a percentage of sales. The patterns are generally the same as in Grid 1. However, the gap between the smaller chains and large chains narrowed in 1964. In fact, in 1964 the group of medium-sized chains earned higher profits as a percentage of stockholders' investment than did the largest chains. It should be noted, however, that all of the chains shown in Figure 20.11 were quite large

---

[33] Profits expressed as a percentage of assets are useful in making comparisons among firms within the same industry because frequently firms of different sizes have different ratios of equity to borrowed capital.

[34] These are the 30 largest chains for which profit information is given in financial manuals. The "large" chain class consisted of 10 chains with sales exceeding $500 million in 1963; the medium-sized chains class consisted of 12 chains with sales between $150 million and $500 million in 1963; the small chain class consisted of 8 chains with sales of $50 million to $150 million in 1963.

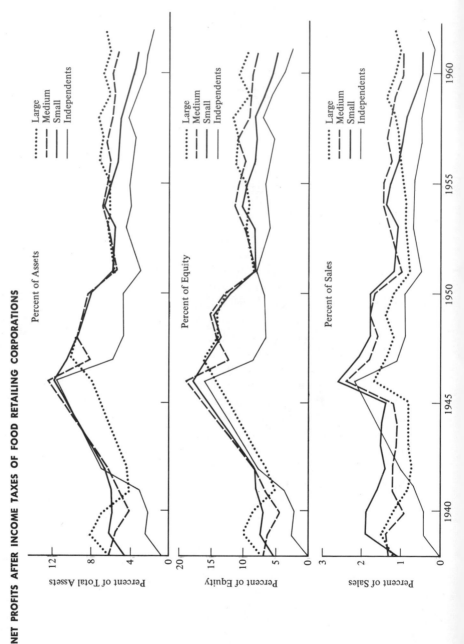

FIGURE 20.10

NET PROFITS AFTER INCOME TAXES OF FOOD RETAILING CORPORATIONS

FIGURE 20.11

POST-INCOME TAX PROFITABILITY OF GROCERY STORE CHAINS

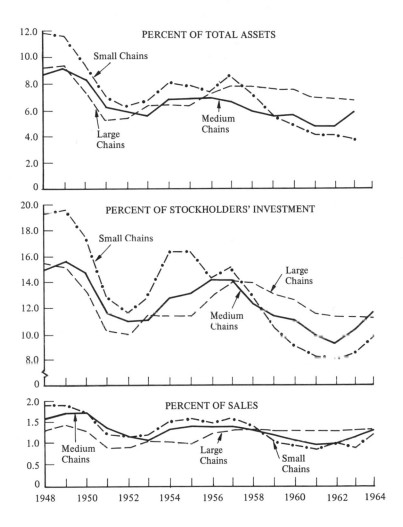

chains. All fell within the "large" and "medium" sized chain category shown in Figure 20.10. In fact, about one-half fell into the "large" category.[35]

SUMMARY OF PEFORMANCE

Substantial changes have occurred in the performance of food retailing over the past four decades. Many of the changes were directly or indirectly associated with the introduction and widespread use of supermarket merchandising.

In the supermarket revolution, gross margins narrowed; but since the mid-1950's, they have widened. Today the gross margins of the largest retailers are not only higher than they were during the early 1950's, but they are higher than they were in the 1920's, when practically all retailers operated very small stores.

Perhaps most significant has been the rapid rise in the largest retailers' gross margins. By 1964 the largest retailers had greater margins than smaller chains and independents. Although most of this increase was due to increasing operating costs, the largest retailers as a group also were more profitable than other retailers as a group. This was in sharp contrast to the situation in the 1930's when large chains generally had lower gross profit margins.

SELECTED READINGS

BOOKS

Harold Barger, *Distribution's Place in the American Economy Since 1869* (Princeton, N.J.: Princeton University Press, 1955).

Reavis Cox in association with Charles S. Goodman and Thomas G. Finchandler, *Distribution in a High-Level Economy* (Englewood Cliffs, N.J.: Prentice-Hall, 1965).

Margaret Hall, John Knapp, and Christopher Winsten, *Distribution in Great Britain and North America: A Study in Structure and Productivity* (London: Oxford University Press, 1961).

Paul W. Stewart and J. Frederic Dewhurst, *Does Distribution Cost Too Much?* (New York: The Twentieth Century Fund, 1939).

Roland S. Vaile, E. T. Grether, and Reavis Cox, *Marketing in the American Economy* (New York: Ronald, 1952), Chapters 31 and 32.

ARTICLES

Joe S. Bain, "Survival-ability as a Test of Efficiency," *American Economic Review*, May 1969, pp. 99 ff.

[35] The "large" chains category shown in figure 38 included the 16 largest chains and the "medium" category included the next 42 largest chains.

James V. Cook, "1970—Can Marketing Measure Up?" in George L. Baker, Jr. (ed.), *Effective Marketing Coordination* (Chicago: American Marketing Association, 1962), pp. 21–27.

Reavis Cox, "Broad Social Forces and the 'Cost Squeeze' in Retailing," in Lynn H. Stockman (ed.), *Advancing Marketing Efficiency* (Chicago: American Marketing Association, 1959), pp. 215–21.

————, and Charles S. Goodman, "Marketing of Housebuilding Materials," *Journal of Marketing*, XXI (July 1965), pp. 33–61.

Edna Douglas, "Size of Firm and the Structure of Costs in Retailing," *Journal of Business*, 25 (April 1962), pp. 158–190.

Horace M. Gray, "Small Business: The Institutional Environment," *A-T Law and Economic Review*, Vol. 1, No. 1 (July-August 1967). (Paper presented to Senate Select Committee on Small Business, March 8, 1967.)

Richard D. Lundy, "How Many Gasoline Service Stations are 'Too Many'?" in Reavis Cox and Wroe Alderson (eds.), *Theory in Marketing* (Chicago: Irwin, 1950), pp. 323–3.

Willard F. Mueller, "Competition, Efficiency, and Antitrust: A Policy Maker's View," in National Industrial Conference Board, *Competition, Efficiency, and Antitrust: Compatibilities and Inconsistencies* (New York: NICB: March 6, 1969).

David A. Revzan, "Evaluation of Channel Effectiveness," *Wholesaling in Marketing Organization* (New York: Wiley, 1961), pp. 151–155.

ADDITIONAL BOOKS

Wroe Alderson, Vern Terpstra, and Stanley J. Shapiro, *Patents and Progress: The Sources and Impact of Advancing Technology* (Homewood, Ill.: Irwin, 1965).

Betty Bock and Jack Farkas, *Concentration and Productivity: Some Preliminary Problems and Findings*, Studies in Business Economics No. 103 (National Industrial Conference Board, 1969).

Richard F. Gift, *Estimating Economic Capacity* (Louisville: University of Kentucky Press, 1968).

Hearings on Economic Concentration, Subcommittee on Antitrust and Monopoly, Committee on the Judiciary, U.S. Senate, Parts 1–6 (Washington, D.C.: Government Printing Office, 1964–1967).

Edwin Mansfield, *Industrial Research and Technological Innovation: An Econometric Analysis* (New York: Norton, for the Cowles Foundation for Research in Economics at Yale University, 1968).

Thomas Marchak, Thomas Glennan, and Robert Summers, *Strategy for R & D: Studies in the Micro-economics of Development* (New York: Springer-Verlag, 1967).

Richard Nelson, Merton Peck, and Edward Kalacheck, *Technology, Economic Growth, and Public Policy*. Washington, D.C.: Brookings Institution, 1967.

Jacob Schmookler, *Invention and Economic Growth* (Cambridge: Harvard University Press, 1966).

W. J. J. Smith and Daniel Creamer, *R & D and Small-Company Growth: A Statistical Review and Company Case Studies*, Studies in Business Economics No. 102 (New York: National Industrial Conference Board, 1968).

C

Market performance:
consumer welfare

Consumer welfare means the extent to which the marketing economy provides satisfaction for consumers. One can take a limited focus and consider
only the satisfaction of immediate wants, that is, first-order effects. Or one
can include all aspects of a consumer's life—the total quality of his life in
the marketing economy. The first two articles—Staff Reports of the Federal
Trade Commission, *Economic Report: On Food Chain Selling Practices in
the District of Columbia and San Francisco* and *Economic Report on Installment Credit and Retail Sales Practices of District of Columbia Retailers*—
offer some problems consumers find in satisfying some immediate wants.
The third article, from Robert Rienow and Leona Train Rienow's *Moment
in the Sun*, discusses part of the total-quality-of-life issue. In both cases,
the reader should remember that these articles are only selections from a
broad assortment of examples in the literature.

Consumer satisfaction in terms of the total quality of life is very complex. In principle, "complete" satisfaction—complete consumer sovereignty
—means a fulfillment of all elements of a want as well as the absence of
any harmful effects. This ideal is often impossible for a number of reasons.

Studies of food prices and margins in low-income areas versus higher
income areas reveal that in many product and geographic markets, the poor
do pay more for the same items. The reason lower-income consumers pay

more is not that supermarket chains and other branch-store operations price discriminate; rather, it is because there are more relatively inefficient stores in ghettos and other low-income areas than in more affluent areas. Also, the quality of produce and meat is frequently lower in low-income stores. Other studies show that ghetto retailers of durables, especially those who offer "easy" credit, have much higher prices than other retailers of the identical items.

Further, if a fully informed consumer perceives a greater net increase in utility from one brand of physically homogeneous offerings, this behavior is not necessarily irrational. Nor is there anything unethical, as long as consumers are informed about the composition of the offerings. In the prescription drug markets, however, some price differences between branded and unbranded offerings of the same drug have not been due to preferences of fully informed consumers. Instead, some very substantial price differences between branded and generic forms of identical drugs have been due to incomplete consumer information, high barriers to entry, and strong control over supply.

With respect to first-order want satisfaction in the marketing economy, the consumer would appear to be well-served in many markets, but there are exceptions, such as the low-income areas. In many markets consumer "sovereignty" is considerable because competition is keen. That is, buyers and sellers are informed, and entry and exit in the market are not artificially blocked.

Although the marketing economy is able in principle and largely in fact to satisfy first-order wants, it probably cannot provide "complete" satisfaction in all aspects of consumers' lives. Burgeoning population and vast, complex industrial processes result in many externalities—air, water, and noise pollution; congestion; and so on. Pollution and contamination continue at a pace which in many cases is now considered almost irreversible.

Psychological states of mind have contributed to the externality problems. For example, the "use-once-and-then-throw-away" and "bigger-is-better" philosophies are now seen as having social costs exceeding their social benefits. All in all, the economic, social, and political orders are closely interrelated in effecting a truly higher *quality of life* for all consumers.

21

Food chain
selling practices in the District of
Columbia and San Francisco

Federal Trade Commission

1. SUMMARY

This study confirms previous Government findings that the distribution
system performs less satisfactorily in low-income areas of our inner cities
than in suburban areas.[1] Many foodstores serving low-income, inner city
areas are small, less efficient, and have higher prices. Consumers in these
areas are frequently sold lower quality merchandise and are provided fewer
services than in other areas. Moreover, the retail facilities of low-income
areas are often old and in a shabby state of upkeep.

On the basis of special investigational surveys and hearings the staff
found no evidence that leading chainstore operators in the District of
Columbia and San Francisco employ discriminatory policies designed to
exploit low-income customers. Each of the largest food chain operators had

[1] *Retail Food Prices in Low and Higher Income Areas*, Bureau of Labor Statistics, U.S.
Department of Labor, February 1969.

From Federal Trade Commission, *Economic Report: On Food Chain Selling
Practices in the District of Columbia and San Francisco* (Washington, D.C.:
United States Government Printing Office, July, 1969), pp. 3–12.

an official policy of price and quality uniformity. To a significant degree, systematic departures from store-to-store price uniformity were discovered. However, for the most part, these involved responses to special competitive situations and could not be interpreted as reflecting an effort to discriminate against low-income customers although that was generally the result.

These findings, however, should not lead one to conclude that food distribution in low-income areas is free of problems, or that the low-income customer does not pay more for food. On the contrary, the reverse is quite likely to be true. Food marketing is not as well organized in low-income areas as in newly developed suburban areas. There simply are not as many modern, efficient supermarkets in low-income areas as there are elsewhere. Thus, the low-income consumer is more likely to do his shopping at a small, independent mom-and-pop store. Such stores generally charge higher prices, whether located in low- or high-income areas. At the same time those supermarkets which are operating in low-income areas generally face less intense competition than they would elsewhere. The lack of competition means there is less pressure to maintain tight managerial control, to improve quality and service, or to lower prices.

Although departures from official company price lists are occasionally authorized to dispose of distressed perishable merchandise, differences in competitive conditions clearly outweigh this as a reason for deviations from official areawide prices. Deviations from areawide prices of chain organizations most frequently occur where stores of one chain meet those of other chains in strong "head-to-head" competition. In these areas special price reductions are frequently authorized, more concern is shown for the appearance of physical facilities and the quality of services provided, and there are more extensive promotional efforts, including the giving away of things of value, such as prizes in promotional games. In many instances authorized price reductions amount to several cents per dollar of total store sales. It is highly significant that not once during the period investigated in this study did a "special competitive situation" occur in an inner-city poverty area in either of the two cities studied.

The structural characteristic that is primarily responsible for ineffective competition in low-income inner-city areas is an inadequate number of supermarket competitors. To a great extent, the condition of entry into the low-income central city is related to entry conditions and the degree of competition in the metropolitan area as a whole. In these aspects of competitive structure there are important differences between the two cities studied —Washington, D.C., and San Francisco—that may in part explain the performance differences found between the two cities. Concentration of grocery store sales is very high in the Washington, D.C., metropolitan area —the highest of all major U.S. cities. The four largest chains of the Washington metropolitan area accounted for 67 percent of total grocery store sales. This percentage was half again higher than the average for other cities ranking among the 20 largest. San Francisco, on the other hand, ranked low in sales concentration among major cities. The four largest chains in the San Francisco metropolitan area accounted for only 33 percent of total grocery store sales. Concentration of supermarket sales in the inner city is much higher. In the District of Columbia, which is somewhat larger than the "inner city" of the metropolitan area, the four largest food chains accounted for 83 percent of supermarket sales.

Entry barriers into the Washington market also appear to be high. Within the last decade two chains have attempted to break into the Washington market. One of these has abandoned its attempt and the other has achieved only marginal success. The Kroger Co., the Nation's third largest grocery chain, entered the market in 1960 with the purchase of a small local chain. After making a substantial effort to expand its market share, Kroger sold its Washington area stores in 1966 to another grocery chain operating in the area.

The second chain that attempted to enter was an aggressive low-margin food retailer from the New Jersey area, which had a history of successful entry into several markets before attempting to enter the Washington market. This chain came into the Washington market by opening three stores. It has since closed two of them. Just prior to this chain's entry into the Washington market, the stores of two leading Washington area chains located near the stores of the new entrant cut their prices substantially below those charged in the rest of the metropolitan area. In doing so, these stores operated on abnormally low margins and—for those stores for which data were available—sustained substantial losses.

Special competitive pricing situations were not the only variations in food chain conduct due to competition. Pricing surveys conducted by the Federal Trade Commission staff reveal that food chain promotional activities also varied according to the competitive setting of the store. Specifically, advertised special items were more frequently unavailable in less competitive, low-income area stores than in more competitive, higher income area and suburban stores.

Prices of advertised special items present substantial savings to purchasers. Sales of advertised special items during a typical week commonly reduce the average price level of a store by 5 percent. Those customers that take full advantage of the specials can save 10 percent or more on their weekly food bills. The availability or unavailability of specials therefore is an important aspect of pricing conduct. Federal Trade Commission price surveys of stores of Washington area chains found that 23 percent of advertised special items were not available in low-income area stores as compared to only 11 percent not available in higher income area stores. In San Francisco the percentages were 7 and 5 percent, respectively. In addition to unavailability, advertised special items were also frequently found to be mispriced. For both cities, an average of 7 to 8 percent of advertised special items available in stores was found to be mispriced. There were three chances in four that the incorrect price was higher than the advertised price.

In addition to advertised specials, variations in many nonprice dimensions of chainstore conduct affecting the values received by customers were also related to competitive conditions. Although the FTC price surveys were primarily designed to record price and availability information, the checkers also observed various quality characteristics. An analysis of these reveals substantial differences in the appearance of perishable products such as produce and meat items packaged in the store.

The policy of the largest chain in the Washington, D.C., metropolitan area in distributing $1,000 winners in its games-of-change promotion further illustrates the manner in which merchandising and promotion policies may be varied depending upon competitive conditions. During 1966, this chain awarded 48 $1,000 winners in the area served by its Washington division. Yet, whereas the central city represented by the District of Columbia contained 30 percent of the division's stores, only two of the 48 $1,000 winners were awarded in stores located in the District. Both prizes were awarded by stores in upper-income areas located at the far Northwest fringe of the District. The winners themselves lived in suburban Maryland. Available information indicates that the distribution of the balance of prize money— 85 percent of the total—approximated the distribution of store locations. Some other leading chains in the Washington area also systematically allocated their major winners to certain stores; however, data were not available to determine how this allocation affected different areas.

During investigational hearings conducted over a 9-month period, the major food chains in the Washington, D.C., and San Francisco metropolitan areas explained their pricing systems and submitted various documents relevant to understanding them. Hundreds of pages of testimony were taken. Although some conflicting evidence was presented, none of the testimony indicated that any of the chains engaged in discrimination aimed specifically at low-income areas. The price and nonprice policies of chains appeared to be attuned to the competitive circumstances in which individual stores operated.

Finally, the evidence indicated that most chains had insufficient central office control over the operations of individual stores to prevent extensive mispricing of individual items. Price surveys indicated that between 5 and 10 percent of the prices found in the stores of a chain differed from those officially authorized by the chain for the dates of the surveys. For items not offered as "specials," there appeared to be a near equal likelihood that the unauthorized prices would be either high or low.

POLICY ALTERNATIVES

There are two general approaches to improving the quality of low-income area food retailing. One focuses on conduct, with a view to preventing excessive mispricing and unavailability of advertised items. The other focuses on changing the structure of the market to make it more competitive. Performance of low-income area supermarkets would likely improve if more supermarket competitors entered the low-income area market.

Before turning to policy alternatives, a word of caution should be raised concerning oversimplified solutions to complicated problems. A frequently proposed reform for lowering food costs to low-income area residents would require food chains to charge the same prices and provide the same product quality and arrays of services in their low-income area stores as in their suburban area stores. This is a simple approach, but like so many simple approaches it may overlook essential facts. The primary reason low-income inner-city residents pay more for food is that there are too few supermarkets in these areas. Most chains serving our major cities avoid operating in the low-income inner city and many chains that once operated in those areas withdrew to the suburbs as the inner city became a less desirable place to operate. Were it not for the few chain and independent supermarkets remaining in low-income inner-city areas, food prices to the poor would be higher. Therefore ill-founded price regulations could hasten the day when many of the remaining supermarket companies will have abandoned the inner city. In situations where costs are higher in the inner city they must be covered. Short of a Government subsidy of some sort, such higher costs must ultimately be reflected in prices charged and services offered. This fact must be recognized in efforts to increase the availability of supermarkets in the inner city.

Regulation of Conduct

This study found that in a great many instances advertised items were out of stock or that prices had not been marked down in accordance with the advertisements.[2] For all chainstores surveyed in Washington, 14 percent of items advertised were unavailable; in San Francisco, 6 percent of items advertised could not be found on the shelves. In both cities unavailability rates were substantially higher in low-income areas.

[2] See . . . pp. 26–32 [of the original article].

The use of advertised "specials" is a key element in the competitive strategy of supermarkets. While many consumers trade at the same supermarket week after week, others comparison shop or can be persuaded by lower advertised prices to switch their loyalties to another store in order to save money. Since consumers cannot make price comparisons for the thousands of items in a supermarket, their attention is most likely to be drawn by specials advertised in newspapers or featured through displays within the store. A study of food store pricing states:

> There are a few items such as coffee, flour, sugar, soap powders, and the like which each store feels must be in a majority of its "ads," since consumers are generally well informed concerning their prices and some will transfer their patronage from one store to another if a substantial price difference on these items are noted.[3]

While such items may be sold at or near cost, the store will profit if additional customers are attracted, as they usually will also buy many other items at regular prices. Even so, customers benefit substantially from low-priced specials. It has been estimated that consumers can save 10 percent or more on their total food bills by taking full advantage of such specials.[4]

To the consumer who is drawn to a store by advertised specials, their unavailability represents both inconvenience and higher costs. Supermarkets, of course, will occasionally run out of an advertised item because of an unexpected heavy demand. However, if a retailer habitually advertises items when quantity is insufficient to meet demand, this constitutes a form of deceptive advertising.

The need for a seller to maintain adequate stocks of advertised items has previously been emphasized in the Federal Trade Commission's *Guides Against Bait Advertising*.[5] These guides define bait advertising as "an alluring but insincere offer to sell a product or service which the advertiser in truth does not intend or want to sell. Its purpose is to switch consumers from buying the advertised merchandise, in order to sell something else, usually at a higher price."[6] The offer that food chains make in their advertisements to sell at stated prices is, of course, not completely insincere, but will still tend to be misleading if adequate stocks of the advertised items are not maintained. Section 3(c) of the guides goes on to point out that one of

---

[3] Bob R. Holdren, *The Structure of a Retail Market and the Market Behavior of Retail Units*, Prentice-Hall, 1960, p. 95.

[4] See . . . p. 26 [of the original article].

[5] *Guides Against Bait Advertising*, adopted by the Federal Trade Commission, Nov. 24, 1959.

[6] *Ibid.*, p. 1.

the factors to be considered in determining if an advertisement is a bona-fide offer is:

> * * * the failure to have available at all outlets listed in the advertisement a sufficient quantity of the advertised product to meet reasonably anticipated demands, unless the advertisement clearly and adequately discloses that supply is limited and/or the merchandise is available only at designated outlets.[7]

Section 5 of the Federal Trade Commission Act, in a broader sense, declares unlawful "unfair methods of competition in commerce, and unfair or deceptive acts or practices in commerce." The Commission can take a variety of steps to combat such practices, including issuance of further guides or the filing of complaints.

It would appear that the simplest and most effective remedy is for food chains themselves to make sure that adequate stocks of advertised items are available. Beyond this, policies can be adopted to deal with infrequent cases where items would be out of stock. At present, some chains have "raincheck" policies that permit the customer to obtain the advertised item for the same price at a later date if it is out of stock. These policies are not an adequate remedy. They impose no real penalty on the store and, thus, no incentive to maintain sufficient stocks. Since many customers will not bother to obtain "rainchecks," the store may still find it advantageous to run out of low-price special items. Also, there is no compensation to the customer for the inconvenience incurred. He may want or need an item now, rather than next week; or he may not want to take the time necessary to obtain a "raincheck." One possible alternative would be to offer the customer an item of like or higher quality if stocks of the advertised item are depleted. Thus, if a store is out of hamburger at a "special" price, it would provide the customer with ground round at the same price. Another alternative would be to permit the customer the same discount on another item if the advertised item is unavailable. Thus, if hamburger is reduced in price 10 percent per pound, the customer would be permitted at least a 10-percent reduction on a substitute cut of meat.

In addition to the maintenance of adequate stocks of advertised items, food chains should also conspicuously post prices of such items in all stores. The price of each advertised item should be clearly indicated on the item and at its position on the shelf. Shelf markers should remain in place during those infrequent instances when the store runs out of stock and a notice could be added indicating an item that could be purchased at the same or greater discount than the advertised item. A list of advertised items should

---

[7] *Ibid.*, p. 2.

be posted at all checkout counters and at other strategic spots throughout the store, such as near the meat counter and on bulletin boards. This will assist consumers in taking maximum advantage of advertised specials, without the necessity of referring to sometimes confusing newspaper advertisements.

Many of the problems of mispricing and unavailability of items appear to occur at the individual store level. There was a great deal of variation from store to store within a given chain, and generally those stores with the highest out-of-stock rates were located in low-income areas. Stores in these areas faced considerably less competition than those in higher income areas. The pressure of competition undoubtedly forces stores in higher income areas to keep advertised items available, because if customers became dissatisfied they would have the alternative of going to another store. In low-income areas the lack of competition allows store managers to become quite careless in maintaining stocks. If the customers are dissatisfied, there is little they can do, as they cannot conveniently shift their patronage to another store. Given this lack of competition, it is the responsibility of the chainstore management to exercise closer supervision over stores in low-income areas. The corporate management of food chains may find it necessary to adopt additional controls over low-income area stores, including more frequent price and inventory checks, stronger supervision at the district level, and changes in the manner in which store managers are assigned and compensated. At present, it appears, that the least efficient managers often are assigned to low-income area stores. These managers may be tempted to cut corners to improve their stores' performance. It would be desirable to organize manager compensation plans so that better quality store managers would be attracted to low-income area stores.

Beyond the question of discrimination against low-income consumers, this study has found that several aspects of food chain behavior in general leave a great deal to be desired. In both low- and high-income areas, items on grocery shelves are mispriced or incorrectly marked far too often. Food chains claimed that a certain amount of mismarking is an inevitable result of human error. Mispricing rates found in our surveys, however, far exceeded those considered tolerable even by the management of some food chains.[8] In both Washington, D.C., and San Francisco, 7 percent of the market-basket items surveyed were mispriced. Several chains had 10 percent or more items mispriced. These error rates indicate a degree of carelessness and laxity which should not be tolerated in the supervision over prices. It is the

---

[8] Other studies have found similar mispricing rates. The Department of Agriculture's six city survey revealed mispricing ranging from 4 to 31 percent. The St. Louis Better Business Bureau study revealed a 5-percent mispricing rate for supermarkets in that city. See app. III [of the original article].

responsibility of food chain management not just to issue general policy directives on pricing but also to see that these policies are implemented in full at the individual store level. Such errors in marking of prices add an element of confusion and make the task of intelligent choice more difficult for shoppers. As an additional means for reducing the frequency of deviations from authorized prices, food chain management might require each store manager to post a list of currently authorized prices at a convenient location in his store.

Action by Consumers

An important source of protection against deceptive advertising and pricing can be provided by consumers themselves. The powers of an agency, such as the Federal Trade Commission or any Government body, to monitor prices of individual stores are limited. However, an educated and aware body of consumers can help to keep store prices in line with advertisements and keep unavailability rates low. Consumer education groups should stress the importance of comparison shopping, of checking to see that actual prices correspond to advertised prices, and of informing consumers where to direct their complaints against unfair or deceptive acts. In addition, a meaningful consumer education program, both within the school system and through adult education groups, can help low-income consumers get more for their dollars. Studies have shown that many low-income consumers buy national brands even when private label items of similar quality are substantially less expensive. Such shopping habits are costly and may lead low-income area stores to place less emphasis on price competition. Low-income consumers also tend to buy in small quantities and to ignore the advantage of low prices on larger size cans and packages.

The Federal Trade Commission, in cooperation with other Government agencies, is developing a collection of consumer information pamphlets.[9] These can alert the consumer to common forms of fraud and deception and inform him as to where he may best direct complaints against unfair or deceptive retail practices. Properly directed consumer complaints are an integral part of any consumer education and protection program. Complaints received from consumers help give direction to educational and informational efforts and, at the same time, assist the Commission in determining priorities in an enforcement program designed to eliminate the most prevalent harmful practices. An alert consumer through his own awareness

[9] Recent publications by the Federal Trade Commission aimed at consumer education include: *Fight Back!*, *Unordered Merchandise—Shipper's Obligations and Consumer's Rights*, and *Pitfalls to Watch for in Mail Order Insurance Policies*. These and other materials may be obtained from the Commission.

can eliminate or forestall many unfair or deceptive retail practices. Failing this, he has both the right and the responsibility to inform a consumer protection agency so that appropriate corrective action may be initiated.

Consumer awareness among low-income persons can be increased further through local buying clubs and similar groups. These groups can study local stores, compare prices and availability, and circulate bulletins about low-cost specials currently available.

IMPROVING MARKET STRUCTURE

Though steps noted above may help to improve the functioning of low-income, inner-city food markets, changes in the competitive structure will also have a salutary impact. An increase in the number of supermarket firms not only would broaden the range of consumer alternatives, but also would tend to intensify price competition and upgrade customer services. The major problems associated with food retailing in low-income areas are not a product of unscrupulous operators, nor are they likely to be corrected simply by consumer protest. Industrial and marketing experience demonstrates that the most dependable method of generating effective services to the consumer is through a favorable competitive structure.

The market structure of food retailing in the inner-city area appears unfavorable to competition, particularly in the District of Columbia. Supermarkets are few and almost all of the supermarkets are owned by one chain. In suburban areas, on the other hand, where several food chains operate, there is pressure on each chain to improve its services and to keep its prices in line. The presence of special competitive zones in some areas where new competition has entered reflects this pressure. Yet, special competitive situations are unlikely to develop in low-income areas where one food chain dominates the market and the market conditions are not conducive to the entry of new competition.

A first step in improving the performance of food retailing in low-income areas, therefore, is to encourage more competitors to enter the market and to build modern supermarkets in such areas. New entrants as noted, however, are faced with substantial barriers to entry into low-income area food retailing. It is unlikely that any large number of supermarkets will be built in low-income areas without some Government incentives or subsidies. These need not be costly, however, and a great deal could be accomplished by simply coordinating planning for supermarkets with present urban renewal and poverty programs.

One of the most serious barriers to entry is availability of land in the inner city. Land is both expensive and hard to obtain. A company must often piece together several properties to get a site large enough to build a moderate size supermarket. Parking space is an additional problem. Urban renewal and model city programs, however, are designed to make major changes in the inner city. Careful consideration should be given in these programs to provision of adequate space for supermarkets. Supermarkets could also be built in conjunction with public housing projects, recreation centers, and schools. The objective should be to provide two or more competing supermarkets within a convenient shopping radius of most inner-city residents.

Although facilities for supermarkets have been provided in previous urban renewal projects, more consideration should be given to competitive structure in allocating space for such facilities. Smaller chains and independent supermarkets should also be encouraged to locate in such areas. To do so may require special efforts by the Small Business Administration. The aim should be not only to build more supermarkets, but also to establish more independent competitors.

A further problem facing new entrants into low-income area food retailing is sources of financing. Banks and financial institutions are often reluctant to make loans for building of stores in low-income areas. A Government program of guaranteeing loans for entrants into low-income area food retailing may, therefore, be desirable.

In addition, new entrants often have problems in obtaining insurance. Fear of loss through theft, vandalism, or riots, for which compensation could not be obtained, therefore deters firms from entering low-income areas. Innovation in insurance plans for protection against such risks appears a necessity. This insurance could either be provided directly by the Federal Government, or could be written by private companies with Government guarantees. One possibility would be for the Government to underwrite all physical losses resulting from civil disorders.

Supermarkets locating in low-income areas may also have manpower problems. Assistance here is potentially available through existing Government programs. The Department of Labor and the Office of Economic Opportunity could train unemployed and unskilled residents of low-income areas to work in supermarkets. This would offer a dual benefit, provide nearby employment and improve retail services.

Management may also need assistance in establishing stores in low-income areas. Product lines and merchandising strategy that are appropriate for middle-income areas may not necessarily be best for low-income areas. Studies should be made of techniques used by those supermarkets that now operate successfully in low-income areas. There are some indications that, in order to operate most effectively in low-income areas, supermarkets need to be especially flexible in adapting their product lines and merchandising strategy to the particular needs of these areas. For this reason some small chains and independents may be better suited for operation in low-income areas than large national chains whose policies have been developed primarily to serve middle-income consumers.

In addition to Government agencies, industry groups and trade associations can conduct studies on means of expanding supermarket operations in low-income areas. Organizations such as the Super Market Institute could make a valuable contribution by studying the requirements for successful operations in low-income areas and by conducting training programs for prospective entrants. At present a number of independent supermarkets and small chains appear to be operating successfully in low-income areas.[10] The management techniques and methods of operation of these successful operators do not appear to be widely known and deserve further study. A forum should be created for the exchange of ideas and techniques among food retailers, Government agencies, and the consuming public. In this way the food industry itself could do a great deal to help reshape the structure of low-income area retailing so that it would serve the consumer more adequately.

Too little is known at the present time as to the most effective mix of public and private effort needed to improve marketing conditions for distributing food and other consumer products in low-income areas. Clearly, improvement is in order, as shown by this study and by an earlier study of household furnishings and appliances.[11] Many new approaches to this problem sponsored by both public and private agencies, are currently subject to experimentation. Certain older programs involving urban renewal and loan guarantee programs are being reevaluated and revised. In a substantive sense, decision-making in these areas is beyond the jurisdiction of the Federal Trade Commission. Nevertheless, the Commission's experience in trade regulation indicates that prominent consideration should be given to competitive effects in evaluating programs for new business to enter or locate within the inner city.

---

[10] For example, low-income area supermarkets have been successful in Boston, Chicago and in the Watts section of Los Angeles. See: "Should Supermarkets Take a New Look at Urban Areas," *Food Topics*, February 1967, pp. 11–22. Also, "Making It In a Ghetto Super," *Chain Store Age*, September 1967, p. 84.

[11] Federal Trade Commission, *Economic Report on Installment Credit and Retail Sales Practices of District of Columbia Retailers, March 1968.*

22

Installment credit
and retail sales practices
of District of Columbia retailers—
summary and conclusions

Federal Trade Commission

This report presents the results of a survey of installment credit and sales practices involving household furnishings and appliances in the District of Columbia. The purpose of the survey was to obtain a factual picture of the finance charges, prices, gross margins and profits, legal actions taken in collecting delinquent accounts, and the assignment relationships between retailers and finance companies. The survey covered those D.C. retailers of furniture and appliances having estimated sales of at least $100,000 for the year 1966. The 96 retailers providing data had combined sales of $226 million, which represented about 85 percent of the sales of furniture, appliance, and department store retailers in the District of Columbia.

USE OF INSTALLMENT CREDIT BY
D.C. RETAILERS

Sixty-five retailers with combined sales of $151 million indicated regular use of consumer installment sales contracts. The remainder sold only for

From Federal Trade Commission, *Economic Report on Installment Credit and Retail Sales Practices of District of Columbia Retailers* (Washington, D.C.: United States Government Printing Office, March 1968), pp. ix–xvi.

cash or on a regular or revolving charge account basis. This report focuses primarily on retailers using installment contracts. These retailers were classified into two groups: those appealing primarily to low-income customers and those appealing to a more general market.

D.C. stores varied widely in their use of installment credit. Some general market discount appliance stores made very few sales on credit. At the other extreme, a number of low-income market retailers sold entirely on installment credit.

Installment credit was used much more extensively by retailers selling to low-income consumers than by retailers selling to other consumers. Low-income market retailers used installment credit in 93 percent of their sales. The comparable figure for general market retailers was 27 percent.

CUSTOMER CHARACTERISTICS OF LOW-INCOME MARKET RETAILERS

A sample of installment sales contracts and credit applications was analyzed to identify the customer characteristics of low-income market retailers. The analysis revealed substantial differences between customers of the low-income market retailers and all residents of the District of Columbia. The average family size was larger—4.3 persons compared to an average of 3.5 persons for the District of Columbia. Almost half of the families of customers in the sample had five or more members. The median family income during 1966 of the sample customers was $348 per month. This is very low considering the larger than average size of the families. The Bureau of Labor Statistics recently estimated that the maintenance of a moderate standard of living for four in Washington, D.C., requires a monthly income of $730.

Most customers were engaged in low-paying jobs. The largest proportion, 28 percent, were Service Workers, such as waitresses and janitors. Second in importance were Operatives (including such occupations as taxi drivers and laundry workers). Laborers and Domestic Workers also represented a significant share of the sample. Together, these 4 major occupational groups accounted for 75 percent of the customer sample. In comparison, only 36 percent of the general population in the District was classified in these low-paying occupational groups. There were 31 welfare recipients in the sample, accounting for 6 percent of all customers in the sample. There were also a number of customers in the sample dependent on social security, alimony, support payments, and income received from relatives.

A review of credit references noted in the 486 contracts subjected to detailed analysis revealed that 70 percent indicated no credit references or references with low-income market retailers only. Only 30 percent of the customers of this retailer, therefore, had established credit with general market retailers.

GROSS MARGINS AND PRICES OF LOW-INCOME MARKET RETAILERS

The survey disclosed that without exception low-income market retailers had high average markups and prices. On the average, goods purchased for $100 at wholesale sold for $255 in the low-income market stores, compared with $159 in general market stores.

Contrasts between the markup policies of low-income and general market retailers are most apparent when specific products are compared. Retailers surveyed were asked to give the wholesale and retail prices for their two best-selling models in each product line. These price data are typical of the large volume of products sold by each class of retailer.

For every product specified, low-income market retailers had the highest average gross margins reported. When similar makes and models are compared, the differences are striking. For example, the wholesale cost of a portable TV set was about $109 to both a low-income market and a general market retailer. The general market retailer sold the set for $129.95, whereas the low-income market retailer charged $219.95 for the same set. Another example is a dryer, wholesaling at about $115, which was sold for $150 by a general market retailer and for $300 by a low-income market retailer.

OPERATING EXPENSES AND NET PROFITS OF RETAILERS SURVEYED

Despite their substantially higher prices, net profit on sales for low-income market retailers was only slightly higher and net profit return on net worth was considerably lower when compared to general market retailers. It appears that salaries and commissions, bad-debt losses, and other expenses are substantially higher for low-income market retailers. Profit and expense comparisons are, of course, affected by differences in type of operation and accounting procedures. However, a detailed analysis was made for retailers of comparable size and merchandise mix to minimize such differences.

Low-income market retailers reported the highest return after taxes on net sales, 4.7 percent. Among the general market retailers, department stores had the highest return on net sales, 4.6 percent. Furniture and home furnishings stores earned a net profit after taxes of 3.9 percent; and appliance, radio, and television retailers were the least profitable with a net profit of only 2.1 percent on sales.

Low-income market retailers reported an average rate of return on *net worth* after taxes of 10.1 percent. Rates of return on net worth varied considerably among various kinds of general market retailers. Appliance, radio, and television retailers reported the highest rate of return after taxes, 20.3 percent of net worth. Next in order were furniture and home furnishings retailers with 17.6 percent and department stores with 13 percent on net worth.

ASSIGNMENT OF INSTALLMENT CONTRACTS

Low-income market retailers typically held their installment contracts and did not assign them to finance companies or banks. Only one-fifth of the total contracts were assigned by low-income market retailers. Among general market retailers, appliance stores assigned almost all (98 percent) of their contracts to finance companies and banks. General market furniture stores assigned somewhat more than half of their contracts (57 percent). Among the retailers surveyed, only the department store category involved no contract assignment.

FINANCE CHARGES ON INSTALLMENT CONTRACTS [1]

There is considerable variation in the finance charges of D.C. retailers of furniture and appliances, particularly among the low-income market retailers. Most of the retailers surveyed determined finance charges in terms of an "add-on" rate based on the unpaid cash balance. When calculated on an effective annual rate basis, finance charges of general market retailers varied between 11 percent and 29 percent, averaging 21 percent when contracts were assigned and 19 percent when retailers financed their own contracts. Finance charges by low-income market retailers imposing such charges ranged between 11 and 33 percent per annum, averaging 25 percent on contracts assigned to finance companies and 23 percent on contracts the retailers held themselves.

One low-income market retailer made no separate charge for installment

[1] These are finance charges as reported by D.C. retailers on their installment contracts. They do not necessarily reflect actual costs of granting installment credit.

credit. All of his finance charges were, in effect, included in the purchase price. Other low-income market retailers kept finance charges below the actual cost of granting credit. This practice of absorbing credit costs can give the illusion of "easy" credit, but the customer may be paying a great deal for such installment credit in the form of much higher prices.

JUDGMENTS, GARNISHMENTS AND REPOSSESSIONS BY RETAILERS

One of the most notable facts uncovered by the study relates to the frequency with which a small group of retailers utilized the courts to enforce their claims with respect to installment contracts. Eleven of the 18 low-income market retailers reported 2,690 judgments in 1966. Their legal actions resulted in 1,568 garnishments and 306 repossessions. For this group, one court judgment was obtained for every $2,200 of sales. In effect, low-income market retailers make extensive use of the courts in collecting debts. While general market retailers may take legal action as a last resort against delinquent customers, some low-income market retailers depend on legal action as a normal order of business.

CONCLUSION

Installment credit is widely used in marketing appliances and home furnishings to low-income families. Often these families purchase durable goods, such as furniture, television sets, and phonographs, through the mechanism of "easy" credit. Low-income market retailers specialize in granting credit to consumers who do not seek or are unable to obtain credit from regular department, furniture, or appliance stores. As a group, low-income market retailers made about 93 percent of their sales through installment credit.

The real cost of this "easy" credit is very dear, however. Primarily it takes the form of higher product prices. Credit charges, when separately stated, are not notably higher than those imposed by general market retailers. Though some low-income market retailers imposed effective annual finance charges as high as 33 percent, others charged much less or nothing at all. Markups on comparable products, however, are often two or three times higher than those charged by general market retailers.

The findings of this study suggest that the marketing system for distribution of durable goods to low-income consumers is costly. Although their markups are very much higher than those of general market retailers, low-income market retailers do not make particularly high net profits. They have markedly higher costs, partly because of high bad-debt expenses, but to a greater extent because of higher salaries and commissions as a percent of sales. These expenses reflect in part greater use of door-to-door selling and expenses associated with the collection and processing of installment contracts.

The high prices charged by low-income market retailers suggest the absence of effective price competition. What competition there is among low-income market retailers apparently takes the form of easier credit availability, rather than of lower prices. Greater credit risks are taken to entice customers. Insofar as the problem for low-income consumers is availability of credit, merchants who sell to them focus on this element.

The success of retailers who price their merchandise on such a high markup in selling to low-income families leads inevitably to the conclusion that such families engage in little comparative shopping. It would appear that many low-income customers lack information or knowledge of their credit charges and credit source alternatives, or of the prices and quality of products available in general market retailing establishments. To the extent that door-to-door sales techniques are utilized, such families frequently make crucial purchases without leaving the home and without seeing the products they commit themselves to buy. The fact that low-income market retailers emphasize the use of door-to-door salesmen both reflects and encourages such behavior. The Commission is well aware that door-to-door selling, as well as home-demonstration selling, provides an opportunity for deceptive and high pressure sales techniques. Moreover, such selling methods are also very high-cost methods of distribution. It would appear, therefore, that the low-income consumers who can least afford mistakes in their buying decisions face two serious problems when they are confronted with a door-to-door or home-demonstration sales approach—(1) the high cost of this sales technique will ultimately be borne by the purchaser, and (2) the opportunity for high pressure or deceptive selling is great, thus discouraging comparative shopping and enhancing the probability that the consumer will agree to purchases he would otherwise not want.

While public policy can help solve the problems of low-income consumers, legislation alone may not be sufficient. Legislation aimed at disclosure and regulation of finance charges will help low-income as well as other consumers make more rational buying decisions. Intensified programs on both state and federal levels to eliminate all deceptions and frauds in the advertising and oral representations of the terms of sale and credit charges will also help to ensure that their money is spent advantageously. The poor, to a considerable extent, however, are not sophisticated shoppers. Many cannot afford the luxury of "shopping around" because their potential sources of credit are limited. Others, because of inadequate consumer education or lack of mobility, simply do not engage in comparison shopping.

Thus, in attempting to deal with the phenomenon of the poor paying more for consumer goods, every effort should be made to improve consumer counseling. Many customers continue to buy from low-income market retailers even though they have sufficient income to qualify for credit at stores selling for less. Greater community effort in consumer education is needed.

Beyond the matter of education is the question of credit availability. Many low-income families are quite capable of making regular payments. They should have the option of making payments on reasonably priced merchandise. Local community effort in the development of effective credit sources could contribute materially to freeing individuals from dependence on "easy" credit merchants.[2] Moreover, perhaps general market retailers can take steps to make it easier for low-income families to apply for and receive credit. Some retailers have already found that they can do so economically. Various community business organizations might consider ways of more actively encouraging low-income families to seek credit from retailers selling for less.

Increased competition for the patronage of low-income consumers would go a long way toward resolving many of the problems confronting them in the low-income market. Public policy should consider the various ways by which new entrants could be encouraged into these markets to increase the competitive viability of these markets.

While the availability of credit is perhaps the major reason why low-income families purchase from the low-income market retailers, it is only logical to conclude that the sales techniques of these retailers are also an important factor. Low-income market retailers have every incentive to continue these techniques since their risk of loss is substantially reduced by their virtually unopposed access to judgment and garnishment proceedings to enforce payment or secure repossession. The 2,600 actions taken by 11 low-income market retailers in 1966 suggest a marketing technique which includes actions against default as a normal matter of business rather than as a matter of last resort. At present, in the face of default, creditors can seek both repossession and payment of the deficiency, including various penalties. It may be appropriate to require creditors to choose one or the other of these legal remedies, and not to have the option of pursuing both courses simultaneously. Repossession would then fully discharge the merchant's claim. It is equally necessary to ensure that purchasers receive *actual*

---

[2] Credit unions organized to serve low-income people may be one answer to the problem. More than 400 Federal credit unions now serve substantially low-income groups. The Bureau of Federal Credit Unions, U.S. Department of Health, Education, and Welfare, is attempting to increase this number through its "Project Moneywise." With proper counseling and organization, credit unions can be successful even with very low-income groups.

notice of any such proceedings and have legal counsel available to defend them in court. Perhaps, consideration should also be given to some form of negotiation before a court-appointed neighborhood referee as a compulsory prelude to a default judgment.

It is apparent that the solution to the problem of installment credit for the poor requires a variety of actions. A requirement that finance charges be clearly and conspicuously stated is a necessary but not a sufficient solution to the problem of installment credit for those consumers who are considered poor credit risks and are unsophisticated buyers. Among the complementary steps which might be considered are the following: (1) make reasonable credit more accessible; (2) provide counseling services which will encourage customers to practice comparison shopping; (3) equalize the legal rights of buyers and creditors in installment credit transactions; (4) encourage additional businesses to enter the low-income market; and (5) intensify consumer protection activities on both federal and local levels to eliminate all fraud and deceptions in the advertising and offering of credit.

23

Our rising
standard
of poisons

Robert Rienow and Leona Train Rienow

Biologist Rachel Carson has been accused, because of her *Silent Spring*, of "pushing the panic button" in regard to the progressive poisoning of our total environment by man-made toxicants. It was not Rachel Carson who pushed the panic button. It was the production experts who have been leaning on this button ever since the baby boom with the cry, "We cannot possibly feed the growing nation or produce the raw materials for their needs without a mammoth program of chemical control." Miss Carson merely exposed our predicament.[1]

[1] Rachel Carson, it must be emphasized, is not without champions in high places. When on May 12, 1964, President Lyndon B. Johnson was signing a pesticides bill, he expressed sorrow that

> "one voice which spoke so often and so eloquently for measures like this is still today— the voice of Rachel Carson. She would have been proud of this bill and of this moment. We owe much to her and to those who still work for the cause of a safer and healthier America." (*New York Times*, May 13, 1964.)

This bill ended the privilege of a manufacturer of pesticides to market his product while protesting the refusal of the Department of Agriculture to register it.

Reprinted from Robert Rienow and Leona Train Rienow, *Moment in the Sun* (New York: Ballantine Books, 1969) pp. 195–214 and 329–334. Originally published in hard covers by The Dial Press, copyright © 1967 by Robert Rienow and Leona Train Rienow and used by permission of The Dial Press.

We are told that our varied diet—indeed, the ability of our producers to feed our growing multitudes at all—depends upon our willingness to accept an ever-increasing dose of poison not only in all that we eat, drink, touch, or wear, but in our muscles, tissues, and even in our brains.[2] If this is so, it would seem that our standard of living has slipped a big notch somewhere.

When we discover (July, 1966) that since the commercial introduction of DDT in 1946, the use of synthetic pesticides has increased from a million pounds annually to the "massive dispersal" in 1965 of nearly *one billion* pounds, we can be confident that we are "living dangerously" at last. When we learn that we are at present ingesting eight times as much poison as we did in 1940 and that by 1975 we will be absorbing four times as much as we are absorbing today, it is evident that the notches are still slipping at an accelerated rate. Again, quantitatively, as in other things, we are at the apex of production; qualitatively, we are starting downhill at a trot.

It is with great emotion that the chemical buffs reiterate that the more than 900 million pounds of unselective pesticides which drench the earth and air each year are *indispensable* to outwit the swarming pest population. How could we conquer the twenty kinds of mites and insects and eight species of diseases of apples, for example, without fifteen or twenty sprays a year? And what foolishness to bend the back to hack out the crab grass around the patio, when 40 million pounds of herbicides soaked into the soil (and possibly thence into the water supply) will do it for all our lawns and patios so neatly?

When grandfather reminds them that fine apples were produced not too many years ago by relying on the "natural enemies" of the pests and then for decades thereafter by relying on only one or two sprays per season, the chemical buffs have an answer for that, too. They respond that the protec-

[2] Emphasis has most generally been on the accumulation of DDT in the fat and muscles of warm-blooded animals; actually, insecticides of every classification lodge, according to the preference of each, in the vital organs as well. For tables detailing the amounts of various poisons found in birds, see U.S. Department of Interior's Circular 167, *Pesticide-Wildlife Studies: A Review of Fish and Wildlife Service Investigations During 1961 and 1962*, especially charts on pp. 48, 49, 51, 68, 73. Toxicity of various insecticides and herbicides to vertebrates and invertebrates is recorded, as well as residues found in dead speciments from both agricultural field application and from controlled tests.

Also found in this bulletin are dozens of references of experiments in the field and laboratory, ranging from Sprunt's and Cunningham's Bald Eagle Projects to Hunt and Bischoff's *Inimical Effects on Wildlife of Periodic DDD Applications to Clear Lake* (California Fish and Game Commission), Frear's *Pesticide Handbook*, a consideration of heptochlor epoxide residues in the organs of living creatures, and many others.

Official defense of pesticide use has shifted sharply from insistence that residues did not exist in any important degree to the insistence on their harmlessness in the quantities now present.

tive species of insects, nature's answer to the pests, have long ago been eliminated by the sprays. Birds, lizards, toads, wasps, and other helpful animals such as skunks have also been killed off around agricultural lands and there is no longer any recourse but to spray more energetically each year. Worse: we are told that as fast as they invent some virulent knockout drops for a species of insect pests, that species become immune to the poison, and the chemists must produce another poison with still more kill-potential. "We not only need [pesticides]," declares a Cornell College of Agriculture bulletin, "we are highly dependent on them."

Apparently the Department of Agriculture and the chemical buffs are right; we are caught in a relentless vise. We are pursuing a path from which there is no longer any retreat and that hourly grows more fraught with danger. If so, we have come to a rather dismal pass. The *Insecta*, some 1,000,000 species of them (possibly 600,000 classified), have endured and flourished on this planet since the Silurian age some 250 million years ago, and it is an excellent bet that they will outlive upstart (1 million-year-old) man.[3] They are "the most successful animal on earth." Unless man comes to terms with the creatures or can enlist some weighty help from nature herself, he is fighting a losing war.[4] Yet undoubtedly he will remain in there slugging it out alone until he is too weak to lift another test tube.

In the meantime, regardless of how "indispensable" the chemicals in our food are, the fantastic amounts of food additives, both "intentional" (661 million pounds in 1965, a 58 per cent rise in ten years) and "incidental" foster a serious and foolhardy situation. As Dr. David B. Hand of the Department of Food Science and Technology at Geneva, New York, and other specialists insist, a volume of incidental additives—pesticides, herbicides, fungicides although "not intended," may well be "unavoidable," *given our present and especially our prospective population demands* and *our philosophy of expediency.*

However, the intentional additives—some 2,600 chemicals used in food

---

[3] A resolution adopted by 2,000 biologists at the final sessions of the 12th International Congress of Entomology (1964) at London predicted that the indiscriminate methods of spraying would cause "drastic reconstructions of local insect faunas," would bring about "the elimination of many species," and result in "vast reservoirs of insect pests."

Yet the commercial sign over the poison counter at our garden store ignorantly proclaims: "The only good bug is a dead bug."

[4] A report on agricultural conditions in *Agway Cooperator*, a farmers' supply house organ (Apr., 1966, p. 7), deplores the resistant strains of rootworms that have developed in response to the intensive use of aldrin, dieldrin, heptachlor, and the like, in the great Midwestern corn belt, which has been "committed to chemical control for years." Northeastern dairy farmers are warned to take heed of the plight of the farmer of the Midwest and "avoid these persistent insecticides which may contaminate forage and milk." Something new has indeed been added in advertising circles.

production by 80,000 or more manufacturers, processors, and packers—which are used to preserve, embalm, flavor, color, emulsify, thicken, bleach, leaven, clarify, acidify, brighten, or change the consistency of foods may well be another story. Dr. Frank Bicknell notes:[5] "Food which cannot go bad is bad food;" i.e., if it won't support weevils or even bacteria, it won't healthfully support you (just another living creature) either.

Many of these strange, unpronounceable chemicals are found on labels; many more (as in the cases of bread and ice cream) are not listed at all.[6] How many housewives realize that we are buying and consuming 8 million pounds of coal tar products in food and cosmetics every year?

When you read a label listing chickle, butadiene-styrene, isopropene, saturated aliphatic hydrocarbons, polyvinyl acetate synthetic resins, butylated hydroxyanisole, butylated hydroxtoluene, propyl gallate,. would you know you were reading a chewing gum label?

Who can keep up with 45,000 or more chemical formulations used in food processing? And when a cow is fed a formulation containing "prednisone acetate, procaine pencillin, dihydrostreptomycin sulfate, methylparaben and propylparaben in peanut oil-aluminum monostearate-polyoxyethylene sorbitan-tristearate vehicle," who among the chemical wizards who dreamed

[5] *Chemicals in Your Food,* New York, 1960, pp. 66ff. Of interest in this post-Carson age is the pontifical attitude displayed by agricultural agents as recently as 1958 and displayed with succinct perfection in Dr. David B. Hand's explanatory piece "Chemical Additives in Foods" in *Farm Research,* Dec., 1958, a quarterly bulletin of the New York State Agricultural Experiment Station at Geneva and the Cornell University Agricultural Experiment Station at Ithaca.

[6] "Some food labels show all the ingredients while others do not because the 1938 Federal Food, Drug, and Cosmetic Act does not require a complete statement of ingredients on foods which are *standardized.*" Sec. 401 states that "in prescribing a definition and standard of identity for any food or class of food in which optional ingredients are permitted, the Secretary shall, for the purpose of promoting honesty and fair dealing in the interest of consumers, designate the optional ingredients which shall be named on the label." Regardless of whether a standard of identity has been established for a food, the Act requires that if it contains any artificial flavoring, artificial coloring, or chemical preservative, it must bear labeling stating that fact, "except that colors used in butter, cheese, and ice cream do not have to be declared." Until the Food Additives Amendment of 1958, says the statement, "Little interest was expressed by consumers in having all optional ingredients listed" on the labels. More recently there has been a public clamor to have labels bear lists of all ingredients. At the same time, industry has set up a clamor for more and a bigger variety of additives. In other words the most common foods, which include bread, butter, and ice cream, may contain a standardized list of additives of all sorts that do not need to be mentioned on the label; only when some adventuresome manufacturer improvises with some new pet chemicals must he declare them on the label. Continues the statement, "From time to time, as the older standards are reviewed, FDA will take into consideration the desire of consumers to have ingredients declared." In other words, we get what we deserve and demand. So long as

up this monstrosity of artificial nutrition is competent to swear that what comes out of the cow and goes into the baby is either wholesome or safe?

When Professor of Civil Engineering Daniel F. Jackson of the University of Syracuse breakfasted with delegates to New York State's annual health conference at the capital in June of 1965, he waited until the last gulp of coffee had been consumed before he analyzed what additives—both incidental and intentional—they had just eaten. In the fruit juice: benzoic acid, dimethyl polysiloxane (antifoaming agent), DDT, parathion (possibly), saccharin. In the bacon and ham: DDT, chlordane, toxaphene or other pesticides, especially in the fatty parts: also stilbestrol (artificial female sex hormone), aueromycin, mineral oil residue from the wax paper. In the eggs: decomposition products from fatty acids, mono- and diglycerides, isopropyl citrate, mono-isopropyl citrate, DDT, various antibiotics. In the rolls: ammonium chloride (conditioner), mono- and diglycerides and polyoxyethylene (softeners), ditertiary-butyl-para-cresol, coal tar dyes, vitamin fortifiers. In the butter: nordihydroguaiaretic acid, oxidation products from interaction with hydrogen peroxide (decomposition), magnesium oxide, AB and OB Yellows (coal tar), diacetyl, DDT or other insecticides. In the coffee, in addition to possible cereals, traces of insecticides.

"You can see," concluded the Professor, "you are really getting more for the money than appeared on the menu."

The Interior Department reveals that one part of DDT in one *billion* parts of water kills blue crabs in eight days;[7] one part per *billion* in more

---

we accept the "secret ingredients" of bread and ice cream, etc., without listing, we shall get them. (*Statement Concerning Declaration of Ingredients on Labels for Standardized Foods*, Department of Health, Education, and Welfare, FDA, Aug. 18, 1965.)

A lengthy article in *Chemical Engineering News* (Oct. 10, 1966) pp. 100ff., deals with "intentional additives" and gives industry's side of the story. Arthur D. Little, Inc., which estimated that 661 million pounds of additives were used in 1965, predicts 852 million pounds will be used in 1970 and 1.03 billion pounds in 1975, not including the ordinary additives of sugar, salt, starch, pepper, cinnamon, citric acid, monosodium glutamate, mono- and diglycerides, and about 575 other such materials exempt from federal control. The additives business has leaped from $172 million at the manufacturers' level in 1955 to $285 million in 1965. "By 1970 these sales are expected to reach about $400 million and by 1975 are likely to exceed $500 million" and many chemical companies are working diligently to develop new chemicals to add to new foods. Years ago chemical companies merely filled orders for chemical additives; today they are eagerly pursuing the additive business as an unlimited bonanza.

[7] Fish and Wildlife Service, Department of Interior news release, Sept. 7, 1965. On the subject of toxicity Massachusetts Audubon Society published a special report, *Pesticide Applications and the Public Welfare*, by William H. Drury, Jr. (reprint from the Sept.–Oct., 1961, magazine), with valuable charts comparing the various toxicities of most-used pesticides. Some of the charts ranged in order of lethal qualities for both fish and birds. Also given were effects of normal field use of pesticides on survival ratio of different species of birds, along with plentiful references of experiments.

understandable phraseology is the relationship one ounce of chocolate syrup would bear to 10 million gallons of milk! The chemical people make a great deal of the "safety" of the various death potions "when used as directed." Yet an analysis of dead wild pheasants in California on lands on which "accepted and normal" sprays had been used showed them to be so saturated that one biologist remarked, "These birds are sizzling hot."

Millions of fish have died in the Mississippi River, reportedly from endrin. While 95 per cent of the fish that die in Missouri streams die from toxaphene poisoning, the swarms and phalanxes of spraying planes dive, whirr, and perform aerial acrobatics, flying from dawn to dusk over the wheat fields in an orgy of soil and water poisoning, says Dr. James Whitley of the Missouri Conservation Commission. In New York State spraying is eliminating the trout in Lake George, Blue Mountain Lake, Paradox, and Schroon; the Finger Lakes are losing thousands of fish from the spraying done at campsites and parks.[8] Few realize that such spray often drifts for many miles. The effects of Sevin, a new organic carbamate substituted for the chlorinated hydrocarbons, are unknown; although its residual life is much shorter, one of its breakdown products is said to be 1-naphthol, listed as "very toxic."[9]

While fish slaughter presents the most dramatic and observable spectacle as the victims float glass-eyed and odorous on rivers and lakes, the bird and wildlife kill is even more serious: pheasants, quail, and mallards at Patuxent, Maryland; ducks, bald eagles, geese, pelicans on the Tule Lake Wildlife Refuge in California; mule deer in Montana and Colorado and New Mexico; shrimps, crabs, and mollusks along the coasts, especially in Louisiana; doves, pigeons, foxes, badgers in the prairie states; salmon, hawks, gulls, golden eagles in Washington and Oregon; the myrtle warblers and red-eyed vireos at Hawk Mountain, Pennsylvania; all the ospreys in the Connecticut River basin; the peregrine falcon utterly vanished from the entire Northeastern states as a breeding bird.

Pesticides are especially concentrated in game animals that roam and feed. "For instance, approximately 70 per cent of the woodcock examined

[8] For effect of pesticide spraying on the salmon of the Miramichi River in New Brunswick, see Ira N. Gabrielson's report in *Pest Control and Wildlife Relationships: A Symposium*, Wildlife Management Institute ("Wildlife—Pesticides Research Needs," pp. 19–25, especially p. 23). This is a publication of the National Academy of Sciences —National Research Council, Washington, D.C., 1961.

[9] Gleason, Gosselin, and Hodge, *Clinical Toxicity of Commercial Products* (Baltimore: Williams and Wilkins, 1963), 2d ed., lists Sevin with a toxicity rating of 4, the same rating as given DDT. *Science* (Apr. 12, 1963, No. 140: pp. 170–71) explains discovery of earlier unsuspected residues as due to more sensitive methods of chemical analysis. Effects of Sevin on wildlife are apparently, as yet, in the balance. An agricultural agent friend of ours who originally was a strong advocate of Sevin has recently reversed his opinion in an equally strong manner.

recently contained heptachlor epoxide (average 1.6 ppm) for which there is a 'zero tolerance' " in domestic meats. Deer collected from an area sprayed with one pound per acre of DDT for spruce budworm control, contained DDT residues, some in excess of legal tolerance for domestic meats, says Dr. John L. Buckley, Director of Patuxent Wildlife Research Center of the Bureau of Sport Fisheries and Wildlife.[10]

The New York State Joint Legislative Committee report continues that in California game birds are so "hot" they have all but closed the hunting season. In Louisiana 186 woodcock contained heptachlor. Both DDT and heptachlor are now present in woodcock in the northern states. "Are we paying too high a price in biological damage for the unquestioned benefits of pest control? I think we are," says Dr. Buckley, "and sometimes, as in use of DDT for Dutch elm disease, we don't even get the benefits we pay for." He adds, "One may well question whether it is rational to eat game meats containing residues that would be unacceptable in domestic foods." Add this to the perils of hunting.

Said Mr. Udall, speaking before the Audubon Society's annual convention in 1963, "The unnerving fact is that pesticide residues have been found in virtually every type of warm-blooded animal across the land. . . . Man himself is slowly building up in his body small, but relentlessly cumulative traces of chemicals." And the chlorinated hydrocarbons possess such "movement" (carried by winds, birds, animals, waters) over the globe that they are now found not only in the flesh of isolated savage tribes (who did nothing to deserve them), but even in arctic penguins, seals, and in the flesh of fish that live 100 miles out in the sea!

A report of the Department of the Interior listed endrin as "about 50 times more toxic than DDT.[11] The other pesticides—dieldrin, aldrin, chlordane, and toxaphene—fell in between." In other words, although we have mountains of evidence of the killing properties of DDT because we have been using it the longest, it is nonetheless far less toxic than the newer poisons of which we as yet know almost nothing. Comments a British Ministry of Health pamphlet for medical practitioners: "*no* specific chemical tests for endrin poisoning exist."

But in addition to "movement" and toxicity the chlorinated hydrocarbons also possess great longevity. Dr. Robert L. Rudd, Associate Professor of Zoology at the University of California, Davis, tells of plots treated experimentally with 100 pounds of DDT in 1947, which still had a residue of 28.2

[10] *Pesticides, Their Use and Effect.* Proceedings of a symposium sponsored by the New York State Joint Legislative Committee on Natural Resources, Albany, N.Y., Sept. 23, 1963, Senator R. Watson Pomeroy, Chairman. This symposium by no means maintains that we can dispense with our poisoning program, but voices pleading for restraint are heard.

[11] U.S. Department of Interior press release, Sept. 7, 1965.

pounds per acre in 1951. Chlordane, dieldrin, heptachlor, and benzine hexa-chloride also last for a long time in the soil.

"Most concern," says Dr. Rudd, "has been directed toward the surviving toxic fraction of the parent chemical. A new phenomenon has shaken dependence on this simple measure. Breakdown or conversion products have been found to be more toxic than, or to complement the toxicity of, the parent residue."[12]

Thus, when heptachlor "breaks down" it converts into epoxide, which is even more lethal; aldrin, said to "disappear rapidly," merely converts into the more poisonous dieldrin. Is the folly of such prolonged poisoning of the earth from which we gain all our sustenance, comprehensible?

Then there are the systemic poisons. A thorough analysis of Cygon 267, a typical systemic, describes how this poison not only keeps killing for two weeks after spraying but also invades the stems and foliage and is circulated to other parts of the plant to kill insects through the plant's juices.[13] (What is the difference, a spokesman for the FDA asks, whether the agricultural poison is *on* the fruit, or *in* the fruit, so long as the "tolerance" rating is the same?) This would seem to knock the last props right out from under all the millions of Americans who have been sedulously scrubbing and peeling their fruits and vegetables in the hope of avoiding the pesticide. They can, however, now save themselves a lot of time and trouble.

Query: Why do Department of Agriculture authorities assure us that systemics are very "short-lived" in their effects, when the ads for farmers stress their "long-lasting" qualities? Doubtless there are comforting answers to all these bewildering questions somewhere.

Because, as mentioned, DDT has been in use far longer than most toxi-cants, we know much more about it, and none of what we have learned is good. We have long known that it builds up in the fatty tissues of warm-blooded animals (including man), seemingly harmless until the host suffers some illness or stress. It has been proved beyond a doubt by many experiments that when something occurs to use up the body fat of an animal or bird, the insecticide accumulation is suddenly released into the blood stream where it often ends the animal's career in a very unpleasant manner.

We are not going to be unscientific enough to extrapolate the results of animals' reactions over to humans.[14] The House Appropriations Commit-

[12] *Pesticides and the Living Landscape* (Madison: University of Wisconsin Press, 1964), pp. 162ff.

[13] *Rural New Yorker*, Mar. 1, 1958, p. 9.

[14] Dr. Theron G. Randolph in his incisive study supported by clinical notes entitled *Human Ecology and Susceptibility to the Chemical Environment* (Springfield, Ill.: Charles Thomas, 1962), points out that toxicity studies on animals are quite remote

tee's *Report on Pesticides*, which came out on April 19, 1965, castigates Rachel Carson for inferring that mammals who breathe, move, eat, drink, and have blood, nerves, cells, and organs alarmingly like man's, might also react like man to unselective poisons.

The Committee agrees with her that certain pesticides do cause cancer, sterility, and other distressing conditions in both man and beast. But it continues, "However, [the book] is unscientific in drawing incorrect conclusions from unrelated facts, and making implications that are based on possibilities as yet unproved to be actual facts." We do not here wish to be guilty of such irrational reasoning.

Nor are we taken in when Dr. Clarence Cottam suggests that "metabolic and physiological processes in man are not greatly different from those found in other vertebrate animals." We stand safely by the House Committee *Report*. Dr. Cottam is Director of the Welder Wildlife Foundation of Texas (and former member of the committee on pesticides of the Ecological Society of America), so he is probably not as unbiased in his observations as, say, some of the medical authorities interviewed by the House subcommittee and subsidized by the national chemical companies.

Yet when we amiably accept the report's repeated statement that it is unscientific to infer that animal bodies react similarly to man's when faced with concentrated poisons, stress, and the like, we find ourselves in the arms of a strange dilemma. What, then, are all the laboratories doing with their millions of experimental animals? What is the excuse, then, for these gigantic outlays of billions of dollars and millions of small (and unimportant, of course) lives? (However, all this is but an irrelevant digression.)

Let us return to the report of the House Committee and its indignation at Miss Carson's "unscientific superficiality." (Witnessing the prolonged death throes of a robin can sometimes move one to irrational deductions.) Certainly man is infinitely superior to all other creatures. Most probably we have some built-in immunity that no other living creature enjoys. Admittedly we have the supreme intelligence, and this should enable us to avoid the consequences of a poison build-up in our bodies by the injection of some powerful antidote or something, to which animals do not have access. And surely the experts in our government would not permit—yes, encourage— us to ingest poisons that build up ominously within us unless they had reliable proof that we could handle them, even under stress?

Moreover, it is not scientific, we are told, to worry about an eventuality until after it has occurred. And the House Appropriations Committee under-

---

from the medical problem. The medical problem is not concerned with the middle of the distribution curve, he says, but with the far end. In other words man is more vulnerable than his animal experiments indicate.

lines that we have as yet documented no single human case of such weird consequences as we have witnessed in thousands of animal tests.[15] Therefore, it is scientific to assume that they will never occur.

But let the biologists carry on their quarrel with the poisoners of life and earth. They are beginning to make an impression. We are concerned here more with the implications of the poison policy to the American way of life.

We have considered the increasing degradation of our standards of wholesomeness in food and environment. But there is more. What is happening to the integrity and trust that should exist between a government and its people? What does it signify that we are willing to accept every year greater compromise with a known evil rather than expend the effort to combat it? What of the bombardment of untruths to which we are submitted by our officials to maintain public complacency? When it becomes more important to sustain the serene upward progress of the economy than to safeguard public health, what happens to a nation's well-being? When it becomes more important not to rock the economic boat than to be honest, what happens to a people's faith in its leaders?

First, there is the "tolerance" fallacy. Pesticides undergo at least two years' testing by their manufacturers, whereupon the FDA usually takes 1/100 of the amount that was found in the two years' tests to have visibly harmed or killed animal subjects and establishes a permissive dose which is then legally acceptable for swallowing *in unlimited doses* by the citizenry over seventy-five years.[16] This little stinger, we are reminded with passionate earnestness, is an absolute essential to "our standard of living."

Very well. But instead of the repeated and highly unscientific avowals

---

[15] One wonders if he might not gain insight by paying special heed to the rabbits who were given DDT by stomach tube when they refused to eat it on food. The two females gave birth to two live rabbits each and killed them on day of birth to escape the punishment. (Fish and Wildlife Service, *Pesticide-Wildlife Studies*, Circular 167 [Washington, D.C.: Government Printing Office, 1963] p. 48.)

[16] For detailed charts of tolerances of all major and many minor pesticides as established under the Food Additives Amendment to the Federal Food, Drug, and Cosmetic Act, complete through Dec. 31, 1965, see *N.A.C. News and Pesticide Review* of the National Agricultural Chemicals Association (1155 Fifteenth St., N.W., Washington, D.C.), dated Feb., 1966. The variation in a poison's permissible residue from food to food leads to the suspicion that the tolerance is based not so much on a scientific evaluation of how much the human body can absorb without undue effects as it is on a realistic bow to expediency: how little can the producer promise while still sustaining his production? For instance, why was but 0.1 ppm (parts per million) of aldrin permitted on cherries, while 0.25 ppm. of the same poison was permitted on apricots? (Aldrin has since been largely discredited anyway.) If the poison tolerances are person-oriented, as claimed, why is Carbaryl, for example, twice as poisonous on beets (tolerance, 5 ppm.) as on apples (tolerance, 10 ppm.)?

that the tolerances set are harmless, we should be frankly told: *This toler-*
ance is a wild guess based on insufficient research. We cannot assure you
that it is "harmless" over a period of time. But since our pesticides have far
outrun our research and we are moreover under great pressure to approve
tolerances for these new poisons, you will have to make the best of it—
that is, if you wish to maintain your supermarkets in their present bursting
splendor.

The finest of our scientists readily (but secretly) admits that the only
effective tests for new pesticides is to release them to the public domain
for a period of several years, where they will be used freely under natural
conditions. This is logical. However, surely the guinea pigs deserve some
warning of what is being done, if only the symbolic skull and crossbones
that used to adorn the iodine and rubbing alcohol bottles of old. Instead,
every agency and dealer assures us that the product is "harmless if used
as directed."

We have been, in fact, almost bludgeoned by the Department of Agriculture into using spray after spray after spray, many of them unnecessarily,
but as "preventives." We are told by Department of Agriculture and chemical company representatives that the ingestion of this insecticide or that
herbicide is very "minimal." They may be right.

However, we have as yet seen no shiny brochures that attempt to estimate the total ingestion—that is, how many and what infinite variety of
"minute tolerance doses" one person on an average diet actually consumes
each day, week, and year.

What do all the thousands of "minute, insignificant" tolerance-doses of
chlorinated hydrocarbons, the antibiotics, organic phosphates, herbicides,
hormones, systemic insecticides, rodenticides, fungicides, preservatives, ar-
senic additives, the omnipresent sodium nitrates and sodium nitrites, tran-
quilizer residues, coal tar colors, the emulsifiers, propionates, and possible
carcinogens add up to in an average American's six-month diet, for instance?
What, exactly, are the biochemical properties of the fifteen additives in a
cake mix? Perhaps it is scientific to declare that all these additives add up
to nothing—because one small tolerance-dose of parathion, for instance, may
add up to nothing?

Although the courage of the federal Food and Drug Administration's
banning of certain dramatic killers is to be commended, it is disturbing that
biocides are often permitted to enjoy extensive sales, Department of Agriculture backing, and the opportunity widely to poison soil and human bodies
over a period of many years before they are banned. Especially irritating
(and dangerous) are the pontifical, positive assurances of minor local officials, who couldn't be more ignorant on the subject, that the man-made
guesses called "tolerances" are dependable and not to be questioned. In

every crisis, on every challenge, the tolerance is cited as though its guarantee was inscribed on a tablet of God instead of being what it is—an expedient compromise of truth with economic interests. *No official is competent to assert honestly that the tolerances permitted by regulation are without harm now or in the future.* We are getting a double dose of poison: literal and verbal.

There is another serious misunderstanding suffered by many regarding the safety of the food they devour. Dr. Robert L. Rudd expresses it concisely when he says: "specialists and advisers maintain the curious illusion that current recommendations actually control residues"[17] and loudly proclaim this misconception to assuage the public.

In other words the FDA "makes rules" that a product shall *not* be marketed with more than so many parts per million of chlorinated hydrocarbon residue on it; that farmers observe strict spraying rules for organic phosphates; that additives shall be harmless.

Then, amazingly enough, salesmen, sprayers, and officials all cite these "rules" as the practice! In the case of milk the FDA long "ruled" that there should be no DDT whatever in the milk fed to babies. In practice, however, whenever a national sampling of milk was taken, DDT turned up in the analysis.[18] Expediency prevailed and the FDA was forced to retract. On June 2, 1966, the Division of Industry Advice of the Bureau of Education and Voluntary Compliance of the FDA responded to our query as follows: "There are no legal pesticide tolerances for milk, cream, or butter at the present time. . . ." *But:* "We have published a proposal to establish tolerances for DDT, DDE, and DDD in milk and other dairy products . . . published in the *Federal Register* of November 16, 1965. . . ."

When a proscribed poison becomes too prevalent in a product, we simply legalize it. It is a convenient system for our purposes. Thus, the tendency when "safe" tolerances are exceeded is toward a "creep-up" of the permitted minimum to conform with reality. But not only are the limits on established poisons creeping up; each day finds new and more virulent ones glutting the markets—and each of these boasts its own tiny contribution of venom to the American smörgasbord, a contribution that may be added to all the others for a poison total that has never been computed and to which there is no limit.

Considering offhand the thirty-seven poisons permitted to be present in minute tolerances on cherries (not to mention a considerable number of

[17] Robert L. Rudd, *Pesticides and the Living Landscape* (Madison: University of Wisconsin Press, 1964), p. 170.

[18] P. A. Clifford, "Pesticide Residues in Fluid Milk Market," Public Health *Report*, LXXII, No. 8, pp. 729ff.

other contaminants, such as the copper compounds, that are also permitted in the field and for which there are no tolerances), the great amount of press attention given to the minor fracas over the addition of more mineral oil and glycerine to the children's peanut butter appears grotesque. All our standards of reasonableness seem to have collapsed. It is not without significance that an FDA release stressing the need for pesticides mentions their importance to "the nation's economics, health and recreational activities," in that order.

Once in a while an unfortunate incident breaks out into print; an·adult man spills a little of a 25 per cent solution of an insecticide on his skin and dies in forty minutes; a carload of carrots is seized containing large amounts of a lethal spray; a few shipments of milk are dumped into the river; a plane pilot spraying a small Minnesota town for mosquitoes gets his cans mixed and accidentally uses parathion intended for crops, and the town has to be evacuated. (Parathion is described as so deadly that if a child rolled in sprayed grass it would probably die, yet there is a one part per million tolerance established for parathion in all our food.)

But in each such report, however, some impressive authority is quoted in the second to the last paragraph, assuring the people that all is well; everything is in hand; the threat of pesticides is "insignificant from a health standpoint." Although DDT has been found "in every complete meal analyzed in this country," testified Dr. Wayland J. Hayes, Jr., Public Health Service toxicologist, before the Committee[19] chaired by Senator Abraham Ribicoff, its concentration is "small and harmless."

We were told that heptachlor was harmless when used as directed and that none of it was appearing in our foods. Then, considerably later, it was revealed that "ten times improved analytical procedures" enabled discovery of minute amounts of this killer in cows' milk, and it was withdrawn from dairy production. Aldrin and dieldrin were registered by our government as safe for years; then on February 2, 1966, after a closed-door conference of U.S. Department of Agriculture officials and the manufacturers' representatives, the registration of these pesticides for use on vegetables, grain, and forage crops was suddenly canceled.

How many other tolerances have been established and the public assured they were "safe" before the scientists even possessed the analytical procedures to detect them on marketed foods? We have no quarrel with the valor that it takes to admit an error and to redress it; but we sometimes wonder wistfully if it is necessary to be deceived with such conviction when the authorities are fully conscious of their own ignorance and are aware that they are responding to organized pressures of interest groups?

[19] See the Senate Governmental Operations Subcommittee's Hearings, July, 1963.

In answer to our query a letter from Senator Everett M. Dirksen, fervent defender of pesticides, assures us that "pesticides we have today have been in use for over twenty years and science has observed no manifestations in man." Let us examine this statement.

First, the avalanche of the most deadly poisons we now use has been conceived in recent years—many of them are but two to ten years out of the test tubes. Second, science has "observed no manifestations in man" probably because it hasn't been looking for them.

The Fish and Wildlife Service found that a number of dead eagles picked up had accumulations of DDT not only in the body fat but also *in the brain.* Zoologist Douglas James at the University of Arkansas found that the same insecticide apparently affected the central nervous system of quail and caused a decline in learning ability. *Query:* How many human brains have been opened after death to investigate whether or not they were so damaged?

Men die from such "natural causes" as liver, heart, or kidney trouble —or so read, in the medical phraseology, the death certificates. *Query:* How extensive has been the research in such unspectacular deaths to determine the victim's poison burden as a contributor to the disease?

We all know the answers. Time and the chemical tide wait for no man, nor for his autopsy either (unless his death presented acute or suspicious poisoning symptoms).

"There are many new chemicals with no analytical techniques set up at all," Dr. William A. Tompkins of the Massachusetts Division of Fish and Game tells us.[20] And, to repeat: decisions which may affect health and life are only too often made on the basis of economics, expediency, and politics, rather than on human welfare. C. P. Snow in his book *Science and Government* comments with some disgust: "Some of the most important choices about a nation's physical health are made, or not made, by a handful of men, in secret, and again, in legal form, by men who normally are not able to comprehend the arguments in depth."

Query: If hot dog colorings are as safe as the federal government presumably certifies, why have seven states (Illinois was the seventh in January, 1966) now banned the red dye used?

Query: If the organic phosphates with their wicked little tolerances are justified on the vast, commercial market, how is it that we just now discover that chick embryos injected with these substances suffer such birth defects as no right wing, skull malformation, and so on?

Senator Ribicoff was deeply shocked to learn that long after poisons in foods and clothing ("You can walk downtown right now and pick up a

[20] *Christian Science Monitor,* May 18, 1964.

sweater with 400 ppm [parts per million] DDT in it")[21] have been in approved use, the Department of Agriculture tells us it cannot set up sound recommendations because it knows too little about them! "The nutritionists among you," he says, "would be interested to know that we are going to *start* finding out whether the over-all nutritional value of the food supply of the nation has been significantly altered through the use of pesticides."

The big argument between the chemical buffs and the protesters may best be illustrated in a comment in the *New Yorker* of May 2, 1964. Secretary Udall wishes to ban the most persistent poisons and those which carry over to effect large kills of wildlife in streams and woods. Secretary Freeman, defensively parroting the Department lines, retorts that it is unwarranted to ban poisons about which "too little is known."

"The Freeman doctrine appears to be that the less you know about a posion the freer you should feel to use it," remarks the *New Yorker*. Did this quaint idea come over from the ancient legal doctrine that the accused person is innocent until proven guilty? With poisons, such a theory is palpably out of place; it is like playing Russian roulette. When the proof comes it is too late to retract.

To which might be added as postscript the memorandum issued by the Rural District Councils Association of Great Britain to the Ministry of Agriculture concerning pesticides: "Long-term effects indirectly harmful to humans have not been assessed and may not be found until the damage is done. . . . There is *no* reliable data so far on how much of these substances the human body can tolerate."

The government is not leveling with the public. A health official high in national circles recently remarked (in private) that "there are times when it is wiser not to tell the truth." We can rail against this treatment, but let us be fair. We have no conception of the pressures put upon the FDA and the administration and especially on our congressmen by the commercial interests involved.

Moreover, all indications have been that we are getting just what we subconsciously want—to be tranquilized and shielded from facts that might disturb us. If the American people rose up and demanded honesty from its officials, not all the commercial interests, economic growth wizards, and moneyed power in the nation could thwart their demands. Our bureaucracies encompass many men of rare vision and principle; they will give us just what we demand of them. We are afraid to face facts. It is easier and more pleasant to skid along without thinking.

We are a society of consumers who insist on a fabulous profusion of

[21] Senator Abraham A. Ribicoff, "Pesticides and Public Policy," *Sierra Club Bulletin*, Apr., 1965, pp. 12ff.

top grade produce (in appearance, not in cleanliness, purity, or essential nutriments). An apple or a peach may not entertain one blemish, but it may be filmed with a deadly spray that lodges in and builds up in our brains, heart, and muscles. We insist on cold cuts that will keep two weeks in the refrigerator, we pay for our convenience by ingesting a steady diet of sodium nitrite and sodium nitrate which, should an accidental "spillage" occur, might (as in New Jersey a few years ago with regard to fish) strike a few customers stone dead.

On top of all this we insist on straining the economy even more with our fecundity, constantly aggravating the problem of supplying great varieties of food to ever larger masses of people.

We are, as a society, entrapped in a pit of seething chemicals, and although the banks seem at present too slippery to climb out, plans abound to control the flood before we are submerged. Senator Ribicoff discovered the basic need for more rigidity and severity of control: organized, periodic pesticide plant inspection, policing of disposal of wastes, policing and stern control of pesticide labeling.

Secretary of the Interior Udall says that although his department is feverishly studying some 70 generally used pesticide compounds, there are more than 500 now on the market needing study, and his staff cannot begin to catch up. As for the popular belief that the vast quantities of food displayed in supermarkets and elsewhere are federally inspected, it is estimated that less than one-third of 1 per cent of all food products that reach the hands of the people suffer this indignity. Writes our FDA correspondent: "We are currently examining approximately 1 per cent of interstate shipments of raw agricultural commodities for pesticide residues. [About 25,000 per year.]"

Intrastate products are subject only to state regulations, whatever they may be or may not be. The Congress, while lavishing sums far beyond what the President asks on medical research, is niggardly indeed with food inspection: fifty inspection stations over the width and breadth of the land offer the spray-happy grower such astronomical odds against detection that even the most timid need lose no sleep.

Dr. Franklin Bicknell (an Englishman) makes a serious charge: "The United States leads the civilized world in chemicalized food and in degenerative diseases." The babies born today are born with "built-in" doses of DDT, heptachlor, and strontium 90; in fact, these virulent guests settle down in the foetus soon after conception.[22] Surely we should foster a better

---

[22] Some support for Dr. Bicknell's worry is found in preliminary report of a study made by four specialists of the University of Miami School of Medicine and Dade Country agencies. They discovered traces of pesticides in unborn babies in excess of those in

environment for the future Americans in whose hands lie the virility and hope of the nation?

A British committee on agricultural pesticides has recently given as its opinion that if all the organochlorines were withdrawn, the annual potential loss of crops would be no more than 250,000 acres out of a total of more than 7,600,000 acres now under cultivation in the British Isles and that the loss could be reduced to about 75,000 acres by the use of less harmful chemicals. With our great ingenuity and greater wealth we could undoubtedly accomplish comparative results if we willed it.

However, the effort would entail an agricultural revolution. It would encompass not only vastly more supervision but new legislation and appropriations for *independent* research, education of the public (and the crazy plane pilots), greater controls on poisons and their users, the outlawing of long-lasting pesticides, increased penalties for violators, new systems of licensing and distribution. Especially would it include research in biological (as opposed to chemical) controls of pests. There would be needed a small army of entomologists, pathologists, geneticists, biochemists, and ecologists to offset the present vast armies of commercial chemists.[23]

The situation, to say the least, is out of hand. As with our other mounting crises, it is the unprecedented population increase that has spurred on this poison carnival in order to meet the emergency of ever more customers with ever bigger appetites. And just so, it is by spiking the population rise that we can take off some of the heat, give society a chance to catch its breath, and perhaps evolve, after some fumblings, a less foolhardy and adventitious method of procedure in the production of its bread.

To the Editor of the [Albany, New York] *Times-Union*:

Give us this day our daily calcium propionate (spoilage retarder); sodium diacetate (mold inhibitor), monoglyceride (emulsifier), potassium bromate (maturing agent), calcium phosphate monobasic (dough conditioner), chloramine T (flour bleach), aluminum potassium sulfate (acid baking powder ingredient), sodium benzoate (preservative),

---

children in the age group from infancy to five years and resembling the burden of the adult population. There is transmission of pesticides from mother to unborn child. (*New York Times*, Jan. 30, 1966, p. 72, and *Industrial Medicine and Surgery*.)

[23] Ira N. Gabrielson, *loc. cit.*, describes a mosquito-control project in Florida where water-level manipulation obviated the need of spraying for salt-marsh mosquitos (p. 24). In the same publication Tom Gill of the Charles Lathrop Pack Forestry Foundation ("Forest Pest Control") instances the protective value of mixed versus pure timber stands in forest management, a new emphasis on planting techniques that can eliminate much wholesale spraying of commercial timber lands (pp. 8–13).

butylated hydroxyanisole (anti-oxidant), mono-isopropyl citrate (sequestrant); plus synthetic vitamins A and D.

Forgive us, O Lord, for calling this stuff BREAD.

Averill Park

J. H. Reed

SELECTED READINGS

A CROSS SECTION OF READINGS ON THE QUALITY OF LIFE OF CONSUMERS

BOOKS

Carolyn Shall Bell, *Consumer Choice in the American Economy* (New York: Random House, 1967).

Federal Trade Commission, *National Consumer Protection Hearings* (Washington, D.C.: U.S. Government Printing Office, 1969).

John Kenneth Galbraith, *The New Industrial State* (New York: Houghton Mifflin, 1967).

Kermit Gordon (ed.), *Agenda for the Nation* (Washington, D.C.: Brookings Institution, 1968).

Michael Harrington, *The Other America* (New York: Macmillan, 1963).

George Katona, *The Mass Consumption Society* (New York: McGraw-Hill, 1964).

Robert J. Lavidge and Robert J. Holloway (eds.), *Marketing and Society: The Challenge* (Homewood, Ill.: Irwin, 1969).

Senator Warren G. Magnuson and Jean Carper, *The Dark Side of the Marketplace: The Plight of the American Consumer* (Englewood Cliffs, N.J.: Prentice-Hall, 1968).

New York State Bar Association, *1967 Antitrust Law Symposium* (Special symposium on consumer protection; reprinted in Commerce Clearing House Trade Regulation Reports).

Lee E. Preston (ed.), *Social Issues in Marketing: Readings for Analysis* (Glenview, Ill.: Scott, Foresman, 1968).

Report of the National Advisory Commission on Civil Disorders (New York: Bantam Books, 1968).

Robert Rienow and Leona Train Rienow, *Moment in the Sun* (New York: Dial Press, 1967).

Clair Wilcox, *Toward Social Welfare* (Homewood, Ill.: Irwin, 1969).

James Harvey Young, *The Medical Messiahs: A Social History of Health Quackery in Twentieth-Century America* (Princeton, N.J.: Princeton University Press, 1967).

ARTICLES

E. B. Weiss, "Marketers Fiddle While Consumers Burn," *Harvard Business Review*, July–August, 1968.

SOME READINGS ON INCOME DIFFERENCES AND PRICING

Bureau of Labor Statistics, U.S. Department of Labor, *Retail Food Prices in Low and Higher Income Areas* (Washington, D.C.: U.S. Government Printing Office, February, 1969).

David Caplovitz, *The Poor Pay More* (Glencoe, Ill.: Free Press, 1963).

Federal Trade Commission, *Economic Report on Installment Credit and Retail Sales Practices of District of Columbia Retailers* (Washington, D.C.: U.S. Government Printing Office, 1968).

————, *Economic Report on Food Chain Selling Practices in the District of Columbia and San Francisco* (Washington, D.C.: U.S. Government Printing Office, 1969).

National Commission on Food Marketing, *Organization and Competition in Food Retailing*, Technical Study No. 7 (June 1966), especially Chapters 16 and 17.

Index

Acton, Lord, 296, 309

Adams, W., 273, 275–305, 307, 307n, 309n, 311, 311n, 315

Adelman, M. A., 108, 122–129, 286n, 305, 310, 310n, 315

Agnew, H. E., 131, 131n

Aithen, H. G. J., 70n

Alchian, A. A., 38n, 69

Alderson, W., 36n, 106, 130n, 131n, 152n, 156, 163n, 326n, 330n, 375

Alexander, R. S., 131, 131n, 136

Andrews, P. W. S., 35n

Arndt, J., 251

Arnold, T. W., 279, 304

Arrow, K. J., 68n

Atkins, W. E., 141n

Ayres, C. E., 104, 105

Bain, J. S., 106, 307, 310, 310n, 312, 315, 317, 349n, 363, 364, 373

Butters, J. K., 300n
Buzzell, R. D., 330, 330n

Cannon, W. B., 97n, 104
Caplovitz, D., 417
Carey, W., 300n
Carper, J., 416
Carson, R., 399, 399n, 407
Carter, W. A., 303
Cassady, R., Jr., 213n, 215
Caves, R., 106
Celler, E., 301n
Chamberlain, N. W., 58, 58n, 59, 59n,
     62n
Chamberlin, E. H., 107, 108, 109,
     111–121, 123, 123n, 141n, 204,
     205, 205n, 214, 214n, 215, 216,
     298n
Charnes, L., 9
Cherington, P. H., 142n
Clark, J. M., 70n, 104, 290n, 308n,
     316
Clarkson, G. P. E., 19
Clewett, R. M., 152n, 216
Clifford, P. A., 410n
Coase, R. H., 50n, 77n
Cohen, K. J., 270
Cole, A. H., 70n, 150n
Cole, R. H., 152n
Coleman, R. P., 270
Collins, N., 106
Comanor, W., 347
Comer, G., 276n
Commons, J. R., 104, 105, 136, 136n
Cook, J. V., 375
Cooper, J. P., 9
Copeland, M. A., 105
Copeland, M. T., 49n, 137, 138
Copernicus, N., 18
Cottam, C., 407
Cox, E. P., 147
Cox, R., 130n, 156, 167n, 172n, 182n,
     216, 251, 320n, 328, 330, 330n,
     331n, 373, 375